From Widgets to Digits

From Widgets to Digits provides an integrated framework with which to understand and address problems generated by the changing nature of the workplace. For most of the twentieth century, employers fostered long-term employment relationships through the use of implicit promises of job security and well-defined paths for career progression. Today, employers no longer value longevity, nor do they seek to encourage long-term attachment. Instead they look for flexibility. The labor and employment laws of the twentieth century are based on an outmoded model of a stable employee-employer relationship. From Widgets to Digits analyzes the impact of the new flexible workplace practices on the issues of employment discrimination, ownership of human capital, worker representation, income distribution, and employee benefits. It proposes legal and institutional reforms to ensure the conditions of success in today's boundaryless workplace. Professor Stone contends that a progressive program for workplace justice must provide continuity in wages, ongoing training opportunities, transferable skills, unambiguous ownership of individual human capital, and portable health and retirement benefits. She also advocates the creation of a reliable social safety net to ease transitions and cushion the fall for those who are left behind by the boundaryless workplace.

Professor Katherine V. W. Stone is an internationally recognized authority in the fields of labor law, labor history, and employment policy. She is Professor of Law and the Anne Evan Estabrook Professor of Dispute Resolution at Cornell Law School and Cornell University's School of Industrial and Labor Relations. Professor Stone has also taught at the Yale Law School, Stanford Law School, the University of Chicago Law School, New York University Law School, and Cardozo Law School. She is the author of Arbitration Law (Foundation Press, 2002) and Private Justice: The Law of Alternative Dispute Resolution (Foundation Press, 2000). Her articles have appeared in the Yale Law Journal, the Stanford Law Review, the University of Chicago Law Review, the UCLA Law Review, and numerous other journals.

For Matthew Drennan and Erica Drennan

From Widgets to Digits

Employment Regulation for the Changing Workplace

KATHERINE V. W. STONE
Cornell University

CAMBRIDGE
UNIVERSITY PRESS

PUBLISHED BY THE PRESS SYNDICATE OF THE UNIVERSITY OF CAMBRIDGE
The Pitt Building, Trumpington Street, Cambridge, United Kingdom

CAMBRIDGE UNIVERSITY PRESS
The Edinburgh Building, Cambridge CB2 2RU, UK
40 West 20th Street, New York, NY 10011-4211, USA
477 Williamstown Road, Port Melbourne, VIC 3207, Australia
Ruiz de Alarcón 13, 28014 Madrid, Spain
Dock House, The Waterfront, Cape Town 8001, South Africa

http://www.cambridge.org

First published 2004

Printed in the United States of America

Typeface Sabon 10/12 pt.   *System* LATEX 2$_\varepsilon$ [TB]

A catalog record for this book is available from the British Library.

Library of Congress Cataloging in Publication Data
Stone, Katherine Van Wezel.
From widgets to digits : employment regulation for the changing workplace /
Katherine V. W. Stone.
   p.   cm.
Includes bibliographical references and index.
ISBN 0-521-82910-0 (hb) – ISBN 0-521-53599-9 (pb)
1. Industrial relations.   2. Labor market.   3. Manpower policy.   4. Human capital.
5. Employees.   6. Organizational change.   1. Title.

HD6971.S865   2004
331 – dc22

2003056855

ISBN 0 521 82910 0 hardback
ISBN 0 521 53599 9 paperback

Contents

Preface   *page* vii

   Introduction   I

PART I   LABOR RELATIONS REGIMES OF THE PAST

  I Artisanal Production in the Nineteenth Century   13

  2 The Labor System of the Industrial Era   27

  3 From Scientific Management to Internal Labor Markets   51

PART II   THE DIGITAL WORKPLACE

  4 The Changing Nature of Employment   67

  5 The New Employment Relationship   87

PART III   IMPLICATIONS OF DIGITAL JOB STRUCTURES FOR LABOR
AND EMPLOYMENT LAW

  6 Implications of the New Workplace for Labor and
     Employment Regulation   119

  7 Disputes over Ownership of Human Capital   127

  8 The Changing Nature of Employment Discrimination   157

  9 Unionism in the Boundaryless Workplace   196

10 Reimagining Employee Representation   217

PART IV   SOCIAL JUSTICE IN THE DIGITAL ERA

11 The Crisis in Benefits and the Collapse of the Private
     Welfare State   243

12 The Working Rich and the Working Poor: Income Inequality
     in the Digital Era   258

     Summary and Conclusion   289

Index   293

Preface

It is difficult to comprehend social change when living in the midst of it. It is easier to study periods of social change in the past – to describe the elements, evaluate the impact, search for linkages, and adumbrate the unintended consequences of change. Many historians have mined these rich veins to describe the changes that occurred in employment relationships as production shifted from an artisan-based system in the nineteenth century to the industrial system of the twentieth century. We are now undergoing another fundamental transformation of the workplace, and this book is an attempt to understand this current metamorphosis, to place it in historical context, and to explore its ramifications.

We are accustomed to thinking of history as divided into a series of parallel realms. Economic history, labor history, history of technology, intellectual history, political history, military history, and legal history are usually treated as separate enterprises, each with its own narratives of stability and change, its own moments of necessity and accident, and its own cast of insiders and outsiders. At times, one type of history imports another to enhance its own story, as when social historians weave in events from economic history to support their narratives or when intellectual historians use examples from legal history to strengthen their assertions of intellectual trends. But by and large, each type of history is studied as a separate story that happens to share with other types of history only a common moment in time. This book is based on a different understanding of how histories fit together and how they together bear on the present.

Both the past and the present look different if you regard all aspects of a production regime as a whole. That is, the technology of production, employment relationships, managerial strategy, worker responses, union organizational possibilities, legal regulation, and social ideology are all interlocking and multidimensional aspects of an era. The interrelationships between these phenomena form a structure, an era, or what I prefer to call a production regime. But the regime is neither static nor predetermined. Each element of the regime conditions the others and defines the realm of possibilities for the people within them. Within the realms of possibilities so framed and constrained, people shape their social lives, form associations, and make their histories.[1] Thus by understanding the interrelationships between the many elements in a production regime, we can understand the prospects for social action and the possibilities for social justice in an era.

I have arrived at this interrelated approach through a personal history of my own. Many years ago as an aspiring labor historian, I set out to study the development of employment relations and work organization in American industry. I used the steel industry as a case study to trace the implementation, transmission, and impact of scientific management and other forms of workplace rationalization in the late nineteenth and early twentieth centuries. My work showed how American corporations adopted the theories of Frederick Winslow Taylor and other industrial engineers of the early twentieth century to develop the internal labor markets that dominated American industry throughout most of the twentieth century. I also showed how issues of work organization are intricately bound up with issues of organization, activism, and power that radiate outward from the shop floor to many aspects of social life. And finally, my study illustrated the contested nature of the transition from the artisanal era to the industrial era, and showed how each group tried to retain its relative position as it was being undermined by changes in technology and the social organization of the workplace.[2]

In a later incarnation, as a legal scholar, I studied the postwar U.S. collective bargaining system and mapped the underlying ideological structure of the regulatory regime. I discovered that through judicial interpretation of the labor law statutes, a legal architecture was constructed in which labor and management were empowered to engage in joint self-regulation of the workplace. I named that system of self-regulation "industrial pluralism" to emphasize its aspiration to form a mini-democracy within the private sphere, and I showed that the practical consequence of the industrial pluralist system of regulation was to subject the unionized workplace to private rule making and to keep external oversight and public policy out. It was a system of deregulatory regulation. I argued that the insular nature of the self-regulatory system of collective bargaining weakened the labor movement by making unionized workplaces impervious to social protective legislation and by isolating the labor movement from other social groups.[3]

---

[1] For an eloquent discussion of the role of human agency in the face of social transformation, see the Preface to E. P. Thompson, THE MAKING OF THE ENGLISH WORKING CLASS (1963).

[2] Katherine Van Wezel Stone, *The Origins of Job Structures in the Steel Industry*, in LABOR MARKET SEGMENTATION 27 (D. Gordon, M. Reich, & R. Edwards, eds., 1975).

[3] Katherine Van Wezel Stone, *The Post-War Paradigm in American Labor Law*, 90 YALE L. J. 1509 (1981); Katherine Van Wezel Stone, *The Legacy of Industrial Pluralism: The Tension Between Individual Employment Rights and the New Deal Collective Bargaining System*, 59 U. CHI. L. REV. 575 (1992).

Only recently have I come to understand that there is a deep relationship between these bodies of work. Because I myself had been operating on separate tracks in my scholarly pursuits, I did not realize initially that they were both part of a bigger story about the U.S. labor relations regime in the twentieth century. But as that twentieth-century regime became eclipsed by another, I began to see how its parts fit together with a new clarity. Thus I came to understand that the regulatory regime of industrial pluralism that I had described in detail was built upon the foundation of the job structures ushered in by scientific management. The industrial pluralist labor law regime assumed the existence of a particular type of workplace. The labor and employment laws we have inherited from the New Deal were built upon the template of an employment relationship characterized by internal labor markets – an employment system that offered long-term attachment between the employee and the firm in which the employee advances up the job ladder of a particular employer for most of his or her working life. Thus the labor law regime was compatible with and tailored to the job structures of the industrial era.

Now the workplace is changing and the teachings of scientific management have been discarded. New ideas about how to organize work have generated new work practices that are proliferating throughout American enterprises. Indeed, the very concept of the workplace as a *place*, and the concept of employment as involving an *employer*, are becoming outdated. As a result of the transformation of work, the regulatory regime is seriously out of alignment with the reality of today's workplace. One consequence of this transformation is that it is necessary to rethink the nature of employment regulation at a fundamental level. Further, it is not only the regulatory regime that is out of alignment – it is also the private organizations, public institutions, social programs, and activist strategies that have constituted progressive politics in the social welfare state. Because of the metamorphosis of the production regime that I describe in the first part of the book, we need to rethink the entire infrastructure of policies and practices that has defined the aspirations of progressive social thought. This book interweaves the story of production techniques, organization of work, managerial ideology, union strategy, and legal regulation in order to make apparent the choices we now face for social policy.

Because we are in a time of transition, many of the particular policy recommendations in this book will no doubt be controversial. Times of transition are challenging because the old structures do not work, but it is difficult for social actors to recognize or respond to the fact of change. This was the problem faced by the American Federation of Labor in the 1920s, when the craft era was giving way to the industrial era but the unions could not alter their craft structures even though craft unionism had little appeal or meaning for industrial workers. As a result, union membership declined from 19 percent of the workforce to 10 percent in less than a decade, and the union movement was powerless to respond to the social crisis of the Great Depression that was just around the corner. We are at a similar moment today, when organized labor is built upon a particular understanding of the production process that makes it institutionally and ideologically difficult to recognize the changes that are occurring in the production regime or to formulate an effective strategic response. At the same time, progressive social thinkers and activists also lack an adequate description of the past or the present that opens up horizons for social policies and effective personal action. This book, by integrating and synthesizing academic disciplines that are normally kept separate, attempts to provide a picture of the present time of transition that can inspire and empower us to reimagine and reengage with the social world.[4]

I want to add one thought about methodology. To write about social change almost invariably requires one to develop a typology of eras. Without eras to designate distinct phases, change is difficult to identify or describe. Minute, evolutionary changes in a rock or a species become notable only when it is possible to say that the rock has transformed from an igneous into a metamorphic rock, or that the species has evolved from a fish to an amphibian. So too with history: the minutiae of everyday life, while ever changing, do not lend themselves to historical description or become objects of analysis unless we can see them as embedded in distinct stages. Whether we call these different stages eras, models, periods, phases, structures, systems, or formations, they are all attempts to give meaning and shape to incremental change. In doing so, we gain an analytic handle on both the past and the present. The typology of change enables us to foreground certain features of daily life as immutable and others as contestable. Yet in doing so, we invariably lose some of the richness of the world we describe. We necessarily simplify, stylize, and tidy up an admittedly messy and ambiguous reality. Any narrative of the past that breaks up time into eras or stages is necessarily oversimplifying; any characterization of a stage in the past or the present is necessarily both over- and under-inclusive.

This books shares in such defects. By organizing my discussion of production and regulatory regimes into periods, I am without doubt oversimplifying both the past and the present. But as with Max Weber's use of ideal types to describe Protestantism and the rise of capitalism,[5] the wisdom of my choice of periods and the accuracy of my characterization of each period should be judged by the plausibility of my story and by the usefulness of my analysis.

The academic enterprise could not occur without the generosity of many selfless people who give hours of their time to listen to, engage with, and

---

[4] Discussions with Elizabeth Long, professor of sociology at Rice University, have helped me to theorize the contribution of a synthetic and integrated approach to the past.
[5] Max Weber, THE PROTESTANT ETHIC AND THE SPIRIT OF CAPITALISM (1968).

improve upon the works of others. As I was writing this book, many friends and colleagues have shared with me their insights, offered me challenging criticisms, and given me support and encouragement. I particularly want to thank Bruce Ackerman, Greg Alexander, Harry Arthurs, Jim Atleson, Rosemary Batt, Richard Bensel, Francine Blau, Barry Bluestone, Jeremy Brecher, Bruno Caruso, Susan Christopherson, Hugh Collins, Alexander Colvin, Simon Deakin, Matthew Drennan, Bill Eskridge, Martha Fineman, Joan Fitzgerald, Mark Freedland, Donald Gibson, Dirk Hartog, Bob Hepple, David Howell, Alan Hyde, Larry Kahn, Harry Katz, David Kennedy, Duncan Kennedy, Alex Keysser, Tom Kochan, John Langbein, Elizabeth Long, Paul Osterman, Jeremy Paul, Dan Raff, Nick Salvatore, Vicki Schultz, Bill Simon, Sasha Skenderija, James Whitman, and Ed Zelinsky.

In addition, a number of exceptionally talented Cornell and Yale law students and Cornell ILR graduate students have helped me with various aspects of the book, including Ariel Avgar, Sarah Burt, Chris McRory, Amanda Meader, Brendan Smith, and Anne Torrey. I want to give special thanks to Virginia Doellgast, Danielle Van Jaarsveld, and Jennifer Clark, who not only did excellent research for me, but also gave up numerous weekends and evenings to help edit the entire manuscript. The dedication and enthusiasm of my students have made this a genuinely collaborative effort.

The intellectual workplace, like the other workplaces I describe, has become truly boundaryless. My work is done not only at my computer, but also in the classroom and in workshops and conferences where ideas are discussed. I am indebted to students in my seminars at Cornell and Yale where I have discussed the ideas of this book, and to participants in numerous faculty workshops and conferences who came, listened, and debated with me about the ideas that have gone into the book. These include workshops at the Yale Law School, Cornell Law School, Connecticut Law School, N.Y.U. Law School, Boston University Law School, Hofstra Law School, UCLA Law School, Georgetown Law School, George Washington School of Law, Emory Law School, Wharton School of Management, Case Western Reserve Law School, Chicago-Kent Law School, Cornell Sociology Department, Cornell University Social Science Seminar, Princeton Program in Law and Public Affairs, St. John's College of Oxford University, Clare College of Cambridge University, the Law and Society Association, the Industrial Relations Research Association, the AFL-CIO Lawyers' Conference, and the law firm of Cohen, Weiss & Simon.

I am also grateful to the Cornell Law School and the Cornell School of Industrial and Labor Relations for giving me the time, resources, and support to carry on my research.

Earlier versions of several chapters of this book have appeared in journals. I want to acknowledge and thank the UCLA LAW REVIEW (*The New Psychological Contract: Implications of the Changing Workplace for Labor and Employment Law*, 48 UCLA L. REV. 519 [2001]), the UNIVERSITY OF CONNECTICUT

Law Review (*Knowledge at Work: Disputes over the Ownership of Human Capital in the Changing Workplace,* 34 Conn. L. Rev. 721 [2002]), Chicago-Kent Law Review (*Employee Representation in the Boundaryless Workplace,* 77 Chi.-Kent L. Rev. 773 [2002]), and the Ohio Journal of Dispute Resolution (*Dispute Resolution in the Boundaryless Workplace,* 16 Ohio St. J. on Disp. Resol. 467 [2001]) for permission to reprint here.

And finally, I am ever grateful to my husband, Matthew Drennan, and my daughter, Erica Drennan, for giving me an abundance of love and support for this project as well as an abundance of amusements and distractions to rejuvenate me along the way. For the sustaining foundation they provide me throughout every day of my life, I dedicate this book to them.

Ithaca, New York
March 2004

Introduction

In January 2000, the London Underground trains carried an advertisement that captures the ambiguity in the employment relationship at the turn of the millennium. The ad, for a leading employment placement agency, pictures a rumpled T-shirt on which appears the slogan "I'm only here for the beer money." Next to the shirt is the following text:

Are you putting in effort or just hours? There's nothing wrong with being in it for the money so long as there's something in it for your employer. Commitment has nothing to do with the hours you work and everything to do with your attitude. Want to work 3 days a week? Go ahead. Fancy 6 months off? It's your life. It ain't what you do, it's the way that you do it. Talk to Brook Street. Whatever you want to do, we'll help you make a career of it.

From the vantage point of the past hundred years, this ad reeks with irony. A "career" involving three days a week? "Commitment" when you are only working for the money? While the ad gives its blessing to this what-me-worry, airhead type of worker, it also speaks of mutual obligations between employer and employee. It says there's nothing wrong with remaining uninvolved *so long as there's something in it for your employer*. Therein lies the irony. How can this three-day-a-week, six months off at a time, beer-drinking, daydreaming employee have something to offer an employer? Clearly the mutual expectations of the employment relationship have undergone a profound transformation.

One does not need to cross the Atlantic to see the changes underway in the nature of work. Recently McDonald's distributed a brochure along with its burgers, called "Good Jobs for Good People." It said:

Looking for a good job? Look no further than McDonald's.

- If you're still in school, we can offer you the chance to learn valuable skills for your future while you earn extra spending money.

- If you have young children and only want to work part time, we can give you flexible hours while you earn the extra income a growing family needs.
- If you're retired and want a job that lets you meet people and have fun while you earn a little extra cash, McDonald's can give you that too.
- If you think a job at McDonald's sounds like a good idea, don't wait. Fill out the attached application and talk to a member of our management team today. Tomorrow you could have a job.

Aimed primarily at students, young mothers, and retirees, this brochure seeks to recruit applicants by promising flexibility and learning opportunities. McDonald's is not seeking long-term, attached, and loyal employees.

Change is apparent in the terminology of work itself. Employees are no longer "workers" – they are professionals in their particular skill or line of work. Cafeteria workers are now called "Culinary Service Professionals;" salespeople are now "Sales Associates;" clerical workers are now "Administrative Assistants;" bank tellers are now "Customer Service Representatives," bank loan officers are "Personal Bankers" or "Financial Specialists," and supermarket cashiers are "Cash Register Professionals." These new professionals have web pages, magazines, and trade conferences with which to network with other professionals and keep abreast of opportunities and developments.

Job seekers today approach the labor market like generals preparing for a strategic air strike. They stake out their target companies on the internet, gathering intelligence from former and current employees about culture and customs of the local worksite. They study the garb of the local population to determine whether casual attire or professional attire is the appropriate camouflage for their interview. And they calibrate their primary weapon – the résumé – to the terrain they expect to encounter.

Résumés are no longer crisp chronological lists of schools attended and positions held. Today, résumés are narratives about skills mastered and tasks performed. Résumé preparation services advise applicants to organize their résumés on a functional rather than a chronological basis, emphasizing abilities and potentials rather than work history. Such a résumé does not highlight either past employers or the sequence of jobs. Indeed, one has to read a resume carefully to find the names of employers or the sequence of jobs.

Evidence of change is also apparent in employer recruitment tactics. Employers are using new approaches to attract applicants, and are offering incentives tailored to the new sensibilities. McDonald's advertises on the radio, offering training in skills such as management and finance, areas that go far beyond the immediate tasks of operating a register or making a hamburger. Burger King offers to help with college tuition.

At the other end of the spectrum, business consultants talk about the "talent wars" of recruitment. They advise firms to restructure human resource policies in order to attract the top talent by offering learning opportunities, lifestyle perks, and performance incentive compensation. For example, in his recent book WINNING THE TALENT WARS, management consultant Bruce Tulgan advises firms that to retain valued employees they need to permit people to customize their jobs to suit their own ambitions and lifestyles.[1] Firms should let their employees select their work tasks, work locations, schedules, and learning opportunities. In Tulgan's view, employees are free agents operating in a free talent market, so they should be offered whatever it takes to attract and keep them – whatever it takes except promotion opportunities or job security.[2]

The popular management writer and Harvard Business School professor Rosabeth Moss Kanter advises firms that to attract a committed workforce they need to make employees feel welcome and valued. She suggests giving employees gifts to welcome them into the workplace community, giving them buddies and mentors to cement their bond, staging periodic formal and informal recognition ceremonies to foster positive feelings, providing family-friendly schedules to accommodate private lives, and in other ways creating a culture of respect and trust.[3] Conspicuously absent are assurances of job security. Rather, Kanter says, firms need to build commitment, not blind loyalty.[4]

These observable trends reflect what management theorists and industrial relations specialists call the "new psychological contract," or the "new deal at work." In the new deal, the long-standing assumption of long-term attachment between an employee and a single firm has broken down. No longer is employment centered on a single, primary employer. Instead, employees now expect to change jobs frequently. No longer does an employee derive identity from a formal employment relationship with a single firm; rather, employment identity comes from attachment to an occupation, a skills cluster, or an industry. At the same time, firms now expect a regular amount of churning in their workforces. They encourage employees to look upon their jobs differently, to manage their own careers, and not to expect career-long job security.

Although there have been many journalistic accounts and academic studies documenting changes in the nature of the employment relationship in recent years, there has been little systemic consideration of the policy implications. From a policy perspective, it is important to define precisely what the new deal is and how it differs from the old deal. Once we understand the terms of the new employment relationship – the explicit and implicit promises, terms, obligations, and expectations that both parties bring to

---

[1] Bruce Tulgan, WINNING THE TALENT WARS 155–57 (2001).
[2] *Id.* at 154–55.
[3] Rosabeth Moss Kanter, E-VOLVE 211–14 (2001).
[4] *Id.* at 225–26.

the relationship – we can evaluate the new workplace from the perspective of fairness to individuals, equity between individuals, and justice society-wide. Such an understanding will force us to revisit labor and employment regulation and enable us to determine which aspects of the current regulatory framework need to be retained, which ones abandoned, and which ones modified, in order to provide employee protection and social justice in the new workplace.

To consider the implications of the change in the workplace for labor and employment regulation, it is necessary to place the new workplace in historical perspective. There have been three distinct phases in the history of American industry over the past two hundred years, each with its own types of job structures, its own form of labor activism, and its own system of employment regulation. These are the eras of *artisanal* production, *industrial* production, and *digital* production. In each era, the labor relations system has had to address certain core issues that arise under any economic system that relies on labor markets for production – issues of worker motivation, skill development, intergenerational transfer of production knowledge, and workplace fairness. If a system cannot deliver with some minimal level of effectiveness in each of these areas, production cannot be efficient and neither growth nor social peace can be maintained. In each era, prevailing custom, technology, and practices addressed each of these issues, with varying degrees of success. Further, in each era, labor organizations emerged that promoted a vision of social welfare and workplace justice that operated within, yet at the same time in opposition to, existing institutional structures. Out of the interaction between employers and labor organizations there emerged legal regulations that were both compatible with and constitutive of the prevailing job structures of the era.

The three eras can be briefly described as follows:

1. *Artisanal Production*

Artisanal production relied upon craft workers who possessed, as a group, complete knowledge about the production process in their particular calling. In the nineteenth century, craft workers typically used their own tools and materials to produce shoes, barrels, horseshoes, steel, and other products manufactured for sale in local and regional markets. The craft workers were often both producers and merchants. Occasionally they had employers who coordinated the raw materials and provided marketing for the finished product, but employers did not direct the work or prescribe the manner of performance. Markets were local and/or regional; unions were producers' associations and guildlike craft unions. The individual employment relationship was governed by master-servant law, and collective action was regulated by the common law doctrine of criminal conspiracy.

2. Industrial Production

Industrial production developed in the late nineteenth and early twentieth centuries. It was characterized by mass production for national markets. Employers sought uniformity in products and processes in order to achieve economies of scale. They utilized assembly line production techniques for manufactured items where it was feasible to do so. In continuous production processes such as steel production, employers established scientific management job structures. In both cases, large firms established internal labor markets with narrow job definitions and clearly defined, hierarchical job ladders. Firms fostered long-term relationships with their employees by curtailing lateral hiring and by giving them an implicit promise of job security. Industrial unions formed in order to regularize and enforce the implicit promises employers made. The role of law in this system was to legalize unions and enable them to exercise countervailing power to employers, to engage in labor-management self-regulation of the workplace, and to enforce explicit and implicit deals in the workplace. These goals were effectuated by the New Deal system of labor regulation that provided labor law to facilitate union formation and establish a self-regulatory framework of collective bargaining. Individual employment law provided a safety net for those left outside the internal labor market system.

3. Digital Production

In the era of digital production, markets are global and highly competitive. Production is also global, as firms locate or operate in networks of firms that are located all over the globe. Profits derive primarily from a firm's intangible intellectual property such as knowledge, patents, copyrights, managerial acumen, and informal networks, rather than from ownership of capital or raw materials. Computers are the central nervous system of global production networks, coordinating the diffuse and disparate parts while at the same time providing the interface between the firm and the external environment. Computerization infuses all aspects of production, from product design to task execution and marketing. Computers are also involved in internal organizational processes, mediating production and human resource tasks. Because of the central role of computers, I call this the era of digital production. In the digital era, frequent shifts in market conditions and consumer demand lead firms to seek flexibility in their labor relations.

One defining characteristic of the digital era is the central role of human intellectual capital – skills, knowledge, information, know-how, tacit knowledge, imagination, and capacity for learning and innovation embodied in employees. Firms believe that value and profitability in the digital era depend upon the intellectual capital of their employees, whether it be the top CEO or the lowliest janitor. Therefore, employers compete for talent, and seek to encourage training, skill upgrading, lifetime learning, and other forms of human capital growth. Scientific management has been superceded by alternate forms of work organization. Rather than reiterating the hierarchies of the past, work is now arranged in fluid workplaces that have permeable borders between firms and within divisions of specific firms.

Presently, the American workplace is poised between the industrial and the digital eras. Some sectors of the American economy, such as the public sector, are still organized into old-fashioned internal labor markets characteristic of the industrial era. However, many private sector firms are moving toward digitalized forms of production and digital-era job structures. Some of these firms are at the vanguard of the technological revolution, such as Microsoft and Hewlett Packard, and some are manufacturers making old-fashioned products, such as the General Electric Company. These firms are characterized as part of the digital era not because of the products they produce but how they produce them. These firms have organized their production, marketing, finance, management, and human resource activities in a new way. They are at the vanguard of a new mode of work organization that has profound implications for the people who work in these firms as well as for the American workplace of the future.

The work arrangements characteristic of the new era place stress on the existing labor laws and employment institutions that were designed for an earlier age. When production arrangements and job structures shift, new types of concerns about workplace fairness and social justice arise. For example, digital production promises high earnings and exciting work for some, but with costs. One cost is job instability. Long-term job security is a feature of an earlier era, yet without it, many face the likelihood of frequent involuntary job loss throughout their working lives. The wave of layoffs of dot.com technology workers in the early 2000s echoed the experience of middle management in the early 1990s and production workers in the 1980s. Job loss invariably imposes high personal costs on the individuals involved. However the dot.com layoffs, unlike the layoffs of the 1980s and 1990s, have not generated intense anger and bitterness, at least amongst younger workers. Rather, journalists report that today's pink slips are accepted as a regrettable but predictable fact of life. Thus the current wave of layoffs reinforces the "no long term" credo that has dominated the workplace in the past decade.[5]

In addition to job instability, the new deal at work involves insecurity about basic social welfare benefits. In the American social welfare system, social safety net programs such as old-age assistance, health insurance, accident and disability insurance, and unemployment insurance are employer based. If employees do not have long-term attachment to an employing unit, they often lose their eligibility for benefits.

---

[5] Louis Uchitelle, *Pink Slip? Now It's All in a Days Work*, NEW YORK TIMES, Aug. 5, 2001, Sec. 3, p. 1; Rick Marin, *Is This the Face of a Midlife Crisis?* NEW YORK TIMES, June 24, 2001, Sec. 9, p. 1.

Yet another cost is found in the changing forms of racial and gender discrimination. The flattened hierarchies and diffuse authority structures of the new workplace present elusive problems for women and minorities that are difficult to remedy under current discrimination laws.

The new workplace also imposes a cost in terms of the loss of employee collective representation. The labor and employment laws of the 1930s were a response to both the advent of scientific management job structures and the rise of industrial unions. Now, as new forms of production and a new set of job structures are emerging, the existing labor laws and forms of collective action are out of date. As a result, employees are devising new forms of collective action to provide employee representation and voice. The labor and employment laws will also have to change in order to accommodate the new issues posed and the new forms of labor-management conflict that arise.

An additional aspect of the digital workplace is rising income inequality. There is considerable evidence of growing income disparity both between sectors of the workforce and within firms, particularly within firms that have adopted digital-era work relations practices. Indeed, the disparity in income between executives and average workers has grown exponentially since the 1970s, and today is at epic proportions.

Yet another, sometimes tragic, cost of the digital workplace is visited upon the cohort of employees who have been caught in the transition from the industrial to the digital era. These tend to be older employees who have seen the rules of the game changed mid-course, leaving them disappointed, embittered, and angry. Disputes over pension plan restructuring have arisen as companies have attempted to convert pension plans that were structured to reward long-term employment into fully portable, vest-as-you-go systems. The rising incidence of violent episodes in the workplace is a dramatic manifestation of the costs of abrupt changes in work practices and expectations that accompany the shift. The plight of this transitional cohort further reminds us that while it is important to devise new concepts of labor and employment regulation, it is also important to ensure that proposals for reform do not leave those working under the old industrial job structures more vulnerable than ever.

The task of labor policy today is to reshape labor law and employment institutions to provide fairness, stability, and justice in the digital era. The task is twofold – to devise a labor and employment law for the new workplace while retaining the protections for workers in the old workplace.

The Structure of the Book

This book begins with a history of the earlier artisanal and industrial eras, and then considers the implications of the shift to the digital era for job structures and labor regulation. It proceeds as follows:

Part I sets out the labor relations systems and the regulatory framework that governed them in the past. Chapter 1 describes the artisan production phase, in which craft workers collectively regulated employment and production. Chapter 2 describes the industrial production era, in which skill was separated from the worker and thinking was separated from doing. In this era, the prototypical worker was the semiskilled machine operative and the prevailing form of labor organization was the industrial union. Chapter 3 describes the advent and spread of internal labor markets, with their origins in the scientific management and personnel theories of the early twentieth century. It shows that internal labor market job structures came to dominate major U.S. manufacturing firms by the mid twentieth century.

Part II describes the emerging new workplace of the digital age. Chapter 4 presents empirical data to document the shift from the industrial production to the digital production era. Chapter 4 also presents sociological accounts of the changing workplace that reinforce the findings of the empirical data. Chapter 5 describes the digital employment system. Drawing on contemporary organizational behavior and management theories, it identifies the terms of the new employment relationship. These terms include the promise of employability security rather than job security; the promise of training rather than lifetime tenure; the promise of opportunities to form networks rather than the promise of promotions; peer group decision making rather than hierarchical supervision and evaluation; broadly defined projects rather than narrowly defined jobs; and opportunities to exercise bounded discretion rather than top-down, command-and-control authority relations.

Part III addresses the implications of digital job structures for labor and employment regulation. Chapter 6 introduces the issue of regulation by describing the many ways in which existing labor and employment laws are based upon assumptions of the industrial era. This background puts into the foreground the misfit between current labor and employment regulation and the new workplace practices. The remainder of Part Three is devoted to discussing particular areas in which existing labor regulation must be revised in light of the new employment relationship.

Chapter 7 addresses a legal issue that was invisible in the past but has become prominent today – the issue of who owns an employee's human capital. Because the new employment relationship relies on employees' intellectual, imaginative, and cognitive contribution to the firm, employers put a premium on human capital development and knowledge sharing within the firm. Yet the frequent lateral movement between firms that typifies the new relationship means that when an employee leaves one employer and goes to work for a competitor, there is a danger that proprietary knowledge will go too. Increasingly, employees and employers have disputes over who owns the valuable human capital that employees gain in the course of their employment. The chapter proposes a framework for deciding disputes about human capital ownership from the perspective of the mutual expectations, understandings, and implicit promises of the new employment relationship.

Chapter 8 addresses the impact of the new employment relationship on employment discrimination. It argues that the nature of employment discrimination has changed in ways that undermine the effectiveness of traditional approaches of discrimination law. Chapter 8 proposes new definitions of employment discrimination and new methods of redress that respond to the challenges of new forms of discrimination in the workplace.

Chapter 9 addresses the consequences of the new employment relationship for employee representation. It argues that many traditional union practices and many aspects of existing labor law are based upon assumptions that were valid under the old employment relationship but no longer pertain.

Chapter 10, entitled Reimagining Employee Representation, presents two new models of labor organization that are better suited than traditional union practices to a boundaryless workplace – new craft unionism and citizenship unionism. It gives examples of both types of organizations in their incipiency, and considers the ways in which each model is able to address current issues of workplace and societal justice.

Part IV addresses the implications of the changing work practices for social justice. Chapter 11 describes the crisis in social insurance that has arisen from the increased job mobility of the digital workplace. The chapter discusses proposals to expand benefit portability that would be necessary to adapt social insurance to the digital-era workplace.

Chapter 12 documents the extent of rising income inequality in the United States in the past two decades. It discusses several theories that have been proposed to explain the widening income distribution, including theories of skill-biased technological change, a shift from manufacturing to service sector production, and increasingly globalized production. The chapter demonstrates that one important cause of growing income inequality lies with the work practices of the digital era. It then considers several approaches for reversing the trend toward greater inequality. It also considers several programs and proposals designed to make it easier for individuals to be flexible and navigate successfully in the face of the new boundaryless workplace.

The Summary and Conclusion addresses the issue of how to bring about change. It suggests that a new legal framework be devised and new organizations formed to ensure that the digital era provides social justice both inside the workplace and throughout society more generally.

PART I

LABOR RELATIONS REGIMES OF THE PAST

I

Artisanal Production in the Nineteenth Century

A 1733 painting by John Heaten depicts eighteenth-century life on the Marteen Van Bergen farm in New York's Hudson Valley.[1] The picture, considered the earliest American genre scene, depicts a family farm set amidst the rolling hills of upstate New York. There is a house and an expansive yard populated by a well-dressed husband and wife, several young children, two black slaves tending livestock, and a white household servant, probably indentured, engaged in a transaction with a Native American. On the roadway in front of the house is a milk-wagon driver, and approaching the house is a well-dressed man followed by two lads, possibly a merchant-craftsman and his apprentices. The painting thus depicts the dominant forms of labor in the early years of the Republic – family members, slaves, indentured servants, craftsmen, and apprentices. There are no wage workers in the picture.

The picture portrays America in its formative years. In the seventeenth and eighteenth centuries, American economic life consisted of the daily travails of people who, like those in the painting, were in relationships defined by fixed legal obligations, such as husband, wife, parent, slave, indentured servant, craftsman, and apprentice. The notion of a labor market in which individuals freely sold their labor did not exist. In fact, until the nineteenth century, there were practically no people in employment relationships.[2] Merchants, artisans, and members of the learned professions all engaged in remunerative activities, but they did not work for wages. Merchants sold their wares, professionals charged fees for their professional services, and artisans were self-employed craftsmen who manufactured items such as barrels, rope, horseshoes, bread, clothing, and glass in their own workshops. Artisans sold the products they produced; they did not sell their labor.

---

[1] The picture, entitled *Overmantel*, is owned by the New York State Historical Society, and is located at the New York State Historical Association Museum in Cooperstown, New York.
[2] Robert J. Steinfeld, THE INVENTION OF FREE LABOR: THE EMPLOYMENT RELATION IN ENGLISH AND AMERICAN LAW AND CULTURE, 1350–1870, at 15–17 (1991).

Wage labor emerged only gradually throughout the course of the nineteenth century, evolving from several sources. One was the perpetual journeymen, the craftsmen-in-training, who never acceded to the ranks of master. In the nineteenth century, master craftsmen, in their quest for cheap labor, abandoned customary norms and began increasing the number of apprentices they kept. Accordingly, by mid century, there were a large number of journeymen who worked for masters and were paid wages, yet lacked any realistic hope of becoming a master themselves. Conflicts over wages, quality standards, and hours frequently arose, leading journeymen to form societies and trade unions to protect their interests. But even with independent trade organizations, journeymen continued to see themselves as the self-employed artisans they aspired to be, rather than as wage labor. For example, in disputes with masters, the journeymen demanded not higher wages but a schedule of prices for the products they produced.[3] These journeymen constituted the skilled workers of the nineteenth century, and their employment relationships shaped the labor system of the artisan era.

Newcomers were another source of wage labor in the second half of the nineteenth century. Some were former slaves who migrated to northern cities after the Civil War to find work. Some were unmarried women who left farms and flocked to factories in industrial centers where they worked as machine tenders until they married and dropped out of the paid labor force. Boatloads of immigrants and their children also arrived and found a place in the urban factories of the New World. These groups, together with the skilled journeymen, comprised the new group known as "free labor."

With the advent of free labor, the factory became the dominant locale of production. Many types of manufacturing activities moved from homes or workshops owned by master craftsmen to factories owned by merchant-manufacturers. Some manufacturing work, such as garment making, continued to be carried out in homes under the "putting out system," in which jobbers distributed raw materials and then collected the finished products. But as the century wore on and production became more capital intensive, more types of production moved into factories where both skilled and unskilled workers were employed.

Life in the factory was grim for unskilled workers. They worked long hours in dangerous conditions for paltry pay. They were vulnerable to sudden layoffs and unannounced pay cuts, and were subjected to harsh disciplinary rules and confiscatory fines.[4] But skilled workers fared differently.

---

[3] David Brody, *Time and Work During Early American Industrialism*, in David Brody, IN LABOR'S CAUSE: MAIN THEMES ON THE HISTORY OF THE AMERICAN WORKER 18–19 (1993). *See also* Mark A. Lause, SOME DEGREE OF POWER: FROM HIRED HAND TO UNION CRAFTSMEN IN THE PREINDUSTRIAL AMERICAN PRINTING TRADES 120–24 (1991).

[4] William A. Sullivan, THE INDUSTRIAL WORKER IN PENNSYLVANIA – 1800–1840, 31–52 (1955).

They retained a dignity that came from their exclusive knowledge of the mysteries of the craft and a power that came from their labor organizations.

A. The Job Structures of Artisanal Production

The nineteenth-century craft workers possessed extensive knowledge, skills, and expertise about the articles they produced. In their work, they utilized considerable experience, dexterity, and judgment, and exercised control over most aspects of the production process. Even inside factories, they determined the nature of the product, the pace of work, the distribution of revenues, and most other aspects of the production process. Often teams of skilled workers determined the process to be used, the division of labor amongst themselves, the division of payment, and even the design of the product.[5] Craft workers also developed their own customs and practices that solved problems of work motivation, skill acquisition, and intergenerational transmission of knowledge.

The nineteenth-century skilled workers possessed extensive specialized knowledge about production of their wares, and their skill gave them independence. Even those hired by merchant-manufacturers saw themselves as independent contractors who were hired to do a job. They usually used their own tools even as they worked on the manufacturers' materials. In these production arrangements, the skilled workers determined the method of work and exercised control over their own time. In such a setting, these men – and they were all men – were able to retain their conception of themselves as self-employed craftsmen.

The skilled workers saw production as a partnership in which they determined what needed to be done and how to do it, while the manufacturers provided the workplace, the raw materials, and marketing. In many occupations, skilled workers had unskilled helpers to do the heavy manual work of lifting, pushing, carrying, and hoisting. Sometimes the skilled workers paid the helpers directly, and sometimes the owner paid the helpers and then deducted the sum from the skilled workers' fees, but in either case, the skilled workers rather than the manufacturer hired the helpers and supervised their work. These skilled workers, termed "inside contractors" were employees of the firm but they hired their own crew to produce a finished product. The inside contractors/skilled workers contracted with the manufacturer to produce a given item at a given cost, using the firm's premises and raw materials. Thus the skilled workers were a hybrid – part employee and part subcontractors, hired to do a job for which they selected, supervised, and paid their less skilled assistants. Historian Daniel Nelson says of these inside

---

[5] I describe the labor practices and wage policies of skilled workers in detail in Katherine Van Wezel Stone, *The Origins of Job Structures in the Steel Industry*, in LABOR MARKET SEGMENTATION 32 (D. Gordon, M. Reich, & R. Edwards, eds., 1975).

contractors that each was at the same time "an employee working for a day wage and an independent businessman working for an anticipated profit."[6]

In the steel industry, for example, steel was made by skilled workers with unskilled helpers, using the companies' equipment and raw materials.[7] The skilled steelworkers hired their own helpers, whom they paid out of their own paychecks. Steelworkers' wages were not set by the employers, but were pegged to the price of the product, and varied according to a sliding scale that automatically adjusted in accord with changes in the market price for iron and steel. The wage pool was determined by a combination of the tonnage produced and the market price for iron and steel so that employers did not have direct control over wage rates.[8] Once the wage pool was established, the distribution of wages within the ranks of the skilled workers, and between the skilled workers and their helpers, was determined by the workers themselves.[9] Thus each individual's wages were set by a combination of market demand for the product, group effort, and intragroup decisions about equity; the employer had no role in the process. The labor system and the sliding scale produced a type of profit-sharing arrangement in which the workers benefited when prices were high but suffered when prices were low. Andrew Carnegie extolled this wage system, stating, "It is the solution of the capital and labor problem because it really makes them partners – alike in prosperity and adversity."[10]

Other craft workers in the nineteenth century had similar job structures to preserve their power and control over the labor process. Glass blowers, potters, coopers, pipe fitters, typographers, coal miners, iron puddlers, steel rollers, metal workers, foundry molders, and many other skilled workers were inside contractors, paid by an employer but retaining broad discretion over their work and their helpers.[11] Until the 1890s, for example, coal miners provided their own tools, set their pace of work, determined the hours of their workday, and used their own judgment about how to timber and where to cut. The miners' customary knowledge and skill were passed down through generations. Their earnings were determined by the tonnage mined and the price of the coal, so that the mine owner had little control over the pace of

[6] *See, e.g.*, Daniel Nelson, Managers and Workers: Origins of the Twentieth-Century Factory System in the United States, 1880–1920, 37 (1995). *See also* John Fitch, The Steel Workers 102 (1920).

[7] Stone, *The Origins of Job Structures* 30–33.

[8] *Id.* at 30–31.

[9] David Montgomery, *Trade Union Practice and the Origins of Syndicalist Theory*, in David Montgomery, Workers' Control in America: Studies in the History of Work, Technology and Labor Struggles (1979), quoted in Stone, *The Origins of Job Structures* 31–32.

[10] Andrew Carnegie, Autobiography 238 (1920).

[11] David Montgomery, *Workers' Control and Machine Production in the Nineteenth Century*, in Montgomery, Workers' Control in America 11; David Brody, *The American Worker in the Progressive Age: A Comprehensive Analysis*, in David Brody, Workers in Industrial America: Essays on the Twentieth Century Struggle 9–10 (1980).

work or the miner's pay. The employer's role was to operate the mine cars, ensure a functioning ventilation system, and transport the coal to market.[12]

Shoe workers also retained their artisan traditions through much of the nineteenth century. Even after the introduction of the factory system in the 1850s, a single skilled journeyman manufactured the entire product and had aspirations of obtaining ownership of his own shop. The spread of the factory system, spurred by government orders during the Civil War, did not become universal in the industry until the 1880s. Yet by then, mechanization had significantly eroded the shoe worker's role in production.[13] Some skilled artisan groups, such as lasters and cutters, retained the prerogatives of their skill into the 1890s, but they came into conflict with the groups whose skills had been degraded.[14]

In brewery work, the printing trades, glass blowing, metal work, and countless other crafts, customs developed that defined and ensured the skilled workers' autonomy. Even within factories, skilled workers often remained exempt from the harsh industrial discipline of driving foremen. Rather, they set their own pace of work, and even the hours of their workdays. Skilled workers had responsibility to produce a requisite minimum amount of product, but they had discretion to enhance their earnings by increasing production beyond the set amount. They came and went throughout the workday, and some, like cigar workers and shoe workers, hired readers to come into the factories and read to them while they plied their craft.[15] The cigar workers in New York City, for example, paid one of their coworkers to read to the others during the workday. The cigar workshops were veritable salons of political and philosophic debates about the issues of the day.[16]

With their monopoly of knowledge of the production process, skilled workers were able to ensure themselves reasonably steady work, fair wages, and considerable social status within their communities. Skilled workers lived in communities that richly affirmed the value of their skill. Labor Day in the nineteenth century was an occasion for great festivities, with bands, parades, parties, dancing, and carousing late into the night. On other days, working-class bars were alive with music and games as well as conversation,

---

[12] *See* John Brophy, *Life in the Mines*, in AMERICAN LABOR: THE TWENTIETH CENTURY 43–49 (Jerold S. Auerbach, ed., 1969).

[13] It has been argued that the innovations in the 1850s, such as the stripper, the sole cutter, and the adjustable last, were aids to the journeyman, but that the inventions of the 1860s and 1870s, such as the McKay sole-stitching machine and the Goodyear welt machine, were not aids to, but rather replacements for, the journeymen's skill. John H. M. Laslett, LABOR AND THE LEFT 60 (1970).

[14] *Id.* at 61–84. *See also* Blanche Evans Hazard, ORGANIZED BOOT AND SHOE INDUSTRY IN MASSACHUSETTS BEFORE 1875, excerpted in WORKERS IN MODERN ECONOMIC SOCIETY 167 (Paul Douglas, Curtice N. Hitchcock, & Willard E. Atkins, eds., 1925).

[15] Harold C. Livesay, SAMUEL GOMPERS AND ORGANIZED LABOR IN AMERICA 19–20 (1978).

[16] Nick Salvatore, Introduction, in SEVENTY YEARS OF LIFE AND LABOR: AN AUTOBIOGRAPHY: SAMUEL GOMPERS, xii (Nick Salvatore, ed., 1984).

debate, and comradery. Fraternal organizations and labor newspapers flourished. Many communities had labor-sponsored baseball leagues and lecture series, and there was even a Workingmen's Library in Muncie, Indiana.[17]

B. Labor Organizations in the Artisanal Era

The nineteenth-century skilled workers' ability to control their wages and working conditions was a result of their skills, their distinctive craft culture, and their unions. In the late nineteenth century, craft unions codified the traditional workplace rules into what they termed "legislation." The legislation was not the result of bargaining with employers; it was unilaterally enacted by unions at their meetings or conventions and enforced through censorship, expulsion, and fines. As the noted Yale professor of labor history David Montgomery observes, the union rules codified but did not create the extensive set of practices and norms that existed within crafts and constituted the power of the craft workers. The craft unions thus articulated and enforced the traditional system of artisanal production.[18]

The craft unions had their origins in the 1830s, when many journeymen felt the need to form separate associations from the master craftsmen. Many trade societies were organized in cities, and there were numerous local strikes of journeymen against masters.[19] In some crafts, there were attempts to join the local associations together into national organizations in the first half of the nineteenth century, but most of these efforts were short-lived. Beginning in the 1850s, national craft unions were formed. The National Typographers Union was formed in 1853; the Cigar-Makers International Union in 1864; the International Association of Machinists in 1888, the United Mine Workers of America in 1890. By the end of the century, sixty-two national craft unions had been formed in diverse trades: they included the Bakers and Confectioners Workers International Union, the International Union of Bicycle Workers, the Boot and Shoe Workers' Union, the United Hatters of America, the Brotherhood of Painters and Decorators of America, the Tin Plate Workers, and so forth.[20]

Journeymen formed national unions in order to resist exploitation not only from masters but also from manufacturers. The late-nineteenth-century craft unions were, first and foremost, guardians of skill. Often unionization was precipitated by the introduction of technology that threatened the journeymen's control of the production.

---

[17] David Brody, WORKERS IN INDUSTRIAL AMERICA 23 (1980). *See also* Alan Dawley, STRUGGLES FOR JUSTICE: SOCIAL RESPONSIBILITY AND THE LIBERAL STATE 37 (1991).

[18] Montgomery, *Workers' Control and Machine Production* 15.

[19] Walter Hugins, JACKSONIAN DEMOCRACY AND THE WORKING CLASS: A STUDY OF THE NEW YORK WORKINGMEN'S MOVEMENT, 1829–1837, 55–57 (1960).

[20] PROC. 20TH ANN. CONVENTION AM. FED'N LAB., LOUISVILLE, KENTUCKY 7–12 (1900).

The craft unions were complex systems for transmitting human capital between generations while restricting access to the craft and protecting its economic value.[21] Knowledge of the craft skill was highly esteemed and fiercely hoarded. The craft unions devised and enforced detailed craft governance rules and apprenticeship arrangements that determined the circumstances under which training was permitted. Senior members of the craft transmitted their knowledge to newcomers through the union-controlled apprenticeship system.

The role of the craft unions in skill acquisition is illustrated by the practices of the machinists' union in the late nineteenth century. The machinists' craft was under severe strain from mechanization in that period. Prior to 1870, the skilled machinist was aptly described as "a carpenter who worked with metal instead of wood."[22] A skilled machinist knew all aspects of the trade, could work on all types of metal in industrial use, and could operate all the tools of the trade. However, the introduction of steam and electrically powered machines for planing, milling, drilling, and lathing so changed the nature of the work that by 1900 few machinists had such all-round skills. Rather, there emerged an important distinction between "the old-fashioned all-around machinist who can interpret a blue-print and execute any part of the work required by it with any tool or on any machine, and the specialist who can only do work of a particular kind on a particular machine."[23] The machinists' union attempted to forestall mechanization by maintaining a strict apprenticeship system for the induction of new machinists. The union constitution limited the number of apprentices to one for each shop and one additional apprentice for every five journeymen. The union required a four-year training period for apprentices and insisted that they be trained as all-around machinists, not as specialists. Thus, all trade agreements between the union and the manufacturers stipulated that apprentices must be given an opportunity to learn all aspects of the trade, and could not spend more than six months on any one machine.[24] The machinists' union waged frequent strikes over employers' attempts to circumvent the apprenticeship system by employing helpers and handymen to do machinists' work. There were also numerous grievances about the number of apprentices.[25]

The elaborate apprenticeship rules limited access to skill and ensured that it remained in the possession of the workers.[26] The apprenticeship system thus protected the skilled machinists' human capital, limited the future labor

---

[21] *See* Stone, *The Origins of Job Structures* 32.
[22] William H. Buckler, *Minimum Wage in the Machinists' Union*, in STUDIES IN AMERICAN TRADE UNIONISM 109, 114 (Jacob H. Hollander & George E. Barnett, eds., 1907).
[23] *Id.* at 116–17.
[24] *Id.* at 132–33.
[25] *Id.* at 132.
[26] *See generally* Stone, *The Origins of Job Structures*; Montgomery, WORKERS' CONTROL IN AMERICA.

supply, and secured their earnings and prestige. However, the craft continued to change and union membership began to decline. In 1903, in order to bridge the divide between the all-around skilled machinists and the specialist, semiskilled, machine operators, the International Association of Machinists changed its constitution to permit the lesser skilled specialists to join. At the same time, it also abandoned its insistence on a standard rate in its trade agreements, instead adopting a wage policy that recognized diversity of skill in the craft.[27]

The typographers' union also attempted to protect their craft against mechanization. When linotype machines threatened to supplant hand type-setting in the 1890s, the International Typographers Union (ITU) convention passed a resolution directing "that in all offices within its jurisdiction where typesetting machines are used, practical printers shall be employed to run them." It also passed a resolution urging members to learn to operate the new machines, and developed a special "learner's scale" so that members would have a chance to learn to use them. Some locals bought or rented machines for this purpose. At first, the ITU prohibited apprentices from operating lino-type machines, but in 1893 it revised its policy and permitted apprentices to work on the machines during the last year of their apprenticeship. The union later limited apprenticeship training on linotype machines to six weeks. In 1899, it again changed the rule to permit apprentices three months' training on the machines, but provided that the product of apprentices could not be used by employers. These efforts of the ITU were successful in retaining control over typesetting work even as the new machines diluted the craft skills of their members.[28]

A similar dynamic was present amongst shoe workers. In 1898, the nascent Boot and Shoe Workers' Union refused to oppose the introduction of lasting machines, so the lasters in many cities seceded from the union and in 1909 formed the rival and more militant United Shoe Workers of America to defend their traditional artisanal role.

C. Radical and Reform Political Programs

While the craft unions strove to protect the skilled workers' skill, status, and privileges, other worker-based reform movements throughout the nineteenth century were formed to secure progressive political and legal reform. Many nineteenth-century labor leaders were social reformers who believed that the ideal society was based on small-scale production and producers' coop-eratives. Some labor leaders were active in both the reformist and the craft unions. For example, William E. Sylvis was both the president of the Iron Molders' International Union and one of the founders of the National Labor

[27] Buckler, MINIMUM WAGE 117–18.
[28] George E. Barnett, CHAPTERS ON MACHINERY AND LABOR 9–15 (1969).

Union (NLU), a prominent national labor organization in the 1860s and 1870s that sought to promote small-scale, regional economic development.[29]

In 1872, a labor organization called the Knights of Labor (KOL) was formed. It was the first mass organization of the American working class, including artisans, unskilled workers, shop-keepers, and small manufacturers as members.[30] The Knights grew quickly, so that by 1884, it had local assemblies all over the country. Its 1884 Declaration of Principles stated that one of its primary goals was "to establish co-operative institutions such as will tend to supersede the wage-system by the introduction of a co-operative industrial system."[31]

The Knights of Labor, the NLU, and other mid-nineteenth-century labor reform organizations have been called "producers' alliances" because they aimed to bring together wealth producers in order to protect themselves against capitalists and those they viewed as idle, corrupt, or parasitic.[32] The producer organizations believed that the economic problems of the era were the result of the rise of monopolies, particularly in the key areas of transportation, communications, and the financial system. Their political program was focused on advocating antimonopoly measures.

In contrast, the national craft unions advocated the creation of organizations strictly for workers and the use of collective action to protect workers from the excesses of modern industry. Such organizations have been called "workingmen's alliances," to distinguish them from the producers' alliance organizations such as the NLU and the KOL.[33] They wanted strong craft-based unions with closed shops that could enforce their own union work rules on employers. In 1866, the American Federation of Labor (AFL) was founded in order to join together the individual national trade and craft unions to further the interests of workingmen.

The national unions favored legislative reforms that would protect labor's right to organize and engage in collective action. Thus, for example, in the 1870s and 1880s, the New York Workingmen's Assembly and the Federation of Organized Trades and Labor Unions (FOTLU), two precursor organizations to the American Federation of Labor, called for state legislatures to enact two measures they believed would assist union efforts to organize: (1) the repeal of the common law doctrine of criminal conspiracy, and (2) the enactment of legislation to permit unions to incorporate. Later the AFL and the national unions became active in a campaign to gain unions an exemption from the Sherman Antitrust Act of 1890, also for purposes of

[29] Victoria Hattam, LABOR VISIONS AND STATE POWER 120–21 (1993).

[30] Leon Fink, WORKINGMEN'S DEMOCRACY: THE KNIGHTS OF LABOR AND AMERICAN POLITICS xii (1983). *See also* T. V. Powderly et al., LABOR: ITS RIGHTS AND WRONGS, 29–33 (1886).

[31] Powderly, LABOR: ITS RIGHTS AND WRONGS 29–33.

[32] Hattam, LABOR VISIONS; Fink, WORKINGMEN'S DEMOCRACY 9. *See also* Gerald Grob, WORKERS AND UTOPIA: A STUDY OF IDEOLOGICAL CONFLICT IN THE AMERICAN LABOR MOVEMENT (1961).

[33] Hattam, LABOR VISIONS 135–36.

facilitating organizing.[34] By the century's end, membership of the Knights of Labor dwindled severely as a result of the difficulty of keeping so many disparate types of workers united in the face of adament employer opposition.[35] The other political labor reform movements also declined in importance, so that by 1900 the national craft unions were the dominant form of American labor organization.

D. Law, Technology, and the Erosion of the Artisans' Autonomy

Much of the history of labor in the nineteenth century can be seen as the history of craft workers struggling to retain the power and social relations that were based on their skill in the face of the triple onslaught of rapid mechanization, the growth of large-scale factories, and hardened management opposition. As the nineteenth century wore on, manufacturers more and more vehemently opposed the union-run apprenticeship systems that controlled access to the trades and limited knowledge of the crafts. In 1887, the cigar manufacturers in New York locked out the cigar makers in order to destroy the apprenticeship system. As reported that year in the Knights of Labor publication THE LABOR LEADER:

> The point involved in the lockout of cigarmakers of this day is a delicate one in trade union ethics. The manufacturers say, shall we not have a right to hire whom we please?
> The answer is No. The men who make cigars have an equal right to a voice in determining the conditions of their work and they cannot be blamed if they refuse to prevent the inundation of their trade with cheap labor.
> Is this selfishness? Perhaps; but do the manufacturers do business for philanthropic reasons?[36]

In some industries, the push to institute labor-saving technology and factory production was driven by opportunities for scale economies. In others, it was driven by the employers' desire to break the strength of the craft unions. For example, mechanization at the International Harvester Company was introduced not to cut costs but rather to destroy the molders' union.[37] Similarly, the factory system in the Massachusetts boot and shoe industry was initially set up to discipline the workforce, and only later did it utilize expensive machinery.[38]

---

[34] *Id.* at 133.

[35] Kim Voss, THE MAKING OF AMERICAN EXCEPTIONALISM: THE KNIGHTS OF LABOR AND CLASS FORMATION IN THE NINETEENTH CENTURY (1993).

[36] 2 LABOR LEADER, no. 11, p. 2 (Sept. 17, 1887).

[37] Robert Ozanne, WAGES IN PRACTICE AND THEORY: MCCORMICK AND INTERNATIONAL HARVESTER 26 (1968).

[38] Hazard, ORGANIZED BOOT AND SHOE INDUSTRY 167.

The skilled workers' unions adopted a number of policies to protect their skills against the onslaught of machines. Some unions, such as the window glass makers and the cigar makers, prohibited the use of machines altogether. Others, such as the soft coal miners, limited the output permitted by machines. The pressmen and stonecutters required several men on one machine, and the printers required that skilled men operate all machines.[39] These were stop-gap measures, however, protecting incumbent workers for a time while strengthening employers' determination to be free of the craft union restraints.

The craft workers' autonomy was eroded not only by technology but also by a change in the legal rules governing the employment relationship. In the late nineteenth century, a new doctrine emerged in state courts, wiping out the semifeudal vestiges of the old master-servant legal framework and making labor more mobile. Whereas previously courts had imposed restraints on employees leaving their employers, state courts in the 1880s adopted the view that both parties to an employment contract could terminate it at any time for any reason. This was termed the "at-will doctrine," and it quickly spread from state to state to become the overwhelmingly dominant common law of employment.[40]

At its inception, the at-will doctrine provided certain benefits for unskilled workers, benefits which can only be understood in relation to what existed before. Throughout most of the nineteenth century, the employment relationship was governed by the master-servant law. One aspect of master-servant law was the "entire contract doctrine," a doctrine that established constructive conditions concerning when payment was due in contracts for services. Under the entire contract doctrine, a worker who quit or was fired before the end of the term of his employment contract forfeited any wages for the time worked. For example, if a worker was hired for a year and left voluntarily after ten months, he would often find himself with no pay for the period he had worked. If the contract was for an unspecified term, courts would imply a time period, such as a harvest season or a year, and thus impose a similar forfeiture on a worker who left prematurely. If the employment was preterminated because the worker was fired, courts also imposed a forfeiture unless they found that the worker had been dismissed without cause. But courts were reluctant to find that a dismissal was not for cause. Instead, they usually upheld dismissals on grounds of insubordination or violation of implicit duties of obedience. For example, in 1845 a worker was fired after

---

[39] Frank T. Carlton, *Restriction of Output,* in Frank T. Carlton, History and Problems of Organized Labor (1911), reprinted in Douglas et al., Workers in Modern Economic Society 662, 665.

[40] On the rapid diffusion of the at-will rule in the 1880s, *see* Jay M. Feinman, *The Development of the Employment at Will Rule,* 26 Am. J. Legal Hist. 118, 126–27 (1976).

she left her worksite to visit her dying mother, and the court found that she was fired for cause.[41]

The entire contract doctrine imposed considerable income insecurity on unskilled workers. Indeed, it gave employers an incentive to impose ever harsher demands on their workers as they neared the end of a fixed-term contract with the hope that the worker would quit and entirely lose his right to be paid.[42]

The at-will rule that swept through the state courts in the 1880s mitigated the harshness of the nineteenth-century entire contract regime. It provided that a worker hired on an indefinite contract had the right to be paid for the time worked, up to the moment he quit or was fired. Because the rule made it easier for workers to quit, the at-will rule gave unskilled workers a degree of autonomy and freedom they had not theretofore possessed.[43] It also gave them income security, at least for the time they worked. It did not give them employment security, but unskilled workers had never enjoyed that in the first place.

The impact of the at-will doctrine on skilled workers was more ambiguous. Skilled workers needed neither income security nor employment security from the law – they already had those benefits by virtue of their knowledge of the craft and the power of their craft unions. For them, job security did not arise from attachment to a particular employer. However, the new mobility of labor heralded by the at-will regime ultimately threatened their craft autonomy. The legal change made it easier for employers to obtain workers, including unskilled workers, to perform the newly deskilled jobs. Thus the at-will rule contributed to the undermining of the craft unions' monopoly over the production process.

E. Confrontation and Breakdown in Artisanal Production

In the late nineteenth century, product markets expanded as a result of rapid domestic growth and increased international trade. To compete in the new arena, employers needed to raise the productivity of labor.[44] However, as

---

[41] Turner v. Mason, 14 M. & W. 112 (1845), discussed in Karen Orren, BELATED FEUDALISM: LABOR, THE LAW AND LIBERAL DEVELOPMENT IN THE UNITED STATES 96 (1991). *See also* Robert Steinfeld, COERCION, CONTRACT, AND FREE LABOR IN THE NINETEENTH CENTURY (2001).

[42] *See* Britton v. Turner, 6 N.H. 481 (N.H. 1834). It is important to note that the Britton v. Turner case was unusual and did not represent the majority approach. *See* Steinfeld, THE INVENTION OF FREE LABOR 151–52.

[43] For a discussion of the progressive potential of the at-will revolution in employment law, *see* Steinfeld, COERCION, CONTRACT, AND FREE LABOR.

[44] Between 1880 and 1910, the United States experienced unprecedented economic expansion at the same time that the population more than doubled. *See* Reinhard Bendix, WORK AND AUTHORITY IN INDUSTRY: IDEOLOGIES OF MANAGEMENT IN THE COURSE OF INDUSTRIALIZATION 254–55 (1956).

discussed, manufacturing employers in the nineteenth century played little role in either the process of production or the establishment of wages, and hence they had little ability to influence the productivity of labor. Efforts to increase productivity led to increased union agitation and increasingly violent labor-management confrontations.[45] Because the craft-dominated labor system did not permit employers to raise productivity, they deliberately set out to destroy the skilled workers' control of the production process.

By the end of the century, American manufacturers in many sectors were determined to break the union work rules and destroy the skilled workers' monopoly of knowledge about production.[46] In the 1890s, many formed industry-specific trade associations and national organizations like the National Association of Manufacturers to wage a concentrated "open shop campaign" against the growing union movement. According to the sociologist Reinhard Bendix:

[T]he employers' endorsement of the need for collective action was a clear-cut departure from established ideas and practices. To be sure, employers had organized in the past in order to have their common interests represented more effectively. But never had they organized in order to solve problems of management within the enterprise....

The outlook of American employers changed in other respects during the open-shop campaign.... One of these changes consisted in the fact that employers were being forced to concern themselves with labor as a problem rather than 'solve' it by simply dismissing the worker who would not do. [47]

The first significant battle over control of the production process between skilled workers and manufacturers in American industry was the lock-out at Carnegie Corporation's Homestead Steel Works in 1892. The Homestead Works was organized by the Amalgamated Association of Iron, Steel, and Tin Workers, a large and powerful organization, dominated by skilled iron workers. Andrew Carnegie and Henry Clay Frick, top executives of the Carnegie Steel Corporation, were determined to eliminate the union from Homestead once and for all. In 1892, just before the contract with the Amalgamated was to expire, Carnegie transferred managing authority of the mill to Frick. Frick was already notorious for his brutal treatment of strikers in the Connellsville coke regions. Frick built a fence three miles long around the entire Homestead Works and topped it with barbed wire. He built platforms for sentinels, put in holes for rifles along the fence, and built barracks inside to house strikebreakers. Frick then retained three hundred guards from the Pinkerton Detective Agency, closed down the Works, dismissed the workforce, and announced that henceforth the Works would operate nonunion.

[45] *Id.* at 265–66.
[46] Montgomery, WORKERS' CONTROL IN AMERICA 24.
[47] Bendix, WORK AND AUTHORITY 269–70.

In the four months that followed, Homestead workers battled Pinkerton guards, the local sheriff, and the state militia. Dozens of men were killed in the bloody battles. Eventually the state and federal troops came in on the side of the Carnegie Corporation and helped it to defeat the union. After four months, the Works reopened with strikebreakers and operated nonunion for the next fifty years. After defeating the Amalgamated in Homestead, the Carnegie Steel Corporation used blacklists and spies to eliminate the union from all of Carnegie's other mills.[48]

Having thus destroyed the union, Carnegie gained the freedom to set the work rules and production techniques within the firm.[49] The company also hastened the pace of technological change in all stages of steel production. In the decade after Homestead, the company introduced a cornucopia of innovations – electric trolleys, the pig casting machine, the Jones mixer, mechanical ladle cars, electric traveling cranes, the Wellman charger, electric cars, and rising-and-falling tables in the rolling mills. These mechanic innovations were heavily capital intensive – they eliminated much manual work and also eliminated much of the human skill required for steel production.[50]

After Homestead, other firms followed Carnegie's lead, taking hard lines against the craft unions and breaking their power.[51] The demise of the craft unions opened up possibilities for employers to abandon the previous system of employment relations and create one that did not depend upon cooperation of skilled workers. In the early twentieth century, they set out to do just that.

---

[48] See Stone, *The Origins of Job Structures* 34.
[49] For a description of the Homestead lockout, *see* David Brody, STEELWORKERS IN AMERICA: THE NON-UNION ERA (1998); Stone, *The Origins of Job Structures* 34–35.
[50] Stone, *The Origin of Job Structures* 34–37.
[51] David Montgomery, THE FALL OF THE HOUSE OF LABOR: THE WORKPLACE, THE STATE, AND AMERICAN LABOR ACTIVISM, 1865–1925 (1987).

2

The Labor System of the Industrial Era

In the late nineteenth and early twentieth centuries, employers' widespread success in breaking the skilled workers' unions caused the entire artisanal system of work organization, wage determination, and training to collapse. As a result, employers had to construct a new labor system. They were determined to build a new system in which production was not dependent upon the knowledge and cooperation of skilled workers. The labor-saving and skill-saving innovations of the preceding decades partially freed employers from the stranglehold of the craft workers, but new technology alone could not create a new labor system. Employers still had to adapt the jobs to the new technology and had to prevent ineptitude, neglect, and sabotage of the new machines. This meant training workers to operate the machines and to ensure that the machines were properly tended, coordinated, and maintained. In addition, employers had to motivate workers to perform the newly deskilled jobs efficiently, rather than begrudgingly. That is, they had to prevent deliberate restriction of output and build a spirit of cooperation. And finally, they had to establish mechanisms and practices that would ensure that employers, rather than workers, maintained lasting control over the pace and quality of production.

A. The Twentieth-Century "Labor Problem"

After the skilled workers' unions were broken and their skills downgraded, employers found themselves with a crisis of discipline and morale on the shop floor. In the artisanal era, skilled workers saw themselves as partners in production, so that the problem of motivation did not arise. The wage structure and the inside contracting system gave skilled workers the sense that they were working for themselves. But with the command and control style of supervision of the post-Homestead era, skilled workers no longer were self-motivated. Instead, the issue of how hard workers worked became an issue of conflict.

At the same time, new technological advances had created a vast new category of workers, the category of the semiskilled. These were primarily machine tenders – people who performed neither the hauling and hoisting work of unskilled workers in the past, nor the highly skilled craft work of the artisans that preceded them. Semiskilled workers required some training to enable them to operate a machine or perform on an assembly line, but they did not require the extensive apprenticeship of the nineteenth-century artisans. Readily available and easily trained, semiskilled workers were, from the employer's point of view, interchangeable.

The homogenization of the workforce produced another problem that employers had not anticipated. With the old skilled/unskilled dichotomy and the exclusiveness of the craft unions disappearing, there was a greater possibility than ever that workers would see their interests in class terms. The early twentieth century was a time when labor radicalism flourished. While the American Federation of Labor (AFL) was conservative and apolitical, the American Socialist Party and the Industrial Workers of the World were growing rapidly. Employers feared anarchism, socialism, and, after 1917, Bolshevism inside the plant gates.

Both the problem of worker motivation and the problem of deterring concerted radical opposition were aspects of what was known, at the turn-of-the-century, as the "labor problem." The labor problem was a ubiquitous topic in academic as well as industrial circles.[1] To solve the labor problem, employers embraced theories of scientific management and personnel management – two complementary and overlapping approaches to the problem of work organization. The approaches resulted in new methods of wage payment, new promotion policies, and paternalistic welfare policies. These practices were designed to bind the worker to the firm, to engender worker loyalty, and to create incentives for hard work. Together they embodied the essence of what are today called internal labor market job structures.

B. Scientific Management and the Problem of Worker Motivation

To help construct a new labor system, employers turned to a newly emerging professional group – industrial engineers. Until the mid nineteenth century, industrial engineers consisted of a motley group of machine designers who made drawings with chalk on factory floors. But in the 1860s and 1870s, industrial engineering matured into a profession. In 1871, the first American technical college devoted to mechanical engineering, the Stevens Institute of Technology, was formed. In 1880, the American Society of Mechanical Engineers (ASME), was organized. The ASME was initially comprised of industrial engineers concerned with technical aspects of machine design and

---

[1] Reinhard Bendix, WORK AND AUTHORITY IN INDUSTRY: IDEOLOGIES OF MANAGEMENT IN THE COURSE OF INDUSTRIALIZATION 266–74 (1956).

operation. At about the same time, departments of industrial engineering were created in business and technical schools to train young men in the applied and practical arts of modern enterprise. These young engineers, together with the more seasoned ASME members, applied themselves to the tasks of mechanical improvement, work flow design, and task routinization. They were dedicated to creating efficiencies in the newly emerging factories of the era. The results of these quests for efficiency were disseminated through academic conferences and professional journals and implemented on the ground by industrial engineering consultants.

Before long the engineers began to search for systematic solutions to human as well as technical problems in production. In 1886, the ASME annual meetings, which previously had been devoted to technical topics, began to include presentations on the subject of work management and organization. When addressing managerial issues and labor problems, the ASME engineers displayed the same optimistic faith in the ability of science to solve social problems that they deployed in attacking mechanical problems. They turned their attention to assisting employers to devise job structures that would free them from the monopoly of knowledge possessed by skilled artisans.

The industrial engineers were rationalizers and systematizers – they wanted to abandon the ad hoc, unsystematic, idiosyncratic practices of the past and replace them with scientifically verifiable, cost-effective, efficiency-enhancing systems for running an enterprise. To this end, they proposed new institutions of wage setting, promotion, training, and job control that would enable employers to transfer skills and knowledge about production from the workers to management.

1. New Methods of Wage Determination

The first step in establishing the new job structures was the development of a new payment system. Factory managers learned early on that when workers were paid by the day, they had no incentive to maintain a reasonable work pace. Instead, workers engaged in "soldiering" – collective, deliberate restriction of output down to the level of the lowest common denominator of the group. To combat soldiering, employers instituted piecework systems, pursuant to which they paid a fixed sum for each unit produced. By 1902, for example, piecework was nearly universal in the steel industry for all types of production work above the lowest unskilled level.[2]

The theory of piecework was that workers would drive themselves to work harder in order to maximize their earnings. However, piecework systems usually failed. This was because with piecework, workers could raise their pay by working harder or finding faster ways to do a job. When managers

---

[2] Katherine Van Wezel Stone, *The Origins of Job Structures in the Steel Industry*, in LABOR MARKET SEGMENTATION 44–45 (D. Gordon, M. Reich, & R. Edwards, eds., 1975). J. Stephan Jeans, AMERICAN INDUSTRIAL CONDITIONS AND COMPETITION 58 (1902).

saw pieceworkers' earnings becoming too high – that is, higher than the rate managers believed the workers should receive – they cut the piece rates. The temptation of managers to cut piece rates was widespread and practically irresistible. Managers' powerful impulse to cut rates stemmed in part from their belief that increases in output under piece rates were the result of their own innovations in methods or technology, not the result of greater worker efforts. Thus managers felt they were entitled to reap the benefit of the increased output, which they could only do by cutting the rates. The other reason for the rate-cutting impulse was the managers' intuitive sense of what was proper for workingmen to earn. Once workers' earnings surpassed this unstated norm, managers felt entitled to cut the rate in order to generate a level of wages commensurate with what the workers had previously earned.

Cuts in piece rates invariably had a devastating impact on workers' productivity. The father of scientific management, Frederick Winslow Taylor, described the effect of rate cuts in a machine shop:

Even the most stupid man, after receiving two or three piece work "cuts" as a reward for his having worked harder, resents this treatment and seeks a remedy for it in the future. Thus begins a war, generally an amicable war, but none the less a war, between the workmen and management. The latter endeavors by every means to induce the workmen to increase the output, and the men gauge the rapidity with which they work, so as never to earn over a certain rate of wages, knowing that if they exceed this amount the piece work price will surely be cut, sooner or later.[3]

Once workers experienced a rate cut, they were thereafter careful to restrict their effort so as not to "spoil the job." Cuts in piece rates also caused tremendous anger amongst the workers and led to bitter conflict. Indeed, most of the major strikes in the early twentieth century were precipitated by a cut in piece rates. The mere threat of a rate cut induced workers collectively to slow down their pace of production, thereby defeating the purpose of the piece-rate system.[4]

The propensity of employers to cut piece rates and the resultant decline in productivity and increase in conflict that rate cuts engendered made piece-rate payment systems an unsatisfactory solution to the labor problem. Thus late-nineteenth-century industrial engineers experimented with

---

[3] Frederick Winslow Taylor, *A Piece-Rate System: Being a Step Toward Partial Solution to the Labor Problem*," presented at the AMSE Meeting, 1895, reprinted in Scientific Management 636, 644 (Clarence Bertrand Thompson, ed., 1972).

[4] On the inevitability of rates-cutting under a piecework system and its effect on work effort, *see* Hugh G. J. Aitken, Taylorism at Watertown Arsenal: Scientific Management in Action, 1908–1915, 39 (1960); Robert Kanigel, The One Best Way 141–42, 210–11 (1997); C. Bertrand Thompson, *The Relation of Scientific Management to the Wage Problem* in Thompson, Scientific Management 706, 709–10, reprinted from 21 J. Pol. Econ. 630. *See generally* Taylor, *A Piece-Rate System*. *See also* Stone, *The Origins of Job Structures* 41–42.

modifications of the piece rate system that would enable employers to avoid the temptation to cut rates. ASME members developed several new wage payment methods, called premium or bonus plans, that gave workers more pay for more output, but less than a full pro rata share of the incremental profit from each additional piece. For example, in 1891, a well-known industrial engineer, Frederick Halsey, proposed a premium plan that involved establishing a base rate based upon the base time period required to do a job. Workers who completed the job faster than the base time period would receive a bonus calculated as a percentage of the monetary value of the time saved by the extra productivity. Halsey maintained that by paying the worker a premium that was less than the value of the increased production, employers would no longer be tempted to cut the rates. The craft unions vigorously opposed Halsey's and other similar premium plans because they undermined the unions' control over wage setting.[5]

In 1895, Frederick Winslow Taylor proposed a different system of wage payment. Called the "differential piece rate," Taylor's system involved setting two rates for a job – a low piece rate for the "average workman," and a high piece rate for the "first class workman." Only the fast workers were entitled to the high piece rate. The high rate was set to give the worker about a 60 percent increase in earnings, in exchange for a 300–400 percent increase in output. While the high rate was a reward for fast work, the low rate was a punishment for slow work. The low rate was set so low that it was difficult to earn a regular day's pay. Part of the idea of the differential piece rate was not only to induce the workers to set a fast pace, but to discourage and eventually weed out those who could not, or would not, do so.[6]

The most significant difference between Taylor's differential piece rate plan and Halsey's premium plan lay in the method each one used to set the base rate for each job. Halsey's plan used existing practices as the norm, thus incorporating existing inefficiencies and restrictive practices into the rates. Taylor, on the other hand, believed it was possible to determine scientifically the "correct" base rate for each job – i.e., the amount of output a typical hard-working worker could produce in a day. He claimed that his system, by using the scientifically correct rate rather than past performance as the base, avoided the problem of perpetuating existing inefficient practices. In 1895, when Taylor first presented his article on differential piece work to the American Society of Mechanical Engineers, Halsey was in the audience. Halsey expressed skepticism about the claim that it was in fact possible to determine scientifically the maximum possible output for each task. Taylor responded by criticizing Halsey's plan for its use of historical rates, stating

---

[5] Daniel Nelson, MANAGERS AND WORKERS: ORIGINS OF THE TWENTIETH-CENTURY FACTORY SYSTEM IN THE UNITED STATES, 1880–1920, 45–46 (1995).

[6] *See generally* Aitken, TAYLORISM; Kanigel, ONE BEST WAY; Taylor, *A Piece-Rate System*.

that such a plan invited the workmen to soldier in order to set a high price per piece at the outset.[7]

Taylor's "scientific" system was comprised of two techniques to develop productivity benchmarks from which to set the "correct" rates for each job – job analysis and time study. Job analysis entailed extensive observation and experiments to determine how long each task should take. Taylor was the chief engineer of the Midvale Steel Company in 1884, and he used his position to engage in extensive experiments to ascertain the various tasks involved in machine-tool work. He and his disciples broke all work tasks into their component motions, identified wasteful motions, and determined the best way to perform each motion. He also redefined the jobs themselves. For example, while an operator of a metal-cutting machine might stop periodically to sharpen his tools, Taylor insisted that the metal-cutter's job was to operate the machine, period. It was someone else's job to keep the tools sharp. Thus Taylor's job analysis led not only to the discovery of efficient work practices, but also to a minute division of labor and a breakdown of job duties into smaller and narrower categories.[8] Robert Kanigel, Taylor's biographer, describes an imaginary Faustian bargain in which Taylor says to the workman, "You do it my way, by my standards, at the speed I mandate, and in doing so achieve a level of output I ordain, and I'll pay you handsomely for it, beyond anything you might have imagined. All you have to do is take orders, give up your way of doing the job for mine."[9]

Taylor also invented systematic time and motion study to give employers a yardstick by which to measure how long each job should take. Time studies were conducted as follows: The time-study man would select a "first-class man," observe his task performance, eliminate all unnecessary motions, and then, once the job was performed in "the one best way," time each motion with a stop watch. Each job was timed several times and the results averaged to account for minor variations in conditions. Then the time required for each motion was added up to arrive at the correct time for the whole job. Taylor discovered early on that it was necessary to add an allowance to the total, and he conducted experiments to determine how great the allowance should be. For example, he determined that in machine shops it was necessary to increase the sum by 67 percent to achieve an accurate base time for the job.[10] Despite the addition of the seemingly arbitrary fudge factor that the allowance introduced into the equation, Carl Barth, one of Taylor's leading disciples, claimed that time study, with the proper adjustment, was

---

[7] *See Discussion*, PROCEEDINGS, 16 AMSE 856, reprinted in Thompson, SCIENTIFIC MANAGEMENT 666, 667–72.

[8] Aitken, TAYLORISM. For a description of how time study changed the nature of the tasks involved in machining a locomotive tire and overhauling a boiler, *see* Kanigel, ONE BEST WAY, 202–9.

[9] Kanigel, ONE BEST WAY 214.

[10] Aitken, TAYLORISM 105–12; Kanigel, ONE BEST WAY 227–30.

"scientific" because "it determines exactly – scientifically – the length of time in which a man can do a piece of work."[11] Taylor touted his differential piecework plan for its success not only in increasing output but also in fostering industrial harmony. Taylor claimed that workers appreciated the higher earnings that they could earn under his system and believed that each man was fairly rewarded according to his own efforts. At the ASME meeting in 1895, Taylor delivered his paper "A Piece-Rate System," in which he boasted that his system "promotes a most friendly feeling between the men and their employers, and so renders labor unions and strikes unnecessary. There has never been a strike by men working under this system."[12] The system spread widely, so that by 1928 the National Industrial Conference Board found in a survey of plant managers that "there was little dissent from the opinion that the [Taylor premium plan] is effective in promoting industrial harmony."[13]

2. Transferring Knowledge from the Skilled Worker to the Firm

Taylor's differential piece-rate system was the opening gambit in his wholesale revolution in management ideology and practice. Taylor believed that so long as valuable knowledge about production was held exclusively by the workers, managers were vulnerable to soldiering and sabotage. Workers could use their superior knowledge as a hostage to extract concessions in wages or other working conditions. Taylor was not satisfied that time and motion studies alone could overcome management's substantial handicap on the shop floor. Management needed more than just time studies, it needed to revise the entire method by which work was organized, supervised, and implemented. In the new method, management instead of workers would decide how and what tasks were to be performed, in what sequence, and at what pace. Taylor called this new method Scientific Management.

In 1905, Taylor published his acclaimed book, PRINCIPLES OF SCIENTIFIC MANAGEMENT, in which he wrote:

In an industrial establishment which employs say from 500 to 1000 workmen, there will be found in many cases at least twenty to thirty different trades. The workmen in each of these trades have had their knowledge handed down to them by word of mouth, through the many years in which their trade has been developed....The ingenuity of each generation has developed quicker and better methods for doing every element of the work in every trade....The ingenuity and experience of each generation – of each decade, even, have without doubt handed over better methods to the next. This mass of rule-of-thumb or traditional knowledge may be said to

---

[11] *Scientific Management*, Tuck School Conference, Dartmouth College (1912), 174–75, quoted in Aitken, TAYLORISM 24. Aitken argues that the allowance factor detracts from any claim that time study is in fact "scientific." *See* Aitken, TAYLORISM 24–25.

[12] Frederick Winslow Taylor, SHOP MANAGEMENT 183 (1911).

[13] National Industrial Conference Board, SYSTEMS OF WAGE PAYMENT 60 (1928).

be the principal asset or possession of every tradesman. Now, in the best of the ordinary types of management, the managers recognize the fact that the 500 or 1000 workmen, included in the twenty or thirty trades, who are under them, possess this mass of traditional knowledge, a large part of which is not in the possession of the management.... And yet these foremen and superintendents know, better than any one else, that their own knowledge and personal skill falls far short of the combined knowledge and dexterity of all the workmen under them.[14]

PRINCIPLES OF SCIENTIFIC MANAGEMENT was a how-to guide for management to systematically transfer that traditional, accumulated, rule-of-thumb knowledge from the worker to the management. According to Taylor's disciple, H. K. Hathaway, "The first great principle of Scientific Management is the establishment of a science in place of rule-of-thumb knowledge."[15]

Taylor's system was designed to promote efficiency by restructuring the location of knowledge in the employment relationship. To this end, Taylor and his followers used time and motion studies not only to set rates but also to provide management with knowledge about production processes. They studied, timed, and recorded the component motions of every task in order to determine the "one best way" to perform each task. Thus, for example, they determined the optimal weight for a shovel, the best method for cutting each type of metal, the ideal thickness and speed for transmission belts, and so forth. Taylor and his followers' exhaustive studies of the minutiae of industrial work were designed to take knowledge out of the exclusive possession of the workers so that management could determine the best way for each task to be performed.

Taylor advised companies to establish a planning department to serve as the central control for the flow of all work through the production process. The planning department, he counseled, should develop a series of flow charts, called routing systems, that would show the path of each piece of material as it progressed through the plant and designate how much time each operation should take. In this way, all production work would be programmed in advance and then reduced to charts. Routing clerks would lay out the exact route each piece was to travel through the shop. The planning department would then issue instruction cards to the foremen, who would then issue directions to the workers. The system separated thinking from doing, with all the thinking done by the planning department. As Taylor admonished, "All possible brain work should be removed from the shop and centered in the planning or laying-out department."[16]

Under Taylor's system, the job of foreman was also subdivided into several functions. One foreman was to prepare the work and machines, another to

---

[14] Frederick Winslow Taylor, PRINCIPLES OF SCIENTIFIC MANAGEMENT 31–32 (1911).
[15] H. K. Hathaway, *The Planning Department, Its Organization and Function*, INDUSTRIAL ENGINEERING, vol. 12, reprinted in Thompson, SCIENTIFIC MANAGEMENT 366, 369.
[16] Taylor, SHOP MANAGEMENT 99.

see that tools were provided, another to oversee the work and ensure it was done in proper sequences, another to oversee machines to ensure that they were operating at optimal speeds, and another to study the work and fix piece rates. In his system, each foreman, like each workman, was given a clear set of instructions and job duties. Thus Taylor's "functional foremanship" was a method for subdividing, and deskilling, the tasks of supervision.

Taylor's system also involved changes in the administrative and technical side of factories. One of his greatest contributions was his discovery of the best types of metal for each cutting task and the optimum speed for drills that could be used. He also determined the optimal size of a shovel, the correct method to organize the toolroom, and so forth. At the same time, he devised systems for cost accounting, record keeping, and administration – means by which knowledge could be retained and retrieved. Taylor even prescribed the type of penmanship to be used in filling out time cards: "plain letters with straight lines must in all cases be written upon the time notes," he wrote in Standard Order No. 27 at Bethlehem Steel. In the Taylorized factory, nothing was left to individual discretion, initiative, or chance.[17]

Scientific management was based upon the belief that all production knowledge could be described scientifically, reduced to written form, and transmitted as discrete instructions to each worker on a need-to-know basis. The routing system assumed a form of production that could be charted in advance, down to the smallest detail. In the scientifically managed factory, humans would operate like well-oiled machines, each one performing its precise role continuously, efficiently, without introducing modifications or qualifications to the task to be performed. This system, in which thinking was totally divorced from doing, was the antithesis of the artisanal labor system in which knowledge was embodied in the workers themselves.

3. The Dissemination of Taylor's Ideas

Taylor's system of scientific management received national attention in 1910. That year, at a hearing on railroad rate increases before the Interstate Commerce Commission, Louis Dembitz Brandeis, the "People's Lawyer" of the Progressive Movement, gave Taylor and his ideas a public showcase. The railroads had applied for a rate increase. In opposing the railroads' rate request, Brandeis argued that if they adopted Taylor's scientific management methods, they would save over $300 million a year and would not need the increase. Brandeis put on a parade of witnesses, all followers of Taylor, who eloquently testified that Taylor's theories and methods were a path to prosperity, efficiency, and social betterment. Taylor was portrayed as an alchemist whose methods could create untold wealth out of the mundanities

---

[17] Kanigel, ONE BEST WAY 349–50.

of machine tools and metal lathes. The case gave scientific management a national stage, and turned scientific management and efficiency into house-hold words.[18]

After the hearings, many firms adopted parts of Taylor's system, and a cult of efficiency took hold in corporate culture. While few firms imple-mented scientific management in its entirety, the differential piece rates, sys-tematic time study, routing cards, and other parts of the system were widely used.

Wherever scientific management was applied, workers and their unions were staunch in their opposition. For example, in 1910, five thousand work-ers at Bethlehem Steel's South Bethlehem Works spontaneously went on strike against the introduction of Taylor's premium plan.[19] Workers had many reasons for opposing scientific management: the speeding up of work, the downgrading of the workers' skills, the reduction of jobs to boring repetitive tasks, and the authoritarian nature of Taylorist factory supervision.

One of the most highly publicized rebellions against Taylor's system oc-curred at the Watertown Armory. In 1909, Taylor scored a major coup when the U.S. Army decided to install scientific management at the Watertown Arsenal. Taylor saw this as an opportunity to get national attention for his theories. He assigned his top disciple, Carl Barth, to oversee the work. Barth and his assistant, Dwight Merrick, spent more than four years at the arse-nal reorganizing operations, setting up a planning department, establishing a routing system, and introducing a time study. In August 1911, however, they ran into trouble when they tried to initiate time studies in the foundry. The molders, with their craft traditions and artisanal sensibilities, refused to cooperate. The molders petitioned management to stop the time studies, and when management refused, the molders went on strike. The strike generated a great deal of public sympathy for the molders who were seen as defying the dehumanizing aspects of Taylorism.[20]

Taylor maintained that resistance to his system by workers was predictable and inevitable. He saw the strike at the Watertown Arsenal as a showdown between the craft workers' desire to hoard information and management's right to information about the work process. As he wrote Barth, "This strike hits at the very foundation of scientific management, and if the owners of the company or the government are not to be allowed to obtain exact in-formation, then scientific management becomes impossible." Taylor insisted that his system was not only in management's interest but in the workers'

---

[18] Id. at 429–36.

[19] Stone, The Origins of Job Structures 45.

[20] See Jean Trepp McKelvey, AFL ATTITUDES TOWARD PRODUCTION 1900–1932, 16 (1952) (de-scribing AFL opposition to Taylorism and AFL President Sam Gompers's attack on Taylor's efficiency schemes in wake of the Watertown strike); Aitken, TAYLORISM; Kanigel, ONE BEST WAY 449–84.

interest as well, and he urged employers to adopt a "tough love" approach to union opposition.[21]

The strike at the Watertown Arsenal was short-lived but it set in motion a public outcry against scientific management that threatened to derail Taylor's whole project. In 1912, Congress's House Committee to Investigate the Taylor and Other Systems of Shop Management initiated a four-city investigation into Taylor's methods. In 1914, Taylorism was again investigated by the U.S. Industrial Relations Commission, at which time Taylor and his disciples were subjected to an exacting and hostile interrogation. As a result of these hearings, Congress attached a rider to the Army Bill in 1915 prohibiting the further use of time study or premium systems in any government arsenals.[22]

Despite such setbacks, Taylor's ideas grew in influence in the corporate world. His primary influence lay not in his specific proposals but in his whole approach to management. He gave employers both a method and a justification for taking knowledge away from skilled workers and appropriating it for themselves. He showed them that it was in the interests of profitability, efficiency, and distributive justice for factories to operate on scientific and rational principles rather than on the basis of the mysteries of the traditional crafts. By insisting on rational methods for organizing everything, his system freed production from the idiosyncrasies of particular individuals, thus making it possible for businesses to expand.[23] Taylor and his followers boasted that scientific management yielded significant results at the companies where his techniques were implemented.[24] For example, the Tabor Manufacturing Company in Philadelphia retained Barth to install Taylor's system when it was faced with imminent failure in 1903. By 1910, Tabor's president reported that the company produced two and a half times as much value in finished product as it had under the old regime, with the same work force.[25] Results such as these demonstrated to the business community that success

---

[21] C. Bertrand Thompson, *Wages and Wage Systems as Incentives*, in Thompson, SCIENTIFIC MANAGEMENT 684, 703–5 (1915), reprinted from SYSTEM, vol. 22 (stating that "[t]hough the results [of Taylorism] read like a fairy tale, to get them requires in investment of time, money and patience which few feel prepared to make"). *See also* H. K. Hathaway in his article *Prerequisites to the Introduction of Scientific Management*, in Thompson, SCIENTIFIC MANAGEMENT 270–78, reprinted from 41 ENGINEERING MAGAZINE 141 (1915) (relating the difficulties encountered by many firms in instituting scientific management and the many temptations to adopt half-way measures instead).

[22] *See* Aitken, TAYLORISM 143–53 (foundry strike), 229–34 (hearings and legislation).

[23] *See* James Mapes Dodge, *The Spirit in Which Scientific Management Should be Approached,* in Thompson, SCIENTIFIC MANAGEMENT 286, 287.

[24] On the successful implementation of Taylor's techniques at certain "Taylorist showcases," *see* Judith Merkle, MANAGEMENT AND IDEOLOGY: THE LEGACY OF THE INTERNATIONAL SCIENTIFIC MANAGEMENT MOVEMENT 56–58 (1980).

[25] Wilfred Lewis, *An Object Lesson in Efficiency,* in Thompson, SCIENTIFIC MANAGEMENT 232, 236, reprinted from W. Lewis, TECHNOLOGY AND INDUSTRIAL EFFICIENCY (1911).

depended upon expertise, science, and professional management, not on the knowledge reposited in skilled workers. Thus over time, many of Taylor's innovations, such as time study, foremanship, planning departments, and narrow job classifications became common management practices.

C. Personnel Management and the "Human Factor" in Production

After the depression of 1914–15, another new school of management science came to the fore – the field of personnel management. Like scientific management, personnel management sought to solve labor problems by restructuring management and administration. However, unlike scientific management, personnel management was linked to the field of psychology rather than to engineering. Personnel management was critical of scientific management for creating impersonal industrial conditions and treating employees merely as machines. Its practitioners sought to increase productivity and industrial performance by attention to the "human factor" in industry. They believed that management needed a cadre of committed long-term employees rather than a revolving set of drifters and roamers. Thus personnel managers advocated that employers institute workplace practices that would build employee loyalty, commitment, and morale.[26] They advocated that corporations establish welfare programs, advancement opportunities, suggestion systems, and grievance procedures. Their most lasting contributions were to advocate that employers create hierarchical job ladders for internal promotion, and to use internal promotion rather than lateral hiring for all vacancies. The use of job ladders was promoted as a solution to the problems of turnover and training, both matters of concern to employers in the post-artisanal era.

1. Addressing the Turnover Problem

Personnel management was initially a response to the growing problem of employee turnover that resulted from the confluence of the demise of the artisanal era job structures, the rise of the at-will regime, and the institution of scientific management. The at-will rule made it easier for employees to change jobs. At the same time, employers diminished the skill requirements of jobs so that they could hire employees into semiskilled jobs and train them to perform well within a short time. Henry Ford boasted that with his assembly line, rank-and-file workers could learn their jobs in a few hours or a few days.[27] Bethlehem Steel's Charles Schwab claimed, in 1902, that he could "take a green hand... and make a steel melter of him in six or eight

---

[26] Bruce E. Kaufman, THE ORIGINS AND EVOLUTION OF THE FIELD OF INDUSTRIAL RELATIONS 23–27 (1993).

[27] Henry Ford, MY LIFE AND WORK 79 (1926).

weeks."[28] Given that the job of melter was then the most highly skilled job in the open hearth department, it is apparent that workers could learn the necessary skills for high level blue-collar jobs rather quickly. As University of Chicago economist Paul H. Douglas observed, "A machine-tender who has learned the general principle of caring for a machine can attend ribbon-weaving machinery as well as shoe-making. He is really an interchangeable part of the industrial mechanism."[29] Hence workers became more likely to quit and move on when jobs no longer suited them. The nascent at-will doctrine aided workers in their new-found mobility.

Turnover rates had been high throughout the nineteenth century, but turnover only came to be perceived as a serious problem after 1910. Several studies confirmed high rates of turnover in manufacturing and railroad establishments, sometimes upwards of 300 percent.[30] For example, it was found that in 1912 the General Electric Company had to hire 42,000 workers in order to expand by 6,700 workers.[31] In 1913, the Ford Motor Company hired 963 men to expand by 100.[32] With turnover came unemployment, and social reformers concluded that turnover and unemployment were two interrelated social ills of the era.[33] Turnover, the social reformers proclaimed, was costly to the firm, the employee, and society.

While social reformers were concerned with the impact of turnover on the social fabric, employers became distressed about the impact of turnover on their firms. Many saw it as a symptom of low morale. University of Chicago's Sumner Slichter warned that high turnover rates were both a cause and a symptom of worker discontent and could easily tip over into labor unrest.[34]

In the early 1900s, a new school of personnel management coalesced around the problem of turnover. To reduce turnover, the personnel management school advocated that firms create personnel departments and give them responsibility for hiring and firing, thus removing such decisions from the foremen. The personnel management theorists also urged firms to institute a systematic promotion plan in order to motivate employees to give greater effort, to build loyalty, to diminish turnover, and to provide a systematic mechanism for skill development. For example, Meyer Bloomfield, a leader in the personnel management field, wrote in his 1921 textbook, "what makes men restless is the inability to move, or to get ahead."[35] Bloomfield

---

[28] Jeans, AMERICAN INDUSTRIAL CONDITIONS 62.
[29] Paul H. Douglas, AMERICAN APPRENTICESHIP AND INDUSTRIAL EDUCATION 124 (1921).
[30] New York Factory Investigation, 1912 and 1915; Russell Sage studies report; U.S. Dept. of Labor Statistics report, 1914.
[31] Sumner H. Slichter, THE TURNOVER OF FACTORY LABOR 17 (1919).
[32] Keith Sword, THE LEGEND OF HENRY FORD 49 (1968).
[33] Alexander Keyssar, OUT OF WORK: THE FIRST CENTURY OF UNEMPLOYMENT IN MASSACHUSETTS 268–70 (1986).
[34] Slichter, TURNOVER 158. *See also* Sanford Jacoby, EMPLOYING BUREAUCRACY 116–21 (1985).
[35] Meyer Bloomfield, LABOR AND COMPENSATION 298 (1921).

referred to a number of major corporations that had established "a liberal system of promotion and transfer [that] has therefore become one of the most familiar features of a modern personnel plan, and some of the most interesting achievements of management may be traced to the workings of such a system."[36]

In a similar vein, in 1919 Sumner Slichter published a study on turnover in which he advocated that employers establish orderly internal promotion schemes as antidotes to excessive turnover. He urged employers to arrange jobs into sequences along which promotion would occur. He argued that these promotion sequences, today called "job ladders," would give workers an incentive to work harder and would therefore discourage turnover. In addition, the ladders would solve the problem of training. According to Slichter, "If the steps of advancement are properly worked out, the men will be advanced to jobs for which by previous experience they are best fitted, and will pass through the series of jobs which will best equip them for the most exacting and most remunerative jobs."[37]

Through the efforts of the personnel management movement, personnel departments were established in many major corporations in the years surrounding World War I. These departments were primarily concerned with the selection, assignment, and compensation of employees. They implemented reforms such as job classification, wage standardization, and rationalization of wage structures. One of their primary initiatives was to establish internal promotion systems to fill vacancies.[38]

Some industrialists discovered the benefits of internal promotion schemes even before the issue was touted by the personnel management movement. For example, Andrew Carnegie boasted in the nineteenth century that his organization only hired from within, and that every worker in his employ had a manager's baton in his lunch pail. In 1922, Judge Elbert Gary, the first president of U.S. Steel Corporation, told the presidents of U.S. Steel's subsidiaries:

We should give careful thought to the question as to who could be selected to satisfactorily fill any unoccupied place; and like suggestions should be made to the heads of all departments. Positions should be filled by promotions from the ranks, and if in any location there are none competent, this fact should be given attention and men trained accordingly.[39]

Consistent with the teachings of personnel management, hierarchical promotion schemes were established in many American industrial firms in the

---

[36] *Id.* at 298.

[37] Slichter, TURNOVER 290–91, 356–57.

[38] Sanford Jacoby, *The Development of Internal Labor Markets in American Manufacturing Firms,* in INTERNAL LABOR MARKETS 23, 38–39 (Paul Osterman, ed., 1984).

[39] Elbert Gary, ADDRESSES AND STATEMENTS, vol. 6 (March 29, 1922), quoted in Stone, *The Origins of Job Structures* 48.

teens and early 1920s. In the model promotion system, employees were hired only for the lowest level job – what is today called the "port of entry." All openings at higher levels were filled from within. Properly structured job ladders were designed not only to address the problems of turnover, but also to address the problem of skill acquisition and transmission, for each job was designed to be a training job for the job above it. That is, job ladders were designed to give employees firm-specific training and to induce them to train newcomers.

2. The Problem of Training

Training became a problem for employers once they destroyed the artisanal labor system with its time-tested mechanisms for intergenerational transfer of knowledge. By the early twentieth century, apprenticeship systems no longer functioned, and workers became reluctant to share knowledge with newcomers who could easily replace them in their jobs. Many employers decried the lack of apprentices and complained about the shortage of trained workers.

Under scientific management, training was not particularly problematic because the planning department and the routing cards were designed to embody all that needed be known about what and how to do each task. Management would determine the one best way to do each job, fully describe each work task, and train the worker to perform it correctly. The worker's job was to follow the detailed instructions. If management and foremen did their jobs properly, each worker would receive the precise amount of training needed for the job, and there would be no need for additional or ongoing training, nor for knowledge transfer between workers.

Despite Taylor's idealized system, many early-twentieth-century employers acknowledged the need for trained workers. Even firms that had gone to great lengths to rationalize production and deskill their jobs along Taylor's lines continued to need some workmen with specific skills such as maintenance, repair, and pattern making. Furthermore, semiskilled workers were just that, *semi*-skilled. They required some minimal training, even at the entry level, to learn the layout of the plant, the flow of materials, the quirks of the machines, and the tricks of the trade. Some of that knowledge was appropriated to management, but not all. Machines have idiosyncrasies, just as people do. They might work one day and require tending the next. Each tending, each tweaking, each modification, makes new quirks that affect future operations. Thus machines have histories that need to be taken into account by their operators.

One solution to the training problem was for employees to learn the skills that industry required before they were hired. To this end, employers established trade schools and advocated vocational education programs in the public schools so that future employees could learn such sought-after skills as machine repair and tool design. Some employers also instituted in-house

vocational training programs for young workers whom they hired.[40] But employers still faced a serious problem. Trade schools and vocational education
programs could not teach the firm-specific skills and specialized know-how
that industry required. Managers knew that their workers possessed crucial
knowledge about the production process that was unique to their shops–
knowledge about causes of bottlenecks and knowledge of opportunities for
efficiencies. Yet workers were reluctant to share this knowledge because they
feared it would lead to a cutback in staffing. Incumbent workers, fearful of
being replaced by "frisky young whipper-snappers," often refused to share
with them know-how, shop lore, and tricks of the trade necessary for successful job performance. Hence managers' needs were less for generalized
vocational training than for a means to induce their workers to share their
existing know-how with newcomers and with the firm.

Numerous approaches to the knowledge-sharing problem were attempted. For example, some firms established suggestion-box systems to
encourage workers to share their knowledge with the firm. These systems
paid workers for suggestions that were adopted and led to cost savings. But
even when the financial incentives were generous, workers were reluctant to
make suggestions that would cost a fellow worker his job.

Personnel management theorists proposed a better approach to the problem of training newcomers. They urged employers to give employees implicit
promises of job security – a tacit understanding that long-term workers were
valued and would not be summarily or arbitrarily discharged. This implicit
promise was conveyed through policies that encouraged longevity, such as
longevity-linked pay and benefit policies and the use of job ladders for pay
and advancement. With the carrot of raising wages and benefits, and the
security of an implicit promise of job security, workers were encouraged to
stay with the employer a long time and develop long-term attachment.

Job ladders, in conjunction with implicit assurances of job security, offered
a solution to the problem of intergenerational knowledge transfer. Hierarchical promotional systems could be designed to make firm-specific training
a part of everyone's job. Employers no longer needed to establish separate
training programs or utilize external apprenticeship programs to train for
the vast bulk of their production jobs. They also did not have to persuade
workers to acquire the firm-specific skills that their firms required, nor pay
unproductive trainees to acquire valuable skills. With job ladders, each job
was a built-in training experience, so that each worker was productive, even
while in training.

Job ladders thus solved the twin problems of encouraging the acquisition
of firm-specific knowledge and encouraging intergenerational knowledge
transfer. Where paths for promotion were fixed, incumbents were guaranteed

---

[40] Sol Cohen, *The Industrial Education Movement, 1909–1919*, 20 AM. Q. (1968); Jacoby, *Development of Internal Labor Markets* 23, 32–33.

a set pattern of advancement without fear that newcomers would be able to jump the queue. When incumbents further believed that their jobs were secure, then they had nothing to fear from sharing their knowledge. Thus job ladders and implicit assurances of job security gave workers the security they needed to share their knowledge.

3. Corporate Welfare Programs

In addition to encouraging the use of hierarchical promotion systems, the personnel management movement encouraged firms to establish social insurance and welfare programs. Several prominent firms established elaborate welfare programs in the early twentieth century that served as inspirations for the personnel management movement. For example, U.S. Steel devised a welfare program in the first years of its existence. In 1903, it established a stock-subscription plan for workers and a profit-sharing plan for executives. It also offered its workers old-age pensions and accident insurance. It engaged in a safety and sanitation campaign and built community housing, education, and recreation facilities. Because they believed that home ownership would encourage permanency in employment, U.S. Steel offered low-interest loans to workers who wanted to buy houses. The corporation also built tens of thousands of rental houses and even entire towns. Gary, Indiana, for example, was built from scratch by U.S. Steel. With a water purification and sewage system, Gary embodied the latest ideas about planning techniques and modern social services. U.S. Steel hired nurses to visit families of employees, employed dentists to visit the children's schools, and often supplemented teacher salaries. It built hospitals, libraries, and public schools. Every plant had its own glee club, band, or orchestra. Unoccupied company land was turned over to the workers for gardens, where with seed provided by the company, about a million dollars' worth of vegetables were produced each year. For its employees' recreation, U.S. Steel built, by 1924, 175 playgrounds, 125 athletic fields, 112 tennis courts, 19 swimming pools, and 21 bandstands.[41]

The U.S. Steel welfare programs were designed to encourage attachment between the workers and the firm. For example, the stock subscription plan was structured to give employees an incentive to stay with the corporation for at least five years, and it required participants to show "a proper interest" in the company's welfare.[42] Similarly the pension plan, established in 1911, offered workers retirement benefits after age sixty unless there was "misconduct on the part of the beneficiaries."[43] The community service programs were designed to help its workers become embedded in the communities and

---

[41] Stone, *The Origins of Job Structures* 51.
[42] *Id.* at 49–50.
[43] *Id.* at 50.

thus less likely to leave. The purpose of these programs was to discourage turnover, promote a spirit of cooperation, and reduce shop-floor opposition.

Other large corporations, such as National Cash Register, International Harvester, and the Ford Motor Company, had comparable welfare programs.[44] Welfare work was advocated by social reformers as a way to restore a personal relationship to the workplace that was lacking in the impersonal mass-production factory. The reformers advocated that firms institute company picnics, glee clubs, company magazines, and athletic teams to foster a "one big happy family" feeling. They also encouraged firms to establish welfare departments with a staff to visit the homes of the workers and offer advice on health concerns, sanitary methods, and family relationships. In part, these outreach programs were animated by a genuine concern for the well-being of employees. But at times, they led to heavy-handed methods of social control. The most famous, and notorious, of these efforts was the Ford Motor Company's sociology department, which conducted intrusive investigations into its workers' home lives, checking their financial stability, monitoring for signs of drinking, smoking, or other immoral conduct, and investigating any union-related proclivities.[45]

Corporate welfare work was promoted enthusiastically by the personnel management movement and embraced by corporate leaders. The latter often boasted that their welfare programs were designed not out of altruism but rather to create loyalty to the company, thereby discouraging turnover and labor unrest.[46] Welfare policies, like job ladders, were a means to encourage long-term ties between the employee and the firm.

D. Job Structures of the Assembly Line

At about the same time that scientific management and personnel management were attracting widespread attention, another major figure in twentieth-century industry developed a work relations system of his own. In 1908, Henry Ford built a technologically advanced automobile factory in Highland Park, Michigan, to mass produce his Model T. After five years, he introduced a moving assembly line so that jobs could be subdivided and materials could move quickly through the production process. This innovation borrowed the concept of a moving belt from the meat-packing industry's use of a disassembly line to slaughter and carve up cattle.[47]

---

44 Robert Ozanne, A Century of Labor-Management Relations at McCormick and International Harvester (1967); Jacoby, Employing Bureaucracy; Edwin P. Norwood, Ford: Men and Methods (1931).

45 Jacoby, Employing Bureaucracy 50, 118. On Ford Motor Company's sociology department, *see* Carl Raushenbush, *Fordism*, 5 Industrial Democracy, no. 7, pp. 14–16 (Oct. 1937).

46 Stone, *The Origins of Job Structures* 51–54; Ozanne, McCormick and International Harvester.

47 Nelson, Managers and Workers.

Ford's assembly line shared many attributes of Taylor's scientific management system. For example, the assembly line, like scientific management, involved breaking down automobile assembly operations into numerous discrete tasks. Also, the assembly line, like the Taylorized workplace, was organized on the premise that jobs should require minimal skill. In words reminiscent of Taylor, Ford wrote:

Along about April 1, 1913, we first tried the experiment of an assembly line. . . . We had previously assembled the fly-wheel magneto in the usual method. With one workman doing a complete job he could turn out from 35 to 40 pieces in a 9 hour day, or about 20 minutes to an assembly. What he did alone was then spread into 29 operations; that cut down the assembly time to 13 minutes, 10 seconds. Then we raised the height of the line 8 inches – that was in 1914 – and cut the time to 7 minutes.[48]

Despite their similarities, Ford's and Taylor's systems differed in significant ways. The Fordist assembly line was not a hierarchical job ladder, but was instead a flattened job structure in which each worker could, with minimal training, perform all the jobs on the line. Rather than inducing workers to train others, Ford's goal was to embody the skills in the technology itself so that the workers needed to acquire little human capital to make the system work. As in Taylorism, the assembly line aimed to remove knowledge from the control of the workers, but, in contrast to Taylorism, knowledge was reposed in the technology of the assembly line rather than in the planning department.[49]

Time and motion studies and differential piece rates were not major factors in the human resource model of the assembly line because with assembly lines it was not important to determine the one best way to do each task. Workers on the assembly line already had little discretion about the pace or process of work. For productivity purposes, what mattered was the speed of the line, which was set by management. There was little need to provide inducements for fast work. On the other hand, because assembly line plants did not have complex, multitiered job ladders, Ford initially experienced severe problems of low morale, high turnover, and aggressive union agitation. These problems were solved by Ford in three ways. First, Ford instituted a high wage – five dollars a day – a wage that was so much greater than what the workers could earn elsewhere that it operated to bind them to the firm.[50] Second, the Ford Motor Company encouraged long-term loyalty by developing a wide range of social services. The company constructed housing, playgrounds, swimming pools, and bandstands. It started orchestras

---

[48] Ford, My Life and Work 81.

[49] *See* Stephen Meyer III, The Five Dollar Day: Labor Management and Social Control in the Ford Motor Company, 1908–1921, 37–38 (1981); Ruth Milkman, Farewell to the Factory: Auto Workers in the Late Twentieth Century 23–24 (1997).

[50] *See* Meyer, Five Dollar Day 1; Daniel M. G. Raff & Lawrence H. Summers, *Did Henry Ford Pay Efficiency Wages?* J. Lab. Econ. S57, S72–S73 (Oct. 1987).

and bands, with instruments provided by the company. It built hospitals and retained nurses to visit employees' families in their homes. It helped build public schools and libraries, and offered night courses in English to immigrants.[51] Third, the company adopted a policy that mitigated against frivolous or arbitrary dismissals, which it advertised to its workers and enforced against despotic line supervisors.[52]

While Ford's assembly line differs in some respects from Taylor's system, Ford's system has been described as a special case of Taylorism, "an application of the Taylor system to mass production."[53] Like scientific management, Fordism involved deskilling tasks, defining jobs narrowly, and encouraging long-term attachment between the worker and the firm. Assembly lines were only feasible in capital intensive industries that produced massive numbers of identical products. Taylorism, on the other hand, had applications in many kinds of industries. According to Robert Kanigel, "Fordism was the special case; Taylorism the universal."[54] Both the assembly line and scientific management became emblematic of large corporations' manufacturing operations in the early years of the twentieth century.

E. The Lasting Impact of Scientific Management and Personnel Management

The ideas of the scientific management and personnel management movements spread rapidly amongst American firms. By 1927, forty percent of firms surveyed by the National Industrial Conference Board reported the use of seniority for layoffs. Many others had welfare programs and personnel departments that instituted promotion ladders and mechanisms to enhance job security. In a study of personnel programs in the 1920s, economist and future dean of the Wharton School of Business C. Canby Balderston found that the firms that pioneered in modern personnel practices – that is, those that provided employment security and formal wage plans – tended to be those that had high and stable profits, and stable employment and product demand. Sanford Jacoby, professor of management and business history at the UCLA Anderson School of Business, has shown that by the mid 1930s many large firms had job classification and evaluation systems as well as measures designed to enhance job security, such as seniority and promotion policies.[55]

---

[51] For a detailed description of the corporate welfare work, *see* Jacoby, EMPLOYING BUREAUCRACY 49–54, and Stone, *The Origins of Job Structures* 49–54. Ford Motor Company's sociology department was heavily criticized in the 1930s because it observed and intruded in the workers' personal and family lives. *See* Meyer, FIVE DOLLAR DAY 164–67.

[52] *See* Jacoby, EMPLOYING BUREAUCRACY 118.

[53] Robert Linhart, quoted in Kanigel, ONE BEST WAY 489.

[54] Kanigel, ONE BEST WAY 489.

[55] Jacoby, *Development of Internal Labor Markets* 49.

Thus by the end of the 1930s, scientific management and personnel management had become the dominant human resource policies within large U.S. manufacturing firms. The industrial relations system that emerged from their overlapping influences had several characteristics that persisted through most of the twentieth century.[56] Throughout corporate America, management reduced the skill level of jobs, while at the same time it encouraged employee-firm attachment through promotion and retention policies, explicit or de facto seniority arrangements, elaborate welfare schemes, and longevity-linked benefit packages. These systems had their origins in the blue-collar workplaces of the smokestack industrial heartland in the 1910s, but in the 1960s they were adapted to large white-collar workplaces such as insurance companies and banks.[57]

Management theorists in the 1930s, 1940s, and 1950s built upon the basic ideas of scientific management and personnel management. The organizational and human resource theorists of those decades did not challenge the assumptions of scientific management, but instead focused on issues of how to design and operate large bureaucratic organizations, manage authority and status hierarchies, and organize large, sprawling organizational structures.[58] The largest innovation in that period was the human relations school, which grew out of a series of experiments at Western Electric about the effects of workplace design on productivity. The experiments yielded a number of insights about the ways in which small informal work groups can restrict production and develop oppositional attitudes. The practical implication of the human relations school's findings was that management could break the counterproductive dynamics of informal work groups by using individualized employment counseling and giving individuals opportunities to let off steam.[59]

In conclusion, in the early twentieth century, many employers reorganized production and instituted hierarchical job ladders, narrow job classification systems, seniority, and elaborate employee retention policies. These new job structures were instituted for the purpose of bolstering employee

[56] Many of Taylor's followers embraced the ideas of the personnel management school. In particular, they approved of the use of scientific selection and internal promotion plans to solve the problems of turnover and workplace discontent. Jacoby, *Development of Internal Labor Markets* 23, 33–34.

[57] *See* Harry Braverman, LABOR AND MONOPOLY CAPITAL: THE DEGRADATION OF WORK IN THE TWENTIETH CENTURY 335, 340 (1974).

[58] *See* Howell John Harris, THE RIGHT TO MANAGE: INDUSTRIAL RELATIONS POLICIES OF AMERICAN BUSINESS IN THE 1940s 60–66 (1982).

[59] *See* F. J. Roethlisberger & William J. Dickson, MANAGEMENT AND THE WORKER: AN ACCOUNT OF A RESEARCH PROGRAM CONDUCTED BY THE WESTERN ELECTRIC COMPANY HAWTHORNE WORKS, CHICAGO (1967) (describing the history and analysis of the results of the Hawthorne experiments). *See generally* Loren Baritz, THE SERVANTS OF POWER: A HISTORY OF THE USE OF SOCIAL SCIENCE IN AMERICAN INDUSTRY 77–116 (1960); Bendix, WORK AND AUTHORITY 308–19.

morale, inducing employee loyalty and motivation, discouraging soldiering and turnover, encouraging job-specific training and knowledge sharing, and transferring knowledge from the worker to the firm. Conceived in Taylor's experiments at Midvale Steel in the 1880s, they matured into the internal labor markets that prevailed in U.S. manufacturing firms throughout most of the twentieth century. They thus comprised the paradigmatic labor practices of the era of industrial production.

F. Law and Social Practices

There is a seeming paradox in the fact that employers instituted practices to encourage worker-firm attachment shortly after the at-will doctrine became the dominant default rule for employment relationships. One might conclude from this sequence that the law is irrelevant to social practice because once the at-will regime proliferated, employers essentially opted out of the at-will regime by establishing internal labor markets. That is, one might conclude that legal change has no impact on social practice, and that changing social practices do not create legal change. However, a closer look at the rise of the at-will regime and the adoption of internal labor markets demonstrates that law and social practice are not mutually autonomous, but are complexly intertwined.

Law shapes and is shaped by practices of individuals and institutions. Law operates as a constraint as well as an enabler, setting the parameters for lawful action and providing incentives and prohibitions that channel social practice. Law also provides a normative framework which subtly permeates the system of values that guide individual and institutional conduct. However, law itself is produced by social practices and external societal values. Struggles about law, whether in courtrooms or in the halls of Congress, grow out of social conflicts that arise prior to and outside of the law. However, the struggles themselves are bounded by existing legal structures that define the realm of possibility. At times, social groups break through previous rigidities and enlarge the realm of possibility.[60]

The history of the at-will rule demonstrates the complex interrelationship between legal and social change. As discussed in Chapter 1, at its inception the at-will rule helped employers escape the tight grip of skilled workers, creating for them a market of available, unskilled workers to staff the newly deskilled jobs. The at-will rule also helped unskilled workers by giving them income security and labor market freedom. They obtained the freedom to change jobs with the assurance that they would be paid for time worked. To be sure, unskilled workers obtained income security and mobility

---

[60] *See* Duncan Kennedy, A Critique of Adjudication: (Fin de Siècle) (1997); Roberto Mangieberra Unger, Politics: The Central Texts (1997).

at the expense of job security, but it had been an elusive job security at best. Employers had usually been able to fire unskilled workers with impunity prior to the at-will regime.

While the advent of the at-will rule in the late nineteenth century did not harm the unskilled, neither did it directly harm the skilled workers. Skilled workers had job security not from an employment relationship with a particular employer but as a result of their skill and membership in a craft union. The at-will rule, at least at its inception, did nothing to change skilled workers' labor market power. Over time, the at-will rule and the free labor market it facilitated enabled employers to reduce their dependence on skilled workers, but this dynamic unfolded over several decades.

Because the negative aspects of the at-will rule were not apparent at the time of its inception, one cannot conclude that the at-will doctrine was adopted by judges in order to free employers from the control of skilled workers. It is more likely that the rise of the at-will doctrine was an adaptation of the law to the changing features of industrial life. In the late nineteenth century, factories proliferated and technological innovations were rampant, making it possible for firms to replace skilled workers with machines. Hence more and more unskilled workers were hired for indefinite-term contracts. In this world, a free labor market, in which workers could come and go with ease and in which firms could hire and fire without constraint, appeared desirable for all concerned.

The at-will rule that emerged in the late nineteenth century did not prevent the subsequent development of internal labor markets. Rather, internal labor markets were privatized regulatory systems that operated within the then-prevailing background of the at-will regime. If there were no at-will rule and if instead the common law gave employees some form of job security, then employers' could not use job security as an inducement for loyalty, longevity, and commitment. Only because employers' promises of job security gave employees something they otherwise did not have did scientific management provide the benefits that employers sought. The at-will rule, then, was a precondition for the effective operation of internal labor markets.

The at-will rule did not become politically controversial until the end of the twentieth century because employees who were in internal labor markets enjoyed job security despite the at-will rule in the background. Thus, despite their lack of legal protections, most employees in internal labor markets assumed they had long-term job security. Only in the 1970s and 1980s, when employers dismantled their internal labor markets and broke their implicit promises of long-term job security, did the at-will rule become a subject of widespread public concern.

Thus the history of the at-will rule demonstrates that the law neither caused the change in social practices nor served as an automatic and predictable response to those changes. Rather, both changes in social practices and legal change had a more complex interaction. Once social practices changed, the law came to appear incongruous and legal change became imaginable. And once the legal rules changed, social practices adapted, albeit in unforeseeable ways. The law did not directly shape the employment relationship – rather it defined the terrain upon which employment practices were built.

3

From Scientific Management to Internal Labor Markets

The job structures that emerged as a result of Taylorism and the personnel management movement deviated in several respects from the way the labor market was predicted to work by neoclassical economic theory. In the labor market of neoclassical theory, workers are assumed to move freely between firms and jobs, constantly seeking and seizing new opportunities to maximize their incomes. Firms likewise hire and dismiss workers freely as demand for their products fluctuates. Firms also raise and lower wages to correspond to changes in product and labor market conditions, all the while paying their employees the value of their marginal product at every point in time. In the theory, wage differentials for any given skill level between firms and within firms disappear over time as wages achieve an equilibrium level. At equilibrium, each worker is paid the prevailing market wage for his or her skill level, each employer has equal labor costs, and the amount of labor hired by any particular firm is determined by the demand for its product and its level of technological and administrative prowess.[1]

In the 1940s and 1950s, a group of labor economists studied the operation of the labor market and found that it did not operate according to the predictions of the neoclassical theory. John Dunlop, Clark Kerr, Lloyd Reynolds, Richard Lester, and others became familiar with the actual operation of labor markets by working for the National War Labor Board. Subsequently, they conducted empirical studies of local labor markets from which they concluded it was necessary to revise neoclassical labor market theory. These revisionist economists found that, contrary to neoclassical theory, employees did not move freely and easily between jobs, always seeking the highest payoff. Rather, they found that most employees stayed with their firms for

---

[1] *See, e.g.,* L. Reynolds, S. Masters, and C. Moser, *Simple Labor Market Models*, in Lloyd G. Reynolds, Stanley H. Masters, and Colletta H. Moser, LABOR ECONOMICS AND LABOR RELATIONS 36–47 (9th ed., 1995); Ronald G. Ehrenberg & Robert S. Smith, MODERN LABOR ECONOMICS: THEORY AND PUBLIC POLICY (6th ed. 1997).

long periods, even when they might command higher wages elsewhere. They also found that firms did not usually lower wages when demand slackened. Rather, firms often maintained wage levels, even if it meant that they had to reduce their workforce. The revisionist economists also found that firms preferred to utilize internal hiring rather than hiring on the open labor market to fill vacancies. Indeed, they found that firms utilized internal promotion to fill vacancies even when more skilled and cheaper workers were available. They reported that promotion took place along formal lines of progression, where each job provided training in the firm-specific skills needed for the next job. This was particularly true, they found, for production jobs in manufacturing establishments. In these firms, they also found that wages were not set by supply and demand, but by administrative policies and in some cases labor-management collective bargaining.[2]

As a result of their findings, the revisionist economists described a picture of firm-level wage setting, hiring, and training policies that differed from that of the prevailing neoclassical theory. They posited that many firms, particularly in manufacturing, had an internal wage structure and system of job assignment that was determined not by supply and demand in the external labor market, but by administrative considerations.

Clark Kerr theorized the findings of the revisionist economists in his famed 1954 article *The Balkanization of Labor Markets*. There Kerr noted that far from being a unified market, the labor market was segmented in a variety of ways as a result of institutional arrangements. Craft labor markets were segmented by hiring halls or other job allocation schemes maintained by the craft unions. Workers admitted to membership through apprenticeship or otherwise could move between establishments, but they remained protected from competition from outsiders by their knowledge of the skill and by the unions' rules. On the other hand, manufacturing labor markets, Kerr found, were segmented vertically by establishment. Firms used internal promotion rather than external hiring to fill all positions except the lowest ones. Kerr described the operation of these systems as "internal markets" that could only be entered at certain "ports of entry." The ports of entry were the only points of contact between the internal and the external labor market.[3]

Through their empirical and theoretical work, the revisionist labor economists thus described and named the phenomenon now known as the "internal labor market" – a concept that has received a great deal of attention from labor economists in the last two decades. The internal labor markets that the revisionist economists found in manufacturing firms were characterized by job ladders, narrowly defined job classifications, firm-specific training, implicit and/or explicit seniority arrangements, and

---

[2] Bruce Kaufman, *The Postwar View of Labor Markets and Wage Determination*, in Bruce Kaufman, How LABOR MARKETS WORK, 169–74 (1988).
[3] Clark Kerr, *The Balkanization of Labor Markets*, in Clark Kerr, LABOR MOBILITY AND ECONOMIC OPPORTUNITY 92–110 (1954).

rising longevity-based wage and benefit policies designed to encourage long-term attachment – the very practices that the Taylorites and personnel management reformers had advocated.

The revisionist economists did not find adminstratively determined job structures to exist in all types of jobs. In clerical jobs they found little evidence of internal promotion along job ladders or firm-specific training. Instead, they found that for clerical work, firms adjusted wage rates to market rates and hiring levels to supply and demand, as the neoclassical model would predict. They also found that clerical workers moved easily and often between firms. They surmised that the difference between market-determined job structures and administratively determined ones was a function of the supply and demand in the product market in which a firm operated, the type of technology used, and the practices of the particular management and union.[4]

A. The Theory of the Internal Labor Market

In the past thirty years, internal labor markets have been further studied, described, theorized, and analyzed by many labor economists. The classic book by Peter Doeringer and Michael Piore, INTERNAL LABOR MARKETS AND MANPOWER ANALYSIS, prefigured much of the latter discussion. Doeringer and Piore define an internal labor market as an administrative unit "within which the pricing and allocation of labor is governed by a set of administrative rules and procedures." The dominant form of internal labor market in manufacturing plants is one in which "production jobs are arranged in seniority districts or lines of progression. Entry job classifications tend to lie at the bottom of these lines and vacancies in other jobs are usually filled by the promotion of workers from the next lowest job classification in the line of progression."[5] A line of progression, according to Doeringer and Piore, is an arrangement of jobs by which "work on one job develops the skills required for the more complex tasks on the job above it, and those at one point in the line constitute the natural source of supply for the next job along the line."[6]

Doeringer and Piore point out that internal labor markets benefit both employees and employers. Employers initially establish them for three reasons: first, internal labor markets offer informal on-the-job training that increases the value of the labor force; second, they reduce turnover; and third, they yield savings in recruitment, screening, and training costs. Employees value the employment security and opportunities for advancement that internal

---

[4] Kaufman, *The Postwar View* 171–72.
[5] Peter Doeringer & Michael Piore, INTERNAL LABOR MARKETS AND MANPOWER ANALYSIS 1–3 (1971). For a review of the considerable literature on internal labor market institutions, *see* Claudia Dale Goldin, UNDERSTANDING THE GENDER GAP: AN ECONOMIC HISTORY OF AMERICAN WOMEN 247 (1990); INTERNAL LABOR MARKETS (Paul Osterman, ed., 1984).
[6] Doeringer & Piore, INTERNAL LABOR MARKETS AND MANPOWER ANALYSIS 58.

labor markets offer, and therefore are willing to sacrifice earnings to gain and retain employment in them. "Wage sacrifices necessary to attain access to an internal labor market thus represent a trade-off between present and future income."[7] The arrangements thus generate a set of customary, unwritten expectations for stability of employment. As Doeringer and Piore write, "The worker accepts employment with the expectation that the rules will operate in the future to improve his income. Such expectations assume a certain stability in the rules, and the employer who later changes them to the detriment of the existing labor force reneges on an implicit contract." Such a violation can lead to sanctions against management, such as a slackening of performance or other oppositional conduct, and it can harm recruitment.[8]

Subsequently, some labor economists developed a model of career wage trajectories to explain the relationship between long-term employment and compensation practices over the course of an individual's employment in an internal labor market. The model reflects the fact that where there is firm-specific human capital, an employee's value to her employer is not the same as her value in the external labor markets throughout her career.[9] Figure 3.1 demonstrates the interaction between an employee's compensation and the value of her marginal product over time.[10]

In the first phase of employment, a new employee in an internal labor market is paid an amount that equals or is slightly greater than the value of her marginal product, and less than the value of her opportunity wage – the amount she could command in the general labor market. This is because she is acquiring human capital, and both she and her employer are investing in its acquisition. Some of this human capital is firm-specific and some is general.

At some point the employee acquires enough human capital to become useful to the employer so that the value of her marginal product rises. This is phase two. In the second phase of employment, the employee is paid less

---

[7] *Id.* at 28.

[8] *Id.* at 28–33.

[9] This model is described in more detail in Katherine Van Wezel Stone, *Policing Employment Contracts Within the Nexus-of-Contracts Firm*, 43 U. TORONTO L.J. 353, 363–9 (1994). *See also* Doeringer & Piore, INTERNAL LABOR MARKETS AND MANPOWER ANALYSIS 13–40; Robert J. Willis, *Wage Determinants: A Survey and Reinterpretation of Human Capital Earnings Functions*, in 1 HANDBOOK OF LABOR ECONOMICS 525, 594 (Orley Ashenfelter & Richard Layard, eds., 1986).

[10] This graph appears in Michael L. Wachter & George M. Cohen, *The Law and Economics of Collective Bargaining: An Introduction and Application to the Problems of Subcontracting, Partial Closure, and Relocation*, 136 U. PA. L. REV. 1349, 1362 (1988). It is a variation on a diagram presented by Edward P. Lazear in *Why Is There Mandatory Retirement?* 86 J. POL. ECON. 1261, 1265 fig.1 (1979); *see also* Gary S. Becker, HUMAN CAPITAL: A THEORETICAL AND EMPIRICAL ANALYSIS, WITH SPECIAL REFERENCE TO EDUCATION 23 chart 1 (2d ed. 1975) (charting the relation of earnings to age).

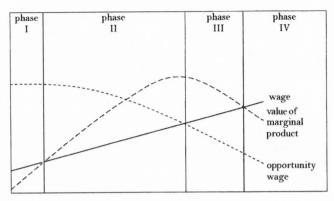

FIGURE 3.1

than the value of her marginal product. Hence the firm is already benefiting from the joint investment in phase one.

What is most notable about phase two is that the employee is paid not only less than the value of her marginal product, but also less than she could obtain in the external labor market. Why, we might ask, would anyone accept a rate of pay that is lower than she could earn elsewhere? The reason is that in this phase, the employee has an expectation that the job will be steady and the wage will keep rising throughout her working career. On the basis of that expectation, she defers compensation. The expectation, created by the employer, is a defining element in the notion of the internal labor market. Thus, in phase two, the employee is investing in acquiring human capital and is deferring compensation.

In the third phase, the firm-specific nature of the human capital the employee has acquired means that she is worth more to her employer than she is to other employers. Hence, the value of her marginal product to her employer is greater than the value of her marginal product to other employers. In this period she is paid more than her opportunity wage, but less than the value of her marginal product.

In phase four – the employee's later years – her productivity begins to lag. However, due to customs, norms, policies, or incentive schemes, her pay is not reduced. Instead, her wage level either continues to rise or levels off. Thus, in this period she is paid more than the value of her marginal product and more than her opportunity wage. This is the recoupment stage in which the employee recovers on her investment in firm-specific training and deferred compensation.

The model is a pictorial representation of the implicit promises within an internal labor market that Doeringer and Piore discuss. During the middle two periods, employees have made an investment for which they have not yet been compensated and for which they anticipate deferred compensation. Their investments in firm-specific human capital and willingness to work for deferred compensation are made not on the basis of some explicit contractual arrangement, but rather take the form of an implicit contract.[11] As modeled, the implicit contract in the internal labor market is that in the early phases of their careers, employees will be paid less than the value of their marginal product and less than their opportunity wage. In exchange, they receive a promise of job security and a wage rate later in their working lives that is greater than the value of both their marginal product and their opportunity wage. Thus employees in internal labor markets are investing in the firm during their training and high productivity periods with the expectation of recouping on the investment in their declining years.[12]

B. The Career Wage Model

The internal labor market career wage model is accompanied by a theory that explains why an employer would make an implicit promise of deferred compensation and why an employee would accept it. As Doeringer and Piore explain, from the employees' perspective, internal labor markets offer the promise of job security, rising wages and benefits, and orderly promotional possibilities. Such a promise has tremendous value for employees, and for that reason employees are willing to defer compensation, develop firm-specific skills, and give cooperation, effort, and loyalty in return. From the employer's perspective, such an arrangement reduces turnover and encourages on-the-job training in firm-specific skills. This explanation is consistent with the history of scientific management and personnel management discussed in Chapter 2.

Several other labor economists have offered similar, but notably different explanations of the development of internal labor markets in American industry. Oliver Williamson posits that the use of job ladders and a rising wage curve operate like a bond, inducing an employee to give a high level of effort and deterring slack performance. Because it is expensive for firms to monitor the level of effort directly, Williamson claims, internal labor markets provide self-enforcing performance incentives. In such a system, the longer

---

[11] For an interesting account of the role of managers in developing and maintaining, and at times breaching, implicit relational contracts, *see* George Baker, Robert Gibbons, & Kevin Murphy, *Relational Contracts and the Theory of the Firm*, Q. J. ECON. 39–84 (2002).

[12] On the implicit contract in the internal labor market, *see* Ehrenberg & Smith, MODERN LABOR ECONOMICS 170–71; Oliver E. Williamson, THE ECONOMIC INSTITUTIONS OF CAPITALISM: FIRMS, MARKETS, RELATIONAL CONTRACTING 249 (1985). *See also* Sherwin Rosen, *Implicit Contracts: A Survey*, 23 J. ECON. LITERATURE 1144, 1147 (1985) ("Wage income is in part an installment payment on specific-investments"); Martin Segal, *Post-Institutionalism in Labor Economics: The Forties and Fifties Revisited*, 39 INDUS. & LAB. REL. REV. 388, 400–401 (1986) (discussing empirical studies that "reinforce the view . . . that many managerial practices concerning hiring, promotions, and wages reflect an approach in which the process of employment is seen as representing a long-term relationship between the firm and its individual workers").

the employee stays on the job, the more he has to lose if he is dismissed because the more difficult it will be for him to find comparable employment. Also, job ladders enable management to observe each worker's performance when workers are at the lower rungs, thus enabling them to make more informed decisions about whom to promote.[13]

Gary Becker has also offered an explanation of internal labor markets in terms of rational employer behavior, but unlike Williamson, who stresses the role of monitoring costs, Becker stresses the role of firm-specific training. Becker assumes that employers need employees to learn techniques and skills that are uniquely tailored to the particular firm. He argues that employers give employees implicit promises of deferred compensation, rising wages, and job security in order to induce employees to self-finance their firm-specific training by accepting lower wages. Without such promises, Becker says, employees will not be willing to invest in firm-specific training. And if employees do not invest, then employers have to pay for the training themselves. But once they do, they bear a risk that the trained employees will leave the firm. In order to discourage turnover, Becker reasons that employers will get employees to share some of the costs of firm-specific training, and to do that employers will offer higher wages after training than could be received elsewhere.[14]

Becker and Williamson both offer plausible explanations for employers' adoption of internal labor market job structures. They both explain the use of internal labor markets as a rational employer response to a particular set of labor relations conditions. Yet missing from their analyses is any recognition that internal labor markets were rational adaptations to labor relations conditions that were themselves historically contingent. As discussed in Chapter 2, employers' need for monitoring and their preference for firm-specific rather than general skills both arose after they destroyed the artisanal era job structures and created a new labor system in its wake. Furthermore, Williamson's and Becker's explanations do not fully account for the use of internal labor markets. Some employers use internal labor market job structures even though they neither utilize firm-specific training nor have difficulty in monitoring employee effort. For example, most assembly-line work involves little firm-specific training and requires little monitoring of effort, yet automobile assembly line work is one of the best documented examples of the use of implicit promises of long-term employment.[15]

Becker's and Williamson's explanations each tell only part of the story of the development of internal labor markets. They need to be supplemented

---

[13] Oliver Williamson, Jeffrey Harris, & Michael Wachter, *Understanding the Employment Relation – The Analysis of Idiosyncratic Exchange*, 6 BELL J. ECON. 250 (1975).

[14] Becker, HUMAN CAPITAL 29–30.

[15] *See, e.g.*, Ruth Milkman, FAREWELL TO THE FACTORY: AUTO WORKERS IN THE LATE TWENTIETH CENTURY (1997).

with an historical understanding of the role of implicit promises of job security and deferred compensation in personnel relations. As seen in Chapter 2, the use of implicit promises of job security has served at least two employer goals. First, it has encouraged employee attachment, discouraged turnover, provided employee motivation, and helped prevent concerted opposition. Employers believe that long-term employees will exhibit high morale and productivity without a proclivity to shirk, sabotage, or unionize. Thus implicit promises were not simply a substitute for monitoring – they were also a means to elicit loyalty and cooperation. This view was expounded by many of the nineteenth- and early-twentieth-century captains of industry, including Andrew Carnegie and Henry Ford.[16]

Second, implicit promises of long-term employment solve the problem of training and knowledge sharing. As discussed in Chapter 2, training became problematic after employers broke the craft unions and abolished the union-controlled apprenticeship systems at the end of the nineteenth century. Firms responded to a lack of skilled workers by adopting methods and processes that relied upon firm-specific rather than generalized skills. However, employers still needed experienced workers to teach those skills and to share their knowledge about production with new recruits. If older workers did not provide new workers with such training, years of valuable knowledge and experience would be lost to the firm. Yet, without some mechanism to ensure them job security, older workers knew that if they trained their juniors, they stood to be replaced as soon as their own speed, dexterity, and strength began to fade.

Throughout the twentieth century, personnel managers have instituted many devices to induce workers to share their knowledge, such as suggestion boxes and quality circles. However, the most effective means to solve the problem has been to promise workers that they will not be fired in their later years, despite some inevitable decline in their faculties. The implicit promise of job security and deferred compensation in the internal labor market thus solved the training dilemma.

As a result of these concerns, there developed within internal labor markets an implicit bilateral deal between the worker and the firm in which the employee received job security in exchange for loyalty, effort, and cooperation. For almost one hundred years, employers have made implicit promises of job security to their employees. They appear in many forms – sometimes as explicit oral promises made by supervisors, sometimes as implied promises of fair treatment contained in recruitment brochures or employment manuals. At other times, the implicit promises are part of the general lore of the shop, transmitted through the in-plant grapevines. They have served as a fundamental fact of life in most medium- and large-sized establishments, whether

---

[16] *See* Sanford Jacoby, EMPLOYING BUREAUCRACY 115–26 (1985).

they be in the industrial or service sectors. These promises, integral to the industrial era job structures, comprise what organizational behavior theorists have come to call the "psychological contract" between the employee and the employer.[17]

Implicit promises of job security were made in both union and nonunion workplaces. Even though employers benefited from the good will and incentives generated by such promises, there have been circumstances in which employers are tempted to renege. For example, when firms undergo takeovers, new managers frequently feel no obligation to honor implicit promises made by their predecessors, and thus they feel free to engage in massive downsizing.[18] In unionized shops, negotiated seniority provisions, just cause for discharge clauses, pension vesting rules, and other mechanisms reinforce the implicit promise.

In the 1980s, some state courts began to enforce employers' implicit promises of job security by creating exceptions to the at-will employment rule. For example, in the case *Toussaint v. Blue Cross & Blue Shield*, the Michigan Supreme Court found that the employer had promoted a "mutual understanding that it was company policy not to discharge an employee 'as long as [he] did [his] job.'" The court reasoned that employers make such implicit promises because "[t]he employer secures an orderly, cooperative and loyal work force, and the employee (secures) the peace of mind associated with job security and the conviction that he will be treated fairly."[19] Therefore, the court concluded, it was only fair and just to hold the employer to the promise.

In another leading case, *Pugh v. See's Candies, Inc.*, the plaintiff was a long-term employee who began as a pot-washer and was repeatedly promoted all the way to vice-president over a thirty-plus year career at the company. When he was fired suddenly and without explanation, he sued for breach of contract despite his evident at-will status. He maintained that when he was originally hired, he had been told by the then president, "if you are loyal to [See's] and do a good job, your future is secure." In addition, the plaintiff argued that the company had a long-standing practice of not terminating management personnel except for good cause. The court found for the plaintiff, stating that there could be an implied-in-fact contract for job security based on the

---

[17] The concept of the psychological contract is developed in Chapter 5. *See generally* Denise M. Rousseau, *Psychological and Implied Contracts in Organizations*, 2 EMPLOYEE RESPONSIBILITIES & RTS. J. 121, 121 (1989).

[18] *See* Stone, *Policing Employment Contracts Within the Nexus-of-Contracts Firm*, 43 U. TORONTO L. J. at 371; *see also*, John C. Coffee, Jr., *Shareholders Versus Managers: The Strain in the Corporate Web*, 85 MICH. L. REV. (1986); Note, *Employer Opportunism and the Need for a Just Cause Standard*, 103 HARV. L. REV. 510, 523 (1989) (student author).

[19] 292 N.W.2d 880, 891–92 (Mich. 1980). *See also* Pugh v. See's Candies Inc., 116 Cal. App. 3rd 311 (1981).

duration of employment, assurances of job security that were given, and the company's past practices.[20]

Pugh, *Toussaint*, and other such cases carved out exceptions to the at-will rule for implicit promises of job security out of a recognition that within some firms the prevailing practices, policies, and assurances of fair treatment were part of the reciprocal exchange of the employment relationship.

C. The Origins of Internal Labor Markets

Doeringer and Piore posited that internal labor markets were established by management in order to realize economies from turnover reduction and savings in recruitment and training costs. Becker and Williamson also posit reasons why employers established internal labor markets. Some economists, however, reject the historical claim that employers voluntarily set up internal labor markets, and argue instead that employers were forced to do so by the industrial unions that organized the mass production industries in the 1930s. The debate about the origin of internal labor markets raises the question of what role, if any, unions can and should play in preserving the internal labor markets of the past.

Paul Osterman, a labor economist at MIT, contends that, as a historical matter, it was often unions that pushed to establish seniority arrangements and other protections for job security that are the hallmarks of internal labor markets, and that employers often resisted. Osterman criticizes Williamson's efficiency-enhancing account of the origin of internal labor markets, and argues that the same phenomenon can just as convincingly be described as efficiency limiting. That is, job ladders involve retaining and promoting people who are not necessarily the best possible subjects for any particular job. The implicit seniority principle in internal labor markets, Osterman argues, means that companies cannot easily lay off the least efficient workers at times of cutbacks. The rising wage trajectory means that many late-life workers are paid more than their marginal product. And the entire structure deprives employers of the flexibility to make agile adjustments to product and labor market developments. Osterman thus reasons that whether internal labor markets are efficiency promoting or efficiency limiting is an empirical question that will vary case by case, and to which the answer cannot ultimately be discerned.[21]

Clark Kerr, in *The Balkanization of the Labor Market*, also attributes the development of internal labor markets to the impact of unions. He argues that unions negotiate rules that protect their members' jobs and livelihoods by constraining the labor market from which the employer can draw. Kerr

---

[20] Pugh v. See's Candies, Inc., *supra* n. 19.

[21] Paul Osterman, *Introduction: The Nature and Importance of Internal Labor Markets*, in Osterman, INTERNAL LABOR MARKETS 1, 9.

states that craft unions shape craft labor markets by insisting that employers use craft-union hiring halls, and that industrial unions help shape enterprise internal labor markets by insisting on seniority arrangements and orderly job bidding promotion schemes. However, Kerr also acknowledges that both craft and industrial firms established internal labor market job structures before there were unions involved.[22]

The historical evidence presented in Chapter 2 suggests that in many instances it was employers, not unions, that established many features of internal labor markets, often before unions were on the scene. While it is also true that some unions sought seniority arrangements, internal promotion systems, and job security in the mid twentieth century, these were union adaptations to the transition from artisanal to industrial forms of production. More frequently, the internal labor market job structures of the industrial era predated unions, often by several decades. Furthermore, internal labor markets are frequently found in nonunion firms. Doeringer and Piore maintain that the role of unions in internal labor markets is to codify and enforce the institutional rules and customs generated by the internal labor market arrangements, and to provide a mechanism by which those rules can be modified.[23]

While unions did not originate the internal labor market form of work organization, they have played an important role in shaping and taming it. Unions have adapted the internal labor market arrangements to workers' needs by regularizing the practices and enforcing the implicit promises they contain. Unions have also achieved, through bargaining, higher wages, more safe and humane working conditions, better fringe benefits, and fairer treatment for workers within internal labor markets. So while employers have benefited from the industrial era job structures, unions have often been successful in adapting the job structures to workers' needs.[24] Thus once internal labor markets had become widespread, both unions and managers sought to stabilize and reinforce their features. According to Doeringer and Piore, internal labor market job structures can explain "[m]uch of the interests of trade unions in seniority, internal promotion, job control and equitable treatment at the workplace."[25]

D. Unions and Internal Labor Markets

When unions entered large manufacturing establishments through the organizing drives of the 1930s, they were not the AFL craft unions of the nineteenth century. Rather, they were industrial unions, affiliated with the

---

[22] Kerr, *Balkanization* 29.
[23] *See* Doeringer & Piore, INTERNAL LABOR MARKETS AND MANPOWER ANALYSIS 13–39.
[24] Jacoby, EMPLOYING BUREAUCRACY 281.
[25] Doeringer & Piore, INTERNAL LABOR MARKETS AND MANPOWER ANALYSIS 40.

newly formed Congress of Industrial Organizations (CIO), uniting workers around a common employer or industry rather than on the basis of a common skill. Many of the newly organized workers in the 1930s were unskilled or semiskilled and did not partake of the craft legacy of the old AFL. In their organizing drives, the CIO unions appealed to a sense of solidarity based not on skill but on employment status. Once established, these unions did not seek to restore workers' skills and power in production, nor did they seek to abolish the internal labor market arrangements that employers had established. Rather, they bargained for terms that were consistent with internal labor market job structures, such as seniority, just cause provisions, and longevity-based pay and benefits.[26]

Since the 1930s, unions have played an active role in policing internal labor markets to make sure that the employers' implicit promises were kept. For while these promises were given, there was frequently a temptation to breach them. Hence the industrial unions insisted upon just cause provisions in collective agreements and arbitration systems to enforce them so that they could make explicit and enforce employer's implicit promises of job security. Also, unions have supported measures that mitigate the potentially unjust effects of internal labor markets – they have attempted to simplify and rationalize the wage structure, to balance intra-workplace claims for equity, to shape benefit packages to workers' needs, and to monitor the workplace for dangerous conditions or excessive production speed. Thus from the 1930s on, industrial unions such as the United Auto Workers and the United Steelworkers of America did not seek to abolish internal labor markets; they sought to mold and tame them instead.[27]

The labor and employment laws that emerged in the 1930s reinforced the Taylorist internal labor market job structures. The Social Security Act of 1935[28] tied old-age assistance and unemployment compensation benefits to employment. The National Labor Relations Act of 1935[29] (also known as the Wagner Act), while facially neutral between the craft and industrial styles of unionism, in operation favored employer-based and plant-based forms of organization.[30]

From the 1930s to the 1950s, both the AFL and the CIO unions fought hard to organize large industrial establishments across America. When they

---

[26] *See* Nelson Lichtenstein, THE MOST DANGEROUS MAN IN DETROIT: WALTER REUTHER AND THE FATE OF AMERICAN LABOR 149–53 (1995) (describing the impact of unionization on the automobile industry); Katherine Van Wezel Stone, *The Origins of Job Structures in the Steel Industry*, in LABOR MARKET SEGMENTATION 70–72 (D. Gordon, M. Reich, & R. Edwards, eds., 1975) (describing the impact of unionization on job structures in the steel industry).

[27] *See* Stone, *The Origins of Job Structures* 63–75.

[28] Ch. 531, Title IV, Part A (1935) (current version at 42 U.S.C. §602 (2000)).

[29] Ch. 372, 49 Stat. 449 (1935) (current version at 29 U.S.C. §§151–69 (2000)).

[30] *See* James A. Gross, 1 THE MAKING OF THE NATIONAL LABOR RELATIONS BOARD 134–37 (1974).

succeeded, they bargained for pay, benefits, grievance procedures, seniority systems, and highly specific, narrow job definitions – all consistent with the Taylorist job structures. Union-negotiated seniority systems dovetailed with existing job ladders. Union-designed grievance and arbitration systems reinforced internal labor markets by enabling unions to enforce employers' implicit promises of job security and orderly promotion.[31] Union-initiated job definitions were a form of protection against foremen's demands for intensified work efforts and thus gave workers some control over the pace of work. Narrow job definitions also forced employers to utilize more workers than might have been necessary to complete specific tasks, and thus were a means for unions to protect job security and overtime pay. Ironically and tragically, however, the price of specific and narrow job definitions in an era of deskilling was that boring jobs became even narrower and more deadening.

---

[31] *See* Textiles Works v. Lincoln Mills, 353 U.S. 448, 456 (1957); *see* Katherine Van Wezel Stone, *The Post-War Paradigm in American Labor Law*, 90 YALE L.J. 1509, 1524–25 (1981); Katherine Van Wezel Stone, *The Legacy of Industrial Pluralism: The Tension Between Individual Employment Rights and the New Deal Collective Bargaining System*, 59 U. CHI. L. REV. 575, 622–24 (1992).

PART II

THE DIGITAL WORKPLACE

4

The Changing Nature of Employment

In the 1970s, the employment practices of most U.S. corporations began to change. The first indication of change was the rapid growth in temporary employment. Prior to the 1970s, temporary employment agencies were generally limited to providing short-term secretarial help, day laborers, and nursing services. However, around 1975, temporary employment agencies began to provide workers for many other types of jobs, including maintenance work, custodial services, legal services, and computer programming. Corporations began to utilize outside contractors to provide workers for jobs that had previously been done in-house, including such core firm tasks as inventory control, bookkeeping, and even human resources. Between 1980 and 1989, the number of employees working for temporary agencies doubled from 518,000 to 1,032,000. In 1993, FORTUNE magazine reported that Manpower, Inc. had become the largest employer in America.[1] The number of employees hired by temporary agencies continued to rise throughout the 1990s, so that by 2001, nearly two million workers worked for temporary employment agencies, many of whom were in highly skilled positions.[2] As of May 2001, according to the U.S. Department of Labor, 9.1 percent of all temporary workers were executives and managers, while only 13 percent were low-skilled laborers.[3] A survey of private firms in all industries and of all sizes conducted by the Upjohn Institute in 1996 found that some 78 percent

---

[1] *The Temping of America,* FORTUNE, 1993.
[2] *See* Labor Force Statistics from the Current Population Survey, *Contingent and Alternative Employment Arrangements,* at http://stats.bls.gov/news.release/conemp.nws.htm (May 24, 2001) (presenting 2001 data); *see also* Sharon R. Cohany, *Workers in Alternative Employment Arrangements: A Second Look,* MONTHLY LAB. REV., Nov. 1998, at 3, 4 ex.1, 5 tbl.1 (presenting 1995 and 1997 data).
[3] Amy Zipkin, *Temporary Work Is Sidestepping Slowdown,* NEW YORK TIMES, July 23, 2001. On the unique perspective of high-skilled contingent workers, *see* Gideon Kunda & Steve Barley, *Why Do Contractors Contract?* 55 ILR REV. 234 (Jan. 2002).

of private sector firms used flexible staffing arrangements – a significant increase from a decade earlier.[4]

In the late 1970s, corporations began to make other changes in their human resource practices. In addition to increasingly relying on subcontractors and temporary help, firms changed the nature of the employment relationship for their "regular" employees. They began to emphasize flexibility and versatility rather than stability and longevity. They sought flexibility in their staffing and compensation practices, and fluidity in their workforces. By the 1990s, it was clear that corporations no longer sought to erect internal labor markets, even for their regular workforces. The world of long-term stable employment, in which an employee was attached to a single large corporation for the duration of his career, was coming to an end.

A. The Growth in Contingent Employment

One method that firms used to gain flexibility in their staffing levels was to utilize temporary rather than regular employees whenever feasible. Temporary workers were easy to dispose of, and thus provided a cushion for changes in product demand. Layoffs of temporary workers were less disruptive of internal labor markets than layoffs of regular workers because such actions did not appear to be a repudiation of a commitment to long-term employment. Furthermore, temporary workers could be let go on the basis of performance criteria rather than seniority. Thus temporary workers gave employers a flexibility to expand and contract the size of their labor forces that the internal labor market job structures did not.

Temporary employment was attractive to employers for legal as well as for organizational reasons. Temporary employment agencies place individuals in positions with "user firms" for an assignment that could be short term but could last months or even years. What characterizes a temporary employment agency job is not the duration of the job, but the relations of power and the locus of legal responsibility. In a temporary employment setting, the agency pays the employee directly and the agency, not the user firm, is considered the employer for purposes of labor and employment laws. That is, even though the individual employee works on the user firm's worksite and utilizes the user firm's tools, the temporary agency is, legally speaking, the employer.

Sociologist George Gonos attributes the tremendous growth of the temporary help industry to its success in securing this triangulated legal arrangement. He has shown that temporary help agencies lobbied Congress and pressured state employment services in the 1960s to ensure that the temporary agency, rather than the user firm, would be deemed the temporary worker's employer for purposes of labor law obligations. Once such

---

[4] Susan Houseman, *Why Employers Use Flexible Staffing Arrangements: Evidence from an Establishment Survey*, 55 INDUS. & LAB. REL. REV. 149 (Oct. 2001).

an arrangement was secured, firms had a powerful incentive to utilize temporary help because it enabled them to avoid expensive legal obligations imposed by labor law and collective bargaining agreements.[5]

In addition to the rapid growth of temporary employment agencies that began in the 1970s, there has been an enormous growth in contract employment and employee leasing firms. Employee leasing firms provide their customers, the user firms, with an entire workforce, while maintaining responsibility for all the employment-related tasks such as payroll, bookkeeping, and supervision. Generally, leased employees have long-term assignments with the user firms, while temporary workers have relatively short assignments. Also, leasing agencies generally provide an entire part of a user's operations, such as landscaping services, computer programming, or security services. Like temporary help agencies, the employee leasing firm is considered the statutory employer for purposes of labor and employment law. According to the most recent U.S. Economic Census, there were nearly nine hundred thousand leased employees in 1997.[6]

Since the 1970s, there has also been an increase in other forms of atypical employment relationships, including part-time work, contract work, on-call work, and independent contracting. In addition, some employers have established their own in-house pools of temporary or provisional workers who fill in when there are short-term vacancies within the organization. These workers are hired under an express understanding that their status is impermanent. For example, Microsoft hires a large number of workers that it terms "temporary" even though they perform the same tasks, often for several years, alongside "permanent" workers. Yet these "permatemps" do not receive the company's stock options and are not permitted to use the company's recreational facilities and stores that are available to the regular workforce.[7] Thus in the past twenty years, a large and growing number of workers have become part of an atypical workforce, a workforce comprised of workers who lack a specific employer and/or have no long-term attachment to a firm.[8]

---

[5] George Gonos, *The Contest over "Employer" Status in the Postwar United States: The Case of Temporary Help Firms*, 31 L. & Soc'ty Rev. 81 (1997).

[6] U.S. Bureau of the Census, 1997 Economic Census, available at www.census.gov/epcd/ec97/industry/E561330.htm.

[7] *See, e.g.*, Vizcaino v. United States Dist. Court, 173 F.3d 713, 716–17 (9th Cir. 1999) (describing Microsoft's in-house temporary workforce). *See also* Danielle Dorice Van Jaarsveld, *Collective Representation Among High-Tech Workers at Microsoft and Beyond: Lessons from WashTech/CWA*, forthcoming in 42 Indus. Rel. (2004) (study of Microsoft temporary workers).

[8] *See* Francoise J. Carré, *Temporary Employment in the Eighties*, in New Policies for the Part-Time and Contingent Workforce 48 (Virginia L. duRivage, ed., 1992) (on growth of temporary employment); Peter F. Drucker, Managing in a Time of Great Change 66–67 (1995) (describing change in the composition of temporary workers); Chris Tilly, *Short Hours, Short Shrift: The Causes and Consequences of Part-Time Employment*, in duRivage, New Policies for the Part-Time and Contingent Workforce 15, 17 fig.1.

In 2001, the U.S. Department of Labor Bureau of Labor Statistics' Current Population Survey (CPS) found that temporary agency employees, on-call workers, and persons employed by contract labor firms together constituted 3 percent of the workforce, or roughly 4 million workers out of a total workforce of 131 million. Independent contractors constituted a larger group – 6.4 percent of the workforce, or roughly 8.6 million workers.[9] Some scholars, using different definitions of atypical employment, have estimated the number of atypical workers to be much larger.[10] Yet under any definition, atypical employment is now a significant factor in the labor market.

B. The Rise of Precarious Employment

In the 1970s and 1980s, temporary work enabled employers to utilize a flexible peripheral workforce and retain a stable core in their internal labor market. But from the mid 1980s, many employers abandoned the goal of maintaining a large core of long-term employees altogether. Instead, they began dismantling their internal labor markets and repudiating any implicit contracts for lifetime employment. As a result, they changed the nature of the employment relationship with their regular workers, those they employed full-time for an indefinite term. These traditional workers had been the beneficiaries of the long-term employment commitment of firms that utilized internal labor markets. They had enjoyed job security, rising wages, stable benefit packages, and predictable advancement opportunities. Since the mid 1980s, many of those long-term employees have been laid off as a result of downsizing or restructuring. Some of those laid off have been rehired in a more explicitly temporary status. Others have received formal or informal notification that they should view themselves as free agents, not as long-term employees. And newly hired "regular employees" are told explicitly that they can be fired at any time and cannot assume a long-term employment relationship. Thus there has been an increase in the number of workers who have full-time "regular" jobs but who lack any explicit or implicit assurance of long-term job security. Work has become contingent, not merely in the

---

[9] See *Contingent and Alternative Employment Arrangements.* This data is almost unchanged from 1995 and 1997. *See* Cohany, *Workers in Alternative Employment Arrangements* 4–6 tbls.1–2.

[10] Richard Belous estimates that between 25 and 30 percent of the workforce consisted of contingent workers in 1988, a number he arrives at by including temporary workers, part-time workers, business service workers, and the self-employed. Richard Belous, THE CONTINGENT ECONOMY 16, tbl 2.1 (1989). *But see* Gillian Lester, *Careers and Contingency,* 51 STAN. L. REV. 73, 79–81 (1998) (criticizing Belous for failing to distinguish atypical employment from contingent employment). Belous includes many whose employment relations may be of long duration. Others include independent contractors in the definition, even though many of these are, by definition, not employees at all. Yet others include long-term employees who work at home. The definition of contingency one uses determines how extensive one finds the phenomena to be and whether one sees it as a growing or declining feature of the labor market.

sense that it is formally defined as short-term or episodic, but in the sense that the attachment between the firm and the worker has been weakened. The sociologist Richard Sennett reported this change after interviewing a number of younger employees about their experiences in the labor market. He wrote:

The most tangible sign of that change might be the motto "No long term." In work, the traditional career progressing step by step through the corridors of one or two institutions is withering; so is the deployment of a single set of skills through the course of a working life. Today, a young American with at least two years of college can expect to change jobs at least eleven times in the course of working, and change his or her skill base at least three times during those forty years of labor.[11]

Sennett also interviewed an AT&T executive, who told him, "In AT&T we have to promote the whole concept of the work force being contingent, though most of the contingent workers are inside our walls. 'Jobs' are being replaced by 'projects' and 'fields of work.'"[12]

The Bureau of Labor Statistics has confirmed Sennett's findings that young workers are changing jobs more frequently than in the past. According to recent unpublished data from the Department of Labor and the Bureau of the Census, the median length of time that workers in their twenties stay in one job has shrunk by half from 1983 to 2001, down from 2.2 years to 1.1 years.[13]

Corporate executives also report that there is a fundamental change in the implicit psychological contract under which most Americans are now employed. For example, Jack Welch, the former chief executive officer and miracle maker at the General Electric Company (GE), was asked by the HARVARD BUSINESS REVIEW in 1989, "What is GE's psychological contract with its people?" He replied:

Like many other large companies in the United States, Europe, and Japan, GE has had an implicit psychological contract based on perceived lifetime employment. People were rarely dismissed except for cause or severe business downturns, like in Aerospace after Vietnam. This produced a paternal, feudal, fuzzy kind of loyalty. You put in your time, worked hard, and the company took care of you for life.

That kind of loyalty tends to focus people inward. But given today's environment, people's emotional energy must be focused outward on a competitive world where no business is a safe haven for employment unless it is winning in the marketplace. The psychological contract has to change.[14]

---

[11] Richard Sennett, THE CORROSION OF CHARACTER 22 (1998).
[12] *Id.*
[13] Rick Marin, *Is This the Face of a Midlife Crisis?* NEW YORK TIMES, June 24, 2001, sec. 9, pp. 1–2.
[14] Noel Tichy & Ram Charan, *Speed, Simplicity, Self-Confidence: An Interview with Jack Welch*, HARV. BUS. REV., Sept.–Oct. 1989, at 112, 120 (emphasis omitted).

The change in the nature of full-time regular employment signifies the undoing of the scientific management and personnel management movements of early twentieth century. In the earlier era, human resource policy was designed to "decasualize" employment – to reduce turnover and transform a transient and mobile workforce into a long-term committed cadre. Today's efforts seek to reverse this trend, to break the assumption of long-term attachment and obligation between the firm and the employee, to "recasualize" the employment relationship. This recasualization of work has reportedly become a fact of life both for blue-collar workers and for high-end professionals and managers.[15]

C. The Empirical Story

To analyze the change in the nature of the employment relationship, it is more helpful to use the term "precarious employment" than the term "contingent employment." By precarious employment, I mean work that has no explicit or implicit promise of continuity – work that is the opposite of long-term stable employment organized in an internal labor market. Thus precarious employment characterizes the employment relations of employees who do not have a long-term attachment to their firm. The term includes many temporary-help agency workers, as well as workers hired as provisional or short-term workers. But, most importantly, it includes workers who have steady, full-time jobs but do not have any implicit or explicit promise of job security. The precariously employed are many of those presently considered contingent workers, as well as many who are regular employees but hired with different tacit or explicit understandings than their predecessors.

1. Measuring the Extent of Precarious Employment

Some economists have questioned whether there has in fact been a trend away from long-term worker-firm attachment toward precarious employment.[16] The empirical debate reflects two types of disagreement – disagreement about

---

[15] *See, e.g., The Future of Work: Career Evolution,* ECONOMIST, Jan. 29–Feb. 4, 2000, at 89; *see also* Drucker, MANAGING IN A TIME OF GREAT CHANGE 71; Rosabeth Moss Kanter, ON THE FRONTIERS OF MANAGEMENT 190 (1997); Sennett, THE CORROSION OF CHARACTER 23. *See also* Chris Tilly & Charles Tilly, WORK UNDER CAPITALISM 223–27 (1998). For a description of high skilled technical workers who left jobs within organizations to become independent contract workers, see Gideon Kunda, Stephen R. Barley, & James Evans, *Why Do Contractors Contract? The Experience of Highly Skilled Technical Professionals in a Contingent Labor Market,* 55 INDUS. & LAB. REL. REV. 2354 (2002).

[16] *See* Henry S. Farber, Are Lifetime Jobs Disappearing? Job Duration in the United States: 1973–1993, 25 (Nat'l Bureau of Econ. Research, Working Paper No. 5014, 1995); Kenneth L. Deavers, *There Is No Evidence "Lifetime Jobs" Are Disappearing* (Employment Policy Foundation Newsletter), available at http://www.epf.org/backg/b981016.htm (Oct. 16, 1998).

what constitutes precarious employment and disagreement about how to measure it. Some researchers include in their estimates all types of atypical employment – temporary employment, part-time employment, on-call employment, and independent contractors. Often such researchers are asking questions for which an expanded definition is appropriate.[17] However, atypical employment is not necessarily precarious. Part-time employment can be long-term and ongoing. If one's goal is to identify trends and changes in internal labor markets, it is necessary to measure not only formal employment relationships, but also employer and employee perceptions regarding job security and long-term employee-firm attachment. Further, it is particularly important to understand those perceptions of typical, rather than atypical, employees.

Because precarious employment is a function of employee perceptions, it presents enormous difficulties for measurement. The category of precarious employment includes not merely workers who are explicitly labeled temporary, but also workers who have steady, full-time work, but lack a reasonable *expectation* of job security. In the past, labor market surveyors did not inquire about employees' subjective expectations of job continuity. Even now, the issue remains elusive. For example, in 1995, 1997, 1999, and 2001, the Current Population Survey conducted studies of contingent employment, defined as "those who do not have an explicit or implicit contract for long-term employment."[18] However, the CPS surveyors were instructed that "Jobs were defined as being short term or temporary if the person was working only until the completion of a specific project, temporarily replacing another worker, being hired for a fixed time period, filling a seasonal job that is available only during certain times of the year, or if other business conditions dictated that the job was short term."[19] In other words, the CPS surveyors only counted as "contingent" those workers who took a job with the explicit understanding that the job itself would end in a relatively short time, that is, people whose jobs had a clear and imminent sunset provision.

---

[17] For example, Rebecca M. Blank has developed an estimate of "problem contingent workers," in which she includes those part-time workers, temporary help workers, and independent contractors who would prefer other employment arrangements. She finds that between 4.6 and 8.5 percent of the workforce is in problem contingent work. While Blank's finding bears on many important labor policy issues, the category of "problem contingent workers" is not the same as the category of precarious workers who may be full-time but lack an implicit promise of long-term employment and thus does not reflect changes in internal labor markets. Rebecca M. Blank, *Contingent Work in a Changing Labor Market*, in GENERATING JOBS: HOW TO INCREASE DEMAND FOR LESS SKILLED WORKERS (Richard Freeman & Peter Gottschalk, eds., 1998).

[18] *Contingent and Alternative Employment Arrangements, February 1999 Technical Note*, available at http://stats.bls.gov/news.release/conemp.tn.htm (Dec. 21, 1999); *see also* Steven Hipple, *Contingent Work: Results from the Second Survey*, MONTHLY LAB. REV., Nov. 1998, at 22 app.

[19] *Contingent and Alternative Employment Arrangements, Technical Note. See also* Hipple, *Contingent Work* 34 app.

They did not include people who believed the job would continue, but with someone else doing it. Using its constricted definition, the CPS found that only a small percentage of workers were "contingent."[20] However, employees of large corporations who believe that they can be fired at any time, but who also know the position will continue, would not be contingent under the CPS definition. Yet, those full-time workers for large and stable corporations are the ones whose employment relationships are undergoing the most dramatic changes.

Another large-scale survey that attempts to collect information on precarious employment is the General Social Survey (GSS) administered by the University of Michigan National Opinion Research Center. The GSS has asked employees periodically since 1972, "How likely do you think you are to lose your job in the next year?" The results have varied in different years, roughly tracking the business cycle. The GSS did find a discernible increase in perceived job insecurity between 1973 to 1998, the latest year for which such data are available.[21] However, because the GSS asks about a one-year time frame, rather than about the prospects for lifetime employment, the question is more likely to elicit a respondent's immediate assessment of the state of the labor market, viewed through the lens of natural optimism. Indeed, the fact that the GSS results track the business cycle suggests that the respondents are simply reporting their observations on the short-term health of the economy.

2. Measuring Job Tenure

Another method that economists use to measure changes in the nature of long-term employment is to track job tenure rates. Since 1983, the Current Population Survey of the Bureau of Labor Statistics has collected data on how

---

[20] The CPS studies used three different definitions of contingent employment and found three different results concerning the percentage of the workforce considered to be contingent. Estimate 1 comprises "[w]age and salary workers who expect their jobs will last for an additional year or less. Self-employed workers and independent contractors are excluded." Estimate 2 comprises "self-employed and independent contractors who expect their employment to last for an additional year or less and who had worked at their jobs...for 1 year or less." Estimate 3 comprises "[w]orkers [including self-employed and independent contractors] who do not expect their jobs to last...even if they already had held the job for more than 1 year and expect to hold the job for at least an additional year." The results, summarized in the following tabulations, suggest that under any of the definitions, contingent employment represents a small percentage of the workforce.

	1995	1997	1999
Estimate 1	2.2	1.9	1.9
Estimate 2	2.8	2.4	2.3
Estimate 3	4.9	4.4	4.3

[21] *See* Douglas Kruse & Joseph Blasi, *The New Employee-Employer Relationship*, in A WORKING NATION: WORKERS, WORK, AND GOVERNMENT IN THE NEW ECONOMY 63 (David Ellwood et al., eds., 2000).

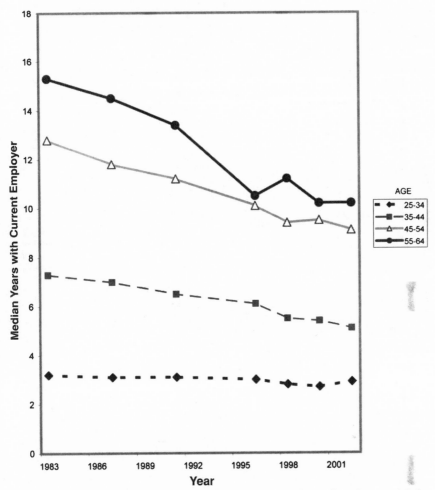

FIGURE 4.1. Median Years of Tenure with Current Employer for Wage and Salary Employees by Age, 1983–2002: Men

long employees stay at their jobs, sorted by gender, age, type of employment, type of establishment, and industry.[22]

The CPS found significant declines in job tenure between 1983 and 2002 among all men over the age of twenty, with the most significant declines among men in the age groups over age forty-five. Figure 4.1 shows the changes in job tenure for all males, by age group from 1983 to 2002.[23] For men ages fifty-five to sixty-four, the median years in their current job declined from 15.3 years in 1983 to 10.2 years in 2002. For men ages forty-five

---

[22] *See* Bureau of Labor Statistics News Release 02-531, *Employee Tenure in 2002*, available at http://146.142.4.23/pub/news.release/tenure.txt (Sept. 19, 2002).

[23] BLS, *Employee Tenure.*

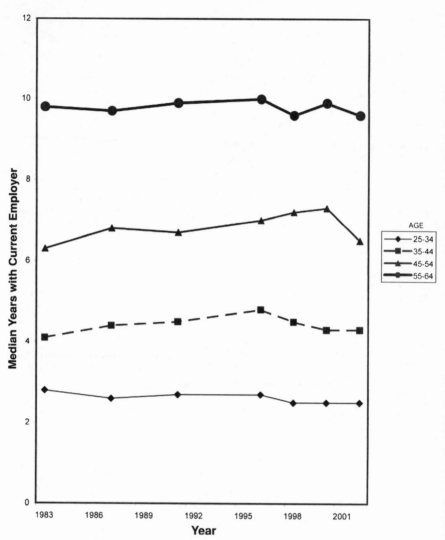

FIGURE 4.2. Median Years of Tenure with Current Employer for Wage and Salary Employees by Age, 1983–2002: Women

to fifty-four, the decline was from 12.8 years to 9.1 years. This is precisely the group that was the beneficiary of the internal labor markets of the past. The CPS's *Employee Tenure* data are derived from a survey of 50,000 households, and they report median results. Because these are medians based on a large sample, they would normally change slowly, so the declines are even more striking.

Figure 4.2 shows the changes in job tenure for women, by age group, between 1983 and 2002. It shows that there was a slight gain in job tenure for women in the middle age groups and a decline for women in the younger and older groups. However, women's job tenure remains far below that of their male counterparts at every step over age twenty. To the extent there are some gains in women's job tenure in the middle years, that trend reflects women's increasing attachment to the workforce – a historical trend since the 1960s. It does not negate the fact that long-term jobs in internal labor markets are declining. Women were not, by and large, the beneficiaries of the implicit promises of the internal labor market job structures in the first place, and when they came in, they entered at the bottom rungs.[24]

In addition to the job tenure data, the CPS publishes data on the percentage of employed workers who have been with their current employer for ten years or more. Figure 4.3 shows that between 1983 and 2002 there was a significant decline in the number of men who had been with their current employer for ten years or more.[25] For men ages forty to forty-four, the percentage declined from 51 percent in 1983 to less than 38 percent in 2002. Similar large declines occurred for men in every age group over forty-five.

As shown in Figure 4.4, the percentage of women who were with their current employer ten years or more did not show a marked decline between 1983 and 2002. Indeed, in some cases there was a modest rise. However, because women were not generally part of the long-term employment system, the overall percentage of women working for ten years or more is significantly lower than that of men at every stage.

The CPS also breaks down changes in job tenure rates by industry and occupational group. It found that between 1983 and 2002 workers in certain industries experienced a much greater decline in job tenure than their counterparts in other industries. The largest declines occurred in those industries that were most heavily unionized and most likely to be characterized by internal labor markets. For example, the largest decline took place in the automobile industry, in which median tenure was down from 13.0 years in 1983 to 7.0 years in 2002.[26] Because the auto industry has been heavily unionized and has undergone substantial downsizing, one would expect that under union seniority arrangements that require the lowest tenure employees to be laid off first, the job median tenure would increase in this period. The fact that the data shows such large declines can be explained by a shift in the nature of the industry itself.

In the past two decades, the auto industry has experienced a shift in employment away from the Big Three automobile manufacturers to independent parts firms. Between 1980 and 2000, employment at the Big Three manufacturers declined 3 per cent, while employment in independent parts

---

[24] *See* Francine D. Blau, Marianne A. Ferber, & Anne E. Winkler, THE ECONOMICS OF WOMEN, MEN AND WORK 113–15 (3d ed. 1998).

[25] BLS, *Employee Tenure.*

[26] *See id.* at tbl. 5 (*Median Years of Tenure with Current Employer for Employed Wage and Salary Workers by Industry, Selected Years, 1983–1998*). *See also* Kruse & Blasi, *The New Employee-Employer Relationship* 50–52.

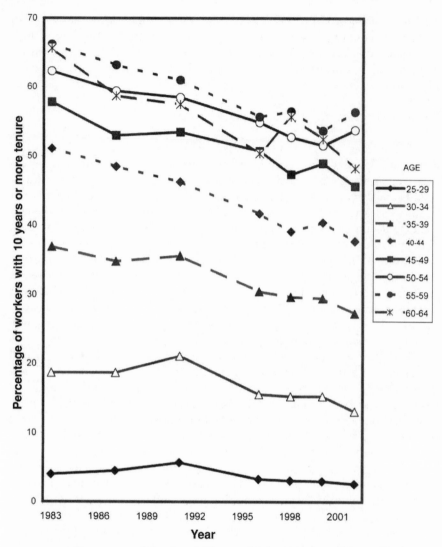

FIGURE 4.3. Percentage of Employed Wage and Salary Workers Who Had Tenure of Ten Years or More with Current Employer, 1983–2002: Men

firms increased 60 percent.[27] In the 1980s and 1990s, competitive pressures led the large firms to outsource more and more of their production, design, and minor assembly functions to nonunion independent parts firms. In 1999, General Motors spun off its internal parts division into a separate firm

[27] Harry C. Katz, John Paul MacDuffie, & Frits K. Pil, *Autos: Continuity and Change in Collective Bargaining*, in CONTEMPORARY COLLECTIVE BARGAINING IN THE PRIVATE SECTOR 55–90 (Paul Clark, John Delaney, & Anne Frost, eds., 2002).

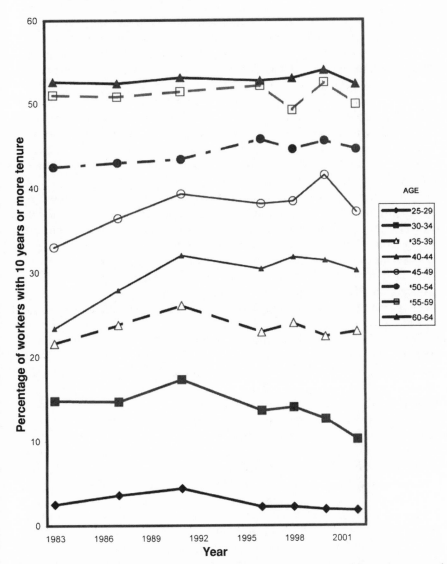

FIGURE 4.4. Percentage of Employed Wage and Salary Workers Who Had Tenure of Ten Years or More with Current Employer, 1983–2002: Women

called Delphi Automotive Systems, and in 2000 Ford similarly transformed its internal parts division into the separate Visteon Corporation. While the independent parts firms had been heavily unionized in the 1950s and 1960s, their unionization rates have declined precipitously since the 1970s. In the 1980s and 1990s, the parts firms adopted more flexible human resource practices than the Big Three. As a result, the bulk of employment in the industry is now concentrated in smaller, nonunion firms that provide lower wages, less stable employment patterns, and lower job tenure.[28]

The same pattern appears to be true of the primary metals industry, in which median job tenure was down from 10.0 years in 1983 to 7.6 years in 2002. Similarly, in the apparel and finished textiles industry, median job tenure declined from 7.0 in 1983 to 5.1 in 2002, and in the communications and public utilities industries, median job tenure was down from 8.3 to 4.7 years in 2002. These industries, like the auto industry, were once heavily unionized and dominated by internal labor markets, and today are increasingly made up of nonunion firms that have substituted flexible employment practices and fluctuating employment levels for internal labor market job structures with long-term employment. For example, union coverage in the iron and steel foundry industry declined from 50.4 percent in 1983 to 32.3 percent in 2002, primarily as a result of a shift from union to nonunion firms.[29] An establishment survey by labor economist Susan Houseman found that the number of private sector firms in all sectors that used flexible staffing arrangements, including temporary workers, on-call workers, and short-term hires, had increased in the 1990s and that "the overwhelming majority of employers expected, in general, that the use of flexible staffing arrangements would grow."[30]

Despite the substantial quantity of empirical evidence that shows that job tenure is declining for male workers, some economists continue to question whether this is a significant trend. For example, Princeton labor economist Henry Farber analyzed the CPS job tenure data from 1973 to 1993 and concluded that "no evidence presented [in the BLS data] supports to [sic] popular view that long-term jobs are becoming less common in the United States."[31] However, Farber's conclusion is an assessment of the combined job tenure data for men and women. When he looked at the data for men alone, Farber reported a "substantial decline in the population-based median [job tenure] for males." Farber also found that "The large decrease in the median for males seems to be due almost entirely to individuals with at most a high school education."[32] He concluded that "long-term jobs are now allocated somewhat differently across the population than they were twenty years ago. Long-term jobs have become more scarce for the least educated (particularly men)."[33] Farber's original article was based on a data set that ended in 1993,

[28] Harry C. Katz & Owen Darbishire, CONVERGING DIVERGENCES: WORLDWIDE CHANGES IN EMPLOYMENT SYSTEMS 34–47 (2000); Harry Katz et al., *Autos: Continuity and Change* 82.

[29] Barry Hirsch & David A. MacPherson, *Union Statistics by Industry*, at www.unionstats.com (visited May 2003).

[30] Houseman, *Why Employers Use Flexible Staffing Arrangements*, 55 INDUS. & LAB. REL. REV.

[31] Farber, *Are Lifetime Jobs Disappearing?* 25.

[32] *Id.* at 16–17. Farber also found a "large increase in the short-job probability for men with no more than a high-school education." *Id.* at 20.

[33] *Id.* at 25.

whereas the most significant trends occurred in the mid and late 1990s. He revisited the issue in 1998, using the Displaced Worker Survey supplements to the Current Population Survey between 1981 and 1996, and he found a dramatic increase in job loss in the mid 1990s, despite a sustained economic expansion. At that time Farber concluded that the evidence was "consistent with the view that there has been a secular decline in job security."[34]

Similarly, in October 1999, labor economists David Jaeger and Anne Huff Stevens analyzed both the Current Population Survey and the Panel Study of Income Dynamics, concluding that "both data sets show an increase in the fraction of men with less than 10 years of tenure starting in the late 1980s."[35]

In 1996, the Russell Sage Foundation sponsored a symposium to bring together labor economists to share and compare their assessments of trends in job stability and job security in the 1980s and the early 1990s. For purposes of the discussion, they distinguished "job stability" – defined as the probability of a worker retaining or leaving a job, from "job security" – defined as the likelihood a worker would experience involuntary job loss. Using data sets that ended in early or mid 1990s, the researchers who focused on job stability all found a decline in the last two decades of the twentieth century. Project editor and project director David Neumark summarized their findings: "Overall, my reading of the evidence is that the 1990s have witnessed some changes in the employment relationship consistent with weakened bonds between workers and firms." However, Neumark added a note of caution, by stating:

Although the magnitudes of these changes sometimes suggest sharp breaks with the recent past, they nonetheless indicate that these bonds have been only weakened, not broken. Furthermore, the changes that occurred in the 1990s have not persisted long enough even to earn the label "trends." ... It is therefore premature to infer long-term trends toward declines in long-term employment relationships, and even more so to infer anything like the disappearance of long-term, secure jobs.[36]

Neumark's caution can be explained on the ground that all studies in the symposium used data sets that ended in the mid 1990s. The addition of the CPS data from the late 1990s and early 2000s data would, no doubt, convince him to elevate his researchers' findings to the status of trends.

For the purposes of tracking changes in internal labor markets, the data concerning males with a high school education or less are of particular

---

[34] Henry S. Farber, *Has the Rate of Job Loss Increased in the Nineties?* Proc. 50th Ann. Meeting Indus. Rel. Res. Ass'n 88, at 92 (1998).

[35] David Jaeger & Anne Huff Stevens, *Is Job Stability in the United States Falling? Reconciling Trends in the Current Population Survey and Panel Study of Income Dynamics*, 17 J. Lab. Econ. S1 (1999). *See also* Robert G. Valletta, *Declining Job Security*, 17 J. Lab. Econ. S170 (1999) (citing numerous studies reaching the same conclusion).

[36] David Neumark, ed., On the Job: Is Long-Term Employment a Thing of the Past? 23 (2001).

significance. Blue-collar men with low educational attainment were the primary beneficiaries of internal labor market practices in the past. This group comprised approximately half of all men, or roughly 25 percent of the entire adult population, as recently as 1990.[37] In the mid 1990s, there was evidence of decline of job tenure among men at all educational levels,[38] but the decline of blue-collar job tenure was far more pronounced than for other men. Farber found that the likelihood that a male worker with less than a high school education would have a short-term job was about 16 percent higher in 1993 than it was in 1973, and that the probability that such a male would have a job of twenty years or more duration declined by about 8 percent.[39] As dramatic as this finding is, it understates the change because it is based on data that ends in 1993. More recent survey data shows significant declines in job tenure for less educated males throughout the 1990s.[40] Whereas a forty-five-year-old male worker with a high school education had a median job tenure of 9.8 in 1991, that same worker's median job tenure was 7.8 in 2002.

The evidence unequivocally demonstrates that there was a significant decline in job tenure for men over the age of twenty-five throughout the 1990s, particularly for those with a high school degree or less. This does not mean that there was a decline in job security for all workers in the 1990s. The significance of a decline in job tenure for this group is that it reflects a decline in internal labor markets. Blue-collar male workers were the beneficiaries of the internal labor market form of job structures – that is, they were the ones who enjoyed de facto job security in long-term employment settings. Evidence that internal labor market models of employment relationships are declining is suggested by the fact that those who were in the long-term employment relationships in the past – blue-collar men – have seen their job tenure decline.

While the job tenure and job loss data are suggestive of an increase in precarious employment and a decline of worker-firm attachment, they do not directly address whether there has been a decline in implicit promises of long-term employment. Job tenure data is an *ex post* measure of how long a worker holds a particular job. Job tenure data can tell us whether

[37] In the period of Farber's study, a full 54.8 percent of *all* adults – men and women – in the United States had an educational level of high school or less. *See* U.S. Bureau of the Census, 1990 CENSUS OF THE POPULATION: SOCIAL AND ECONOMIC CHARACTERISTICS, CPH-L-96 (1993). Thus we can estimate that males comprised approximately half of that group.
[38] Using the data since 1996, we see that males between the ages of 25 and 65 with a college education experienced the following changes in their job tenure:

	1997	1998	2000
25 to 34 years	2.7	2.7	2.5
35 to 44 years	5.7	5.4	5.0
45 to 54 years	9.4	9.7	9.9
55 to 64 years	12.2	14.2	10.8

[39] *See* Farber, *Are Lifetime Jobs Disappearing?* 22–24.
[40] *See* Jaeger & Huff Stevens, *Job Stability*, J. LAB. ECON. at S24–S25.

jobs today are in fact of shorter duration than they were in the past, but they do not show whether a worker has an *ex ante* expectation that his or her job will be long-term. What characterized internal labor markets, from an employee's point of view, was the *expectation* of long-term job security. Job tenure data are, at best, a proxy for this subjective understanding. If the prevalence of employment relationships that embody such an implicit understanding is declining, that fact might or might not show up in job tenure data. A person who works at McDonald's for twenty years, always knowing that they might be fired at the end of the week, has a different understanding of their employment contract – a different "psychological contract" – than a person who worked for General Motors in the 1950s. Job tenure data, while suggestive of a trend, are a post hoc account of employee labor market experience, and do not tell the whole story about changes in employee perceptions or expectations. For that reason, it is necessary to supplement the data with journalistic accounts and academic studies by those in disciplines such as organizational behavior and the sociology of work. In addition, it is necessary to study the subjective views and expectations of employees and employers.

Organizational behaviorists and industrial sociologists have studied the expectations of employees who have full-time steady jobs, and have posited that there is a "new deal" at work, a new set of expectations that people have about their jobs. This new deal, or "new psychological contract," refers to the changes in the subjective understandings of both parties about the terms of their employment relationship. Part of the new expectation is, in the words of Richard Sennett, "no long term." The specific factors that comprise this new deal are explored in the next chapter.

D. Accounting for the Transformation

Before examining the expectations and understandings of the new employment relationship, it is necessary to consider why employers are abandoning the internal labor markets of the past century. The decline of job stability and the rise of precarious employment in the past two decades is the result of an increase in both voluntary and involuntary job loss. The rise in voluntary job change reflects the new sensibility that Richard Sennett and others report, in which employees increasingly seek out labor market prospects beyond the boundary of their current firms. The rise in involuntary job loss is a function of both downsizing and workforce churning, two characteristics of the labor relations practices of large firms in the past two decades.[41]

Some scholars have argued that the change in the employment relationship is a function of changes in the legal framework governing employment. In the 1970s and 1980s, many state courts in the United States revised their

---

[41] Peter Cappelli & David Neumark, *External Job Churning and Internal Job Flexibility* (Nat'l Bureau of Econ. Research, Working Paper No. 8111, Feb., 2001).

at-will doctrines and restricted employers' right to fire employees. Most state courts adopted a tort of unjust dismissal, in which a court imposes tort liability when an employer discharges an employee for a reason that violates public policy. Thus, for example, courts found an employer liable in tort when an employer fired an employee for serving on a jury or for refusing to commit perjury.[42] In addition, a small number of states implied a covenant of good faith and fair dealing into employment contracts, thus finding that an employer breached an employment contract by discharging an employee in a situation that demonstrated egregious bad fath. The prototype situation in which a court found an employer liable for breaching an implied covenant was when an employer discharged a salesman just before a large commission became due and payable.[43]

A third type of exception to the at-will doctrine, adopted by forty-three states, was an implied-in-fact contract exception. In these cases, courts found employers for breach of contract if they made express or implicit promises of job security and then broke their promise. For example, in 1984, the Supreme Court of Washington held that an employer who distributed an employee handbook that promised its employees fair treatment and relinquished its right to engage in arbitrary dismissals was obligated to act in accordance with its promises.[44] The court explained:

While an employer need not establish personnel policies or practices, where an employer chooses to establish such policies and practices and makes them known to its employees, the employment relationship is presumably enhanced. The employer secures an orderly, cooperative and loyal work force, and the employee the peace of mind associated with job security and the conviction that he will be treated fairly.... This may create an atmosphere where employees *justifiably rely* on the expressed policies and, thus, justifiably expect that the employers will do the same. Once an employer announces a specific policy or practice, especially in light of the fact that he expects employees to abide by the same, the employer may not treat its promises as illusory. Therefore, we hold that if an employer, for whatever reason, creates an atmosphere of job security and fair treatment with promises *of specific treatment in specific situations* and an employee is induced thereby to remain on the job and not actively seek other employment, those promises are enforceable components of the employment relationship.[45]

In addition to holding that employee handbooks can create enforceable obligations to discharge employees only for just cause, some courts find that other employer conduct can create enforceable promises of job security. Thus, for example, one employer was held liable for breach of contract for arbitrary dismissal when the employer had given verbal promises of lifetime

[42] Needs v. Hocks, 536 P.2d 512 (Or. 1975) (jury duty); Petermann v. International Bhd. of Teamsters, 174 Cal. App. 2d 184 (1974) (refusal to commit perjury).
[43] Foley v. National Cash Register Co., 364 N.E. 2d 1251 (Mass. 1977).
[44] Thompson v. St. Regis Paper Co., 685 P.2d 1081 (Wash. 1984).
[45] Id. at 1087–89.

employment and had fostered a corporate culture that assured its employees that they would not be fired unfairly.[46]

The first two exceptions to the at-will doctrine have had very little impact on employers' personnel practices. Both the tort of unjust dismissal and the covenant of good faith and fair dealing impose liability on employers for actions that are taken after an employee is hired – actions that are usually taken under ad hoc and sui generis circumstances. In addition, courts have limited those exceptions to cases of extremely abusive employer conduct, so that there have been relatively few cases in which employers were found liable either for unjust dismissal or breach of an implied covenant of good faith. In contrast, the implied-contract exception applies to the employer's regular personnel policies, particularly those communicated to an employee at the time of hire. As a result of the implied-contract exception, many employers who made promises of job security either explicitly in their employment handbooks or implicitly in their corporate cultures have found themselves bound by them when they tried to dismiss long-term workers.[47]

Some have argued that the implied-contract exception to the at-will doctrine induced employers to cut back on implied promises of job security. For example, labor economist David Autor attempted to test this proposition in a study of the use of temporary help agencies between 1979 and 1995.[48] Autor found that the use of temporary help agencies increased substantially in states that adopted the implied-contract exception to the at-will rule. Using a regression analysis, Autor found that states that had adopted an implied-contract exception to the at-will doctrine saw an increase in temporary employment in the magnitude of 20 percent. From this, Autor concluded that employers responded to the legal change in the at-will doctrine by increasing their use of temporary employees, and affirmatively disavowing any long-term employment commitments. Without a reliable right to discharge at will, Autor claims, employers have increasingly turned to temporary employment agencies to give them the flexibility to reduce their workforces on short notice.[49]

Autor acknowledges that his finding does not explain the tremendous growth in the use of temporary help agencies. As he says, "only a modest percentage of the growth of THS (Temporary Help Supply) over this period is explained."[50] Furthermore, Autor's study does not explain why employers

---

[46] *See, e.g.*, Pugh v. See's Candies, 171 Ca. Rptr. 917 (Ca., Ct. App. 1981), *overruled in part on other grounds by* Guz v. Bechtel Nat'l, Inc., 24 Cal. 4th 317 (2000).

[47] Some of the other cases in which courts have found and enforced an implied contract for long-term employment are Fletcher v. Wesley Med. Ctr., 585 F. Supp. 1260, 1263–64 (D. Kan. 1984); Salimi v. Farmers Ins. Group, 684 P.2d 264, 265 (Colo. Ct. App. 1984); Toussaint v. Blue Cross & Blue Shield, 292 N.W.2d 880, 892 (Mich. 1980); Woolley v. Hoffman-La Roche, Inc., 491 A.2d 1257, 1268 (N.J. 1985).

[48] David H. Autor, Outsourcing at Will: Unjust Dismissal Doctrine and the Growth of Temporary Help Employment (Nat'l Bureau of Econ. Research, Working Paper No. 7557, 1999).

[49] *Id.* at 10.

[50] *Id.* at 34.

are dismantling their internal labor markets for their "regular employees." One subsequent study found that the adoption by states of implied-contract exceptions to at-will employment did not have a discernible impact on the structure of internal labor markets.[51]

Other changes in the employment law make it implausible that modifications in the at-will rule are what have caused employers to abandon internal labor markets job structures. Employers who are anxious to avoid liability in implied-contract jurisdictions can do so without losing valued long-term employees or dramatically restructuring their human resource practices. All they have to do is place an explicit disclaimer of just cause liability and a clear statement that the employment relationship is at will in their employment manuals. There is evidence that employers are increasingly doing just that.[52] In addition, an employer can avoid liability for unjust dismissals by establishing a mandatory arbitration system for disputes concerning terminations and designing the systems to make it difficult for employees to prevail. The use of employer-promulgated arbitration systems has been growing at a rapid rate as employers seek to limit their liability both for employment discrimination and for wrongful dismissal.[53] In 2001, the Supreme Court gave its approval to the use of these systems in the case of *Circuit City Stores v. Adams.*[54] By utilizing explicit at-will contracts or by establishing an internal arbitration system, firms can continue to make implicit promises of job security and at the same time avoid any liability that might be assessed against them under implied-contract exceptions to the at-will rule. The fact that employers are dismantling their internal labor markets despite these other methods for liability avoidance suggests that the changes in the at-will rule alone do not explain the current changes in work practices.

A better explanation for the change in the employment relationship and the recasualization of work is that work practices are being adjusted to production requirements. As firms find themselves in a more competitive environment through increased trade and global competition, they have to pay more attention to short-term cost reduction. In addition, the market for corporate control forces firm managers to be responsive to short-term changes in revenues and demand. Part of this responsiveness involves just-in-time production, just-in-time product design, and just-in-time workers.

[51] Max Schanzenbach, *Exceptions to Employment at Will: Raising Firing Costs or Enforcing Life-Cycle Contracts?* 5 AM. L. & ECON. REV. 470, 501 (2003).

[52] Mark Berger, *Unjust Dismissal and the Contingent Worker: Restructuring Doctrine for the Restructured Employee,* 16 YALE L. & POL'Y REV. 1, 5–6 (1997).

[53] *See* Katherine Van Wezel Stone, *Employment Arbitration Under the Federal Arbitration Act,* in EMPLOYMENT DISPUTE RESOLUTION AND WORKER RIGHTS IN THE CHANGING WORKPLACE 27 (Adrienne E. Eaton & Jeffrey H. Keefe, eds., 1999); Katherine Van Wezel Stone, *Mandatory Arbitration of Individual Employment Rights: The Yellow Dog Contract of the 1990s,* 73 DENVER L. REV. 1017 (1996).

[54] Circuit City Stores, Inc. v. Adams, 532 U.S. 105 (2001). *See also* Gilmer v. Interstate/Johnson Lane, 500 U.S. 1 (1991).

5

The New Employment Relationship

For the past ten years, labor relations professionals have been advocating and implementing changes in the organization of work. Chapter 4 reviewed empirical studies of the U.S. labor market that are indicative of a departure from internal labor market job structures. However, in order to understand these changes in the workplace, the empirical data must be supplemented with information about the expectations and experiences of employees and employers. Organizational psychologists and industrial sociologists have developed a vocabulary for describing these subjective aspects of the workplace and a methodology for studying them. At the same time, management consultants have devised innovative human resource practices and approaches that create and reflect these subjective understandings. This chapter summarizes these bodies of work in order to extrapolate the essential elements of the new employment relationship as it is described and designed by organizational theorists, industrial sociologists, management consultants, and corporate executives. Each of these professional groups, from its own distinct vantage point, is engaged in the creation of a new digital workplace. While some of their writings are aspirational rather than descriptive, they express the aspirations of those who are actively and self-consciously engaged in creating the new institutional structures of the workplace. These structures then shape the aspirations, opportunities, and expectations of today's workforce.

A. Imagining the New Workplace

Even the most routine types of work involve the exercise of discretion. Sometimes an employee has discretion over what to produce or how to produce it. Professionals, for example, have a great deal of discretion to select the tasks they perform, set their own pace of work, and even determine their own level of compensation. Most lower-level employees – those for whom the choice of product and process is determined by others higher up in the organizational pecking order – also have discretion in some areas. Low-level workers can choose how hard to work, whether to make suggestions for improvements in work methods, whether or not to pitch in and help when unanticipated problems arise, whether to teach new employees the tricks of the trade, and whether to help build team esprit. These kinds of discretionary choices involve intangible aspects of work performance that are difficult to specify in advance, select for, and monitor, yet they are an important component of effective firm performance. Therein lies the essential fallacy of Taylorism, which tried but was ultimately unable to remove all discretion from those on the shop floor. The persistence of discretion reflects the fact that the employment relationship is more than a contract – it has elements of a gift exchange in that both sides have numerous important yet unspecified rewards that they can choose to bestow or withhold.

Rather than attempt to eliminate discretion, human resource professionals and organizational theorists have, since the Hawthorne experiments at Western Electric in the 1930s, studied intangible aspects of job performance such as motivation, commitment, and morale in order to determine how best to induce employees to exercise their discretion on behalf of the welfare of the firm. In doing so, they have developed a conceptual framework that forms both a descriptive and a prescriptive vision of the workplace today.

1. The New Psychological Contract

Organizational theorists have coined the term "psychological contract" to characterize the nature of employees' expectations and perceptions of their work. They posit that most employees have a psychological bond with their employer based on a perceived pattern of mutual obligation. The concept of a psychological contract is a subjective one, expressing an individual's belief in the existence of a bilateral relationship with his or her employer and his or her beliefs about the terms of the reciprocal exchange. According to organizational theorists Sandra Robinson and Denise Rousseau, a psychological contract is "an individual's beliefs regarding the terms and conditions of a reciprocal exchange agreement."[1] It is not the same as expectations, but rather consists of "beliefs in paid-for promises or reciprocal obligations," a "belief that some form of a promise has been made and that the terms and conditions of the contract have been accepted by both parties."[2] A psychological contract may include beliefs or perceptions regarding performance requirements, job security, training, compensation, and career management issues.[3] Some psychological contracts are written and highly

[1] Sandra L. Robinson & Denise M. Rousseau, *Violating the Psychological Contract: Not the Exception but the Norm*, 15 J. ORGANIZATIONAL BEHAV. 245, 246 (1994).
[2] *Id.*
[3] Marcie A. Cavanaugh & Raymond A. Noe, *Antecedents and Consequences of Relational Components of the New Psychological Contract*, 20 J. ORGANIZATIONAL BEHAV. 323, 323 (1999).

formalized, but it has been found that "for the most part, [the psychological contract between employee and employer is] implicit, covertly held and only infrequently discussed."[4]

A central element in the concept of a psychological contract is the perception of a bilateral exchange.[5] Scholars distinguish a psychological contract from mere expectations according to the reciprocal nature of the belief in the former. Expectations, they find, reflect an employee's hopes and aspirations but not beliefs in the existence of mutual obligation. When expectations are not met, an employee is disappointed; when a psychological contract is breached, an employee feels wronged. Researchers find that "[f]ailure to honor a [psychological] contract creates a sense of wrongdoing, deception and betrayal with pervasive implications for the employment relationship."[6]

In one study, Robinson and Rousseau examined the reaction of recent MBA graduates to employers who promised but failed to provide adequate training, compensation, prospects for promotion, job security, feedback, responsibility, and other desirable attributes of their jobs. They found that those who believed their employer breached such a contract experienced heightened levels of distrust of their employers and job dissatisfaction, and were more likely to leave.[7] Another study of 800 managers found that psychological contract violations increased exit, voice, and neglect behaviors and decreased loyalty to the organization.[8] Yet another study of postgraduation MBAs found that psychological contract violations led employees to reevaluate, and downgrade, their view of their obligations to their employers. The authors concluded that "[organizational] citizenship may, in fact, result from the employees' perceptions of their obligations to organizations and the degree to which they are reciprocated rather than from attachment, loyalty, or satisfaction, as has been most frequently suggested."[9]

Academic interest in the notion of psychological contracts developed during the 1980s, the period in which middle-management employees in large

---

[4] Neil Anderson & René Schalk, *The Psychological Contract in Retrospect and Prospect*, 19 J. ORGANIZATIONAL BEHAV. 637, 637 (1998).

[5] Initially there was some disagreement amongst theorists as to whether the term referred to an actual exchange within an organization, or merely the individual's perception of an exchange. However, in recent writings, a subjective definition has prevailed. *See* David E. Guest, *Is the Psychological Contract Worth Taking Seriously?* 19 J. ORGANIZATIONAL BEHAV. 649, 649–58 (1998); Denise M. Rousseau & Snehal A. Tijoriwala, *Assessing Psychological Contracts: Issues, Alternatives and Measures*, 19 J. ORGANIZATIONAL BEHAV. 679, 679–80 (1998); Anderson & Schalk, *Psychological Contract*, 19 J. ORGANIZATIONAL BEHAV. at 638–39.

[6] *See* Robinson & Rousseau, *Violating the Psychological Contract*, 15 J. ORGANIZATIONAL BEHAV. at 247.

[7] *See id.* at 248.

[8] *See* William H. Turnley & Daniel C. Feldman, *The Impact of Psychological Contract Violations on Exit, Voice, Loyalty, and Neglect*, 52 HUM. REL. 895, 908, 917 (1999).

[9] *See* Sandra L. Robinson et al., *Changing Obligations and the Psychological Contract: A Longitudinal Study*, 37 ACAD. MGMT. J. 137, 149–50 (1994).

American corporations were the victims of large-scale downsizing and corporate restructuring. In studying those left standing after massive layoffs in their firms – a group referred to by the evocative term "layoff survivors" – as well as those who lost their jobs but were later reemployed at new firms – a group termed "expatriate managers" – organizational researchers found that both groups experienced an intense sense of unfairness and anger. They hypothesized that the employees' reactions resulted from the fact that the changes in their employment were inconsistent with their tacit assumptions about the terms of their employment contracts.[10]

Although most of the early studies on psychological contracts looked at management employees, subsequent studies have found that such contracts exist with lower-level employees as well. Indeed, some scholars have hypothesized that even contingent and temporary workers have a psychological contract with their employers, albeit a different one than that of full-time, long-term employees.[11]

The term "psychological contract" is useful to theorists of organizational behavior because it both captures the fact that parties bring expectations of reciprocal obligation to the employment relationship and accounts for the intense sense of injustice that can result when these expectations are not met. Thus, for example, it helps to explain the oft-observed fact that most at-will employees believe that it is unfair, and illegal, for an employer to fire them without good cause.[12] Despite their formal at-will status, such employees have a psychological contract that leads them to expect job security. Indeed, some courts have acknowledged the existence of psychological contracts for long-term job security and have modified the at-will rule in situations in which an employer had deliberately led an employee to believe that his job was secure.[13]

Because the concept of a psychological contract is capable of measurement, it is a valuable tool for studying employee expectations, job satisfaction, attachment, commitment, and morale. These factors are all related to job performance and hence to profit-linked outcomes such as productivity,

---

[10] *See generally* Anderson & Schalk, *Psychological Contract*, 19 J. ORGANIZATIONAL BEHAV. at 643–44 (summarizing studies of the impact on employees of employer breach of psychological contracts).

[11] *See, e.g.*, Judi McLean Parks et al., *Fitting Square Pegs into Round Holes: Mapping the Domain of Contingent Work Arrangements onto the Psychological Contract*, 19 J. ORGANIZATIONAL BEHAV. 697 (1998).

[12] *See* Pauline T. Kim, *Bargaining with Imperfect Information: A Study of Worker Perceptions of Legal Protection in an At-Will World*, 83 CORNELL L. REV. 105, 133–40 (finding in an empirical study that employees regularly overstate their degree of job security).

[13] *See, e.g.*, Pugh v. See's Candies, Inc., 116 Cal. App. 3d 311, 324–30 (1981), *overruled in part on other grounds by* Guz v. Bechtel Nat'l, Inc., 24 Cal. 4th 317 (2000); Toussaint v. Blue Cross & Blue Shield, 292 N.W.2d 880, 892 (Mich. 1980); Woolley v. Hoffman-La Roche, Inc., 491 A.2d 1257, 1268 (N.J. 1985); Thompson v. St. Regis Paper Co., 685 P.2d 1081, 1089 (Wash. 1984).

turnover, and organizational effectiveness. Thus the concept of a psychological contract has received considerable attention in recent years.[14]

For present purposes, the most important aspect of the psychological contract is that it is undergoing a profound transformation. While there was initially some disagreement as to whether the old contract has simply been breached or whether a new contract has taken its place, there is now a consensus among organizational theorists that a new psychological contract is emerging.[15] The change has been described by organizational theorists Marcie Cavanaugh and Raymond Noe as follows:

> According to the old psychological contract, the employer was seen as a caretaker for the employee.... Employees who were good performers were virtually guaranteed a job by their employer until retirement.... [Under the old psychological contract] the employer gave career development and promotions and the employee gave loyalty and commitment to the job and the organization. In the new psychological contract, both employees and employers have lower expectations for long-term employment, employees are responsible for their own career development, and commitment to the work has replaced commitment to the job and organization.[16]

Denise Rousseau, Snehal Tijoriwala, and other scholars similarly report that employees no longer assume that the employment contract offers job security and promotional opportunity within a single employer's internal labor market, but rather assume that it offers job opportunities with other employers and marketability in the external labor market.[17]

Management theorists and consultants have also noted the change in the psychological contract. For example, Peter Drucker writes, "there is no such thing as 'lifetime employment' anymore – such as was the rule in big U.S. or European companies only a few years ago."[18] Thomas Davenport of the Towers Perrin consulting firm writes, "Has the psychic contract evolved since 1983? You bet it has."[19]

The change in the psychological contract is accompanied by an explicit critique of Taylorist production techniques on the part of many managers and

---

[14] *See, e.g.*, Robinson et al., *Changing Obligations*, 37 ACAD. MGT. J. at 149 (reporting on an empirical study that found compliance with psychological contracts to be linked to employee commitment and citizenship behavior).

[15] Mark Roehling et al., THE NATURE OF THE NEW EMPLOYMENT RELATIONSHIP(S): A CONTENT ANALYSIS OF THE PRACTITIONER AND ACADEMIC LITERATURES 2 (Cornell Ctr. for Advanced Human Res. Studies, Working Paper No. 98-18, 1998).

[16] Cavanaugh & Noe, *New Psychological Contract*, 20 J. ORGANIZATIONAL BEHAV. at 324.

[17] *See* Rousseau & Tijoriwala, *Assessing Psychological Contracts*, 19 J. ORGANIZATIONAL BEHAV. at 683. For a survey of over fifty articles on the new employment relationship in scholarly journals and trade publications, *see* Roehling et al., NATURE OF THE NEW EMPLOYMENT RELATIONSHIP(S), Cornell Center for Advanced Human Resource Studies, Working Paper 98–18 (1998).

[18] *Id.*

[19] Thomas O. Davenport, HUMAN CAPITAL: WHAT IT IS AND WHY PEOPLE INVEST IN IT 26 (1999).

executives. Taylorism, with its emphasis on deskilling and narrow, rigidly organized job classifications, not only bred boredom and instilled resistance among workers, it also deprived management of workers' creative contributions. The new psychological contract literature expresses a desire of managers to harness employees' knowledge and imaginative capacity in the production process. That desire is coupled with a new set of expectations that managers impart to their employees, expectations not of long-term job security and continuous promotion along a job ladder, but of something else. The terms of the new contract can be found in the literature about competency-based organizations, total quality management, and other high-involvement work practices that define the new workplace as it is imagined, and currently being constructed, by management scholars and management consultants. In order to explore this new contract, it is first necessary to introduce two other concepts in organizational theory – the concept of the boundaryless career and the concept of organizational citizenship behavior.

2. The Boundaryless Career

In the early 1990s, General Electric's Jack Welch characterized the modern corporation as a "boundaryless organization." In a similar vein, FORTUNE magazine editor Thomas Stewart urged companies to transcend the boundaries of the firm and instead to foster "learning communities [that] cannot be contiguous with the boundaries of the corporation, business unit, or department." As Stewart admonished, "Boundaries don't just keep information in. They keep it out, too."[20] Organizational scholars, echoing the practitioners, have also used the notion of boundarylessness to describe the career trajectory of today's workers. The concept of the boundaryless career has become an important part of the description of the new employment relationship.[21]

A boundaryless career is defined as "a career which unfolds unconstrained by clear boundaries around job activities, by fixed sequences of such activities, or by attachment to one organization."[22] It is a career that does not depend upon traditional notions of advancement within a single hierarchical organization. It includes an employee who moves frequently across the borders of different firms, such as a Silicon Valley technician, or a professional whose career draws its validation and marketability from professional and extraorganizational networks. A boundaryless career also refers to career paths within organizations in which individuals are expected to move laterally,

---

[20] Thomas A. Stewart, INTELLECTUAL CAPITAL: THE NEW WEALTH OF ORGANIZATIONS 102 (1997) (quoting Jim Euchner of Nynex).
[21] See Michael B. Arthur, *The Boundaryless Career: A New Perspective for Organizational Inquiry*, 15 J. ORGANIZATIONAL BEHAV. 295 (1994).
[22] Anne S. Miner & David F. Robinson, *Organizational and Population Level Learning as Engines for Career Transitions*, 15 J. ORGANIZATIONAL BEHAV. 345, 347 (1994).

without constraint from traditional job ladders or hierarchical career lattices. As one prescient theorist wrote in 1994, "The old picture of stable employment and associated organizational careers is fading. A new picture of dynamic employment and boundaryless careers calls for our attention."[23]

The development of boundaryless careers corresponds to the growth in joint ventures, outsourcing, and other forms of network production that permit and sometimes even encourage mobility between related enterprises. It is also related to changes within firms in which departmental boundaries and job definitions are becoming blurred. For example, many firms are using broadbanding rather than narrow job definitions to determine job duties and compensation levels. With broadbanding, jobs are defined by generalized competencies and workers are placed in a band rather than within a narrow job category. There is a range of compensation for each job within a band, so that workers can move up in pay while staying within the band. Further, broadbanding allows managers to assign workers to a wide range of tasks without formal reclassification. In addition to the increased use of broadbanding, firms are utilizing cross-functional teams that cut across departmental lines for many projects. In these and other ways, horizontal mobility has become ubiquitous in the transfer and deployment of personnel. All of these are features of the boundaryless workplace.

Boundarylessness has become a reality for many in America's workforce. Whereas previously careers were understood to unfold in structured ways – by movement up job ladders in internal labor markets or along fixed lattices on organizational flowcharts – recent research on careers has found organizational fluidity instead. As organizational theorists Anne Miner and David Robinson write, "Inside firms in the United States, decentralization, increasing emphasis on cross-functional coordination and teams have blurred previously rigid departmental boundaries. Many American employers have moved to more general job descriptions, emphasizing key values, rather than precise, predetermined duties."[24]

Professor Charles Heckscher of Rutgers' School of Management and Labor Relations describes post-bureaucratic organizational forms as organizations that are open at the boundaries. Unlike the situation in large bureaucracies, Hecksher claims that in today's organizations "there is no expectation that employees will spend their entire careers in one organization. There is far more tolerance for outsiders coming in and for insiders going out." Heckscher dates the change in career patterns from the 1980s, when there were widespread managerial layoffs. Also, at about that time, firms experienced pressures to innovate their processes and products. This led them to look for employees who had the requisite technical skills and to hire them

[23] Arthur, *Boundaryless Career*, 19 J. Organizational Behav. at 297.
[24] Miner & Robinson, *Organizational and Population Level Learning* 347. *See also* Arthur, *Boundaryless Career* 345.

laterally. Thus firms departed from the job ladder arrangements that had previously defined the shape of careers within organizations.[25]

Peter Drucker notes a historical shift throughout the twentieth century in career patterns. In his book MANAGING IN A TIME OF GREAT CHANGE, Drucker points out that while most adults still work for large organizations, "increasingly they are not *employees* of that organization. They are contractors, part-timers, temporaries." In addition to the rise of temporary work and outsourcing, Drucker notes that there has been a dramatic increase in alliances between firms, such as joint ventures, co-licensing agreements, and partnerships. Thus, he predicts that within twenty years a sizeable minority of managers and professionals will not be employees of the firms with whom they do business.[26]

The concept of a boundaryless career, like that of the new psychological contract, reflects the shift in job structures away from Taylorist, internal labor markets. Instead of job ladders along which employees advance within stable, long-term employment settings, there are now possibilities for lateral mobility between and within firms, with no set mobility paths, no established expectations, and no tacit promises of job security.

3. Commitment and Organizational Citizenship Behavior

In any employment relationship, firms need to motivate employees to perform efficiently, reliably, and with a high level of quality. As described in Chapter 2, internal labor markets performed an important motivational function in the past by promoting skill acquisition, giving employees a stake in the well-being of their firms, and discouraging employee resistance. Today, without implicit promises of job security, management's concern for motivation and commitment is more acute than ever. Today's managers believe they need not merely predictable or even excellent role performance, they need what has been termed "spontaneous and innovative activity that goes beyond role requirements."[27] Firms can no longer succeed if employees simply perform their tasks in a reliable but routine manner. They need employees to commit their imagination, energies, and intelligence on behalf of the firm. They want employees to innovate, to pitch in, to have an entrepreneurial attitude toward their jobs, to behave like owners. Current management theorists counsel managers to give employees discretion, but to do so in a way that ensures that discretion is exercised on behalf of the firm. Thus managers want to elicit behavior that goes beyond specific rules

---

[25] Charles Heckscher, *Defining the Post-Bureaucratic Type*, in THE POST-BUREAUCRATIC ORGANIZATION: NEW PERSPECTIVES ON ORGANIZATIONAL CHANGE 14, 27 (Charles Heckscher & Anne Donnellon, eds., 1994).

[26] Peter F. Drucker, MANAGING IN A TIME OF GREAT CHANGE 66–71 (1995).

[27] John R. Deckop et al., *Getting More Than You Pay For: Organizational Citizenship Behavior and Pay-for-Performance Plans*, 42 ACAD. MGMT. J. 420, 420 (1999).

and job demands, and gives the firm something extra. Organizational theorists describe the willingness to give that something extra as commitment. Commitment is a willingness to exert effort on behalf of an organization, a spirit of cooperativeness, and a willingness to contribute.

Among organizational theorists, commitment is generally divided into two types: affective commitment and continuance commitment. Continuance commitment is commitment to stay with an organization. It is fostered by human resource policies such as longevity-based benefits, long vesting periods for pensions, and seniority systems – all policies that make it worthwhile for an employee to stay and costly to leave. Affective commitment, on the other hand, involves identification with the firm's goals and a desire to do what is best for the organization. Employees who display affective commitment not only perform their assigned tasks, they engage in extra-role behavior on behalf of the firm.[28]

Researchers have found that affective commitment is positively correlated with job performance and firm productivity, while continuance commitment is negatively correlated with those same goals. For example, practices such as long vesting periods for pensions, rapid promotion, and skill-specific training – that is, traditional features of an internal labor market – may develop continuance commitment, but "may not instill . . . the desire to contribute to organizational effectiveness."[29] Thus, in an implicit critique of Taylorism and internal labor markets, organizational theorists advise firms to structure their human resource practices to increase affective rather than continuance commitment.

The extra-role behavior that results from affective commitment is termed organizational citizenship behavior, or OCB. OCB is defined as discretionary behavior that goes beyond the requirements of specific role definitions and that is not rewarded through the formal reward structure of the firm. It does not mean excellence in in-role performance, but rather performance that goes beyond formal role requirements to further organizational goals. OCB involves engaging in extra acts of helpfulness such as spontaneously rendering assistance to a coworker, taking on extra duties when a colleague is out sick, or demonstrating a technique to a novice. OCB can also involve extra conscientiousness, such as coming in during a snowstorm or meeting deadlines under adverse circumstances when performance would be excused. A scale commonly used for measuring organizational citizenship behavior

---

[28] *See, e.g.*, Dennis W. Organ, ORGANIZATIONAL CITIZENSHIP BEHAVIOR: THE GOOD SOLDIER SYNDROME 105–6 (1988); John P. Meyer et al., *Organizational Commitment and Job Performance: It's the Nature of the Commitment That Counts*, 74 J. APPLIED PSYCHOL. 152, 152 (1989); N. J. Allen & J. P. Meyer, *The Measurement and Antecedents of Affective, Continuance and Normative Commitment to the Organization*, 63 J. OCCUPATIONAL PSYCHOL. 1, 1–18 (1990); *see also* Dennis W. Organ & Mary Konovsky, *Cognitive Versus Affective Determinants of Organizational Citizenship Behavior*, 74 J. APPLIED PSYCHOL. 157, 157 (1989).

[29] *See* Meyer et al., Organizational Commitment, 74 J. APPLIED PYCHOL. at 153–55.

asks supervisors to rate their employees on the basis of several factors that address the employees' altruistic willingness to assist others and the conscientiousness that they bring to their tasks.[30]

Today, it is generally believed that OCB is a crucial component of organizational effectiveness. While organizational effectiveness is comprised of features such as efficiency, ability to attract valuable resources, good will, external image, reputation, innovativeness, and adaptability, many contend that OCB is the most important feature of those companies rated as excellent in their managerial practices. The challenge for today's human resource policy makers is to encourage organizational citizenship behavior without promising employees job security. That is, the goal of today's management is, in the words of one management theorist, to elicit commitment without loyalty.[31]

In their efforts to instill affective commitment and elicit organizational citizenship behavior, some firms encourage employees to take an entrepreneurial approach toward their jobs. Thomas Davenport writes that corporations should "think of workers not as human capital but rather as human capital owners and investors."[32] Consultants advise management to encourage each employee, at every level, to feel that they are in control and making decisions about profitability. Nordstrom gives its salespeople personalized professional business cards in order to encourage them to think of themselves as "salesperson professionals"; Wal-Mart gives departmental financial reports to employees down to the lowest level.[33] One corporate advisor illustrated how to elicit OCB amongst lower-level employees by recommending that supermarket cashiers should be given discretion over decisions about which magazines to place on the top of the display and which sundry items – flashlights, razor blades, car air fresheners, key chains, or candies – to feature.[34]

4. Procedural Justice

One way that employers attempt to foster OCB is to create mechanisms to ensure employees on-the-job fairness. Researchers have found that employees' subjective appraisal of their employer's fairness is one factor in generating OCB. Employees who perceive their employer as unfair reduce their OCB, triggering a downward cycle in which the employees' diminished

---

[30] *See* Organ, GOOD SOLDIER SYNDROME 4–5, 9–10, 115–17 app.; Organ & Konovsky, *Organizational Citizenship Behavior* 157–58.

[31] *See* Peter Cappelli, THE NEW DEAL AT WORK: MANAGING THE MARKET-DRIVEN WORK FORCE 217 (1999).

[32] Davenport, HUMAN CAPITAL 7.

[33] James C. Collins & Jerry I. Porras, BUILT TO LAST: SUCCESSFUL HABITS OF VISIONARY COMPANIES 117, 213 (1994).

[34] I am grateful to Jeremy Paul, who used this example while serving as special advisor to the chief executive officer of a major insurance company.

OCB leads the supervisor to withdraw informal types of affirmation, causing the employees to experience additional feelings of unfairness and to further decrease their OCB.[35]

Concern for generating OCB has led theorists to focus on the role of procedural justice and employee perceptions of fairness.[36] Organizational theorist Dennis Organ explains that people in organizations perceive themselves as involved in a social exchange relationship in which they contribute effort and citizenship in return for formal and informal rewards. When they encounter what they perceive to be unfair treatment, they revise their assessment of the nature of the overall exchange, retreat from an assumption of reciprocity, and reinterpret the relationship as an economic transaction.[37]

A number of organizational behavioral theorists have proposed definitions of procedural fairness. One widely used measure of procedural fairness uses six criteria to determine whether a procedure is fair – it must

(a) be consistently applied
(b) be free from bias
(c) ensure that accurate information is collected and used in the decision-making process
(d) have a mechanism to correct flawed decisions
(e) conform to personal or prevailing standards of ethics
(f) ensure that the opinions of various affected groups have been taken into account.[38]

All of these criteria are about the *process* by which rules are applied and disputes are resolved; they are not about substantive outcomes.

There is evidence that as firms disavow promises of job security, procedural fairness becomes more important than before. For example, a study of three thousand employees by the Towers Perrin consulting firm in 1997 found that the changes in the employment relationship had made employees more sensitive to whether they were treated with fairness and respect.[39] It is understandable that employees would focus on procedural fairness when they lack promises of long-term employment because, in this new employment relationship, employees are required to bear many of the risks that

---

[35] *See* Organ & Konovsky, *Organizational Citizenship Behavior* 76–77, 162. *See also* Robinson et al., *Changing Obligations*, 37 ACAD. MGMT. J. at 149 (finding that citizenship may result from employees' perceptions of the company's performance of its obligations under the psychological contract).

[36] *See* Jerald Greenberg, THE QUEST FOR JUSTICE ON THE JOB 32–39 (1996). *See generally* Jason Colquitt et al., *Justice at the Millennium: A Meta-Analytic Review of 25 years of Organizational Justice Research*, 86 J. APP. PSYCHOL. 425, 435–36 (2001).

[37] Dennis W. Organ, *The Motivational Basis of Organizational Citizenship Behavior*, in 12 RESEARCH IN ORGANIZATIONAL BEHAVIOR: AN ANNUAL SERIES OF ANALYTICAL ESSAYS AND CRITICAL REVIEWS 43, 63–66 (Barry M. Staw & L. L. Cummings, eds., 1990).

[38] *See* Colquitt et al., *Justice at the Millennium*, 86 J. APPLIED PSYCHOL. at 426.

[39] Roehling, NATURE OF THE NEW EMPLOYMENT RELATIONSHIP(S) 16.

were previously borne by the firm. Employees increasingly have to bear the consequences of firm failure or market fluctuations, so that they at least want to be confident that the incidence of the risks is fairly applied.

Because there is a link between procedural justice and organizational performance, employers have attempted to devise procedures for hearing complaints and resolving disputes that foster a perception of fair treatment. They have instituted a wide range of dispute resolution procedures designed to address employee complaints.[40] For example, some corporations maintain open-door policies that encourage an employee to bring a problem or grievance to a high-level manager outside the chain of command. Some have hired specialized corporate officers, called ombudsmen, whose job it is to hear complaints, conflicts, and disputes and to reach across status and departmental lines to seek resolution. Some have established management appeals boards to permit an employee to appeal an objectionable decision of an immediate supervisor to managers in other departments or divisions. Peer review procedures, in which disputes are resolved by panels comprised of fellow employees who hear and decide specific employee grievances, are also becoming a common practice. In addition, the more conventional forms of alternative dispute resolution – mediation and arbitration – are becoming more prevelant in the workplace.[41] A common characteristic of these employer-initiated dispute resolution techniques is that they all utilize decision makers who are outside the employees' normal chain of command. For this reason, the disputes can be resolved in a manner that does not reinforce hierarchy.

Peer review is one of the fastest growing forms of nonunion dispute resolution. A recent survey of over three hundred firms in the telecommunications industry found peer review procedures in place in 15.9 percent of the firms in the sample, a surprisingly high incidence.[42] The peer review plan at TRW

---

[40] See Lisa B. Bingham & Denise R. Chachere, *Dispute Resolution in Employment: The Need for Research*, in EMPLOYMENT DISPUTE RESOLUTION AND WORKER RIGHTS IN THE CHANGING WORKPLACE, 103–13 (Adrienne E. Eaton & Jeffrey H. Keefe, eds., 2000); David B. Lipsky, Ronald L. Seeber, & Richard D. Fincher, EMERGING SYSTEMS FOR MANAGING WORKPLACE CONFLICT: LESSONS FROM AMERICAN CORPORATIONS FOR MANAGERS AND DISPUTE RESOLUTION PROFESSIONALS, esp. ch. 3 (2003) (discussing the growth of ombudsmen, mediation, and arbitration programs amongst nonunion firms); Alexander J. S. Colvin, *Adoption and Use of Dispute Resolution Procedures in the Nonunion Workplace*, in 13 ADVANCES IN INDUSTRIAL & LABOR RELATIONS (David Lewin and Bruce E. Kaufman, eds., 2004) (discussing the development of peer review, open door policies, management appeal boards, mediation, and arbitration at TRW in the 1990s). *See also* Alexander J. S. Colvin, Citizens and Citadels: Dispute Resolution and the Governance of Employment Relations 126–44 (1999) (unpublished Ph.D. dissertation, Cornell School of Industrial and Labor Relations).

[41] *See* Katherine Van Wezel Stone, PRIVATE JUSTICE, THE LAW OF ALTERNATIVE DISPUTE RESOLUTION (2000).

[42] Alexander James Colvin, *Institutional Pressures Human Resource Strategies, and the Rise of Nonunion Dispute Resolution Procedures*, 56 INDUS. & LAB. REL. REV. 375, 385 (2003).

illustrates how these new systems are designed to promote procedural justice without reinforcing hierarchy. At TRW, peer review can be invoked by any employee who wants to challenge a serious disciplinary measure, including termination. The review panel consists of two managers and three peer employees, selected by the employee from a list provided by TRW. Under the guidance of a facilitator from the human resource department, the panel holds a hearing, accepts evidence, and then issues a decision. The panel has no authority to change company policy – merely to ensure that it is applied correctly. If it was not, the disciplinary measure is revoked.

The purpose of peer review and other new nonunion employee dispute resolution procedures is to create a perception of procedural fairness and thus to encourage the OCB of employees and enhance performance outcomes of the firm. The degree to which the dispute resolution mechanisms succeed in doing so is yet to be definitively determined.[43]

B. Converting Theory into Practice: Two Contemporary Management Theories

Contemporary management literature, like the organizational behavior scholarship, is riddled with explicit critiques of Taylorism and its emphasis on hierarchy and rigid job ladders. Management theorists claim that internal labor market job structures stifle the creativity and organizational citizenship behavior that are necessary to succeed in today's competitive markets.[44] These theorists advocate the creation of organizations that embody flexibility, promote skill development, and foster organizational citizenship behavior.

We can look to the writings of management theorists and consultants about the internal organization of firms to learn about the terms of the new psychological contract. This section examines three of the most comprehensive and influential proposals for restructuring the workplace – the competency-based organization, total quality management, and high performance work practices. These three approaches have different starting points and different foci, but are remarkably similar in their prescriptions and implications.

---

[43] In one TRW plant between 1992 and 1997, Alexander Colvin found that 160 employees took cases to peer review, but only 10 were successful in overturning a supervisory decision. The low employee win rate nonetheless was sufficient to promote a sense of procedural fairness by the firm. *See* Colvin, *Adoption and Use of Dispute Resolution*.

[44] Today's management literature is replete with critiques of Taylorism. *See, e.g.*, Eric E. Anschutz, TQM AMERICA: HOW AMERICA'S MOST SUCCESSFUL COMPANIES PROFIT FROM TOTAL QUALITY MANAGEMENT 48–49 (1995); Edward E. Lawler III, HIGH-INVOLVEMENT MANAGEMENT 5–11 (1986); Stewart, INTELLECTUAL CAPITAL 48; James C. Worthy, LEAN BUT NOT MEAN: STUDIES IN ORGANIZATION STRUCTURE 93–116 (1994).

1. Competency-Based Organizations

Edward E. Lawler III, of the University of Southern California, has written extensively about the new employment relationship, and is the originator of many of its key elements. Lawler advocates that firms shift from being job-based organizations to being what he calls competency-based organizations. He points out that ever since Frederick Winslow Taylor and the era of scientific management, organizations have used job-based approaches to employment. The emphasis on jobs assumes that jobs can be studied, tasks can be rationalized, and human performance can be measured. As large-scale bureaucratic forms of organization developed, scholars devised various approaches toward designing job hierarchies and evaluating the performance of workers within them. The job paradigm, Lawler claims, has been central to human resource theorists' approaches to employee selection, training, performance management, and compensation – tasks designed to ensure that employees are motivated and capable of performing their jobs.[45] He writes:

There is good reason to believe that the concept of an individual holding a job is no longer the best way to think about organizing and managing individuals. Instead of thinking of people as having a job with a particular set of activities that can be captured in a relatively permanent and fixed job description, it may be more appropriate and more effective to think of them as human resources that work for an organization.[46]

According to Lawler, the scientific management and bureaucratic approaches of the past emphasized selection tests and training programs that were designed to fit individuals into a preset job within a predetermined organizational structure. "The implicit assumption [was] that the best way to optimize organizational performance [was] to fill jobs with appropriately skilled individuals and motivate them to perform effectively through pay and other rewards." This in turn assumed a hierarchy of duties and responsibilities within a command-and-control form of organization. Lawler contends that such forms of work organization were dominant throughout most of the twentieth century but are no longer appropriate.[47]

Lawler warns that globalization has enabled many firms to shift production and assembly tasks to lower-wage workers in developing countries. Workers in developed countries are increasingly performing knowledge and service work. Global competition, he argues, forces companies to focus on quality, speed, and adaptability to customer desire. Because there is increased instability in the product market, companies need flexibility to alter their products quickly in anticipation of changes in demand. To survive, companies must become "learning organizations." They must also constantly

---

[45] *See* Edward E. Lawler III, *From Job-Based to Competency-Based Organizations*, 15 J. ORGANIZATIONAL BEHAV. 3, at 3–4 (1994).
[46] *Id.* at 4.
[47] *Id.*

change their structure. In this environment, Lawler writes, "[individuals] become a key competitive asset. Their knowledge and skills become critical to the ability of the organization to perform.... [S]kills, capabilities, and learning become an important part of the organization's ability to compete and are at the heart of an organization's adaptability and ability to learn."[48]

Lawler argues that organizations that rely on capabilities as a source of competitive advantage have had to abandon the idea of using jobs and job definitions as the basis for managing individuals within them. In today's environment, earlier models of routine work in mass production settings underutilize employees and fail to develop the capabilities necessary to perform successfully. Individuals have moved "front and center as the key resource of an organization," so it is necessary to motivate individuals and develop their capabilities.[49]

What do competency-based organizations look like, and how do they differ from job-based organizations? First and foremost, Lawler maintains, an effective competency-based organization should not use a functionally based structure. Rather, it should emphasize cross-functional teams that facilitate lateral operation. However, it must do so without sacrificing functional excellence. For a competency-based approach to maintain excellence while capturing the benefits of flexibility and cross-utilization, it must attend to work design, selection, career movement, and pay systems. Lawler makes the following programmatic recommendations:

1. *Work Design.* Organizations should base human resource policy not on the job but on the individual. They should use skill and person descriptions rather than job descriptions. Organizations need to "focus on what individuals need to be able to do in order to make the work processes operate effectively."[50]

2. *Selection.* Organizations should select individuals for membership in the organization rather than for specific jobs. The challenge is to find individuals who "fit the learning environment that is provided by the organization."[51] When general skills are required, an organization can use a "realistic job preview" as a selection device. When individuals with specific skills are required, it can use assessments by existing workers.[52]

3. *Pay the Person.* Lawler urges organizations to adopt a skill-based approach to payment, in which they pay individuals according to the skills they have. Traditional pay systems rely heavily on the practice of job evaluation. In job evaluation, each job is broken down into factors, which include working conditions, knowledge required, accountability, and so forth. The factors

---

[48] *Id.* at 5 (citations omitted).
[49] *Id.* at 6.
[50] *Id.* at 7–8.
[51] *Id.* at 9.
[52] *See id.* at 9.

are assessed and assigned weights. Each job is given a total point score based upon the specific factor it involves, and each point score is translated into a level of pay.[53] Lawler is critical of job evaluation because it relies upon fixed job descriptions. He maintains that "inherent in any job description system is a message to an individual about what is not included in his or her job responsibilities. . . . It does not fit well . . . with an orientation that says that an individual should do what is right in the situation rather than what is called for by a job description."[54] Also, Lawler points out that job evaluation tends to measure jobs according to their hierarchical power and control, so that it reinforces hierarchical relations that are dysfunctional, at least for professional or high-technology organizations.[55]

In place of job evaluation, Lawler advocates skill-based pay. Skill-based pay systems were initially instituted in firms utilizing blue-collar workers as part of their attempts to break out of narrow job definitions. More recently, skill-based pay has become a prominent feature in the compensation packages of white-collar and professional workers as well.[56] As Lawler writes:

In simple skill-based pay systems, employees may be rewarded for learning what in essence are multiple jobs. For example, members of a factory work team may be given a pay increase for each machine they learn to operate as well as for each support job they learn, such as inspection, maintenance, and material handling. In complex work systems individuals may be rewarded for learning more abstract collections of skills. For example, in information services organizations employees may be rewarded for learning hardware-related skills, programming (software) skills, and skills in consulting to line managers, rather than for performing a single job within one of these areas. Skill blocks in skill-based pay systems become analogous to jobs in job-evaluation systems.[57]

Lawler contends that skill-based pay would induce firms to focus on people and their value to the firm. It would also motivate employees to acquire skills, particularly those skills that the organization needs. By encouraging employees to develop a variety of skills, a skill-based pay system makes them available for cross-utilization and horizontal career tracks typical of competency-based organizations.[58]

4. *Assessment.* To use skill-based pay, it is necessary to assess each person's skills and capabilities. Lawler suggests using peer review, technical experts,

---

[53] *See* Edward E. Lawler III, The Ultimate Advantage: Creating the High-Involvement Organization 144–45 (1992).

[54] *Id.* at 148.

[55] *See id.* at 148–49.

[56] *See* Mary Rowland, *It's What You Can Do that Counts*, New York Times, June 6, 1993, p. F17.

[57] Lawler, *From Job-Based to Competency-Based Organizations*, 15 J. Organizational Behav. at 9–10.

[58] *See* Lawler, The Ultimate Advantage 156.

and tests, rather than simply relying upon a supervisor's opinion. Once an employee's skills are assessed, he says, they should be priced to the market.[59]

5. *Pay for Performance.* While pay for performance has become a popular means of increasing productivity, it does not fit easily within competency-based organizations. In such settings, it is often difficult to identify each individual's contribution, especially when the individual is part of a team effort. Lawler suggests the use of peer ratings to appraise an individual's contribution to a team. Alternatively, he advocates that team performance, business unit performance, or organizational performance be used as a factor in pay.[60]

6. *Training and Career Development.* Skill-based pay systems have the virtue of providing an incentive for individuals to acquire new skills. "[W]hen individuals are paid for skill acquisition, they place a great emphasis on being able to learn and develop their abilities."[61] Thus organizations need well-developed training programs and arrangements to give individuals the time to attend.[62]

7. *Career Systems.* Rather than promoting hierarchical mobility within an organization, the organization should see careers as involving multiple "skill acquisition tracks," where different types of workers have different tracks. As an example, Lawler contrasted a producer's career track that could involve mastering a limited set of skills with a managerial career track that "might involve the acquisition of a broad understanding of how the organization operates and training in various types of managerial activities."[63]

Lawler's competency-based organization emphasizes employee skill development and deployment. After detailing the conception in all its parts, Lawler raises but does not answer a crucial question – whether the opportunity for skill acquisition can provide the same motivational effects as the hierarchical promotion opportunity formerly provided in jobs-based organizations.[64] He acknowledges that the shift to a competency-based organization can be difficult for some employees.

Other contemporary theorists and practitioners echo Lawler's emphasis on the need to design organizations that generate knowledge and adapt to change. The notion of a "learning company" has become a common organizational mantra. For example, the influential management theorist Rosabeth Moss Kanter writes, " 'The learning organization' promises to become a 1990s business buzzword as companies seek to learn more systematically

[59] *See* Lawler, *From Job-Based to Competency-Based Organizations* 10.
[60] *See id.* at 11. Edward Lawler acknowledges that studies in job-based systems find that group incentive plans like profit sharing and gain sharing are less effective motivators than individual pay-for-performance systems, but he suggests that the result of group-based performance measures may be more effective within a competency-based organization.
[61] *Id.*
[62] *See id.*
[63] *Id.* at 11–12.
[64] *See id.* at 12.

from their experience and to encourage continuous learning for their people."[65] To become "learning organizations," she counsels firms to invest in learning and to recognize and reward knowledge that is generated at all levels of the firm. Rather than foster hierarchy, organizations should build social networks that exchange knowledge across divisions. "Change-adept organizations make competence an organizational asset, rather than just an individual attribute, by stressing the need to make tacit knowledge explicit."[66] Kanter advocates that organizations create opportunities for knowledge exchanges, such as informal lunch seminars, conferences, internal trade fairs, education benefits, and training programs.[67]

2. Total Quality Management

Just as the competency-based organization tries to enhance competitiveness by harnessing employees' abilities and imagination, the total quality management (TQM) approach does so by enhancing the quality of the product. Each approach aims to design an organization that can compete effectively in a global marketplace.[68]

TQM was developed by W. Edwards Deming, an American accountant who consulted with Japanese managers in the postwar era about how to achieve industrial success. Deming urged the Japanese to focus on product quality. He claimed that quality could be achieved by stressing customer focus, workforce empowerment, and planning. Deming's teachings were widely adopted in postwar Japan, and Deming himself became an important figure in Japanese public life.[69] The Japanese created a highly esteemed award, called the Deming Prize, which is awarded on an annual basis to the company that most successfully embodies Deming's ideas.[70] It was not until the 1980s that these ideas took hold in the United States, but since that time TQM concepts have permeated management ideology and practice.

Deming's management philosophy is based on fourteen points. The fourteen points sound like slogans for bumper stickers or advertising banners, but they tell a story. Several of Deming's points stress the importance of maintaining a high level of product and service quality. For example, point number one is: "Create constancy of purpose toward improvement of product and service, with the aim to become competitive, stay in business, and

---

[65] Rosabeth Moss Kanter, ON THE FRONTIERS OF MANAGEMENT 53 (1997).

[66] *Id.* at 17.

[67] *See id.* at 16–19.

[68] *See, e.g.*, Geoff Mason, *Product Strategies, Workforce Skills and "High-Involvement" Work Practices: US-European Comparisons*, in EMPLOYMENT STRATEGIES: WHY EMPLOYERS MANAGE DIFFERENTLY 193, 212 (P. Cappelli, ed., 1999) (finding that those firms that move to high-involvement practices, increased employee training, and Total Quality Management (TQM) work practices are those that are faced with foreign competition for their products).

[69] *See* James P. Womack et al., THE MACHINE THAT CHANGED THE WORLD 277 (1990).

[70] *See* Anschutz, TQM AMERICA 16–17.

provide jobs." Point number two is: "Adopt the new quality philosophy." Point number five is: "Improve constantly and forever." Several other points advocate enhancing worker skills. For example, point number six is: "Institute training on the job." Point number thirteen is: "Institute a program of education and self-improvement."[71]

For present purposes, the most interesting of Deming's points is the last one, point number fourteen, which says: "Put everybody to work to accomplish the transformation."[72] This expresses the goal of moving concerns about product quality, customer satisfaction, and organizational effectiveness down the structure away from top management to employees at all levels. As one TQM consultant writes, "At successful TQM organizations, everyone is involved in the corporate transformation. Partnership breeds involvement, and involvement breeds partnership."[73]

In practice, TQM has many similarities with the competency-based organization. TQM involves a flattening of management positions and a shift in authority to cross-functional work teams. It advocates widening jobs and instituting "horizontal management" practices, in which managers focus on broadly defined tasks rather than narrowly defined departments.[74] TQM also advocates giving ordinary workers responsibility for many core functions of the firm.[75] For example, TQM advocates that workers have direct contact with customers. "[M]anagement should seek to create conditions whereby every worker, at least from time to time, sees and talks with real customers, with actual users of the company's product or service."[76] In addition, workers should be provided with the results of customer satisfaction surveys and focus groups. Workers should also have direct contact with external suppliers and should be involved in the selection of new employees.[77]

Another aspect of TQM is an emphasis on training. Training makes employees available for horizontally defined tasks. Training employees in their organization's products, techniques, markets, goals, and competitive environment is necessary if employees are to interact with customers and be involved with core organizational decisions. One TQM consultant describes the role of training as follows: "[Training] creates a covenant between the organization and the person by conveying a bonding message: 'The company is investing in your professional growth because your future is with us, as a

---

[71] *Id.* at 17–27.
[72] *Id.* at 28.
[73] *Id.*
[74] *Id.* at 50.
[75] *See* Joshua G. Rosett & Richard N. Rosett, *Characteristics of TQM: Evidence from the RIT/USA Today Quality Cup Competition* 4–5 (Nat'l Bureau of Econ. Research, Working Paper No. 7241, 1999).
[76] Anschutz, TQM AMERICA 53.
[77] *See id.*

partner; the organization's well-being depends on the collective ability and effort of its people.'"[78]

Related to its emphasis on training, TQM advocates the Japanese concept of *Kaizen*, which means improvement. TQM encourages constant, small, incremental improvements rather than splashy one-shot innovations. Some TQM companies give prizes or other formal marks of recognition for teams of workers who devise improvements.

Related to its emphasis on improvement, TQM gives a central role to the research and development department. Two industrial relations scholars described TQM as "an unparalleled symbiosis between R & D and continuous improvement in the production process, premised on the active mobilization of the knowledge and intelligence of all employees."[79]

TQM is also associated with human reengineering, including the consolidation of managerial functions and elimination of redundant positions. As one TQM consultant writes:

Organizations across the country have taken note that there is a cadre of mid-level (and even senior) managers that neither lead nor decide, whose sole function is to collect information from performers, analyze it, provide it to decision makers, and convey decisions back to performers.... In TQM organizations, these non-managing managers have become redundant and excessive. Workers are now empowered to collect data about their jobs and to make job-related decisions; they also deal directly with corporate decision makers, and even with suppliers and customers as necessary. There is no longer a need for many of the mid-management people formerly "required." They can be, and are being, assigned to more productive work.[80]

Deming was critical of conventional human resource practices such as setting numerical goals, using performance-based pay, or using annual performance appraisal. He said these techniques tended to encourage employees to compete with each other rather than build teamwork and mutual support. Furthermore, he believed that these techniques encouraged employees to work to meet the specific goals set and then relax.[81] They do not encourage "discretionary effort,"[82] or organizational citizenship behavior.

The ideas embodied in TQM have had a major impact on American companies. By 1995, it was estimated that 67 percent of American organizations were focused on product quality.[83] In 1987, the Baldridge Award was established, in imitation of the Japanese Deming Award, to reward American

[78] *Id.* at 95.
[79] Tony Elger & Chris Smith, *Introduction* to GLOBAL JAPANIZATION? THE TRANSNATIONAL TRANS-FORMATION OF THE LABOUR PROCESS 1, 3–4 (Tony Elger & Chris Smith, eds., 1994) (summarizing and adopting the conclusion of Martin Kenney & Richard Florida, BEYOND MASS PRODUCTION: THE JAPANESE SYSTEM AND ITS TRANSFER TO THE U.S. (1993)).
[80] Anschutz, TQM AMERICA 132.
[81] *See id.* at 17–28.
[82] *Id.* at 46–48.
[83] *See id.* at Foreword.

firms that excelled in implementing total quality management programs. The Baldridge Award quickly became so prestigious that the number of companies requesting applications to compete for it increased from 12,000 in 1988 to 180,000 in 1990. The award is administered by the National Institute of Standards and Technology, a branch of the U.S. Chamber of Commerce. Every year, the agency disseminates the award criteria widely so that firms applying for the award can model their practices on the ideal TQM practices. Each year, two awards are given for each of three categories – manufacturing, service, and small business. In 1999, additional categories for education and health care were added. The Baldridge Award has become a coveted prize and its impact has been widely felt. Beyond those applying for the award, many companies use the Baldridge scoring system to evaluate and improve their own practices.[84]

In sum, the management systems of competency-based organizations and total quality management (TQM) are two prominent examples of comprehensive proposals for restructuring the workplace, promoting skill development, and fostering organizational citizenship behavior without promising long-term attachment. Advocates of the competency-based organization emphasize skill development by insisting that employees be paid for the skills they have, rather than according to lock-step job evaluation formulas.[85] Advocates of TQM, meanwhile, counsel firms to involve every employee, at every level, in continuous product and service improvement. Some of the specific recommendations of TQM are to provide continuous training and opportunities for individual improvement, and to give workers direct contact with customers, external suppliers, and others who do business with the firm.[86]

3. High Performance Work Systems
A third approach to workplace restructuring falls under the umbrella term "high performance work systems" (HPWS). High performance work systems take many different forms, including self-managing teams, quality circles, performance-based pay, increased delegation of decision making, and increased training.[87] Despite the many variations, they share certain characteristics. First, fundamental to HPWS is the reorganization of work in such a

---

[84] R. R. Gehani, *Quality Value-Chain: A Meta-Synthesis of Frontiers of Quality Management Movement*, 7 ACAD. MGMT. EXECUTIVE 29 (1993); Richard Blackburn & Benson Rosen, *Total Quality and Human Resource Management*, 7 ACAD. MGMT. Executive 49; Zbigniew Przasnyski & Lawrence Tai, *Stock Market Reaction to Malcom Balderidge National Quality Award Announcements*, 10 TOTAL QUALITY MGMT. 391 (1999).

[85] *See* Lawler, THE ULTIMATE ADVANTAGE 156 (1992).

[86] *See* Rosett & Rosett, Characteristics of TQM; Anschutz, TQM AMERICA. *See generally* Stone, *The New Psychological Contract*, 48 UCLA L. REV. 565–68 (2001).

[87] See Gerard F. Farias & Arup Varma, *High Performance Work Systems: What We Know and What We Need to Know*, 21 HUM. RESOURCE PLAN. 50 (1998); Amy Varma, Richard W. Beatty,

way as to increase employee participation in organizational decision making throughout the hierarchical levels of the organization. Eileen Appelbaum, an economist at the School of Management and Labor Relations of Rutgers University, refers to HPWS as creating an employee-based "opportunity to participate."[88] At the root of the management's interest in participatory employment patterns is the belief that nonauthoritarian methods of control hold the potential for increasing employee input and therefore improving productivity and performance.[89] While this objective is clearly not a novel one, HPWS have attempted to develop a systemic and comprehensive method for eliciting employee contributions.[90] Furthermore, HPWS have been touted for their ability to tap into underutilized employee potential such as creativity and imagination.[91] Thus HWPS substantially increase the discretionary prerogatives of the front-line employees vis-à-vis internal and external agents.[92] They involve giving employees more opportunity to obtain information, to take part in the decision-making process, and to influence the work process itself.[93]

The high performance organization is therefore characterized by a flattening of the organizational hierarchical control alongside increased employee empowerment.[94] The opportunity to participate in organizational decision making is aimed at increasing employee discretionary effort, which in turn is claimed to improve organizational performance.[95]

In addition, the HPWS are associated with an expansion of the range of employee skill and authority and thus they stress employee training. They also tend to relax job classifications and increase employee versatility.[96] Many of the HPWS advocates maintain that this organizational design promises gains for both employers and employees.[97]

HPWS human resource practices are geared at insuring that employees are motivated to take on their new organizational role and that the system's

Craig Schneier, & David Ulrich, *High Performance Work Systems: Exciting Discovery or Passing Fad*, 22 HUM. RESOURCE PLAN. 26 (1999).

[88] Eileen Appelbaum, Thomas Bailey, Peter Berg, & Arne L. Kallenberg, MANUFACTURING ADVANTAGE: WHY HIGH-PERFORMANCE WORK SYSTEMS PAY OFF 39 (2002).

[89] *See, e.g.*, J. Pfeffer COMPETITIVE ADVANTAGE THROUGH PEOPLE: UNLEASHING THE POWER OF THE WORK FORCE (1994).

[90] Appelbaum et al., MANUFACTURING ADVANTAGE 26.

[91] Paul Osterman, *Work Reorganization in an Era of Restructuring: Trends in Diffusion and Effects on Employee Welfare*, 53 INDUS. & LAB. REL. REV. 179 (2000). *See also* Appelbaum et al., MANUFACTURING ADVANTAGE 26.

[92] Appelbaum et al., MANUFACTURING ADVANTAGE 8.

[93] These components are discussed in detail as part of Appelbaum et al.'s conceptual framework. *See* Ch. 2.

[94] Varma et al., *High Performance Work Systems* 27 (1999).

[95] *See* Appelbaum et al.'s flow chart on p. 27 of MANUFACTURING ADVANTAGE. *See also* Varma et al., *High Performance Work Systems* 31.

[96] Appelbaum et al., MANUFACTURING ADVANTAGE 103.

[97] *See, e.g.*, A. T. Kochan & Paul Osterman, THE MUTUAL GAINS ENTERPRISE (1994).

reward structure is aligned with its mode of production.[98] Hence they use performance-based pay, profit sharing, and a variety of individual and group incentive pay techniques to motivate employees. Managerial literature refers to this as a "holistic" approach to human resource practices.[99]

The opportunity to participate advocated by HPWS can take many different forms, from individual employee consultation to fully self-managed teams. However, many proponents of HPWS believe that the hallmark of the approach is the implementation of some form of teamwork.[100] However, as will be discussed, there is some evidence that suggests that the team aspect of the HPWS may be declining in significance.[101]

Some advocates of HPWS contend that unlike other forms of workplace restructuring, high performance techniques are associated with increased job security. For example, in their book, MANUFACTURING ADVANTAGE, Eileen Appelbaum et al. place employment security and training at the core of HPWS. They write:

Employment security provides front-line workers with a long-term stake in the company.... Employment security and incentive pay motivate workers to expend extra effort on developing skills and participating in decisions. Embedding work organization practices such as broader job definitions, team production, and responsibility for quality in a human resource system that provides increased training, employment security, and pay incentives for nonmanagerial employees has the greatest effect on plant performance.[102]

To determine the effectiveness of HPWS, Appelbaum et al. examined HPWS in forty-four plants in three different industries – steel, apparel, and the medical electronic and imaging industry. They looked at three HPWS component practices – participation in teams, skill enhancement, and incentives to increase motivation – and they examined the effects of these practices both on employer-centered outcomes such as performance and on employee outcomes such as job satisfaction and stress reduction. The researchers found a significant positive correlation between the implementation of HPWS practices and organizational performance in all three industries. Productivity, quality, and financial performance increased in firms that instituted high performance practices. As for employee outcomes, the researchers found that HPWS components improved employee trust in management and enhanced the intrinsic rewards from work. They also found that the implementation

---

[98] For an in-depth discussion on the implementation of systemic HR practices alongside new work systems *see* J. P. MacDuffie, *Human Resource Bundles and Manufacturing Performance: Organizational Logic and Flexible Production Systems in the World Auto Industry*, 48 INDUS. & LAB. REL. REV. 197–221 (1995).

[99] *See, e.g.*, Varma et al., *High Performance Work Systems*.

[100] *See id.* at 29.

[101] Osterman, *Work Reorganization*, 15 INDUS. & LAB. REL. REV. at 183, 186.

[102] Appelbaum et al., MANUFACTURING ADVANTAGE 8.

of HPWS increased organizational commitment and job satisfaction, and reduced work-related stress. In addition, the study provided evidence that in the steel and apparel industries HPWS were associated with increased wages. Finally, the researchers found that HPWS improved performance without increasing the demands on employees.[103]

Despite the findings of positive employee outcomes from HPWS, the Appelbaum study did not measure the impact of HPWS practices on job security. Rather, the researchers assumed that HPWS practices augment job security. Such an assumption is reasonable if one defines HPWS as involving primarily the use of team production, particularly self-managed teams. Team production requires continuity – it is not compatible with a high degree of workplace churning. Employers who adopt self-managed teams must make a significant investment in plant and process redesign. They also must provide considerable training for the team members. And team members can only work productively if they have time and experience working together.

If one strips the team component away from HPWS, it is not clear that the high performance approach entails increased job security. And this may indeed be the trend. Some advocates of HPWS question whether team production is worth the costs. For example, one recent survey of thirty-nine firms that implemented HPWS practices found that there were no significant benefits from teams, and concluded that the benefits from HPWS could be achieved without the formation of teams.[104]

C. The Terms of the New Employment Relationship

The preceding examination of some of the dominant trends in organizational theory helps to illuminate the terms of the new employment relationship. All three approaches represent changes to the hierarchical job ladders and narrow job structures advocated by the practitioners of Taylorism and personnel management. These approaches attempt to resolve a fundamental paradox: firms need to motivate employees to provide OCB, commitment, quality, productivity, efficiency, and continuous improvement while at the same time they are dismantling the job security and job ladders that bound people to their employers for the past one hundred years. As we saw in Chapter 2, Taylorist hierarchies and job ladders were adopted by firms to solve problems of employee motivation, encourage skill acquisition, and discourage employee opposition. Now it is important to determine what in the new employment systems will accomplish these goals.

Rosabeth Moss Kanter acknowledges that the new high-commitment management models are colliding with the "job-insecurity reality" found

---

[103] For a detailed discussion of these results *see* id. at ch. 9.
[104] Varma et al., *High Performance Work Systems* 35.

in American corporations.[105] She resolves the paradox by advocating that firms offer "employability security" instead of employment security. She says firms should provide lifetime training and retraining opportunities in order to enable them to attract high-caliber talent and to give those employees who are downsized other opportunities.[106] To this end, she proposes a model employability contract in which the firm promises to upgrade worker skills and to help provide new job opportunities should those at the firm disappear.[107] Kanter also urges firms across industries and across countries to develop standard human resources policies for items such as fringe benefits, vacations, and bonuses, and to ensure portability of benefits and skills so as to enable workers to function in the new employment setting.[108]

Peter Drucker also tries to confront the problem of eliciting employee motivation in the world of no long-term job security.[109] Drucker recommends that employees market themselves on the basis of their knowledge and their human capital. They should plan to work in networks – for corporations, but not as employees of corporations. He says top management needs to stop emphasizing loyalty and instead needs to learn how to instill trust.[110]

Janice Klein, a former GE executive who became a professor at MIT's Sloan School of Management, also attempts to provide an answer to the paradox.[111] While she acknowledges that promises of job security are a powerful means to inculcate loyalty, she maintains that loyalty can be fostered in other ways as well. The task, according to Klein, is for managers to "find other means to convince employees that they are in the same boat together."[112] She suggests that commitment can come through the personal

---

[105] Kanter, FRONTIERS OF MANAGEMENT 190.

[106] *Id.* at 192.

[107] *See id.* at 194. In her model employability security "contract," Rosabeth Moss Kanter recommends that companies make a written pledge that states, inter alia:

- Although we cannot guarantee tenure in any particular job or even future employment, we will work to ensure that all our people are fully employable.... We promise to:
- Recruit for the potential to increase in competence, not simply for narrow skills to fill today's slots.
- Offer ample learning opportunities, from formal training to lunchtime seminars – the equivalent of a month a year.
- Provide challenging jobs and rotating assignments that allow growth in skill even without promotion to "higher" jobs....
- Retrain employees as soon as jobs become obsolete....
- Provide three-month educational sabbaticals or external internships every five years.
- Find job opportunities in our network of suppliers, customers, and venture partners.

[108] *See id.* at 195.

[109] *See* Drucker, MANAGING IN A TIME OF GREAT CHANGE 71–72.

[110] *See id.*

[111] *See* Janice Klein, *The Paradox of Quality Management: Commitment, Ownership, and Control,* in Heckscher & Donellon, THE POST-BUREAUCRATIC ORGANIZATION 178.

[112] *Id.* at 179.

relationship between a supervisor and a worker, or between peers, especially in self-managed teams.[113] She claims that management can also obtain commitment by providing employees with ownership-like experiences, such as autonomy, voice, and profit sharing.[114] She advocates a flattening of hierarchies and a visible commitment to equity of sacrifice in times of workforce reductions. Klein also advocates narrowing wage differentials between top management and low-level employees, and increasing the use of employee stock ownership plans and profit sharing.

These management theorists articulate some of the ways in which corporations are attempting to make the shift away from long-term career employment not only acceptable, but desirable. By promising employees the opportunity to develop their human capital, a new psychological contract is being created. Employers promise employability and training so that, in return, employees will see themselves as entrepreneurs marketing their own human capital in a marketplace.[115] Rosabeth Moss Kanter observes that "[t]he chance to learn new skills or apply them in new arenas is an important motivator in a turbulent environment."[116] Towers Perrin counseled employers in its November 1999 newsletter: "[T]o attract the right people, organizations are adopting total reward strategies that include learning and development opportunities and the creation of better work environments, in addition to the traditional pay and benefits."[117]

Another feature of the new employment relationship involves opportunities for networking. Not only can employees raise their human capital, they can raise their social capital by meeting and interacting with others in different departments within the firm, with customers and suppliers of the firm, and with competitors. When jobs are redefined in competency terms, each employee is a professional in his or her particular area. They are sent to trade meetings or other professional gatherings to network and keep up to date.

The new employment relationship also involves compensation systems that peg salaries and wages to market rates rather than relying upon internal institutional wage-setting factors. The emphasis is on differential pay to reflect differential talents and contributions.[118] Thus, for example, Towers Perrin says an excellent company is one that "rewards results, not tenure, even at the hourly level." The consulting firm also advocates allocating

---

[113] *See id.* at 178–79.

[114] *See id.* at 182.

[115] *See* Davenport, HUMAN CAPITAL 7–16 (touting the importance of encouraging workers to see themselves as investors in human capital).

[116] Kanter, FRONTIERS OF MANAGEMENT 53.

[117] *Global Survey Highlights Growth in Variable Pay*, TOWERS PERRIN MONITOR (Nov. 1999), at http://www.towers.com/towers/publications/publications_frame.asp?target=mon.htm.

[118] *See, e.g.*, Kanter, FRONTIERS OF MANAGEMENT 175 (reporting that the tide is moving "toward more varied individual compensation based on people's own efforts").

a "[s]ignificantly disproportionate share of all pay programs for high-performing employees," and giving "[d]ifferen[t] deals based on employee contribution." Towers Perrin acknowledges that these recommendations will create dissatisfaction among lower-performing employees, and says:

> Top companies also plan for and achieve higher turnover rates. This strategy is based on the hypothesis that significant pay differentiation provides more motivation for the average and poor contributors to leave as they can get a better deal at other companies which tend to offer higher levels of base pay.[119]

In jobs where performance is highly variable, the trend is to base wages on individual performance wherever possible. Thus in today's workplace it is not uncommon for workers doing identical tasks to have different pay. In jobs where performance is routine and predictable, benchmarking is used to set wages according to the going market rate for the particular job, and thus break the lock-step wage patterns of internal labor market or union compensation schedules.

Benchmarking began as a technique for evaluating work design and enhancing technical efficiencies, but it has become a mechanism by which compensation levels are reassessed and pegged to market rates. With benchmarking, an expert identifies discrete tasks or functions that are performed within a firm and compares them to the same functions in other firms. The comparison yields information about work design and also about costs. With benchmarking, a firm can compare its labor costs for a particular task to those of other firms even in other industries. A firm can identify the going rate for a particular collection of tasks, and then apply that rate inside its own operations so as to set the rate for those jobs in accordance with the external market. Benchmarking thus removes the protective shield of internal wage-setting devices and makes workers within the firm vulnerable to competition from similarly tasked workers on the outside. In other words, benchmarking imports wage dispersion from the external labor market into the wage structure of the firm.[120]

Other features of the new employment relationship involve flattening hierarchies, through such means as the elimination of executive dining rooms, management parking spaces, and other status-linked perks. It also involves the development of company-specific dispute resolution devices to redress perceived instances of unfairness. We can thus make a table comparing the new employment relationship to the old (see Table 5.1).

---

[119] *Pay Attention! How to Reward Your Top Employees: Sleep Well Last Night?*, PERSP. ON TOTAL REWARDS (Jan. 2000), at http://www.towers.com/publications/publications_frame. asp?target=pubs_date.htm.

[120] *See* Peter Cappelli and David Neumark, *Do "High-Performance" Work Practices Improve Establishment-Level Outcomes?* 54 INDUS. & LAB. REV. 737, 767 (2001).

TABLE 5.1

Old Employment Relationship	New Employment Relationship
Job security	Employability security
Firm-specific training	General training
Deskilling	Upskilling
Promotion opportunities	Networking opportunities
Command supervision	Microlevel job control
Longevity-linked pay and benefits	Market-based pay
Collective bargaining and grievance arbitration	Dispute-resolution procedures for individual fairness claims

D. The Geography of the Boundaryless Workplace

The new work practices described in this chapter are pervasive but by no means universal. In order to make predictions or formulate policy, it is important to determine in what sectors of the economy the boundaryless workplace is located, in which jobs, for which types of workers. While some have suggested that the practices described above are located in the new high-tech economy but not in the brick-and-mortar world of manufacturing, the evidence suggests no such clean divide. There have been some surveys that have attempted to determine how widely various new work practices have diffused throughout the economy. In addition, there are some industry studies and case studies, all of which point to the conclusion that the new workplace, while boundaryless, is quite extensive.

One of the national studies of the new work practices was conducted by the Bureau of Labor Statistics in its 1993 Survey of Employer Provided Training. Nearly eight thousand establishments from all sectors and sizes were asked about six practices: worker teams, TQM, quality circles, employee involvement in technology and purchase decisions, and job rotation.[121] The survey found that of the 3,400 establishments with more than fifty employees, almost seventy percent had one or more of the practices. In particular, almost half had implemented TQM, almost one-third had implemented worker teams, and almost one-quarter had implemented job rotation.[122] It also found that those establishments that had implemented alternative work arrangements had also made significant investments in worker training.[123]

A large study by Paul Osterman called the National Establishment Survey traced the incidence and spread of new work practices over time. In 1992, his survey team conducted telephone interviews with over eight hundred

---

[121] Maury Gittelman, Michael Horrigan, & Mary Joyce, *Flexible Workplace Practices: Evidence from a Nationally Representative Survey*, 52 INDUS. & LAB. REL. REV. 99, at 104–05 (1998).

[122] *Id.* at 105.

[123] *Id.* at 110–11.

establishments having fifty employees or more. The establishments were a representative sample of private sector firms, including firms of all sizes and in all sectors of the economy. The surveyors asked about work practices of core employees, defined as nonsupervisory workers directly involved in production. They asked the firm which, if any, of four practices were used by over more than fifty per cent of the core employees. The four practices were (1) self-managed teams, (2) TQM, (3) quality circles, and (4) job rotation. The surveyors found that approximately 40.5 percent of the firms used self-managed teams, 24.5 percent had adopted TQM, 27.4 percent had adopted quality circles, and 26.6 percent had adopted job rotation. Osterman concluded that a significant minority of firms had adopted some features of high performance work practices.[124]

Osterman's results were corroborated by several other surveys in the early and mid 1990s that also found various types of high performance work practices to be in widespread use.[125] Case studies in the early 1990s of the apparel industry, auto assembly plants, and many other types of manufacturing firms similarly found that a significant minority of establishments had implemented some aspects of high performance work systems.[126]

In 1997, Osterman repeated his survey, following up on those establishments that had responded in 1992. The 1997 survey found increasing evidence of diffusion of the specific work practices identified earlier in this chapter as aspects of the new psychological contract.

Osterman's 1997 National Establishment Survey included 462 enterprises from the 1992 survey and 221 new establishments, designed to be representative of all private sector firms. As before, the surveyors asked whether particular practices were in use for over half of the core employees. In this

[124] Paul Osterman, *How Common Is Workplace Transformation and Who Adopts It?* 47 INDUS. & LAB. REL. REV. 175 (1994). *See also* Paul Osterman, SECURING PROSPERITY 95–96 (1999).

[125] In 1994, the Bureau of the Census surveyed a national representative sample of private sector establishments with twenty or more employees and found somewhat lower usage of high performance techniques. The census survey differed from the Osterman one in that it did not limit questions to "core employees." Also, it asked about numbers of workers involved in certain work practices, rather than number of firms using the practices in question. It found that 13 percent of workers were involved in self-managed teams and 18 percent were involved in job rotation. *See* Osterman, *Work Reorganization*, 53 Indus & Lab. Rel. Rev. at 180–82.

[126] *See, e.g.*, Peter Berg et al., *Modular Production: Improving Performance in the Apparel Industry*, in C. Ichniowski, D. Levine,, C. Olsen, & G. Strauss, THE AMERICAN WORKPLACE 62–80 (2000); Maryellen R. Kelley, *A Participatory Bureaucracy: A Structural Explanation for the Effects of Group-Based Employee Participation Programs on Productivity in the Machined Products Sector*, in Ichniowski et al., AMERICAN WORKPLACE 81–110; Davis Jenkins & Richard Florida, *Work System Innovation among Japanese Transplants in the United States*, in REMADE IN AMERICA: JAPANESE TRANSPLANTS AND THE DIFFUSION OF JAPANESE PRODUCTION SYSTEMS (Paul Adler, Mark Fruin, & Jeffery Liker, eds., 1999); Thomas Bailey, Peter Berg, & Carola Sandy, *The Effects of High-Performance Work Practices on Employee Earnings in the Steel, Apparel, and Medical Electronics and Imaging Industries*, 54 INDUS. & LAB. REL. REV. 525 (2001).

later survey, Osterman found that 38.4 percent of the firms used self-managed teams, 57.2 percent used TQM, 57.7 percent used quality circles, and 55.5 percent used job rotation. That is, he found that in a five-year period there was a marked increase in the use of all forms of high performance work practices *except* the use of teams, which showed a slight decline.[127] The high performance practices that were growing – quality circles, job rotation, and TQM – are compatible with the new employment relationship because they involve up-skilling and enhanced opportunities for networking, yet they do not require long-term employment.[128] The use of autonomous teams, on the other hand, requires stability and long-term commitment to function effectively, so it is understandable that as firms shifted to more boundaryless practices the use of teams would decline.

Osterman also found that firms using high performance work practices provided less employment stability than other firms of their type. By the late 1990s, the workplaces that used high performance work practices in 1992 had experienced more layoffs than those that did not. Yet he also found that the layoffs were not accompanied by overall downsizing.[129] The 1997 survey also found that there was a disproportionate loss of managerial jobs, reflecting a movement away from hierarchy and toward placing more authority in the hands of frontline workers.[130] The constant churning of the workforce and the flattening of hierarchy suggest that those firms are not engaged in downsizing, but in building a boundaryless workplace.[131]

The National Establishment Survey, together with industry and firm-level case studies provide evidence that the new employment practices are widespread and growing throughout most sectors of the American economy.

---

[127] Osterman, *Work Reorganization*, 53 Indus & Lab. Rel. Rev. at 179.
[128] *Id.* at 186.
[129] *Id.* at 190–91.
[130] Osterman, SECURING PROSPERITY, 105–13.
[131] *Id.* at 192.

PART III

IMPLICATIONS OF DIGITAL JOB STRUCTURES FOR LABOR AND EMPLOYMENT LAW

6

Implications of the New Workplace for Labor and Employment Regulation

The new employment system described in Part II has many implications for labor and employment regulation. The basic framework of today's labor and employment law originated in the New Deal period, when President Franklin D. Roosevelt and a Democratic Congress took affirmative steps to assist American workers who had been devastated by the Great Depression. In that decade, three significant labor statutes were enacted and two major Supreme Court opinions rendered that together established a framework for governing labor relations that persists to this day. This framework was based upon the employment relationship that prevailed during the New Deal period – the Taylorist job structures of the internal labor market. It was a framework that was appropriate to long-term employment relationships in stable work environments, but it is a framework that it is becoming increasingly out of date.

A. The New Deal Labor Law Framework

In 1932, Congress enacted the Norris-La Guardia Act, which declared it to be the public policy of the United States to support workers' rights to organize and engage in collective bargaining.[1] The act made it unlawful for federal courts to issue injunctions in many types of labor disputes. In 1935, the National Labor Relations Act (NLRA) was passed by Congress, giving workers an enforceable right to engage in concerted action for mutual aid and protection, to organize unions of their own choosing, and to engage in collective bargaining.[2] The NLRA also established an administrative agency, the National Labor Relations Board (NLRB), to enforce those rights. In 1937, Congress enacted the Fair Labor Standards Act, which established

---

[1] 29 U.S.C. §§ 101–15.
[2] 29 U.S.C. §§ 151–68.

a federal minimum wage and set maximum hours for employment.[3] These three statutes, taken together, established a two-tiered system in which labor and management were encouraged to bargain to establish the terms of the employment relationship, while at the same time, individual employees not covered by collective bargaining were guaranteed certain minimal employment terms.

In the same decade, the Supreme Court decided two cases that greatly expanded the power of the federal government to regulate private employment. In 1935, in *West Coast Hotel v. Parrish*, the Supreme Court held that it was constitutional for a state to enact legislation setting minimum wages for women's labor.[4] In so holding, the Court overturned a previous decision, *Atkins v. Children's Hospital*, in which it had found a state minimum-wage law to be an unconstitutional infringement on freedom of contract and hence a violation of the Due Process Clause.[5] The Court justified its reversal in *West Coast Hotel* by declaring that there was a public interest in ensuring an adequate level of wages for working people. The Court's reasoning in the *West Coast Hotel* decision opened the door for state and federal governments to enact a host of statutes regulating the terms of the employment contract.

Two years later, in 1937, the Supreme Court held, in *Jones and Laughlin v. NLRB*, that the NLRA was a constitutional exercise of Congress's power under the Commerce Clause.[6] The Court rejected previous interpretations of the Commerce Clause that had placed severe limits on Congress's power to pass laws that intervened in private economic life. The *Jones and Laughlin* decision signified a monumental shift in the power of the federal government in all fields of regulation.

The legislative and judicial developments of the 1930s provided the legal infrastructure for the two-tiered regime of labor law that dominated the post-war era, a regime comprised of legal support for collective bargaining combined with government-mandated minimum terms of employment. Despite many subsequent developments in the interpretation of the NLRA, and the many new employment protections enacted since the 1930s, this basic structure has survived to this day.[7]

The labor laws of the 1930s were written in the industrial era, and used industrial era labor relations as the template for the employment relationship they were intended to regulate. The present system of labor and employment

---

[3] 29 U.S.C. §§ 201–19.
[4] 300 U.S. 379 (1937).
[5] 300 U.S. 399.
[6] NLRB v. Jones & Laughlin Steel Corp., 301 U.S. 1 (1937).
[7] For an overview of the history of labor law in the United States, *see generally* Katherine Van Wezel Stone, *Labor and the American State: The Evolution of Labor Law in the United States*, in Marcel van der Linden & Richard Price, THE RISE AND DEVELOPMENT OF COLLECTIVE LABOUR LAW (2000).

law thus assumes the existence of strong firm-worker attachment, long-term jobs, and promotion ladders to define progress throughout a career. Indeed, for most of the twentieth century, the law and the institutions governing work in America have been based on the assumption that workers were employed in stable jobs by corporations that valued long-term attachment between the corporation and the worker – that is, based on the internal labor market model of employment.

1. The Operation of the Collective Bargaining Laws

The primary objective of the NLRA was to promote the joint regulation of the workplace by organized labor and management. The collective bargaining laws were designed to promote the self-organization of workers to enable them to constitute a countervailing power that could bargain with employers about the operation of internal labor markets. In the bargaining process, labor and management were permitted, indeed encouraged, jointly to determine the rules by which the workplace would be governed.

Under the NLRA, the unionized workplace was divided into discrete bargaining units, each unit a well-defined, circumscribed, and economically stable group. While the individuals working within the unit could and did change, the bargaining rights and bargaining agreements applied to the unit. Unions negotiated agreements that specified wages, work rules, and dispute resolution systems for those individuals working in the unit. The terms and benefits applied to the job – they did not follow the workers to other jobs when they left the unit. Job-centered benefits were not problematic in a workplace in which jobs themselves were stable and long-term.

The assumption of long-term employment permeated union bargaining goals. Many of the benefits and work rules unions negotiated rewarded long-term employment and were thus consistent with the implicit lifetime employment commitment. Wages, vacations, and sick leave policies, for example, were often based on length of service. Long vesting periods for pensions also assumed and reinforced the norm of long-term employment. At the same time, the New Deal social security and unemployment programs tied those crucial social insurance protections to employment, thereby reinforcing the bond between the employee and the firm. Health insurance was not mandated nor provided by the government. When it existed it was provided by individual employers, usually as a product of labor-management negotiations.

Unions also protected employees against employer breaches of their implicit promises of long-term employment. Seniority and just-cause-for-discharge clauses enabled unions to enforce the firms' promises of employment security. At the same time, unions negotiated grievance and arbitration systems that gave workers an expeditious and inexpensive mechanism to enforce the psychological contracts of the industrial era workplace.

Under the NLRA, there thus evolved an employment system comprised of rising job security, longevity-based wages, employer-based health insurance, and employment-linked retirement security. For many unionized American workers, this employment system of the industrial era was the epitome of a good life.[8] These promises were not given freely or gratuitously – workers fought hard to secure them. Nonetheless, once in place, the lifetime employment system, with its multiple forms of job and livelihood security, was beneficial to both management and labor.[9]

The collective bargaining system gave unions little input into strategic corporate decision making.[10] However, labor's circumscribed role in corporate policy was not particularly problematic in an era of growing firms, expanding employment opportunities, and tacit agreements for long-term employment. Furthermore, the implicit promise of job security and the longevity-based system of benefits gave employees a stake in the financial well-being of their firms. Thus the American unionized corporation offered its workers an American variant of the Japanese lifetime employment system.[11] The tacit promise of lifetime employment in American industry was supported by the confluence of prevailing human resource policy, union bargaining strategy, and the legal framework of the labor laws.

2. Statutory Protections for Individual Employees

While the New Deal employment system provided job security and relative prosperity to many, it also created an invidious division between insiders and outsiders, a division that often fell along racial and gender lines. The primary sector – the unionized workforce within large firms – was the privileged core, made up primarily of white men. As a core, it generated a periphery in which women, minorities, migrant workers, and rural Americans were clustered. The labor laws and the employment practices of large firms reinforced a sharp divide between those inside and those outside the corporate family.

---

[8] *See, e.g.*, Ruth Milkman, FAREWELL TO THE FACTORY: AUTO WORKERS IN THE LATE TWENTIETH CENTURY 1 (1997) (describing the labor system at a pre-1980s unionized auto plant as "the best America had to offer to unskilled, uneducated industrial workers").

[9] *See* Ray Marshall, *Work Organizations, Unions, and Economic Performance*, in UNIONS AND ECONOMIC COMPETITIVENESS 287, 289–90 (Lawrence Mishel & Paula B. Voos, eds., 1992) (describing the period from World War II until the late 1960s as "the longest period of equitably-shared prosperity in U.S. history").

[10] *See* Katherine Van Wezel Stone, *Labor and the Corporate Structure: Changing Conceptions and Emerging Possibilities*, 55 U. CHI. L. REV. 73, 74 (1988).

[11] *See* Ronald Dore, BRITISH FACTORY – JAPANESE FACTORY 31–41 (1973) (describing the Japanese system of lifetime employment). It is important to note that the Japanese employment system is undergoing transformation similar to that in the United States. According to the ECONOMIST, "[f]ull-time, lifetime employment in big companies is disappearing.... Since early 1998 Japan has lost more than [one million] full-time jobs; meanwhile it has slowly been creating part-time and temporary ones." *The Amazing Portable Sarariman*, ECONOMIST, Nov. 20, 1999, at 71.

Insiders benefited from the collective bargaining laws and the implicit job security of the internal labor market; outsiders had neither. However, in the New Deal system, outsiders were covered by two other types of labor laws – minimal employment standards and, from the 1960s, employment discrimination laws.

Federal and state employment laws provided a safety net and set a floor of benefits for those workers who remained outside the bilateral collective bargaining system. The minimum wage and unemployment compensation laws were originally conceived as a safety net to set a floor for labor conditions for those not protected by the collective bargaining system. Over the past thirty years, the employment laws have expanded in number and scope as the extent of the collective bargaining system has contracted. In the 1970s, individual employment protections were expanded by national legislation to provide occupational safety and health protection and pension insurance, expanded protection against discrimination for government employees and pregnant women, and, in the Civil Service Reform Act of 1978,[12] protection for federal employee whistleblowers who reported employer wrong-doing.[13] In the 1980s, the federal government enacted the Worker Adjustment and Retraining Notification Act (WARN)[14] requiring that employers give their employees advance notice of plant closings and mass layoffs, and the Employee Polygraph Act[15] to provide protection for worker privacy interests. In the same period, numerous states enacted legislation to protect the job security, privacy, dignity, and other concerns of employees. Thus, as union density declined in the private sector, statutory protections became the main source of worker rights.[16]

In addition to these legislative developments, in the 1980s some state courts began to create exceptions to the at-will employment doctrine, thereby giving workers in those states judicial protection against unfair dismissal. The exceptions were not uniform – some states recognized a tort of unjust dismissal, some imposed implied terms of good faith and fair dealing into employment contracts, and some expanded the situations in which they would enforce implied contracts for job security. Some courts became more receptive to the application of conventional torts to workplace harms. Thus, for example, some workers could recover for mistreatment under theories of tort of intentional infliction of emotional distress or defamation in job references. Despite these exceptions, however, the bulk of American nonunion workers remained subject to the at-will doctrine and largely unprotected for their job-related grievances.

---

[12] 5 U.S.C. §§ 7101 et. seq.
[13] 5 U.S.C. §§ 1211–1222, 3352.
[14] 29 U.S.C. §§ 2102–2109.
[15] 29 U.S.C. §§ 2001–2009.
[16] *See* Katherine Van Wezel Stone, *The Legacy of Industrial Pluralism: The Tension Between Individual Employment Rights and the New Deal Collective Bargaining System*, 59 U. CHI. L. REV. 591–93 (1992).

3. Employment Discrimination Laws

In the 1960s, the U.S. Congress established a third type of labor regulation: the employment discrimination laws. These laws were not part of the New Deal labor legislation, but in recent decades they have significantly reshaped the American workplace. The Equal Pay Act of 1962,[17] Title VII of the Civil Rights Act of 1964,[18] the Age Discrimination Act of 1967,[19] the Americans with Disabilities Act of 1990,[20] and other related statutes have helped women and minorities remove barriers to employment and promotion. Both as a result of enforcement of these laws and as a result of other cultural and market factors, the position of women and minorities in the labor market has improved in recent decades. The gender pay gap narrowed from the 1970s to 2001, and the difference between women's and men's unemployment rates has virtually disappeared.[21] Also, the segregation of jobs along gender lines has diminished, and women's job tenure rates have increased while men's have declined. The wage gap between minorities and white workers has also declined since the 1970s, but not as dramatically.[22] However, there remain many pernicious residues of the exclusionary policies of the past, such as continuing pay gaps, differential unemployment rates, and glass ceilings that limit women's and minorities' upward progress within firms.

B. The Demise of the New Deal System

The changes in workplace practices described in Chapter 5 have rendered many features of existing labor regulation obsolete. The former regulatory structure was based on the template of long-term employment relationships and strong employer-employee attachment, and thus it is not well suited to the newly emerging employment system comprised of implicit promises of employability security, human capital development, lateral employment mobility, and networking opportunities. Therefore, as internal labor markets decline in importance, many features of the regulatory framework need to be reconsidered.

First, in the industrial era, employers did not rely on the imaginative or cognitive facilities of their workforce. Indeed, they wanted to suppress any thinking work on the part of workers. Taylor insisted that all "brainwork"

---

[17] Pub. L. No. 88-38, 77 Stat. 56 (1963) (codified as amended at 29 U.S.C. §§201, 206).

[18] Pub. L. No. 88-352, §701, 78 Stat. 253 (1964) (codified as amended at 42 U.S.C. §2000e (1994)).

[19] 29 U.S.C. § 621 et. seq.

[20] 42 U.S.C. §12101 et. seq.

[21] *See* Francine D. Blau, Marianne A. Ferber, & Anne E. Winkler, THE ECONOMICS OF WOMEN, MEN AND WORK 239-42, 247-48 (3d ed. 1998) (discussing the pay and unemployment gap).

[22] *See* Alan Hyde, CLASSIFICATION OF U.S. WORKING PEOPLE AND ITS IMPACT ON WORKERS' PROTECTION 2-3 (Jan. 2000) (Report to the International Labour Office) (citing ECONOMIC REPORT OF THE PRESIDENT ch. 4 (1998)).

should be removed from the shop floor and placed in the planning department. Today's human resource practices are the complete reverse. Today employers want to use and enhance the intellectual contributions of their employees. They hire individuals for their talents, pay them for their skills, and offer incentives so they will engage in training to increase their knowledge and abilities. As a result, an epidemic of disputes has arisen when employees depart. Employers fear that valuable knowledge possessed by the employee will fall into the hands of a competitor, so they seek to prevent the departing employee from taking a new job or utilizing the valuable knowledge. Yet employees understand that their employability depends upon their knowledge and skills, so that they assume that they can take their human capital with them as they move around in the boundaryless workplace. As a result of these conflicting perspectives, disputes about employees' use of intellectual property in the post-termination setting have increased. It is therefore necessary to develop a framework for analyzing and deciding disputes involving the ownership of human capital in light of the promises, explicit and implicit, involved in the new employment relationship.

Second, the new employment system has important implications for women and minorities, posing not only new possibilities but also new obstacles to achieving equality in the workplace. Much of current equal employment law is designed to assist women and minorities in their efforts to move up orderly job ladders. In a workplace with fewer job ladders and with flattened hierarchies, discrimination takes new forms, such as patronage networks and cliques that exclude, ostracize, and marginalize newcomers. These types of workplace harms can be not only psychologically devastating to women and minorities, but also damaging to their career success. However, under current discrimination law they are difficult to remedy. In order to make further strides toward equality, it is necessary to understand the new face of employment discrimination and devise antidiscrimination strategies that are appropriate to the new workplace.

Third, the new employment relationship was initially constructed in nonunion environments and has proven remarkably resistant to unionization efforts. In part this may be because many of the core features of American unionism, such as narrowly defined bargaining units and seniority systems, are antithetical to boundaryless careers. If we want to preserve institutions for employee representation, then we must define which aspects of current labor law and union practice are incompatible with the new employment relationships, and then devise a new labor law and a new model of employee representation that can provide employee voice and protection in the new workplace.

Fourth, the boundaryless workplace is not compatible with the existing framework of employee benefits. In the United States, retirement security, health insurance, and many other benefits assume a long-term employment relationship with a single employer. When workers make frequent movements between firms, and even between industries, they lose these important safety nets. Thus the issue of benefit portability and broader forms of social safety nets need to be placed squarely on the national policy agenda.

Fifth, the new workplace is emerging at the same time that income distribution is becoming increasingly unequal. The incomes of the less educated portion of the population have deteriorated in the past twenty years.[23] The pay gap between the top quintile and the bottom quintile of the work force is the greatest it has been at any time since 1947 when the U.S. Department of Labor first collected such statistics.[24] In addition, there have been widening pay disparities within firms.[25] There is evidence that the rising pay gap and deteriorating income distribution are related to the new work practices described in Chapter 5. The impact of the new employment relationship on income equality is an important issue of social welfare that needs serious attention.

The following chapters are devoted to these issues.

[23] *See* L. Blackburn McKinley et al., *Declining Economic Position of Less Skilled American Men,* in A FUTURE OF LOUSY JOBS? THE CHANGING STRUCTURE OF U.S. WAGES 31 (Gary Burtless, ed., 1990).

[24] *See* Hyde, CLASSIFICATION OF U.S. WORKING PEOPLE 2.

[25] *See* Steven J. Davis & John Haltiwanger, *Employer Size and the Wage Structure in U.S. Manufacturing* (Nat'l Bureau of Econ. Research, Working Paper No. 5393, 1995).

7

Disputes over Ownership of Human Capital

While it may be true that knowledge is power, in the current era it is more accurate to say that knowledge is value – economic value. In this information age, individual knowledge, expertise, skill, and the ability to acquire additional knowledge, expertise, and skill, are the primary sources of institutional and individual advancement. Most firms believe that the knowledge possessed by their employees is their major asset and their primary source of competitive advantage. In the words of FORTUNE magazine editor Thomas Stewart, "Information and knowledge are the thermonuclear competitive weapons of our time."[1]

Today's firms value not merely specific technical knowledge, such as computer code or biotechnical discoveries, but also more mundane types of knowledge, such as how the business operates, how the goods are produced, how paperwork flows, and how files are organized. Employees also have valuable knowledge about the firm's product, the context in which it is produced, and the environment in which the firm competes, including knowledge of business plans, upcoming projects, past projects, and past experience. There is also enormous value in employees' knowledge about customers, markets, and competitors. One particularly valuable type of knowledge is called "negative knowledge" – knowledge of products tested or systems tried that proved to be unproductive. Such knowledge in the hands of a competitor can save huge expenditures in duplicative and wasteful efforts in pursuit of dead ends.[2]

---

[1] Thomas A. Stewart, INTELLECTUAL CAPITAL: THE NEW WEALTH OF ORGANIZATIONS ix (1997).
[2] On the role of intellectual capital in organizations, *see generally* Bruce A. Lehman, *Intellectual Property: America's Competitive Advantage in the Twenty-First Century*, 31 COLUM. J. WORLD BUS. 6, 10 (1996); Stewart, INTELLECTUAL CAPITAL 71–78 (describing the importance of tacit knowledge and other informal forms of intellectual capital to organizations). On negative knowledge, *see* Nathan Hamler, *The Impending Merger of the Inevitable Disclosure Doctrine and Negative Trade Secrets*, 25 J. CORP. L. 383, 384 (2000); Thomas J. Methvin, *Business Torts*

As firms and employees have come to recognize the enormous value of employees' human capital, disputes over ownership of human capital have increased. Such conflict may well be endemic to the information-based workplace, where the unique nature of human capital defies simple legal categories. Employees bring knowledge and capabilities to their jobs and expect that their jobs will further increase their human capital, whether by providing experience and learning on the job, or by providing more formal training opportunities. Employees see the growth of their human capital and the enhancement of their labor market opportunities as one of the benefits of their job. Jobs are often evaluated and selected on the basis of whether and how much opportunity for learning and skill enhancement they provide. Employees accordingly assume that whatever skill or knowledge they acquire on one job "belongs" to them in the sense that they take it with them when they depart.

Employers, on the other hand, believe that if they have imparted valuable skills or knowledge to employees, they should "own" that human capital in the sense of being able to ensure that it is utilized only on their firm's behalf. While they cannot compel an employee to remain with their firm, employers attempt to prevent former employees from using knowledge obtained in their employ on behalf of a competitor. Thus employers increasingly impose and seek to enforce post-employment restraints such as covenants not to compete, and they attempt to obtain judicial protection for trade secrets.

The conflicting perspectives of employees and employers about the ownership of human capital has generated an increasing number of legal disputes. More and more, employers are requiring employees to accept covenants not to compete and covenants not to disclose confidential information at the outset of an employment relationship. And increasingly, employers are suing their former employees at the end of an employment relationship, seeking to enjoin them from taking knowledge acquired on the job to use on behalf of a competitor. In the past decade, there has been an exponential increase in the volume of court cases between employers and former employees involving the ownership of information and knowledge. Indeed, disputes over ownership of human capital are becoming one of the most frequently litigated issues in the employment law field.[3]

---

from a Plaintiff's Perspective, 60 ALA. LAWYER 415, 415 (1999). *See also* Brunswick Corp. v. Jones, 784 F.2d 271, 275 (7th Cir. 1986).

[3] *See* Phillip J. Closius & Henry M. Schaffer, *Involuntary Nonservitude: The Current Judicial Enforcement of Employee Covenants Not to Compete – A Proposal for Reform*, 57 S. CAL. L. REV. 531, 532 (1984) (noting an increased use of covenants not to compete in employment contracts); Tracy L. Staidl, *The Enforceability of Noncompetition Agreements When Employment Is At-Will: Reformulating the Analysis*, 2 EMPLOYEE RTS. & EMPLOYMENT POL'Y J. 95, 118 (1998) (describing how postemployment noncompetition agreements have become typical additions to employment contracts and an increasingly frequent basis for litigation); Peter J. Whitmore,

The law of post-employment restraints has been described as a "sea – vast and vacillating, overlapping and bewildering [from which] [o]ne can fish out of it any kind of strange support for anything, if he lives so long."[4] In this primal soup, one finds a murky mass of intertwined and conflicting interests – employees' interest in job mobility, employers' interest in protecting their business secrets, society's interest in a free and competitive labor market, and judicial commitment to enforcing contracts. While the case law on restrictive covenants has been tangled in the past, today many courts, legislatures, and commentators are confronting post-employment constraint issues anew, and many new approaches have been advocated.[5] No uniform consensus has yet emerged.

The increased number of disputes over post-employment restraints is the result of two developments – first, the recognition of the central value of employee human capital in the production process, and second, the fact that changing work practices have caused a decline in job security and a corresponding increase in employee mobility. Both of these developments are functions of the new human resource practices described in Chapter 5. These new practices embody new sets of expectations and understandings about the employment relationship that are relevant to the question, who owns employees' human capital?

This chapter explores the current state of the law of post-employment restraints from the vantage point of the implicit and explicit promises that make up the new employment relationship. It argues that it is not possible to determine the appropriate scope for judicial enforcement of post-employment restraints without an understanding of the nature of the new employment relationship. It advocates that courts inquire into the terms – tacit and explicit – of the new employment contract in determining whether to enforce post-employment restraints or protect an employer's alleged trade secret.

A Statistical Analysis of Noncompetition Clauses in Employment Contracts, 15 J. CORP. L. 483, 489 (1990) (noting that "noncompetition covenants continue to be used with ever-increasing frequency"); Suellen Lowry, *Inevitable Disclosure Trade Secret Disputes: Dissolutions of Concurrent Property Interests*, 40 STAN. L. REV. 519, 519 (1988) (noting the dramatic increase in trade secret litigation).

4 Arthur Murray Dance Studios of Cleveland, Inc.v. Witter, 105 N.E. 2d 685, 687 (Common Pleas, Ohio, 1952).

5 *See* Outsource International, Inc. v. Barton, 192 F.3d 662, 670 (7th Cir., 1999) (Posner dissenting) (advocating enforcement of all postemployment covenants so long as there was contractual consent, and no fraud, duress, or unconscionability); Paul H. Rubin & Peter Shedd, *Human Capital and Covenants Not to Compete*, 10 J. LEGAL STUD. 93 (1981); Michael J. Trebilcock, THE COMMON LAW OF RESTRAINT OF TRADE: A LEGAL AND ECONOMIC ANALYSIS (1986). *See generally* Gillian Lester, *Restrictive Covenants, Employee Training and the Limits of Transaction-Cost Analysis*, 76 IND. L. J. 49, 59–71 (2001).

A. The Evolving Law of Post-Employment Restraints

Because of the importance of employees' knowledge in today's business world, a growing number of disputes have arisen when employees leave their jobs and try to take their knowledge with them. Employers use a variety of legal theories to restrain former employees from using knowledge obtained at their firms, including misappropriation of trade secrets, breach of a duty of loyalty, industrial espionage, breach of nondisclosure agreements, and breach of covenants not to compete. The various legal doctrines offer different types of protection for valuable information. Trade secret protection prevents an employee from disclosing knowledge that qualifies as a trade secret – a vague and uncertain standard at best. Breach of duty of loyalty and industrial espionage claims involve allegations that an employee used knowledge gained from one employer on behalf of a competing enterprise. A covenant not to disclose confidential information can protect the particular information that is the subject of the agreement. Covenants not to compete have the potential to prevent an employee from using *any* of her knowledge for a competitor. Despite their differences, all of these doctrines implicate the underlying question: Who owns the employee's human capital?

Recent judicial and legislative approaches to the issue of ownership of human capital generally favor employers. However, as will be seen below, these approaches are out of step with the new employment relationship, in which skills, training, networking, and horizontal mobility are important terms of the employment contract. The analysis presented here suggests that courts should carefully scrutinize any efforts by employers to place restrictions on the portability of the employee's human capital in order to assure that the employer has not breached the explicit and implicit terms of the employment contract.

1. Covenants Not to Compete

Covenants not to compete and covenants not to disclose information have become commonplace in employment contracts over the past ten years. In addition to their increased presence in negotiated, fixed-term employment contracts, restrictive covenants have also been inserted into at-will employment relationships. And there has been a corresponding increase in litigation over them.[6] A search on the legal database, Westlaw, for cases involving covenants not to compete and trade secrets revealed the number of reported cases to be as shown in Table 7.1.[7]

---

[6] *See* Lowry, *Inevitable Disclosure*, 40 Stan. L. Rev. at 519; Staidl, *Enforceability of Noncompetition Agreements*, 2 Employee Rights & Employment Pol'y J. at 95.

[7] *See generally* ABA Section of Labor & Employment Law, Covenants Not to Compete: A State-by-State Survey (Brian M. Malsberger et al., eds., 2d ed. 1996); ABA Section of Labor & Employment Law, Employee Duty of Loyalty: A State-by-State Survey (Brian

TABLE 7.1

	1970–1974	1975–1979	1980–1984	1985–1989	1990–1994	1995–1999
All states file						
Covenants not to compete	127	235	314	47	512	509
Noncompete covenants	40	68	123	178	171	193
Trade secrets	156	233	367	510	312	719
All federal file						
Covenants not to compete	125	135	185	264	340	368
Noncompete covenants	29	33	45	66	99	161
Trade secrets	258	328	546	779	1011	1256

Admittedly, these data do not represent a scientific survey – Westlaw does not contain all the decisions, the search terms do not capture all the cases, and there is no doubt substantial overlap in the cases and hence double counting. However, the data do reveal an unequivocal trend and are consistent with observations by scholars and practitioners.[8]

At the same time that cases have proliferated, courts have become increasingly receptive to employer efforts to limit employee use of human capital. As will be shown below, courts have adopted expansive definitions of trade secrets and have expanded the circumstances under which they will enforce covenants not to compete. In addition, forty-four states have changed their unfair competition laws in recent years so as to make it easier for employers to enforce covenants not to compete.[9]

(a) Restrictive Covenants and At-Will Employees. Covenants not to compete occupy a peculiar legal never-never land between contract and tort, in which party consent and externally imposed obligation are intimately but complexly intertwined. When an employment relationship includes a covenant not to compete or not to disclose specific information, it is reasonable to assume that the employee has consented to restrictions on his or her post-employment activities. Accordingly, there is a strong argument for courts to enforce the covenant, perhaps with some scrutiny to ensure that the agreement was the product of actual consent and that the terms

M. Malsberger et al., eds., 2d ed. 1998); ABA SECTION OF LABOR & EMPLOYMENT LAW, TRADE SECRETS: A STATE-BY-STATE SURVEY (Arnold H. Pedowitz et al., eds., 1997).

[8] *See* Lowry, INEVITABLE DISCLOSURE; Staidl, *Enforceability of Noncompetition. See also* Jeff Nachtigal, *Tech Worker Says Agency Used Non-Compete Agreements to Bully, Intimidate* WASHTECH NEWS, May 23, 2003 (reporting an increase in the use of noncompete agreements by employment agencies that provide high-skilled contract employees for Microsoft).

[9] *See, e.g.,* West's Florida Statutes Annotated, F.S.A. §542.335 (1999); Texas in TEX. BUS. & COM. CODE ANN. 15.50–.52 (Vernon Supp. 1999); Michigan in MICH. COMP. LAWS ANN. 445.771–.778 (West Supp. 1988).

were disclosed. A consent-based approach to noncompete and nondisclosure covenants might, for example, permit courts to ensure that a covenant was not buried in fine print in an employment handbook or otherwise hidden from view. It might also be legitimate for a court to require an employer to identify the confidential information that is subject to a nondisclosure agreement with particularity at the outset, so that employers cannot use such agreements to impose far-reaching restrictions on employees at the point of termination. A consent-based approach would impose no further scrutiny in determining whether a noncompete and nondisclosure covenant is enforceable.[10]

However, with covenants not to compete, the existence of consent is only the beginning of a court's analysis. Historically, courts were suspicious of noncompete covenants in the employment setting because they believed they were often the result of vastly unequal bargaining power and thus contracts of adhesion.[11] While the existence of one-sided or oppressive terms in an employment contract are not usually grounds to vacate a contract, courts have historically scrutinized noncompete promises with a jaundiced eye. One reason for this special treatment was that noncompete clauses implicated the right of an individual to earn a living. For example, in one case of obvious employer overreaching, a court invalidated a covenant that restricted a janitorial employee from working as a janitor for ten years.[12] Courts are also suspicious of noncompete clauses because they impose costs on society as a whole by suppressing employee mobility, interfering with the labor market, and restraining trade.[13]

As a result of these concerns, courts historically did not enforce noncompete covenants as a matter of course, but rather held that post-termination covenants were presumptively void. But over time, most state courts have become more receptive to enforcing covenants not to compete, but with a "rule of reason" approach. This approach says, quite simply, that to be enforceable an employment covenant not to compete must be reasonable. Reasonableness has been defined to mean a covenant must be no broader

---

[10] A strict consent-based approach is advocated by Richard Posner in his dissenting opinion in Outsource International, Inc. v. Barton, 192 F.3d 662, 669–75 (7th Cir. 1999). Posner said, "I can see no reason in today's America for judicial hostility to covenants not to compete. It is possible to imagine situations in which the device might be abused . . . but the doctrines of fraud, duress, and unconscionability are available to deal with such situations." *Id.* at 670 (Judge Posner, dissenting) (citations omitted).

[11] Rachel Arnow-Richman, *Bargaining for Loyalty in the Information Age: A Reconsideration of the Role of Substantive Fairness in Enforcing Employee Non-Compete Agreements*, 80 OR. L. REV. 1163, 1165 (2001). In one case of obvious employer overreaching, a court held that a ten-year covenant restricting a janitorial employee from working in eight counties was unreasonable. Frederick v. Prof'l Bldg. Maint. Indus., Inc., 344 N.E.2d 299 (Ind. App. 1976).

[12] *See* Frederick v. Prof'l Bldg. Maint. Indus., Inc., *id.*

[13] *See, e.g.*, Insulation Corp. of Am. v. Brobston, 667 A.2d 729, 733 (Pa. Super. Ct. 1995). *See generally* Closius & Schaffer, *Involuntary Nonservitude*, 57 S. CAL. L. REV. at 531.

than necessary to protect a *legitimate* interest of the employer, and must be reasonable in duration and geographic scope.[14] In addition to these factors, courts traditionally required that the covenant not unduly burden the employee or unduly harm the public.[15]

What a court considers reasonable duration and geographic scope varies from state to state and from case to case. Some courts have upheld extremely broad covenants, and some have struck down very narrow ones.[16] Recently some courts have upheld covenants that are wider in geographic scope than those they would have upheld in the past on the grounds that the firm seeking to enforce the covenant competes in a nationwide or worldwide market.[17] Some courts have restricted the time of an allowable covenant on the grounds that in today's fast-moving and competitive environment, an employee's knowledge loses its value quickly.[18]

Restrictive covenants involving at-will employees are particularly problematic and sometimes receive additional scrutiny. An at-will employee is one who can be fired for a good reason, a bad reason, or no reason at all. If an at-will employee is fired without cause, she has no redress for her unjust dismissal, yet, if there is a covenant in effect, she can be prevented from performing another job. Because courts usually enforce noncompete covenants

---

[14] *See, e.g.*, RESTATEMENT (SECOND) OF CONTRACTS §188(1)(a) and (b)(1981) (stating that a covenant not to compete is only enforceable if "the restraint is [no] greater than is needed to protect the promisee's *legitimate* interest." *See also* Ronald J. Gilson, *The Legal Infrastructure of High Technology Industrial Districts: Silicon Valley, Route 128, and Covenants Not to Compete*, 74 N.Y.U. L. REV. 575, 603–04 (1999) (describing the origin of the rule of reason approach). A few states, including California, still refuse to enforce covenants not to compete. *See* Bayer Corp. v. Roche Molecular Sys., Inc., 72 F. Supp. 2d 1111 (N.D. Cal. 1999).

[15] *See* Edward T. Ellis et al., *Protection for an Employer's Investment in its Key Employees: Recent Caselaw on Covenants Not to Compete and Trade Secrets*, in 3 CURRENT DEVELOPMENTS IN EMPLOYMENT LAW, ALI-ABA COURSE OF STUDY 1324 (1998).

[16] *Compare* Shipley Co. v. Clark, 728 F. Supp. 818, 828 (D. Mass. 1990) (upholding a one-year covenant for salesman's dealings with former customers); Loranger Constr. Co. v. C. Franklin Corp., 247 N.E.2d 391, 393 (Mass. 1969) (upholding a three-year restriction on a natural gas service employee); Superior Gearbox Corp. v. Edwards, 869 S.W.2d 239, 248 (Mo. Ct. App. 1993) (upholding a five-year restriction); *and* Karlin v. Weinberg, 372 A.2d 616, 619 (N.J. Super. Ct. App. Div. 1977) (stating that a five-year restriction on a doctor was reasonable); *with* Blalock v. Perfect Subscription Co., 458 F. Supp. 123, 127–28 (S.D. Ala. 1978) (finding a 120-day covenant against a magazine salesman unreasonable); *and* Birmingham Television Corp. v. DeRamus, 502 So. 2d 761, 764 (Ala. Civ. App. 1986) (finding a six-month restriction of an at-will employee unreasonable).

[17] *See, e.g.*, Intelus Corp. v. Barton, 7 F. Supp. 2d 635 (D. Md. 1998) (upholding covenant with no geographic restriction because plaintiff works for clients on a global basis); Ackerman v. Kimball Int'l, Inc., 652 N.E.2d 507, 510 (Ind. 1995) (upholding a worldwide covenant not to compete).

[18] *See, e.g.*, EarthWeb v. Schlack, 71 F. Supp. 2d 299, 313 (S.D.N.Y. 1999) (holding that a covenant not to compete of one-year's duration was unreasonably long due to the "dynamic nature of the industry, its lack of geographical borders," and the fact that the employee's knowledge would lose its value quickly if he did not keep abreast of constant changes).

with injunctions, an at-will employee who has been fired unfairly can be barred from accepting all subsequent employment in the type of work that she is best able to perform. That is, an at-will employee subject to a restrictive covenant who is fired unfairly is left without a job and unable to take another one.[19]

To avoid these harsh consequences, some courts have imposed stricter requirements for enforcing noncompete covenants against at-will employees than they do against employees on fixed-term contracts. One way that some courts do so is by requiring that to be enforceable, a covenant must be "ancillary to an otherwise valid transaction," that is, part of a real exchange or supported by valid consideration. The "ancillary to an otherwise valid transaction" requirement is intended to ensure the presence of a real bargain and prevent an employer, particularly in an at-will employment context, from getting something for nothing.[20]

Recently, many courts have either abandoned or modified this requirement in order to permit enforcement of noncompete covenants against at-will employees.[21] The courts do so by defining an initial offer of employment, even at-will employment, as valid consideration for the covenant.[22] For a time, some courts refused to enforce noncompete covenants that were presented to at-will employees after employment had commenced on the grounds that consideration was lacking. But most courts now believe that the post-employment situation should not be treated any differently than the initial hiring.[23] Thus, for example, an Ohio appellate court recently noted that "[a]s a practical matter every day is a new day for both employer and employee

---

[19] See, e.g., Aero Kool Corp. v. Oosthuizen, 736 So. 2d 25, 27 (Fla. Dist. Ct. App. 1999).

[20] *See, e.g.,* Loewen Group Int'l, Inc. v. Haberichter, 912 F. Supp. 388, 392 (N.D. Ill. 1996); Applied Micro, Inc. v. SJI Fulfillment, Inc., 941 F. Supp. 750, 753 (N.D. Ill. 1996); Creative Entm't, Inc. v. Lorenz, 638 N.E.2d 217, 219 (Ill. App. Ct. 1994); Insulation Corp. of Am. v. Brobston, 667 A.2d 729, 733 (Pa. Super. Ct. 1995); *see also* Staidl, *Enforceability of Noncompetition Agreements,* 2 EMPLOYEE RIGHTS & EMPLOYMENT POL'Y J. at 97–98. *See also* RESTATEMENT (SECOND) OF CONTRACTS §188(1).

[21] *See, e.g.,* Woodfield Group, Inc. v. DeLisle, 693 N.E.2d 464, 466 (Ill. App. Ct. 1998); Fin. Dimensions, Inc. v. Zifer, Nos. C-980960, C-980993, 1999 WL 1127292, at *3 (Ohio Ct. App. Dec. 10, 1999); Abel v. Fox, 654 N.E.2d 591, 597 (Ill. App. Ct. 1995) (repudiating *Creative Entertainment* and finding a covenant in an at-will contract enforceable); *see also* Uli Widmaier, *Covenants Not to Compete,* in ANTITRUST AND UNFAIR COMPETITION (Ill. Inst. for Continuing Educ., 1998) (stating that the *Creative Entertainment* decision has been "roundly criticized" in Illinois).

[22] *See* Staidl, *Enforceability of Noncompetition Agreements* at 102.

[23] *See* Fin. Dimensions, Inc. v. Zifer, Nos. C-980960, C-980993, 1999 WL 1127292, at *3 (Ohio Ct. App. Dec. 10, 1999) (stating that since 1985 the majority of courts have rejected the distinction between covenants presented at the time of commencing at-will employment and those presented after employment has begun, and "hold[ing] that the employer's continued employment of the employee after the employee signs or agrees to the restrictive covenant is sufficient consideration to support the employer's later enforcement of the agreement").

in an at-will relationship. [Thus] we see no substantive difference between the promise of employment upon initial hire and the promise of continued employment subsequent to 'day one.'"[24]

The recent trend of relaxing the "ancillary to a valid transaction" requirement revives the concern that enforcing covenants against at-will employees can yield harsh and unfair results. An employee who is subject to a restrictive covenant and is then fired unfairly is left without a job and unable to take another one. To avoid such a harsh result, some courts have taken to protecting at-will employees by refusing to enforce a covenant against an at-will employee if the dismissal was unfair.[25] These courts inquire into the circumstances of the dismissal, and only enforce a post-termination covenant when they find that the dismissal was justified. This approach is a major departure from an at-will regime. It has been proposed that if courts enforce restrictive covenants against at-will employees, they should automatically impose a corresponding obligation on the employer not to discharge the employee except for just cause.[26] To date, this proposal has not been adopted. Indeed, some courts continue to enforce covenants against at-will employees, notwithstanding the circumstances of their dismissal.[27]

As discussed, the expanded enforcement of restrictive covenants in employment contracts has occurred through judicial reinterpretation of the meaning of reasonableness in time and space, as well as through a relaxation of the requirement of consideration in the at-will context. In addition, expanded enforcement has occurred through a change in judicial attitudes toward revision. In the past, courts usually refused to enforce a covenant not to compete if any part of it was invalid. This all-or-nothing approach gave employers an incentive to draft their covenants narrowly. The current approach of a majority of courts is either to rewrite an invalid covenant and enforce it as rewritten or to delete the invalid portions and enforce the remainder.[28]

The conflicting interests involved in the enforcement of noncompete covenants for at-will employees is illustrated by a sharply drawn battle in

---

[24] *Id.* at *4 (quoting Copeco, Inc. v. Caley, 632 N.E.2d 1299, 1301 (Ohio Ct. App. 1992)).

[25] *See, e.g.,* Cent. Adjustment Bureau, Inc. v. Ingram, 678 S.W.2d 28, 37 (Tenn. 1984); Insulation Corp. of Am. v. Brobston, *supra* n. 20 at 729, 738.

[26] *See* Staidl, *Enforceability of Noncompetition Agreements* at 118.

[27] Examples of cases in which a court looks to see whether the at-will employee was fired unfairly are Cent. Adjustment Bureau, Inc. v. Ingram, 678 S.W.2d 28, 37 (Tenn. 1984) Insulation Corp. of Am. v. Brobston, *supra* n. 25. Cases in which the court enforced a restrictive covenant notwithstanding the fairness of a dismissal are Olliver/Pilcher Ins., Inc. v. Daniels, 715 P.2d 1222, 1224 (Ariz. Ct. App. 1985), *vacated on other grounds by* 715 P.2d 1218 (Ariz. 1986) (enforcing covenant); Allen v. Rose Park Pharmacy, 237 P.2d 823 (Utah 1951).

[28] *See* Ellis et al., *Protection for Employer's Investment* 1330–32.

the late 1980s and early 1990s in Texas.[29] In the late 1980s, the Texas Supreme Court handed down four decisions in which it refused to enforce restrictive covenants. In response, in 1989, the Texas legislature enacted a law designed to reverse the state court's approach to restrictive covenants and to expand the situations in which such covenants would be enforced. Senator John Whitmire, who introduced the legislation, complained that the Texas Supreme Court had pursued a policy "of [putting] free movement of workers above...the increased investment in business."[30] Whitmire argued that the legislation was necessary to encourage investment in the state. The Texas Business Bar Foundation, one of only two groups to testify on the bill, also argued that enforcement of noncompete covenants was necessary for business. They contended that, by protecting confidential information, the covenants encouraged firms to engage in research and development.[31]

The new statute was passed in 1989, but almost immediately the Texas Supreme Court refused to apply it to at-will employees. In response, in 1993, the legislature amended the 1989 statute to state explicitly that restrictive covenants involving at-will employees were enforceable.[32] The amended statute provided that courts should enforce covenants even against at-will employees, so long as they are reasonable with regard to time, geographic area, and scope of activity, and narrowly tailored to protect the good will or other business interest of the employer. And notably, the statute stated that when a covenant is unreasonably broad in time, space, or scope of activity, the court should rewrite the covenant to render it enforceable.[33]

Even after the 1993 amendment, the Texas Supreme Court was reluctant to enforce restrictive covenants against at-will employees. The first case under the new statute, *Light v. Centel Cellular Co.*, involved a salesperson who had agreed to a noncompete agreement after working for the company as an at-will employee for two years.[34] After the company changed hands, she quit and the company attempted to enforce the covenant. When the case first came before the Texas Supreme Court under the 1989 statute, the court refused to enforce the covenant on the grounds that the employee was at-will. The opinion was later withdrawn in light of the 1993 statute, and the case was reheard. In 1994, the court applied the 1993 statute, but gave it a razor-thin interpretation. The court held that because Light's at-will employment agreement contained several terms, the covenant was ancillary

---

[29] The recent history of noncompete clauses in Texas is recounted in detail in Jeffrey W. Tayon, *Covenants Not to Compete in Texas: Shifting Sands from Hill to Light*, 3 Tex. Intell. Prop. L.J. 143 *passim* (1995). *See also* Light v. Centel Cellular Co., 883 S.W.2d 642, 643–44 (Tex. 1994) (recounting the history of the Texas noncompete statute).

[30] *See* Tayon, *Covenants* at 180 (quoting Senator John Whitmire).

[31] *See id.* at 179–80.

[32] *See id.* at 147–48.

[33] *See* Tex. Bus. & Com. Code Ann. §15.50 (Vernon Supp. 2001).

[34] Light v. Centel Cellular Co., *supra* n. 29 at 642.

to an enforceable agreement. However, the court also concluded that the covenant not to compete was not ancillary to the enforceable aspects of the agreement, and so it did not enforce the noncompete covenant.[35]

(b) Legitimate Employer Interests and the New Employment Relationship. Another area in which judicial enforcement of noncompete covenants has changed is in the conception of what constitutes a legitimate protectable employer interest. A court will not enforce a covenant if it is solely a means to restrain trade. Rather, the long-standing view has been that to be enforceable, a covenant not to compete must protect an employer's interest in a trade secret or in other "confidential information."[36]

The historical linkage between noncompete covenants and trade secrets is somewhat paradoxical because disclosure of trade secrets and confidential information can be restrained in the absence of a covenant.[37] However, it has been argued that for procedural reasons it is difficult to obtain meaningful protection for trade secrets so that a restrictive covenant provides employers with important additional protection.[38] At the same time, some scholars have posited that courts are more likely to enjoin misappropriation of a trade secret or confidential information in the face of a covenant not to compete because the existence of a covenant permits the court to avoid the difficult legal issue of determining what constitutes a trade secret. A case in point is *Comprehensive Technologies International, Inc. v. Software Artisans, Inc.,*[39] in which the Fourth Circuit enforced a very broad covenant, one that would prevent a former executive employee from working in any capacity for a competitor, even as a janitor or file clerk. The court justified its decision on the ground that the employee had access to confidential information concerning both the products and customers of the former employer, so that "it will often be difficult . . . to prove that a competing employee has misappropriated trade secret information belonging to his former employer."[40] This rationale suggests

---

[35] *Id.* at 647.

[36] Edmund W. Kitch, *The Expansion of Trade Secrecy Protection and the Mobility of Management Employees: A New Problem for the Law*, 47 S.C. L. REV. 659, 667 (1996); Lowry, *Inevitable Disclosure*, 40 STAN. L. REV. at 524–25.

[37] *See* Kitch, *Expansion of Trade Secrecy Protection* at 667 (noting "circular[ity] when the scope of trade secrecy is defined by the scope of the confidentiality obligation, and the permissible scope of the confidentiality obligation is defined by the scope of trade secrecy protection"); *see also* Closius & Schaffer, *Involuntary Nonservitude*, 57 S. CAL. L. REV. at 547–48 (arguing that because the only circumstance in which courts should enforce a covenant is when there is a trade secret or confidential information, the existence of a noncompete covenant is superfluous).

[38] *See* Gilson, *Legal Infrastructure of High Technology Industrial Districts*, 74 N.Y.U. L. REV. at 605–06 (1999).

[39] 3 F.3d 730, *vacated and case dismissed pursuant to settlement*, No. 92-1837, 1993 U.S. App. LEXIS 28601 (4th Cir. Sept. 30, 1993).

[40] *Id.* at 739.

that the court was acting to protect a trade secret, not to enforce the parties' agreement, and that the presence of a covenant enabled the court to sidestep the difficult trade secret issue. In these cases, courts enforce restrictive covenants in order to protect trade secrets, not to effectuate party consent.[41]

Courts have recently expanded the types of employer interests that they consider legitimate subjects of noncompete covenants beyond the narrow trade secret rationale. Many courts no longer require that there be a trade secret involved at all.[42] For example, courts have enforced covenants when a manicurist left to work for another nail salon,[43] a carpet salesman took a job with another carpet retailer,[44] and a liquor deliveryman went to work for another distributor.[45] In doing so, the courts have expanded the set of interests they consider legitimate to protect with a noncompete covenant. Two factors that are now cited with increasing frequency as legitimate employer interests are (1) contact with customers, and (2) employer provision of training. Courts use the presence of either factor as evidence from which to infer that a covenant has a legitimate, rather than an anticompetitive, purpose.[46] However, each of these factors is inconsistent with the terms and implicit understandings of the new employment relationship.

(c) Customer Contact. Firms operating in competitive markets place great value on relationships with customers, viewing their customers as important assets of the firm. Yet they are vulnerable assets because a departing employee who has dealt with a firm's customers has the ability to steal them away. Companies often use noncompete covenants to try to protect customer information from falling into the hands of competitors through the agency of a departing employee. As a result, customer information is the most commonly litigated post-employment issue.[47] Increasingly, courts rule that customer contact provides a basis for enforcing a covenant not to compete, whether or not they consider customer information to be a trade

---

[41] *See also* Water Servs., Inc. v. Tesco Chems., Inc., 410 F.2d 163, 170–71 (5th Cir. 1969) ("[S]ince it may be difficult to determine, as a matter of law, what is a trade secret, the covenant not to compete is a pragmatic solution to the problem of protecting confidential information.").

[42] *See* Fin. Dimensions, Inc. v. Zifer, *supra* n. 23 at *5–*11.

[43] *See* Nail Boutique, Inc. v. Church, 758 S.W.2d 206, 210–11 (Mo. Ct. App. 1988).

[44] *See* Reardigan v. Shaw Indus., 518 S.E.2d 144, 148 (Ga. Ct. App. 1999).

[45] E. Distrib. Co. v. Flynn, 567 P.2d 1371 (Kan. 1977).

[46] *See* Closius & Schaffer, *Involuntary Nonservitude*, 57 S. Cal. L. Rev. at 547–48. *See, e.g.,* Aero Kool Corp. v. Oosthuizen, *supra* n. 19 at 25, 26; *see also* Freund v. E.D. & F. Man Int'l, Inc., 199 F.3d 382, 385 (7th Cir. 1999) (Posner, C.J.) (suggesting that under Illinois law, an employer's investment in its employees' training is grounds to enforce a covenant not to compete).

[47] *See* Henry J. Silberberg & Eric G. Lardiere, *Eroding Protection of Customer Lists and Customer Information Under the Uniform Trade Secrets Act*, 42 Bus. Law. 487, 487 (1987).

secret.[48] For example, some courts find that a customer list is a trade secret when it has been compiled from information that was difficult to obtain and has been kept strictly confidential.[49] When a customer list is a trade secret, enforcing a restrictive covenant to prevent the use of a customer list falls within the trade-secret-as-legitimate-interest rationale for enforcement of covenants. However, even courts that do not consider a customer list to be a trade secret will usually enforce a covenant against an employee who has knowledge of a customer list or customers' preferences, and is likely to use the knowledge on a new job.[50] Thus, while trade secret law alone does not always protect customer lists, noncompete covenants almost always do.[51]

As states have adopted a solicitous view of customer lists, they have also expanded it to other forms of customer contact. In doing so, they have greatly expanded the legitimate interest test so that it barely operates as a constraint on naked anticompetitive concerns. One sees the courts' changing approach to customer contact and its impact on the legitimate interest test in the judicial opinions in Maryland over the past thirty-five years. In 1967, in *Ruhl v. F. A. Bartlett Tree Expert Co.*, the Maryland Court of Appeals enforced

---

[48] Whitmore surveyed 105 cases involving noncompete covenants from 1966 through 1988 from 27 states showing that an employee's relationship with customers is a very important factor given by courts as a reason for enforcing or not enforcing covenants. *See* Whitmore, *Statistical Analysis of Noncompetition Clauses*, 15 J. CORP. L. at 503–06. Cases that treat customer lists as a trade secret include N. Atl. Instruments, Inc. v. Haber, 188 F.3d 38 (2d Cir. 1999); Suncoast Tours, Inc. v. Lambert Group, Inc., No. CIV. A. 98-5627 (JEI), 1999 WL 1034683, at *8 (D.N.J. Nov. 10, 1999); Merrill Lynch, Pierce, Fenner & Smith, Inc. v. Ran, 67 F. Supp. 2d 764, 775 (E.D. Mich. 1999); Nobel Biocare USA, Inc. v. Lynch, No. 99 C 5774, 1999 WL 958501, at *1 (N.D. Ill. Sept. 15, 1999); Wright v. Power Indus. Consultants, Inc., 508 S.E.2d 191, 196 (Ga. Ct. App. 1998). *See generally* Lowry, *Inevitable Disclosure*, 40 STAN. L. REV. at 522–23 (noting that states vary as to whether or not they treat customer lists as a trade secret).

[49] *See, e.g.*, Alagold Corp. v. Freeman, 20 F. Supp. 2d 1305, 1315–16 (M.D. Ala. 1998); AmeriGas Propane, L.P. v. T-Bo Propane, Inc., 972 F. Supp. 685, 698 (S.D. Ga. 1997); Trans-Clean Corp. v. Terrell, No. CV 9703480395, 1998 WL 142436, at *8 (Conn. Super. Ct. Mar. 17, 1998). Conversely, if the information is publicly available, courts generally do not give it trade secret protection. *See, e.g.*, Ability Search, Inc. v. Lawson, 556 F. Supp. 9, 15 (S.D.N.Y. 1981); Templeton v. Creative Loafing Tampa, Inc., 552 So. 2d 288, 290 (Fla. Dist. Ct. App. 1989); Hamer Holding Group, Inc. v. Elmore, 560 N.E.2d 907, 918–19 (Ill. App. Ct. 1990).

[50] *See, e.g.*, Standard Register Co. v. Cleaver, 30 F. Supp. 2d 1084, 1094 (N.D. Ind. 1998); Roto-Die Co. v. Lesser, 899 F. Supp. 1515, 1522 (W.D. Va. 1995); Chem-Trend Inc. v. McCarthy, 780 F. Supp. 458, 461 (E.D. Mich. 1991); Osage Glass, Inc. v. Donovan, 693 S.W.2d 71, 74 (Mo. 1985) (en banc); Cont'l Res. Corp. v. Schloz, 595 S.W.2d 396, 401 (Mo. Ct. App. 1980).

[51] In a review of cases seeking trade secret protection for customer lists under the UTSA as of 1987, Henry J. Silberberg and Eric G. Lardiere, attorneys with Stroock, Stroock & Lavan, concluded that the UTSA provides less trade secret protection for customer contacts than the preexisting common law. As a result, they advised "people-oriented businesses" to impose covenants not to compete on employees who have significant contact with customers on the assumption that courts will enforce these clauses even though the information so protected is not a trade secret. *See* Silberberg & Lardiere, *Eroding Protection*, 42 BUS. LAW. at 505.

a restrictive covenant to prevent a manager of a tree service from working in his trade for two years in a six-county area.[52] Although the court conceded that Ruhl, the manager, did not possess any trade secrets and his work did not involve solicitation of customers, the court said that it was necessary to examine the employer's business interest on a case-by-case basis and consider the extent and importance of personal relationships in the particular business in deciding whether a covenant is reasonable. In a much quoted phrase, it said:

There is no arbitrary yardstick as to what protection of the business of the employer is reasonably necessary, no categorical measurement of what constitutes undue hardship on the employee, no precise scales to weigh the interest of the public. The decisions in this State and in other jurisdictions are helpful, but, as in so many other fields of the law, the determination must be made on the particular circumstances.[53]

In the case at hand, the court justified the injunction on the ground that the tree service business was highly competitive and that personal relationships between Ruhl and the employer's customers were important to a firm's success.[54] The court emphasized the fact that Ruhl had voluntarily quit.

The *Ruhl* court gave lip service to the principle that a covenant to protect an employer's legitimate interest should not be enforced if it is "unduly restrictive of the employee's freedom."[55] In this case, the court recognized that the employee would suffer hardship from the injunction as he had only a high school education, had learned the tree business from his uncle at age fourteen, and knew no other trade. However, the court stated:

Two years is a long time in the life of a young man with a family to support to be precluded from engaging in the only business which he knows in the area in which he grew up and lives. Had Ruhl's employment been terminated by Bartlett through no fault of Ruhl's, a different legal situation might well have been presented.[56]

Despite the *Ruhl* court's departure from the narrow trade secret rationale for covenant enforcement, and despite the cavalier treatment of the hardship to the employee, for several years the Maryland courts interpreted *Ruhl* as consistent with a narrow approach to restrictive covenants. Thus, for example, in 1973 in *Becker v. Bailey* the Maryland Court of Appeals stated that "Maryland follows the general rule that restrictive covenants may be applied and enforced only against those employees who provide unique services, or

---

[52] 245 Md. 118, 225 A.2d 288 (Md. App. 1967).
[53] *Id.* at 123–24.
[54] *Id.* at 124.
[55] *Id.* at 126.
[56] *Id.* at 128. The court also mentioned that Ruhl had received training and experience while working for Bartlett, but it did not rely on that factor to justify the injunction.

to prevent the future misuse of trade secrets, routes or lists of clients, or solicitation of customers."[57]

In the mid 1970s and 1980s, the Maryland court began to relax its approach to covenants and, in particular, to relax the application of the legitimate interest test when customer contacts were involved. For example, in *Hebb v. Stump, Harvey & Cook,*[58] the Maryland Court of Appeals enforced a restrictive covenant to prevent a former employee from soliciting customers that he himself had generated. In contrast to *Ruhl,* the *Hebb* court's rationale for protecting customer contacts did not depend upon an analysis of the competitive nature of the business or a special feature of the customer relationship. Rather, the court reverted to reasoning from an antiquated master-servant law doctrine, stating:

> The customers and patronage thus secured were for the benefit of the employer, and the increased good will became the property of the master, however much their procurement was to be attributed to the servant's energy, personality, and skill. Since the servant was hired and rewarded to produce these results, the employer had a right to their enjoyment.[59]

By the late 1990s and early 2000s, the Maryland courts had adopted an even more expansive interpretation of the legitimate interest test and a correspondingly narrower view of the role of employee hardship. For example, in 2002, in *Padco Advisors v. Omdahl,* the Maryland federal district court applied Maryland law to enjoin Omdahl, a former employee of a mutual fund company, from working for a competitor for two years.[60] The court found that in *Padco,* as in *Ruhl,* there was a highly competitive industry in which the employer had a legitimate interest in protecting customer relationships. The court found the covenant to be reasonable despite the fact that it had no geographic restriction because it only limited the employee's employment with the two mutual fund companies with which Padco competed. The Padco court did not mention a key difference between the cases – that Omdahl was fired, while Ruhl had quit. Thus the court ignored the language in *Ruhl* that a court should weigh the circumstances of a dismissal into the balancing of hardship of a covenant on an employee.

---

[57] 299 A.2d 835, 939 (Md. App., 1973). Similarly, in Servomation Mathias v. Englert, 333 F. Supp. 9 (M.D. Pa. 1971), the Pennsylvania District Court applied Maryland law to refuse to enjoin a food service installer from working at the installations of former clients of his former employer. The court scrutinized the claims of customer contact strictly and held that the covenant did not prohibit the defendant-employee from working at installations of other former customers with whom he had had no contact in the course of his previous employment. *See also* Food Fair Stores v. Greeley 264 Md. 105 (1972).

[58] 25 Md. App. 478 (1975).

[59] *Id.* at 492. Internal quotations and citations omitted.

[60] 179 F. Supp. 2d 600 (D. Md. 2002) (applying Maryland law).

In addition, in *Padco Advisors v. Omdahl,* the court did not require that the covenant be carefully tailored to the employer's legitimate purposes of protecting trade secrets or customer lists. The employee had argued that the covenant was overbroad because it was not limited to preventing him from marketing the particular products about which the two firms competed but rather attempted to preclude him from continuing relationships with his former clients. The court rejected this argument on the ground that because Omdahl was working for a competitor, "it would be impossible for Padco to monitor whether he is disclosing protected information to its direct competitor."[61] Thus in *Padco,* the court justified its injunction on the basis of the need to protect the employer from competition itself, rather than on a need to protect some independent legitimate employer business interest.

The court gave an unusually candid discussion of its new approach in the case of *Intelus Corp. v. Barton.*[62] In that case, the employee-defendant Barton worked as an account manager for a company that sells medical software to health-care organizations. When Barton was hired, he signed a confidentiality agreement and an agreement not to compete for six months when and if his employment with Intelus should terminate. After working for Intelus for three years, Barton received a poor performance review and a pay cut, so he resigned. Shortly thereafter, he accepted a position as an account manager with MedPlus, another purveyor of medical products. There Barton's work was exclusively with clients already under contract with MedPlus. Nonetheless, Intelus received an injunction to enforce the restrictive covenant.

In balancing the hardships, the court found that the plaintiff Intelus had demonstrated that its business successs depended largely on its account managers. The court concluded that "[t]hrough his direct client contact, Barton had the opportunity to establish close working relationships with Intelus clients and surely played a major role in developing good will on behalf of Intelus."[63] It found that by working for MedPlus, Barton had the potential to inflict harm on the plaintiff. The court conceded that Barton, too, would suffer if he were forced to find another employer or remain unemployed for the period of the restriction, yet it concluded that the *potential* harm to Intelus outweighed the *actual* harm to Barton.

In determining the likelihood of success on the merits, the *Intelus* court dismissed the fact that the covenant had no geographic limit by pointing out that Intelus competed for clients on a national, if not global basis. "Competition unlimited by geography can be expected where the nature of the business concerns computer software and the ability to process information."[64] It

---

[61] *Id.*
[62] 7 F. Supp. 635 (D. Md.1998).
[63] *Id.* at 639.
[64] *Id.* at 641–42.

thus found that the lack of geographic restriction did not render the covenant unreasonable. Rather, it stated:

Intelus has a protectable interest in preventing a loss of good will, and such a loss could easily result from Barton's employment with a direct competitor. The loss could occur even if the competitor is located somewhere other than where Intelus is located or where Barton was based... [65]

The court then considered the final factor, the public interest, and expressed its view about where the law should go:

"[T]he public has an interest in the enforcement of reasonable restrictive covenants. Restrictive covenants can play an important role in the growth of a business that depends upon the development of good will through effective customer service. See Ruhl, 245 Md. at 127.... The Court anticipates that restrictive covenants will grow in importance with the continued emergence of technology driven and information based industry. An employee who can use a computer and a modem to solicit and service customers anywhere in the world is an employee who can easily jump from competitor to competitor, potentially taking with him a collection of clients. As long as employers do not restrict employees from earning a living and do not limit fair competition, they must be given the opportunity to provide a service to their customers without risking a substantial loss of business and good will every time an employee decides to switch employment."[66]

The reasoning in *Intelus* demonstrates that in enforcing a covenant, the Maryland courts no longer confine covenant enforcement to the protection of an independent interest of the employer, such as a trade secret or confidential information, to which the restraint on competition is intricately, if regrettably, intertwined. Rather, the court will protect an employer's interest in being free of competition, period. And, as the *Intelus* court candidly acknowledged, in the contemporary production milieu in which employees interact with customers all over the world to provide knowledge and services, such restrictions will not only be commonplace but will almost always be enforced.

Courts that expand the legitimate interest test to include customer lists do so because they view a firm's customers as the property of the firm and an essential element of the firm's good will.[67] Such courts accord customer contact a high level of protection, permitting firms to control and constrain its use.[68] However, the view that the employer has an exclusive property interest in customer contacts is inconsistent with the terms of the new employment

---

[65] *Id.* at 642.

[66] *Id.*

[67] *See, e.g.,* Hebb v. Stump, Harvey and Cook, Inc., 25 Md. App. 478 (Md. Ct. of Spec. App. 1975).

[68] *See* Edmondson v. Am. Motorcycle Ass'n, 54 F. Supp. 2d 544, 550 (W.D.N.Y. 1999); Carriage Hill Health Care, Inc. v. Hayden, No. CIV.96-101-SD, 1997 WL 833131, at *5 (D.N.H. Apr. 30, 1997); Morlife, Inc. v. Perry, 56 Cal. App. 4th 1514, 1526 (1997); *see also* Standard

relationship. As discussed in Part II, the new employment relationship involves promises by employers to provide employees with networking opportunities – opportunities to interact and build contacts among suppliers and customers of the firm. At the same time, new work practices such as total quality management (TQM) dictate that employees should meet customers and become familiar with their needs. Customer contact is promoted as a means to improve the firm's performance as well as to facilitate the employee's horizontal flexibility in the boundaryless workplace. Opportunities to network with customers are often part of the implied promise of employability. The courts, by treating customer lists and knowledge of customer needs as the firm's exclusive property and a basis for enforcing restrictive covenants, are unwittingly undermining one of the most important terms of today's employment contract.

(d) Employer-Provided Training. The second factor that courts have begun to use to justify enforcement of covenants not to compete is the presence of employer-provided training. Under the courts' traditional approach, if an employee's knowledge is not a trade secret, the knowledge belongs to the employee and its use cannot be restrained regardless of who paid for its acquisition.[69] But recently, courts have justified enforcing covenants on the ground that the employer paid for an employee's training to acquire skills and thus is entitled to prevent the employee from utilizing those skills on behalf of a competitor, even when there was no trade secret involved.[70] The "who pays" factor in covenant cases is relatively new. In a 1990 survey of 105 cases involving employment-restrictive covenants, Professor Peter Whitmore did not find the presence of an employer's investment in training to be sufficiently significant to warrant discussion.[71] But now employer-provided training is a frequently cited rationale for enforcing noncompete covenants.[72]

Register Co., 30 F. Supp. 2d at 1094–97 (refusing to protect a customer list as a trade secret, but enjoining competition because of employer's good will).

[69] *See* Robert Unikel, *Bridging the Trade Secret Gap: Protecting "Confidential Information" Not Rising to the Level of Trade Secrets,* 29 Loy. U. Chi. L.J. 841, 867–75 (1998) (describing the current two-tiered approach, in which an employee's knowledge is classified either as general and thus not subject to judicial protection, or as a trade secret and entitled to judicial protection).

[70] *See, e.g.,* Aero Kool Corp. v. Oosthuizen, *supra* n. 19 at 25, 26. Even in Texas, where the state supreme court has been reluctant to enforce covenants not to compete, they do enforce covenants when the employer has provided the employee with training. *See* Hill v. Mobile Auto Trim, Inc., 725 S.W.2d 168, 171 (Tex. 1987), *superseded by* Tex. Bus. & Com. Code Ann. §§15.50–15.51 (Vernon Supp. 2001).

[71] *See* Whitmore, *Statistical Analysis of Noncompetition Clauses,* 15 J. Corp. L. at 524–25 and n. 243. Rather, that factor was one of 15 variables clustered along with trade secrets, exposure to customer information, and geographic restriction under the general heading, "hardship to the employer."

[72] *See, e.g.,* Aero Kool Corp. v. Oosthuizen, *supra* n. 19; Freund v. E.D. & F. Man Int'l, Inc., 199 F.3d 282, 1999 WL 1085870 (7th Cir., 1999).

Legal economists Paul Rubin and Peter Shedd have analyzed restrictive employment covenants in terms of the distribution of training costs and the incentives that training creates, using Gary Becker's human capital model as their point of departure.[73] Becker's model of employee training and human capital distinguishes two types of training – specific and general.[74] Specific training is defined as training that has value only to the specific firm. General training, on the other hand, is training that has value to other firms either in the industry or in the economy more generally.[75] Becker posits that employers will pay most of the costs of specific training because they benefit from providing this training, which is, by definition, of value to them but not to other firms. Once they pay for specific training, employers will encourage employees to stay on the job long enough to make the employer's investment in the training worthwhile. Indeed, some have argued that a desire to recoup the cost of specific training is what led firms to establish internal labor markets and encourage long-term employment relationships in the first place.[76]

General training, on the other hand, enhances the labor market power of employees because it makes them more valuable to other firms. Becker surmises that employers will not be willing to pay for general training because they have no way to ensure that employees will remain on the job and use the training on the employer's behalf.[77] Instead, employees will self-finance general training by accepting lower wages.[78]

Rubin and Shedd adopt the Becker framework, but they modify Becker's model by positing that there are actually two types of general training. Some general human capital, they claim, consists of both general skills and knowledge that an employee is willing to finance through lower wages, and some consists of specialized trade secret information that is far too valuable and too costly for an employee to self-finance.[79] This latter type of information is not firm-specific in Becker's typology because it is information that other firms would benefit from having. Rubin and Shedd claim that most employees obtain training in both types of general human capital – general training that they self-finance and trade secrets that the employer finances.

Rubin and Shedd posit that an employer will be willing to finance the acquisition of general human capital of the latter type so long as the employer

[73] *See* Rubin & Shedd, *Human Capital* 10 J. LEGAL STUD. at 94.

[74] Gary S. Becker, HUMAN CAPITAL: A THEORETICAL AND EMPIRICAL ANALYSIS, WITH SPECIAL REFERENCE TO EDUCATION 26 (2d ed., 1975).

[75] *Id.* at 26.

[76] *See id.* at 29–30; Peter Doeringer & Michael Piore, INTERNAL LABOR MARKETS AND MANPOWER ANALYSIS (1971); Sherwin Rosen, *Implicit Contracts: A Survey*, 23 J. Econ. Literature 1144, 1147 (1985).

[77] *See* Becker, HUMAN CAPITAL at 19–20.

[78] *See id.*

[79] *See id.* at 96–97.

can protect it with a restrictive covenant that prevents an employee from opportunistically obtaining valuable knowledge and then leaving and using it on behalf of a competitor. If courts do not enforce such covenants, Rubin and Shedd contend, employers will be discouraged from developing this type of information or will be forced to utilize it in a guarded and inefficient manner.[80] Thus it is efficient for a court to enforce a restrictive covenant when doing so encourages the development of specialized trade secret information.

However, Rubin and Shedd also point out that if there is a restrictive covenant, employees are vulnerable to opportunistic behavior by employers. Specifically, there is a danger that employers might use a covenant to restrain the employee from using not merely the trade secret that the employer paid for, but also the general training that the employee self-financed.[81] Furthermore, Rubin and Shedd argue that, as a practical matter, it is impossible to draft a covenant that distinguishes between the two types of general human capital.[82] Thus they argue that to enforce all covenants would be inefficient, just as it would be inefficient to enforce none of them. They conclude that it is appropriate for courts to limit enforcement of covenants to information that comprises a trade secret. They counsel courts to determine what information is within the covenant on a case-by-case basis, and only enforce covenants involving training in trade secrets or confidential information provided by the employer.[83]

Rubin and Shedd's application of Becker's human capital model argues for a return to the view that restrictive covenants should only be enforced to protect knowledge that involves a trade secret. Only in those cases can a court be sure that the employer has paid for the acquisition of the knowledge being protected. They claim that their analysis explains why noncompete covenants are found primarily in industries and occupations in which specialized training is important.[84] They also use their analysis to explain customer list cases. When a customer list involves specialized knowledge that was expensive to obtain, Rubin and Shedd argue, it is a type of specialized general human capital that is a legitimate subject of a covenant.[85]

Under Rubin and Shedd's analysis, the court's function when asked to enforce a noncompetition covenant is to ascertain whether the covenant is limited to protecting knowledge that an employer paid for. When a covenant is properly limited in its scope, the court should enforce it to prevent the

---

[80] *See id.* at 97–98.
[81] *See id.* at 98.
[82] *See id.* at 98.
[83] *See id.* at 98–99.
[84] *See id.* at 99.
[85] *See id.* at 99–104.

employee from appropriating general knowledge that the employer did not intend to impart for the employees' own use. They propose that by limiting enforcement of noncompete covenants to trade secrets or other specialized knowledge, courts can best approximate this efficient result.[86]

While Rubin and Shedd's analysis makes sense in theory, it must be evaluated in light of the new employment relationship. Today it is more difficult than before to ascertain whether an employer or an employee has paid for the acquisition of certain knowledge. As seen in Chapter 5, today's employers often promise to provide general training as part of the new employment relationship. There is a great deal of empirical evidence to suggest that in today's labor market many employers do offer this deal, and pay for general training and skill development for at-will employees.[87] This evidence is consistent with one of the most important terms of the new psychological contract – the employers' promise of general training and employability security in exchange for employee motivation, commitment, and organizational citizenship behavior (OCB). Employers also promise to provide general training in order to attract applicants. Thus many firms offer to pay for some types of employee education as an inducement for recruitment.

When an employer has promised to give employees skill development and general knowledge as part of the employment deal, then it cannot be said that the employer has paid for its acquisition, nor can it be assumed that the employer intended to preclude the employees from using knowledge for their own advantage. Rather, when such promises are present, the employees have paid for the training, not with reduced wages in the Gary Becker sense, but with increased effort, commitment, and OCB. Hence, when human capital development is part of what an employee is promised in the employment deal, then it must be assumed that the human capital thereby obtained belongs to the employee.

There are occasions in which an employer provides training, not as part of a psychological contract to elicit OCB or attract high quality applicants, but merely to give employees the skills to perform specific work tasks. In cases in which a firm is only willing to provide training if it can realize a short-run profit from the training investment, then it has a means to make such intent explicit and protect that interest without resorting to a broad covenant

---

[86] *See id.* at 110.

[87] *See* Daron Acemoglu & Jorn-Steffen Pischke, *Beyond Becker: Training in Imperfect Labor Markets* 4–5 (Nat'l Bureau of Econ. Research, Working Paper No. 6740, 1998) (giving examples of firms bearing the full costs of general training); John M. Barron et al., *Do Workers Pay for On-the-Job Training?* 34 J. HUM. RESOURCES 235, 250 (1999); Mark A. Loewenstein & James R. Spletzer, *General and Specific Training*, 34 J. HUM. RESOURCES 710, 729–31 (1999). *See generally* Ronald G. Ehrenberg & Robert S. Smith, MODERN LABOR ECONOMICS: THEORY AND PUBLIC POLICY 162–66 (6th ed. 1997) (presenting empirical studies that suggest employers bear much of the costs of on-the-job training, including training that is general).

not to compete. An employer can request that the employee agree to repay the training costs if the employee departs prior to the time when the training costs are recouped.[88] However, to be enforceable, a training repayment agreement must be written narrowly. If a training repayment agreement only requires repayment in circumstances in which the employee goes to work for a competitor, then courts will view the agreement as a disguised covenant not to compete, and subject it to the same scrutiny they apply to noncompete covenants.[89] For example, in *Heartland Securities Corp. v. Gerstenblatt et al.*, the court stated:

> The fact that Heartland will forgive the entire repayment of training costs if the employee does not compete with the company in any way for a four year period from the start of his employment further supports this Court's finding that the true purpose and intent of the provision is to discourage an employee from leaving the company. If the refund of training costs provision was intended merely to recoup training costs, those costs to the company should be the same no matter what the employee does after leaving Heartland.[90]

Similarly, if a training repayment agreement calls for repayment in amounts that are not reasonably related to the actual costs of the training, courts will treat it as a penalty provision and refuse enforcement.[91] However, if an employer requires employees to sign a clear and narrow repayment agreement that applies only to the cost of training provided, is not excessive as to amount, and is triggered by departure before a specified date regardless of the employees' subsequent employment, it is enforceable.[92] When an employee accepts a narrowly crafted training repayment agreement, she is on notice that training is not an implicit term of the employment contract, but rather something that she is required to pay for by her continued employment.[93] In such event, enforcement of such an agreement, unlike enforcement of a broad covenant not to compete, does not undermine her psychological contract.

In sum, courts should take the implicit terms of the new psychological contract into account when deciding whether or not to enforce noncompetition covenants. When employers argue for enforcement of noncompete

---

[88] *See, e.g.*, Anthony W. Kraus, *Repayment Agreements for Employee Training Costs*, 1993 LAB. L.J. 49. *But see* Arnow-Richman, *Bargaining for Loyalty*, 80 OR. L. REV. (questioning whether such retraining agreements can be written with sufficient particularity to avoid the pitfalls of a noncompetition covenant).

[89] *See* Brunner v. Hand Indus., 603 N.E. 2d 157 (Ind. Ct. App. 1992).

[90] Heartland Securities Corp. v. Gerstenblatt et al., 2000 WL 303274 (S.D.N.Y. 2000).

[91] Brunner, *supra* n. 89 at 159–60; Heartland Securities, *id.* at 6–7; Heder City of Two Rivers, 149 F.Supp.2d 677 694 (E.D. Wisc. 2001).

[92] *See* Milwaukee Area Joint Apprenticeship Training Committee for the Electrical Industry v. Howell, 67 F.3d 1333 (7th Cir., 1995).

[93] *See* Lester, *Restrictive Covenants*, 76 IND. L.J. at 75–76 (advocating statutory provisions permitting training repayment contracts subject to an explicit statutory cap).

covenants on the grounds that the employer paid for the training, courts should inquire whether the promise of general training was expressly or tacitly part of a larger employment deal. If it was, then they should not restrain employees from subsequently using the knowledge so obtained.

B. Trade Secrets and Inevitable Disclosure

Employers can obtain judicial protection for specialized knowledge, even without a restrictive covenant, when the knowledge consists of a trade secret. However, a trade secret is not a self-defining term. Different courts, at different times, have used different definitions of what constitutes a trade secret. For example, at present courts differ as to whether they consider negative knowledge to qualify as a trade secret.[94] Obviously the broader the definition of trade secret used, the more protection an employer has for knowledge about its products and operations.

Until the late 1980s, trade secrets were protected under the common law with guidance from the Restatement of Torts, an influential treatise prepared by the prestigious American Law Institute. At that time, the Restatement of Torts defined a trade secret as "any formula, pattern, device or compilation of information which is used in one's business and which gives [one] an opportunity to obtain an advantage over competitors who do not know or use it."[95] Pursuant to this approach, trade secret protection was available for specific inventions, formulas, devices, and other technical information that was only known to a firm but that would be valuable in the hands of a competitor. Under the Restatement of Torts's definition, a trade secret did not include general business information, market plans, or customer contacts.[96]

In the past fifteen years, the definition of trade secret has expanded dramatically. In 1985, the National Conference of Commissioners on Uniform State Law amended its Uniform Trade Secrets Act (UTSA)[97] to include a broader definition of trade secrets. The Uniform Conference of Commissioners of State Laws, also comprised of distinguished jurists, drafts model

---

[94] *Compare* Novell Inc. v. Timpanogos Res. Group, Inc., 46 U.S.P.Q.2d (BNA) 1197, 1216–17 (D. Utah 1998) (using negative knowledge to justify applying inevitable disclosure doctrine), *with* EarthWeb v. Schlack, *supra* n. 18 at 299, 315 (rejecting the argument that "gaps or holes" in knowledge is a trade secret).

[95] RESTATEMENT OF TORTS §757 (1934). This section was not included in the RESTATEMENT (SECOND) OF TORTS (1979).

[96] *See, e.g.,* AMP, Inc. v. Fleischhacker, 823 F.2d 1199, 1203–04 (7th Cir. 1987) (stating that there is no trade secret protection for general confidential business information, including information about business and strategic planning, new product development, manufacturing processes, cost and capacity, financial information, budget information, or marketing and customer information).

[97] UNIF. TRADE SECRETS ACT §1(4)(i)–(ii), 14 U.L.A. 463 (1990).

statutes that are often adopted by state legislatures. Under the UTSA, a trade secret is defined as information that (1) "derives independent economic value, actual or potential, from not being generally known... or not being readily ascertainable" and that (2) an employer uses reasonable efforts to keep secret.[98] This definition extends trade secret protection beyond technical information to all commercially valuable information. As of 2001, forty-four states had adopted the definition of trade secrets recommended in the UTSA.[99]

In 1995, another committee of the American Law Institute drafted the Third Restatement of Unfair Competition, which also adopted an expansive definition of trade secrets. The Restatement of Unfair Competition (RUC) defined a trade secret as "any information that can be used in the operation of a business or other enterprise and that is sufficiently valuable and secret to afford an actual or potential economic advantage over others."[100] By focusing on economic value rather than specific concrete technical innovations, the UTSA and RUC approach makes the definition of trade secret almost infinitely expandable. The modern trend has generated great uncertainty in practice.

As courts expand the types of information they call trade secrets, it becomes increasingly difficult for an employee to avoid learning them. Even an employee who does not want to be exposed to his employer's trade secrets has no way of knowing which nugget of information that he learns on a job might later be the subject of a successful claim of protected trade secret status. When such an employee changes jobs, he is at risk of a lawsuit for misappropriation.

The expansion in the definition of trade secrets is closely linked to the highly controversial doctrine of inevitable disclosure. The doctrine of inevitable disclosure became prominent in 1995, in the case of *Pepsico, Inc. v. Redmond*.[101] In that case, the Seventh Circuit Court of Appeals enjoined William Redmond, a high-level management employee of PepsiCo, Inc. (PepsiCo), from working for Gatorade, Inc., a competitor, even though Redmond's employment contract did not contain a covenant not to compete, and despite the fact that Pepsico had no trade secret at risk. The court reasoned that Redmond had valuable knowledge about the Pepsico operations, including knowledge about its business and marketing plans, that he would "inevitably disclose" in the course of doing his new job. As a result,

---

[98] *Id.*

[99] Andrew Beckermen-Radau, *Trade Secrets: The New Risks to Trade Secrets Posed by Computerization*, 28 RUTGERS COMPUTER & TECH. L.J. 227, 233 (2002).

[100] RESTATEMENT (THIRD) OF UNFAIR COMPETITION §39 (1995). The Third Restatement of Unfair Competition also expands the remedies available to employers to protect their confidential information.

[101] 54 F.3d 1262 (7th Cir. 1995).

Redmond was enjoined from accepting a position with Gatorade to do the type of work that he was most qualified to do. The *Pepsico* decision has been widely criticized, yet it remains good law in most jurisdictions.[102]

California is one of the states that has refused to adopt the inevitable disclosure doctrine. According to the California court:

> The inevitable disclosure doctrine permits an employer to enjoin the former employee without proof of the employee's actual or threatened use of trade secrets based on an inference (based in turn upon circumstantial evidence) that the employee inevitably will use his or her knowledge of those trade secrets in the new employment. The result is not merely an injunction against the use of trade secrets, but an injunction restricting employment.
>
> ...[T]he doctrine of inevitable disclosure 'creates a de facto covenant not to compete.'...The chief ill in the covenant not to compete imposed by the inevitable disclosure doctrine is its after-the-fact nature. The covenant is imposed after the employment contract is made and therefore alters the employment relationship without the employee's consent.
>
> ...As a result of the inevitable disclosure doctrine, the employer obtains the benefit of a contractual provision it did not pay for, while the employee is bound by a court-imposed contract provision with no opportunity to negotiate terms or consideration.[103]

The doctrine of inevitable disclosure is a natural outgrowth of employers' aggressive efforts to restrict employees' use of knowledge. The California court identified one respect in which the inevitable disclosure doctrine alters the contractual relationship between the parties. An understanding of the new employment relationship makes it possible to see an even more fundamental conflict between the new employment relationship and the inevitable disclosure doctrine.

In today's workplace, employees are expected to participate in many aspects of the firm, develop knowledge about the firm's overall operation, create cross-departmental links, and engage in a wide variety of tasks. Flexibility and cross-utilization are essential elements of the new work practices. Furthermore, employees are expected to interact with and to develop knowledge about business practices, customers, competitors, and the larger context

---

[102] *See* Lumex, Inc. v. Highsmith, 919 F. Supp. 624, 631 (E.D.N.Y. 1996); Cardinal Freight Carriers, Inc. v. J.B. Hunt Transport Servs., Inc., 987 S.W.2d 642, 643–44 (Ark. 1999). *But see* Bayer Corp. v. Roche Molecular Sys., 72 F. Supp. 2d 1111, 1120 (N.D. Cal. 1999) (noting that California does not recognize the doctrine of inevitable disclosure because to do so would create a "de facto covenant not to compete," which is unenforceable in California). *See generally* Whyte v. Schlage Lock Co., 101 Cal. App. 4th 1443, 14460–61 (Cal. App. 4th Dis. 2002) (reporting the majority of jurisdictions have adopted the inevitable disclosure doctrine, and listing cases). *See also* Jay L. Koh, *From Hoops to Hard Drives: An Accession Law Approach to the Inevitable Misappropriation of Trade Secrets*, 48 Am. U. L. Rev. 271, 281–84 (1998) (summarizing positions in debates over the inevitable disclosure doctrine).

[103] Whyte v. Schlage Lock Co., *id.* at 1461–63.

of the firm. Indeed, as discussed in Chapter 5, compensation practices often reward such knowledge. The more employees know, the more valuable they are to their firm, yet the more risk they run of acquiring knowledge that they could "inevitably disclose."

In addition, the new employment relationship requires employees to construct their own boundaryless careers. Rather than promising job security, employers encourage them to depart and to seek employment in related firms. If employers expect employees to network beyond the boundary of the firm, it would be a bitter irony if they were not free to enjoy the benefits of the contacts and opportunities that such networks provide. They should not find themselves unemployed and unemployable when they set out to construct their careers.

Under current trends, the most successful employee in the new workplace is the one who is most at risk from the inevitable disclosure doctrine. The more successful an employee is on the employer's own terms, the more likely she is to be penalized for obtaining information when she departs. Courts have expanded their definition of trade secrets and restricted disclosure of knowledge that does not rise to the level of a trade secret at the same time that employees are expected to gain as much knowledge as possible about the overall operation of their firms. Successful employees will be frozen out of subsequent employment opportunities in their field. In this area, the law is clearly out of step with business practice.

C. The Role of Implicit Contracts in Employment Regulation

It has been argued in this chapter that courts should take cognizance of the implicit promises in the employment relationship when deciding whether or not to enforce restrictive covenants and in determining the scope of trade secret protection. Employment contracts are famously incomplete, particularly when they are at-will and made pursuant to an oral agreement. It is well understood that employment contracts embody shared understandings and mutually agreed terms that are not a part of the formal contractual apparatus. Hence it is common for courts to take implicit understandings into account when determining the rules for employment regulation. Two examples are presented below to illustrate how courts can be sensitive to implicit understandings when determining the rules for employment regulation. These examples concern the refusal of the English courts to enforce restrictive covenants in the sixteenth and seventeenth centuries and the trend in some U.S. courts to modify the at-will employment relationship in the 1970s and 1980s.

1. The Origin of Judicial Attitudes Toward Restrictive Covenants
The current disputes about ownership of human capital are analogous to disputes in the sixteenth and seventeenth centuries involving employee

training and mobility. The historic refusal of the English courts to enforce employment covenants not to compete arose from the ancient common law courts' desire to enforce the unwritten, customary terms of guild apprenticeship arrangements and thus to prevent masters from circumventing them.[104]

The medieval European craft guilds had apprenticeship systems that provided master craftsmen with a labor force while at the same time serving as a system of technical training for young men. In the guild system, some of the obligations of both master and apprentice were specified in a contract, termed an indenture, but most were based on custom. Later, statutes were enacted to set some of the terms of the apprenticeship relationship. For example, the Statute of Apprentices in 1563 set the duration of apprenticeships at seven years.

Disputes arose in the fifteenth and sixteenth centuries when masters began to take on more and more apprentices and bind them for longer periods of time. As a result, there was a large increase in the number of journeymen seeking to become craftsmen, something the established craftsmen wanted to prevent. That is, the master craftsmen wanted the cheap labor that apprentices provided without having to endure competition from the resulting increase in the numbers of craftsmen. Hence the master craftsmen tried to restrict the number of future craftsmen by making entrance examinations more difficult and by charging exorbitant entrance fees. Some craftsmen also extracted promises from their apprentices and journeymen not to assume the role of craftsmen upon expiration of the indenture term.[105] These were early forms of employment covenants not to compete.

Because the guild system was a deep part of the social and moral fabric of society, there was general outrage against unethical masters who tried to subvert the customary rules of apprenticeship. Statutes were enacted to protect apprentices, and some apprentices challenged post-apprenticeship restraints contained in the indentures.[106] The courts held that the restraints were void. According to legal historian Harlan Blake, "These cases represent reactions by the judges against erosions in the customs of the guilds by aggressive craftsmen, [and]...[t]hey show judicial support of the customary concepts of 'fair' commercial activity of the late medieval period."[107] Thus in the seventeenth century, courts became suspicious of covenants not to compete because they viewed them as attempts by employers to breach customary understandings of the terms of the employment relationship.

---

[104] *See* Harlan M. Blake, *Employee Agreements Not to Compete*, 73 HARV. L. REV. 625, 631–37 (1960).

[105] *Id.* at 634.

[106] *See id.* at 634–35.

[107] *Id.* at 637.

2. Judicial Modification of the At-Will Regime in the 1980s

Closer to home, today's problem of employers' tendency to breach psychological contracts for training and networking finds a parallel in the judicial developments in the at-will employment area in the 1980s. In the recession of the early 1980s, many employees who had been in their jobs for long periods and held what they believed to be implicit contracts for long-term job security were shocked to find themselves dismissed or downsized. This trend fueled the movement within many state courts and some state legislatures to modify the at-will rule and bring it into congruence with the implicit psychological contracts of the then-dominant employment relationship – the internal labor market model of long-term job security. Some courts in the 1980s recognized that employers often gave employees an implicit promise of long-term job security in exchange for commitment and loyalty. Where such an implicit promise had been given, those courts enforced the implicit contract by imposing a just cause restriction on the employer's power to dismiss.[108]

Since the early 1990s, the disputes over at-will employment have been less numerous despite the fact of continuing lay-offs and workforce churning.[109] In part this is because many employees no longer have psychological contracts for long-term employment. With the new employment relationship, implicit promises of job security, while still used in some workplaces, are not so widespread. In fact, to avoid ambiguity, many employers now make explicit statements to employees, orally and in writing, that the employment relationship is at-will and that there are no implicit promises of long-term job security.[110]

Today, the problem of unfairness for individual employees is different than it was in the 1980s. As shown in Chapter 5, some of the most important terms of the new employment relationship are that employers will provide employees with training, skill development, networking opportunities, and general human capital development. Under the new employment relationship, the problem is no longer employer breaches of implicit promises of job security, but rather employer breaches of the other promises implicit in the employment relationship. Networking, training, and lateral mobility

---

[108] *See, e.g.,* Fletcher v. Wesley Med. Ctr., 585 F. Supp. 1260, 1263–64 (D. Kan. 1984); Pugh v. See's Candies, Inc., 116 Cal. App. 3d 311, 316–19 (1981), *overruled in part on other grounds by* Guz v. Bechtel Nat'l, Inc., 24 Cal. 4th 317 (2000); Salimi v. Farmers Ins. Group, 684 P.2d 264, 265 (Colo. Ct. App. 1984); Toussaint v. Blue Cross & Blue Shield, 292 N.W.2d 880, 892 (Mich. 1980); Woolley v. Hoffman-La Roche, Inc., 491 A.2d 1257, 1268 (N.J. 1985); Thompson v. St. Regis Paper Co., 685 P.2d 1081, 1089 (Wash. 1984).

[109] *See, e.g.,* Louis Uchitelle, *Pink Slip? Now It's All in a Day's Work,* NEW YORK TIMES, Aug. 5, 2001, Sec. 3, p. 1 (noting that despite a new round of layoffs, "the usual protests and anger are largely missing").

[110] *See* Max Schanzenbach, *Exceptions to Employment at Will: Raising Firing Costs or Enforcing Life-Cycle Contracts?* 5 AM. L. & ECON. REV. 470 (2003).

are a fundamental aspect of today's employment system. Yet it is often in the interest of individual employers to breach these new psychological contracts, just as it was at times in the interest of employers to breach the old psychological contracts through unjust dismissals.

3. Post-Employment Restraints and Economic Growth

Recently legal scholars Ronald Gilson and Alan Hyde, in separate works, have argued that the success of Silicon Valley as a high-growth agglomeration economy is the result of California's refusal to enforce covenants not to compete.[111] They each show that it is in the public interest for employees to move freely between firms, taking their knowledge with them. They argue that courts should adopt a permissive attitude toward employee mobility and a restrictive approach toward noncompete covenants and trade secret protections. My argument adds a slightly different, albeit compatible, perspective.

The new employment relationship includes an employer's promise of human capital development through the acquisition of knowledge. As seen in Chapter 5, for firms to remain dynamic, they need to promote citizenship, commitment, creativity, and effort in their workforce. And to do that, they need to honor the psychological contracts they offer. Yet, it is often in the interest of individual employers to breach these new psychological contracts, just as it was at times in the interest of employers to breach the old psychological contracts through unjust dismissals. It is therefore incumbent upon courts to enforce the new psychological contract, or at the very least, restrain employers' efforts to renege.

Labor history demonstrates the serious social costs that occur when individual employers renege on their psychological contracts. The current flood of post-termination employment litigation parallels the history of piece rates in the early twentieth century. As discussed in Chapter 2, employers adopted piece rates to motivate workers to increase the pace of work. Employers assured employees that with piece rates they could increase their earnings by increasing their work pace. But once workers increased their pace enough to earn a decent wage, employers almost invariably cut the piece rates. The rate cuts were experienced by workers as a breach of the psychological contract that the piece-rate system embodied. Most of the major strikes in the early years of the twentieth century were precipitated by such rate cuts.[112]

---

[111] AnnaLee Saxenian, REGIONAL ADVANTAGE: CULTURE AND COMPETITION IN SILICON VALLEY AND ROUTE 128 (1994) (comparing the industrial districts of Silicon Valley and Route 128 in Boston, Massachusetts); Gilson, *Legal Infrastructure of High Technology Districts*, 74 N.Y.U. L. REV.; Alan Hyde, WORKING IN SILICON VALLEY: ECONOMIC AND LEGAL ANALYSIS OF A HIGH-VELOCITY LABOR MARKET (2003).

[112] *See, e.g.*, Steven Fraser, LABOR WILL RULE: SIDNEY HILLMAN AND THE RISE OF AMERICAN LABOR 41 (1991) (noting how sudden cuts in piece rates and changes in production quotas precipitated numerous strikes in the needle trades between 1880 and 1920, making it the

Today's courts should insist that employers honor their psychological contracts and perform their part of the bargain. Otherwise, the implicit reciprocity will be discredited, trust will evaporate, and serious labor relations problems will ensue.

D. Conclusion

The lessons from the past demonstrate that courts can and should take psychological contracts and implicit understandings of the employment relationship into account when regulating the employment relationship. Thus they should reassess the trend toward giving ever wider enforcement to covenants not to compete. They should recognize that in the new employment relationship, employees have been promised not only training, up-skilling, and networking, but also the ability to use their newly acquired skills in subsequent employment. While individual employers may have an incentive to offer these benefits and then renege, the courts should not support them in doing so. In today's marketplace, for firms to remain dynamic, they need to promote citizenship, commitment, creativity, and effort in their workforce. And to do that, firms need to honor the psychological contracts they offer. If they do not do so voluntarily out of short-term, opportunistic motives, courts should force them to do so by refusing to permit them to renege.

In conclusion, courts should address today's disputes over ownership of human capital in the same spirit as their predecessors have done. Just as courts in the seventeenth century enforced customary and tacit understandings, today's courts should develop an approach to human capital cases that prevents employers from violating the tacit understandings of today's employment contract. When forced to decide who owns employees' general human capital, courts should factor the implicit terms of the new psychological contract into their determination. Thus they should adopt a narrow definition of trade secrets, limit enforcement of noncompete covenants to the protection of trade secrets narrowly defined, reject the doctrine of inevitable disclosure, and thereby give employees broad rights to acquire, retain, and deploy their own human capital.

third most strike-prone industry in the country at that time); Roger Waldinger, *Another Look at the International Ladies' Garment Workers' Union: Women, Industry Structure and Collective Action,* in WOMEN, WORK, AND PROTEST: A CENTURY OF WOMEN'S LABOR HISTORY 86, 96 (Ruth Milkman, ed., 1985) (describing how changes in piece-rate calculations reduced earnings and thereby triggered the "uprising of the 20,000" in New York in 1909).

8

The Changing Nature of Employment Discrimination

Over the past three decades, civil rights laws have made a major contribution to reducing employment discrimination in the workplace in the United States. Since the enactment of the Civil Rights Act of 1964, women and minorities have entered many previously all-white, all-male occupations and have made significant gains in employment levels and pay relative to white males. For example, the pay of white women working full time relative to that of their white male counterparts increased from 57.9 percent in 1965 to 71.3 in 1995. Similarly, the earnings of black males relative to white males increased in the same period from 62.8 to 72.8 per cent.[1] While some of these changes might be the result of changes in general attitudes, mores, and social practices, it is clear that they are, in large part, attributable to the law.[2]

Despite the success of civil rights efforts, discrimination still exists in the workplace, although it now often takes new forms. The diffused and decentralized authority structure of the new boundaryless workplace can give rise to bias and favoritism that is more subtle than discrimination in internal labor markets. Women and minorities in formerly white male workplaces often encounter passive hostility and subtle harassment from coworkers as well as glass ceilings and other de facto barriers to advancement. The civil rights laws were designed to eliminate discrimination as it was manifest in the old

---

[1] Francine D. Blau, Marianne A. Ferber, & Anne E. Winkler, THE ECONOMICS OF WOMEN, MEN AND WORK 139, tbl. 5.11 (3d ed. 1998).

[2] On the effectiveness of equal employment laws in reducing employment discrimination on the basis of gender, *see* COMMITTEE ON WOMEN'S EMPLOYMENT AND RELATED SOCIAL ISSUES, WOMEN'S WORK, MEN'S WORK: SEX SEGREGATION ON THE JOB 128–29 (Barbara F. Reskin & Heidi I. Hartmann, eds., 1986). On change in black-white earnings differential due to the enactment of the Civil Rights Act of 1964, *see* William A. Darity Jr. & Patrick L. Mason, *Evidence of Discrimination in Employment: Codes of Color, Codes of Gender*, 12 J. ECON. PERSP. 63, 63–90 (1998). *See also* John Donahue & James Heckman, *Continuous vs. Episodic Change: The Impact of Civil Rights Policy on the Economic Status of Blacks*, 29 J. ECON. LITERATURE 1603, 1604 (1991).

employment relationship, and therefore may be less effective to redress new forms of discrimination. In particular, the new workplace practices described in Chapter 5 threaten both to make liability for discrimination more difficult to establish and to render many of the old remedies ineffective. Further, contemporary human resource practices that involve delegation of important decisions to peer groups intensify the problem of coworker harassment and raise the specter of discrimination without a discriminator, an injured plaintiff without a legally accountable defendant.

This chapter argues that changes in workplace practices described in Chapter 5 force us to rethink conceptions of liability and the remedies that should be used to eliminate employment discrimination as it is manifest in the new workplace. It begins by explicating the ways in which the civil rights laws of the past decades were tailored to the forms of discrimination that existed in the old workplace. It then describes the new forms of employment discrimination that are emerging as workplace norms and practices change, and the problems they pose for existing Title VII law. Finally, it explores some approaches that could redress discrimination in the new workplace.

A. The Relationship Between Employment Discrimination and Internal Labor Markets

Historically, employment discrimination has taken the form not merely of pay differentials between men and women and blacks and whites, but also of job segregation along gender and racial lines. Jobs occupied primarily by women or minorities almost invariably have offered lower pay, fewer benefits, and lesser status than jobs occupied by white males.[3] Because of these historical forms of discrimination, the civil rights legislation of the 1960s was aimed at eliminating discrimination that took the form of disparate pay for the same work and job segregation into different types of work. The Equal Pay Act of 1962 addressed the pay differential between women and men by requiring equal pay for men and women performing the same work.[4] Title VII of the Civil Rights Act of 1964 addressed the issue of equal employment opportunities for women and minorities by prohibiting discrimination in regard to hiring, testing, promotion, training, remuneration, benefits, and other aspects of the employment relationship.[5] Because of its focus on equal employment opportunity, Title VII became the primary weapon in the struggle to achieve equality in the workplace.

---

[3] Reskin & Hartmann, WOMEN'S WORK; Jerry A. Jacobs, REVOLVING DOORS: SEX SEGREGATION AND WOMEN'S CAREERS 28–30 (1989) (finding significant gender segregation of workplaces throughout the 1980s). *See generally* Vicki Schultz, *Reconceptualizing Sexual Harassment*, 107 YALE L. J. 1683, 1756–57 (1998); Vicki Schultz, *Life's Work*, 100 COLUM. L. REV. 1881, 1894–95 and n. 40 (2000) (summarizing data on sex segregation and pay differentials).

[4] 29 U.S.C. § 206.

[5] 42 U.S.C. §§ 2600e–2000e-17.

There is a direct link between the antidiscrimination legislation of the 1960s and internal labor market job structures of the past. Internal labor markets have played an important role in the creation and perpetuation of employment discrimination in the twentieth century – indeed, arguably one of the most important causes of women's disadvantaged position in the labor market has been the internal labor market structure of American industry. Therefore the antidiscrimination laws were designed to assist in the elimination of discrimination as it operated within internal labor markets. Understanding the link between internal labor markets and employment discrimination makes it possible to see how discrimination has changed under the new employment relationship, and to consider the ways in which the new forms of discrimination can be redressed.

1. Causes of Employment Discrimination

Long ago, Gary Becker explained employment discrimination as a product of employers' "taste for discrimination."[6] He hypothesized that some employers had an irrational taste for an all-white or an all-male workforce, and that this taste factored into their utility function when making profit-maximizing employment decisions. Those employers, he posited, were willing to pay higher wages for their taste preference. In this view, discrimination is both irrational and inefficient.

A number of economists have since pointed out that if discrimination were merely a product of irrational employer behavior – namely, the result of employers exercising a nonmarket preference – then over time competition would eliminate it. Employers of white men would find that they could operate just as well and enjoy lower labor costs by using minorities or women workers. Rational employers would thus lay off white men and hire minorities and women. Eventually wages of white males would fall and those of minorities and women would rise until parity was achieved. However, this has not occurred. Therefore, various modifications of Becker's theory have been offered to explain the intractable nature of discrimination in the labor market.[7]

One concept that has been used to explain the persistence of employment discrimination is the concept of statistical discrimination. Statistical discrimination occurs when two groups vary on average in terms of some relevant characteristic, and an employer treats all members of each group as if they all possess that average characteristic. For example, if employers assume all women will have short job tenure and treat all women on the basis of that belief, then employers will avoid hiring women for jobs for which they

---

[6] Gary S. Becker, THE ECONOMICS OF DISCRIMINATION 14–15 (1957).
[7] *See* Kenneth J. Arrow, *What Has Economics to Say About Racial Discrimination?* 12 J. ECON. PERSP. 91, 92–98 (1998); Darity & Mason, *Discrimination in Employment*, 12 J. ECON. PERSP. at, 63–76, 84–87 (1998).

value longevity.[8] In particular, they will not hire women for jobs that require on-the-job training or that are organized into job ladders.[9]

As discussed in Chapter 3, internal labor markets came to dominate American industry in the early twentieth century. Under the internal labor market employment system, employers valued longevity; they wanted to hire employees who would stay on the job for a long time. Yet for most of this century, women as a group have had a pattern of short job tenure relative to men.[10] Labor economist Claudia Goldin found, on the basis of available data, that in 1900, males had almost three times the job duration that women had in their current occupations, and one and a-half times the years with their current employer than women. According to Goldin, "firms often used sex as a signal of shorter expected job tenure."[11] Thus, by operation of statistical discrimination, employers avoided hiring women for jobs within internal labor markets.[12] In this way, the system of job ladders, internal promotion, and limited ports of entry operated to keep women out of the best jobs.

The interaction between statistical discrimination and internal labor markets is explained by sociologists Patricia Roos and Barbara Reskin as follows:

> With respect to women, [statistical discrimination] is most often manifest in employers' reluctance to hire *any* woman for jobs that require appreciable on-the-job training, because they believe many young women leave the labor force to have children. As a result, newly hired females are often assigned to low-skilled dead-end jobs. Because transferring across internal labor markets is very difficult, if not impossible, . . . statistical discrimination has long-lasting implications for women's occupational outcomes.[13]

Internal labor markets not only limited women's entry level job prospects, they limited women's later employment prospects as well. This is because internal labor markets required that employers hire only at the bottom rung

---

[8] See Arrow, *Racial Discrimination,* 12 J. Econ. Persp. at 96–97; Francine D. Blau, *Occupational Segregation and Labor Market Discrimination,* in Sex Segregation in the Workplace 117, 122–23 (Barbara F. Reskin, ed., 1984); Karen Oppenheim Mason, *Commentary: Strober's Theory of Occupational Sex Segregation,* in Reskin, Sex Segregation in the Workplace 157, 165.

[9] See Blau, *Occupational Segregation.* Historically, women tended to be placed in jobs that required few skills and were provided little or no on-the-job training. *See* Claudia Dale Goldin, Understanding the Gender Gap: An Economic History of American Women 100–103 (1990).

[10] Goldin, Understanding the Gender Gap 101.

[11] *Id.* at 116.

[12] See Jeremy I. Bulow & Lawrence H. Summers, *A Theory of Dual Labor Markets with Application to Industrial Policy, Discrimination, and Keynesian Unemployment,* 4 J. Lab. Econ. 376, 401 (July 1986); *see also* Lester C. Thurow, Generating Inequality: Mechanisms of Distribution in the U.S. Economy 178 (1975).

[13] Patricia A. Roos & Barbara F. Reskin, *Institutional Factors Contributing to Sex Segregation in the Workplace,* in Reskin, Sex Segregation in the Workplace 235, 241 (citations omitted).

of the job ladder and then promote from within existing employment ranks.[14] Therefore, when women were excluded from entry-level jobs within internal labor markets, they were excluded from the best jobs forever.

For these reasons, a great deal of contemporary employment discrimination has its roots in the internal labor market job structures of the past. Employers that utilized promotion ladders did not hire women because they wanted workers who would learn skills as they went along. Those that utilized Fordist-style assembly lines, in which job ladders were flat, did not hire women because their early-twentieth-century human resource practices were designed to discourage turnover and encourage longevity.[15]

One can see evidence of women's exclusion from internal labor market jobs in the pattern of women's employment. In the past, women workers have tended to cluster into two types of jobs.[16] First, women were heavily concentrated in jobs for which they could obtain the necessary training *outside* the workplace. For example, women have been overwhelmingly clustered in occupations such as child care, nursing, cooking, and sewing – all of which involved skills learned in the traditional gendered home. Similarly, women were hired for jobs for which they received training through the public school system, such as teaching or bookkeeping. Thus as late as 1949, three-quarters of the white women who worked were occupied in the fields of garment and textile manufacturing, sales, teaching, nursing, cooking, waitressing, and beauty care.[17]

Second, women have historically been hired into jobs for which employers do not value longevity. Indeed, in some jobs, employers had policies that prevented women from remaining for long. For example, airlines hired women as flight attendants from the early days of commercial air flight, but until the early 1970s the carriers required women to quit as soon as they reached age thirty or were married.[18]

Throughout most of the twentieth century, women were not hired by large corporations with internal labor markets. Rather, the dominant labor

---

[14] *See* Katherine Van Wezel Stone, *The Origins of Job Structures in the Steel Industry*, in LABOUR MARKET SEGMENTATION 45–49 (D. Gordon, M. Reich, & R. Edwards, eds., 1975); Peter Doeringer & Michael Piore, INTERNAL LABOR MARKETS AND MANPOWER ANALYSIS 2 (1971).

[15] *See* Sanford M. Jacoby, MODERN MANORS: WELFARE CAPITALISM SINCE THE NEW DEAL (1997).

[16] On the clustering of women's jobs throughout the twentieth century, *see* Blau, *Occupational Segregation* 134.

[17] Frank Levy, THE NEW DOLLARS AND DREAMS: AMERICAN INCOME AND ECONOMIC CHANGE 16 (1998).

[18] *See* Georgia Panter Nielsen, FROM SKY GIRL TO FLIGHT ATTENDANT: WOMEN AND THE MAKING OF A UNION 83–89 (1982) (writing on the pervasiveness of the no-marriage rule and the protracted struggle by the flight attendants' union to eliminate it). Other women's occupations also had no-marriage policies, including teaching, nursing, and secretarial work. *See* Jacobs, REVOLVING DOORS; *see also* Zipes v. Trans World Airlines, Inc., 455 U.S. 385, 388 (discussing the airline's no-children rule); United Airlines, Inc. v. McDonald, 432 U.S. 385, 387 (1977) (discussing the airline's no-marriage rule).

relations practices, based on the theories of early-twentieth-century scientific management and personnel management scholars, kept women out of the better jobs in manufacturing. The use of internal labor markets and the operation of statistical discrimination led employers to hire men for primary labor market jobs. When women finally were permitted in, union-negotiated promotion rights and job ladders dictated that they come in at the bottom.[19]

Some economists have argued that statistical discrimination might explain short-term employment discrimination, but it cannot explain persistent discrimination because employers will ultimately find it inefficient to hire on the basis of average group characteristics if there are better methods of assessment available. Thus, some economists have claimed, employers have an incentive to improve their assessment methods rather than rely upon statistically average characteristics.[20] However, even if better assessment methods were available, statistical discrimination can explain the *initial* exclusion of women and minorities from internal labor markets on the basis of hiring decisions made before improved assessment techniques became available, or exclusionary hiring decisions made as a rough first cut in a time of rapid expansion. Once that first cut occurs, a vicious cycle develops. Women and minorities learn they are not eligible for primary labor market jobs and do not invest in the necessary training to get them. Because women and minorities underinvest in education and training, employers come to believe, sometimes correctly, that these workers lack the necessary human capital for primary labor market jobs.[21] At that point, even improved, individualized assessment techniques do not lead to equal labor market opportunities.[22]

Labor economist Francine Blau suggests an additional dynamic at work for women. She concedes that it might be true that women, knowing that certain better jobs are not available to them, do not invest in the training necessary to perform them. However, she argues that:

[It is possible that] employers' view of female job instability leads them to give women less training and to assign [women] to jobs where the cost of turnover is minimized. [As a result,] women may respond by exhibiting the unstable behavior employers expect. This in turn confirms employer perceptions. . . . Viewing the matter somewhat differently, the employers' *ex post* "correct" assessment of sex differences in average productivity may be seen to result from their own discriminatory actions.[23]

---

[19] *See, e.g.*, Ruth Milkman, Farewell to the Factory: Auto Workers in the Late Twentieth Century 37 (1997) (noting that women in General Motors auto plants do not get the highly desirable jobs because their average seniority is considerably less than that of men).

[20] *See, e.g.*, Darity & Mason, *Discrimination in Employment*, 12 J. Econ. Persp. at 83–84.

[21] *See id.* at 84.

[22] William Darity and Patrick Mason describe this dynamic as a "self fulfilling prophecy." *Id.* at 176–77.

[23] Blau, *Occupational Segregation* 117–23.

Under either scenario, employers' initial perceptions that women's labor market characteristics are not suited to internal labor market job structures set in motion a feedback loop that leads employers to refuse to hire women for primary labor market jobs.

2. White and Male Privilege as a Psychological Contract

There is another respect in which work practices under internal labor market job structures have played a role in sustaining job segregation. Sociologist Jerry Jacobs has posited that the implicit contract between employers and employees under the Taylorist labor system involved not only a promise of job security, but also a promise that existing working conditions and status and pay differentials would be maintained. Jacobs argues that male workers derived both tangible and symbolic benefits from sex-segregated workplaces, including status rewards, camaraderie, and the job and income security that resulted from not having to compete with lower paid women workers. These implicit contracts were used to instill morale, motivation, and trust. They operated within internal labor markets to induce employees to invest in firm-specific human capital and to expend effort on behalf of the firm. Thus, if an employer were to integrate a formerly all-male workplace, he ran the risk that the existing workforce would see it as a violation of these implicit contracts, with a resulting cost in terms of morale, productivity, and labor peace.[24]

A similar dynamic of discrimination that has limited women's employment opportunities operates with respect to minorities. Minority opportunities have been curtailed by the same pernicious combination of internal labor markets, implicit contracts, and statistical discrimination that generated the exclusion of women. In addition, they were excluded from internal labor markets by the overtly racist policies of American employers and unions. Until the 1960s, many unions either excluded minorities altogether or kept them in low-wage, low-skill job categories. In the building trades, for example, unions kept minorities and women out of apprenticeship programs and out of union hiring halls. Thus minorities, like women, were excluded from the core good jobs and relegated to the secondary labor market periphery in which the pay was low, the jobs were dirty, and job security did not exist.[25]

---

[24] *See* Jacobs, REVOLVING DOORS 153–55, 179–81. For a description of male workers' reaction to the presence of women auto workers, *see* Milkman, FAREWELL TO THE FACTORY 37.

[25] *See* Steele v. Louisville & Nashville R.R. Co., 323 U.S. 192, 195 (1944) (holding that a whites-only railroad union that negotiated collective agreement designed to exclude blacks from desirable jobs violated the duty of fair representation). *See generally* William B. Gould, BLACK WORKERS IN WHITE UNIONS: JOB DISCRIMINATION IN THE UNITED STATES (1977); THE NEGRO AND THE AMERICAN LABOR MOVEMENT (Julius Jacobson, ed., 1968); Joseph F. Wilson, TEARING DOWN THE COLOR BAR: A DOCUMENTARY HISTORY AND ANALYSIS OF THE BROTHERHOOD OF SLEEPING CAR PORTERS (1989).

3. Changes in Employment Patterns

In the 1970s and 1980s, employment patterns began to change. First, women became more attached to the labor market so that employers had less reason to practice statistical discrimination. Also, equal employment opportunity laws forced many firms to hire women and blacks for previously all-white, all-male jobs.[26] Early in its history, the Equal Employment Opportunity Commission (EEOC) took the position that Title VII prohibited statistical discrimination by declaring that it was unlawful for employers to make hiring decisions based upon real or perceived group characteristics.[27] Overt discrimination in hiring became unlawful unless it was pursuant to a "bona fide occupational qualification," which was narrowly defined.[28] For all of these reasons, the sex segregation of jobs as well as the pay gap between men and women declined.[29]

The pay gap between blacks and whites also declined from 1965 to 1975, but the trend flattened somewhat after that.[30] Nonetheless, the pay gap between black and white women continued to narrow substantially, so that by 1981 black women were earning 90 percent of what white women earned – a dramatic increase from the mere 69 percent of 1964. In the same period, the gap between the earnings of black men and white men narrowed from 66 percent in 1964 to 71 percent in 1981. Occupational segregation, which was not as extreme for minorities as it was for women, also declined.[31]

Even after the most blatant pay differentials and explicit barriers to hiring women and minorities were broken, those groups continued to be disadvantaged within major corporations. Because jobs were arranged in hierarchical progression, latecomers came in at the bottom and had the farthest to rise. They did not have access to the higher rungs of the internal labor markets. Also, because they were at the bottom, latecomers were the first to be laid off in times of cutbacks. Efforts by women and minorities to jump over established arrangements for hierarchical progression generated intense and bitter disputes about affirmative action. White male workers resisted because they felt that they were entitled to a certain sequence of advancement and that

---

[26] On the change in women's labor force participation, *see* Blau et al., ECONOMICS OF WOMEN, MEN AND WORK 207–8; Blau, *Occupational Segregation* 125. On changes in black-white employment and earnings differentials, *see* Darity & Mason, *Discrimination in Employment*, 12 J. ECON. PERSP. at 63–90.

[27] *See* EEOC Guidelines, 29 C.F.R. §1604.2(a)(1) (1968).

[28] 42 U.S.C. §§2000e to 2000e-17. The bona fide occupational qualification (BFOQ) exception permits employers to make hiring decisions based on otherwise prohibited reasons, if such decisions are necessary to the "essence of the business." Int'l Union, UAW v. Johnson Controls, Inc., 499 U.S. 187, 203 (1991).

[29] *See* Blau et al., ECONOMICS OF WOMEN, MEN AND WORK 127–29 (noting decline in job segregation and pay gap).

[30] *See* Donahue & Heckman, *Continuous vs. Episodic Change*, 29 J. ECON. LITERATURE at 1604.

[31] *See* Blau, *Occupational Segregation* 126, 135–36.

affirmative action was thus a violation of their psychological contracts and their legal rights.

B. The Nature of Discrimination in the Boundaryless Workplace

Because many aspects of employment discrimination originated in or were perpetuated by the old employment system, there is reason to believe that discrimination might subside in the future. The new workplace, with its rejection of implicit long-term employment guarantees and its repudiation of rigid job ladders, offers the possibility of creating new opportunities for women and minorities. To the extent that the old labor system locked them out, it might appear that the demise of that system is a major improvement. The new employment relationship could spell the end of labor market dualism and the beginning of more egalitarian job structures. However, there are new impediments to the achievement of equal opportunity for women and minorities in the new workplace that need to be addressed.

1. The Problem of Diffused and Invisible Authority

As discussed, in the past much employment discrimination was rooted in the hierarchical job structures of internal labor markets. Today's workplace does not have as much formal hierarchy, so there are less formal impediments to advancement. In the boundaryless workplace, everyone makes lateral movements, but some move in circles while others spiral to the top. Because there are not defined job ladders and the criteria for advancement are not clearly specified, it is difficult for someone to claim that she has been bypassed for advancement because of her gender or race. That is, the diffuse authority structure of the new employment relationship makes discrimination hard to identify and difficult to challenge.

In addition to the hidden nature of the decision-making process, there is also a hidden element to the decision criteria in the modern corporation. The decentralization of authority and the flattening of hierarchy means that decisions are delegated to a wide range of people who are permitted to use their individual, often idiosyncratic, discretion. Also, when jobs are defined in terms of competencies and employees are valued for their varied skills and flexibility, it is difficult for firms to articulate clear criteria for advancement. Often social credentials are used in lieu of objective performance measures. These social credentials include such things as prestigious education, membership of social clubs, participation in certain sports – all activities that have traditionally excluded women and minorities. Thus under a system that rewards social credentials, women and minorities are disadvantaged.[32]

---

[32] *See* Edward S. Adams, *Using Evaluations to Break Down the Male Corporate Hierarchy: A Full Circle Approach*, 73 Colo. L. Rev. 117, 167–68 (2002).

A growing number of employment discrimination class action lawsuits allege that informal and decentralized promotion practices foster covert discrimination against women and minorities. For example, in a suit filed in 2001 against Johnson & Johnson, the plaintiffs alleged that the giant conglomerate knowingly engaged in racial discrimination by maintaining promotion policies that allowed supervisors to " 'handpick white candidates, resulting in fewer promotions for African-Americans and Hispanic-Americans and perpetuating a glass ceiling and glass walls,' thereby blocking advancement of these employees into 'visible and influential roles within the organization.' "[33] Similar complaints against informal promotion policies are becoming widespread.

In addition, the new nonhierarchical workplace makes power and lines of authority less visible. Thus it is often difficult to know to whom to make appeals, with whom to lodge complaints, or how to bring about change. For example, there are numerous cases in which an employee experiences sexual harassment and wants to complain, yet loses her discrimination case because she did not know to whom to report the offensive conduct or because she reported to the wrong person.[34]

When there is no visible power structure, the invisible structures rule. In the new workplace, these invisible power structures may well turn out to be more remote and impenetrable for women and minorities than the old power structures. The difficulties of identifying discrimination and locating the responsible party in the face of decentralized and dispersed decision-making structures are recurrent themes in contemporary employment discrimination litigation, as will be seen.

2. The Problem of Cliques

The new workplace exacerbates the age-old problem of cliques because it involves delegating major employment decisions to peers. For example, Ed Lawler's proposed competency-based organization, described in Chapter 5, calls for using peers to decide issues such as hiring, evaluation, job allocation, and pay. While peer-based decision making may work well in some situations, it can also promote cliquishness, patronage systems, bigotry, and corruption. In such a workplace, women and minorities could again find themselves excluded. The growing popularity of peer-review procedures for handling disciplinary infractions could similarly reinforce in-groups and exacerbate the exclusion of newcomers such as minorities and women.[35]

---

[33] Beth M. Mantz, *J & J Discrimination Suit May Be One of Largest Ever*, Dow Jones News Wires, 15:40 (Dow Jones News Service, Nov. 16, 2001).

[34] *Schrean v. Chicago Transit Authority*, 1999 WL 977068 (N.D. see. 1999); *Montero v. Agco Corp.*, 192 F.3d 856 (9th cir. 1999); *Watkins v. Professional Security Bureau, Ltd.*, 203 F.3d 439 (4th Cir. 1999).

[35] *See, e.g.*, Masanori Hashimoto, *Employment-Based Training in Japanese Firms in Japan and the United States: Experiences of Automobile Manufacturers*, in Training and the Private Sector

Title VII remedies, such as decrees requiring employers to promote women and minorities up job ladders, are not useful for redressing these forms of discrimination.

Several sociologists of work have focused on the role of informal networks in perpetuating sex and racial segregation in employment. Mark Granovetter, Jerry Jacobs, and others have observed that workplaces are social organizations in which people interact with each other to learn the tricks of the trade, share necessary information, assist in tasks, and coordinate performance.[36] The need for cooperation and teamwork makes it difficult for employers to incorporate women and minorities when there is resistance from incumbent white males.[37] Yet when women and minorities are denied access to informal forms of training and networking, their ability to succeed is severely compromised.[38] The phenomenon of women being shunned, ignored, and frozen out of the loop when they enter predominately male workplaces has been well documented. Many accounts attest to the power of workplace cliques to exclude, disempower, demoralize, or otherwise disable those who are targeted for exclusion.[39] Clique members use the tools of ostracism, belittlement, verbal harassment, innuendo, nefarious gossip, and shunning – tools that are difficult to identify or remedy. And usually the targets are those who are not part of the old crowd, namely women and minorities. Reports of such conduct are becoming increasingly prevalent.[40]

3. The Problem of Lawlessness

The problem of workplace cliques is not new, but it is exacerbated by the new workplace practices. In the past, one of the achievements of unionism was to facilitate the introduction of rules into industrial life. The mass organizing drives of the Congress of Industrial Organizations in the 1930s were

---

109, 140 (Lisa M. Lynch, ed., 1994) (describing peer review at a Honda plant in Ohio); *id.* at 142 (describing peer review at a Toyota Motor plant in Kentucky).

[36] *See* Mark S. Granovetter, GETTING A JOB: A STUDY OF CONTRACTS AND CAREERS 45–48 (1974); Jacobs, REVOLVING DOORS 182.

[37] *See* Jacobs, REVOLVING DOORS 181–82.

[38] Susan Sturm, *Race, Gender and the Law of the Twenty-First Century Workplace*, 1 U. PA. J. LAB. & EMP. L. 639, 642 (1998).

[39] *See* Kathryn Abrams, *The New Jurisprudence of Sexual Harassment*, 83 CORNELL L. REV. 1169, 1196–98 (1998) (citing numerous cases, studies, and other examples).

[40] *See* Jacobs, REVOLVING DOORS 181–82; Rosabeth Moss Kanter, MEN AND WOMEN OF THE CORPORATION 207 (1977); Roos & Reskin, *Sex Segregation in the Workplace* 235, 236–56 (citing studies); Chris Tilly & Charles Tilly, WORK UNDER CAPITALISM 223 (1998) (discussing studies about networks within firms that marginalized women and minorities). *See also* Schultz, *Reconceptualizing Sexual Harassment*, 107 YALE L. J. at 1704 (citing examples of ways in which gender dynamics can sabotage women's ability to function on the job); Vicki Schultz, *Telling Stories About Women and Work*, 103 HARV. L. REV. 1750, 1832–39 (1990) (citing first-person accounts); David C. Yamada, *The Phenomenon of "Workplace Bullying" and the Need for Status-Blind Hostile Work Environment Protection*, 88 GEO. L.J. 475, 477–78 (2000)) (citing first person accounts).

often precipitated by acts of petty tyranny and arbitrary mean-spiritedness by lower-level supervisors.[41] The industrial unions created an industrial jurisprudence, a common law of the shop, enforceable by outside arbitrators. This law of the shop remained invisible to outsiders, but it enabled third-party neutrals – arbitrators – to erect a rule-based system for the day-to-day conduct of affairs in unionized workplaces. While it has been argued that the grievance and arbitration system did not go far enough in bringing external norms into the workplace, the system did bring some modicum of external scrutiny and judgment to bear on what was otherwise an insulated and autocratic domain.[42]

Later, equal employment laws also provided a mechanism for orderly, rule-based, and accountable decisions about such matters as hiring, promotions, and pay rates. These rule-based systems injected an external order into the otherwise private and often anarchic domain of the workplace. In particular, equal employment laws provided rules by which women and minorities could break into workplaces that had been white, male, privileged clubs.[43]

These former systems of rules helped prevent favoritism, cronyism, and patronage networks on the part of supervisors and managers. The need to prevent abusive supervisory patronage practices remains as important as ever, but a growing problem today involves not supervisor, but coworker favoritism. As will be shown, Title VII is not particularly effective against coworker forms of preference and exclusion. Thus as unions decline and the effectiveness of other systems of external rules to govern the workplace fade, there is an even greater danger that the workplace will become a bastion of cliques and favoritism.

C. Applying Title VII to the Boundaryless Workplace

Title VII and the Equal Pay Act embodied an approach to eliminating discrimination that was appropriate to long-term, stable employment relationships and well-defined, hierarchical paths of advancement. As will be shown, today's flexible work practices make it difficult to establish liability under the

---

[41] *See, e.g.*, Clinton Golden & Harold Ruttenberg, The Dynamics of Industrial Democracy (1942).

[42] On the centrality of grievance and arbitration procedures to the postwar system of collective bargaining, *see* Archibald Cox, *Some Aspects of the Labor Management Relations Act, 1947*, 61 Harv. L. Rev. 274, 276–77 (1948); Harry Shulman, *Reason, Contract, and Law in Labor Relations*, 68 Harv. L. Rev. 999, 1001 (1955). For a critique of the grievance and arbitration system, *see* Katherine Van Wezel Stone, *The Post-War Paradigm in American Labor Law*, 90 Yale L. J. 1509, 1523–25, 1531–35, 1559–65 (1981); Katherine Van Wezel Stone, *The Legacy of Industrial Pluralism: The Tension Between Individual Employment Rights and the New Deal Collective Bargaining System*, 59 V. Chi L. Rev. 575, 577 (1992).

[43] *See* Cynthia L. Estlund, *Working Together: The Workplace, Civil Society and the Law*, 89 Geo. L. J. 31–32 (2000) (arguing that Title VII has supplied a normative vision of equal opportunity that has helped transform discriminatory workplace practices).

conventional Title VII approaches. In addition, the new workplace practices foster forms of discrimination that elude existing Title VII remedies.

1. Establishing Liability

For a plaintiff to prove an allegation of discriminatory treatment under Title VII, he or she must show that the employer made an adverse decision or took an adverse action with a discriminatory intent. The employer's intent can be established with direct or indirect evidence. Direct evidence of discrimination means overt statements such as a supervisor saying, "I did not hire you because you are black," or, "You cannot be promoted because we only give managerial jobs to men." Such direct evidence is rare today because most employers have trained their supervisors to disguise any overt discriminatory motives they might harbor.[44]

Because of the difficulty of finding direct evidence of discriminatory intent, the Supreme Court, in *McDonnell Douglas Corp. v. Green*, established a method of establishing discriminatory motive with indirect evidence.[45] Under the *McDonnell Douglas* test, as elaborated in subsequent decisions, a plaintiff who claims she was dismissed or denied a particular job because of her gender or race can establish a prima facie case by showing that (1) she was a member of a protected class; (2) she was qualified for the job; (3) she applied for but was not given the job; and (4) the job was given to someone who was not a member of a protected class.[46] If she can establish these factors, the burden switches to the employer to produce evidence showing that the action was taken for a legitimate nondiscriminatory reason. If the employer offers no evidence of a legitimate motive, and if the factfinder believes the plaintiff's prima facie case, then the plaintiff will prevail. However, if the employer offers such evidence, the plaintiff can try to rebut the employer's articulated reason by showing that it is a pretext and that the employer acted

---

[44] The requirement to show discriminatory intent is sometimes called the "causation requirement" – i.e., the requirement of showing that the employer took the adverse action against the plaintiff *because* of the plaintiff's race or gender. David S. Schwartz, *When Is Sex Because of Sex? The Causation Problem in Sexual Harassment Law,* 150 U. PA. L. REV. 1697, 1709–1710 (2002). A plaintiff does not need to show that the employer had an intent to discriminate when she alleges that the employer engaged in a neutral practice that had a disparate *impact* on a protected class. *See* Griggs v. Duke Power Co, 401 U.S. 424 (1971). However, disparate impact theories are difficult to prove because an employer can defend by showing that the challenged practice was "job related and consistent with business necessity." 42 US.C. 2000e-(2)(k). The business necessity requirement has been interpreted as a relatively light burden which an employer can satisfy by showing that the challenged practice serves its legitimate goals.

[45] 411 U.S. 792 (1973).

[46] McDonnell Douglas was modified in Texas Dept. of Community Affairs v. Burdine, 450 U.S. 248 (1981), St. Mary's Honor Center v. Hicks, 509 U.S. 502 (1993), and Reeves v. Sanderson Plumbing Products, Inc., 120 S. Ct. 2097 (2000).

on the basis of a discriminatory motive instead. The factfinder must then decide whether the real motive for the action was discriminatory or not.

In practice, the essential factor in establishing liability under the *McDonnell Douglas* framework is the employer's reason, that is, motive, for the adverse employment action. If the employer can convince the court that it acted from a legitimate rather than a discriminatory motive, it will prevail. Thus most cases turn on whether the employer establishes that it acted from a legitimate, nondiscriminatory motive, or whether instead the plaintiff can demonstrate that the employer's stated motive was a pretext that was asserted to disguise the true, discriminatory motive.[47]

Because, as Justice David Souter says, "employers who discriminate are not likely to announce their discriminatory motive,"[48] a Title VII plaintiff must usually establish her case by means of circumstantial evidence. One method to establish that an asserted motive is a pretext is to show that it is false. For example, if an employer refuses to promote a woman on the ground that she has only worked for the firm for five years and thus lacks sufficient experience, that claim can be refuted if it can be shown that the same employer routinely promotes men with four years or less experience to the same position. Or, if an employer refuses to hire a black woman on the stated ground that she does not have a high school diploma, that reason can be impugned by showing that the employer routinely hires white males without a high school diploma for the same job.

In general, it is reasonable to presume that if an employer's proffered nondiscriminatory motive is shown to be false, the employer has utilized a pretext to disguise its true, discriminatory, motive. For years, the EEOC and many lower federal courts took this position. The Supreme Court appeared to adopt this reasoning in *Texas Department of Community Affairs v. Burdine,* when it stated that once an employer asserts a nondiscriminatory motive for its action "the plaintiff now must have the opportunity to demonstrate that the proferred reason was not the true reason for the employment decision. This burden now merges with the ultimate burden of persuading the court that [the plaintiff] has been the victim of intentional discrimination."[49] However, in 1993, in *St. Mary's Honor Center v. Hicks,* the Supreme Court held that a Title VII plaintiff cannot prevail simply by establishing a prima facie case and then demonstrating that the employer's proffered nondiscriminatory motive is false. Rather, the Court said that the plaintiff must *both* refute the employer's stated motive *and* prove that the real motive was discriminatory.[50] The Court conceded that "the factfinder's disbelief of the reasons put

[47] *See* Ann C. McGinley, *¡Viva La Evolucion! Recognizing Unconscious Motive in Title VII,* 9 CORNELL J. L. & PUB. POL'Y 415, 448–465 (2000).

[48] St. Mary's Honor Center, 509 U.S. at 534 (J. Souter, dissenting).

[49] 450 U.S. 248, 256 (1981).

[50] 509 U.S. 502, 514–15 (1993) ("[N]othing in law would permit us to substitute for the required finding that the employer's action was the product of unlawful discrimination, the much

forward by the defendant...*may*, together with the elements of the prima facie case, suffice to show intentional discrimination," but that such findings do not *compel* a judgment for the plaintiff.[51] The *St. Mary's Honor Center* case was widely criticized as making it nearly impossible for plaintiffs to prevail.[52]

Subsequently, in *Reeves v. Sanderson Plumbing Products*, the Supreme Court retreated from its position in *St. Mary's Honor Center* position and reaffirmed that it is "*permissible* for the trier of fact to infer the ultimate fact of discrimination from the falsity of the employer's explanation."[53] The Court went on to explain:

Proof that the defendant's explanation is unworthy of credence is simply one form of circumstantial evidence that is probative of intentional discrimination, and it may be quite persuasive. . . . In appropriate circumstances, the trier of fact can reasonably infer from the falsity of the explanation that the employer is dissembling to cover up a discriminatory purpose. Such an inference is consistent with the general principle of evidence law that the factfinder is entitled to consider a party's dishonesty about a material fact as "affirmative evidence of guilt." Moreover, once the employer's justification has been eliminated, discrimination may well be the most likely alternative explanation, especially since the employer is in the best position to put forth the actual reason for its decision. *Furnco Constr. Corp. v. Waters*, 438 U.S. 567, 577, 98 S.Ct. 2943, 57 L.Ed.2d 957 (1978) ("[W]hen all legitimate reasons for rejecting an applicant have been eliminated as possible reasons for the employer's actions, it is more likely than not the employer, who we generally assume acts with *some* reason, based his decision on an impermissible consideration"). Thus, a plaintiff's prima facie case, combined with sufficient evidence to find that the employer's asserted justification is false, may permit the trier of fact to conclude that the employer unlawfully discriminated.[54]

The Supreme Court opinions in *St. Mary's* and *Reeves* underscore the conceptual centrality of employer motive in Title VII cases. Proving a discriminatory motive is the single most important task of the Title VII plaintiff. However, the available techniques for demonstrating an unlawful motive

different (and much lesser) finding that the employer's explanation of its action was not believable").

[51] *Id.* at 511 (emphasis supplied).

[52] Ruth Gana Okediji, *Status Rule: Doctrine as Discrimination in a Post-Hicks Environment* 26 FLA. ST. U.L. REV. 49 (1998); Karen W. Kramer, *Overcoming Higher Hurdles: Shifting the Burden of Proof After Hicks and Ezold*, 63 GEO. WASH. L. REV. 404 (1995); Maria Therese Mancini, *Employment Law: Providing Pretext May Be Insufficient in Title VII Employment Discrimination Cases*, 28 SUFFOLK U.L. REV. 235 (1994); Shannon R. Joseph, *Employment Discrimination: Shouldering the Burden of Proof After St Mary's Honor Center v. Hicks*, 29 WAKE FOREST L. REV. 963 (1994); Harvard Law Review Association, November 1993, *The Supreme Court, 1992 Term 2, Title VII – Burden of Persuasion in Disparate Treatment Cases*, 107 HARV. L. REV. 342, 344 (1993).

[53] 530 U.S. 133, 147 (2000) (emphasis in original).

[54] 530 U.S. at 147–48 (internal citations omitted).

only make sense in a world in which employers make employment decisions on the basis of uniform policies and practices that can be articulated. In such a world, if an employer departs from its uniform policy or preexisting practices, then the plaintiff can use that fact to show that the employer's proffered reason is a pretext. When employers have uniform policies and practices, these policies establish a baseline against which an employer's actions can be measured and a pretext can be identified. *St. Mary's Hospital* ostensibly curtailed the impact of such evidence, but *Reeves* made it clear that such evidence remains highly probative. Indeed, without evidence that an employer's practice is a departure from a uniform baseline, it is practically impossible for a plaintiff to prove that an employer's asserted motive is a pretext.

The *McDonnell Douglas* methodology of proof is undermined by many new employment practices. In the boundaryless workplace, employment decisions are decentralized. Rather than promoting uniform policies and centralized decision-making, many firms today delegate job assignment decisions to disparate, decentralized decision-makers. Sometimes these decision makers are peers. In the boundaryless workplace, decision makers are expected to exercise subjective, often ad hoc, judgments. In this setting, it is difficult to establish whether a particular decision is pretextual because there is no uniform baseline from which the employer's deviation can be identified. The baseline is constantly changing.

Under the *McDonnell Douglas* test, an employee cannot win simply by showing that the employer's reasons were inefficient, irrational, or even tyrannical. The court does not judge the reasonableness or sagacity of the business decisions. As one judge said, "The court does not sit as a super-personnel department that reexamines an entity's business decisions."[55] Rather, to prevail, the plaintiff needs to show that the reason was discriminatory – that is, a departure from a baseline because of the plaintiff's race or sex. Given today's world of work, in which employees are hired, reassigned, and laid off on a frequent and unsystematic basis, a plaintiff cannot easily refute an employer's asserted legitimate reason for its actions. Employers seek flexibility in their staffing decisions, and that flexibility often means the freedom to make ad hoc judgments that are not part of a uniform preestablished plan. This does not mean that the employer's decisions are arbitrary or random, but rather that they are made on the basis of factors that are difficult to articulate.

One example of the difficulties of disproving a pretext in the new workplace is found in the case of *Gentry and Whitley v. Georgia-Pacific Corp.* in which Katherine Whitley alleged that the company discriminated against her

---

[55] Watt v. New York Botanical Garden, 2000 U.S. Dist. LEXIS 1611, *15 (S.D.N.Y. 2000), quoting Scaria v. Rubin, 117 F.3d 652, 655 (2d Cir. 1977).

by failing to promote her to a supervisory position.[56] Whitley began working as an hourly employee in the shipping department in 1991. In 1995, in
response to a notice of vacancy, she applied for a position of shift supervisor. The selection process involved a structured interview, with numerical
scores given by a mixed-gender panel. She did not get the position. In 1996,
the company posted another shift supervisor position, for which she also
applied. By then the company changed its selection process. Under the new
process, an application involved a test of basic education skills, a structured
interview, and a creative expression exercise. Those that completed these requirements successfully were then required to participate in a workshop with
other applicants, from which a selection was made by a panel, which in turn
made recommendations to the superintendent of the shipping department.
The panel recommended three male candidates. One was awarded the job
at hand, and the other two were awarded the next available vacancies. In
1998, another vacancy was posted, again Whitley applied, and again a male
was selected and hired. Whitley then filed a discrimination complaint.

While the court conceded that Whitley had made out a prima facie case
under *McDonnell Douglas*, it found that she had not shown that the employer's stated ground – merit as revealed in a nondiscriminatory selection
procedure – was a pretext. Because the selection process had multiple components, the court refused to give credence to evidence about how the plaintiff's
score compared to the other applicants on any particular component. In addition, the court disregarded affidavits from two former supervisors which
alleged that the superintendent said he designed the multicomponent process as he did because "that is the surest way of getting the one I want and
they cannot come back on me." The court also refused to give weight to
the fact that the Georgia-Pacific Corporation had never promoted a female
production worker to a shift supervisor in the shipping department. Rather,
the court held that Whitley had not met the burden of showing that the
panel's recommendations were based on anything other than neutral criteria. In effect, the court imposed on the plaintiff an insuperable burden to
prove discrimination in the face of the multicomponent selection procedure
and the subjective element in the final decision making.

In the new workplace, claims of discrimination in promotion are particularly difficult to establish. A plaintiff who believes she has been passed
over for a promotion on the grounds of her sex or race must show that the
employer awarded the position to a male or white employee who was less
qualified. That is, the plaintiff must show that the employer's claim that the
successful applicant had superior qualifications was a pretext. Yet, courts are
reluctant to decide cases based on the relative qualifications of candidates

---

[56] 250 F.3d 646 (8th Cir. 2001). Bettye Gentry also sued for discriminatory failure to promote
to supervisor positions, but the court dismissed her claim on the ground that she had not
applied for the positions.

because they do not want Title VII to be used as a vehicle for second-guessing an employer's business judgment. Employers can make incorrect and even irrational decisions without violating Title VII – what they cannot do is make discriminatory decisions. Thus an employer's choice of an inferior candidate does not *prove* a discriminatory intent – it could merely demonstrate bad business judgment. As one court stated, "the bar is set high for this kind of evidence because differences in qualifications are generally not probative evidence of discrimination unless those disparities are of such weight and significance that no reasonable person, in the exercise of impartial judgment, could have chosen the candidate selected over the plaintiff for the job in question."[57]

In all these respects, the change in work practices makes it more difficult than ever for a plaintiff to establish a case of discriminatory treatment. When employer decisions are decentralized, unsystematic, and ad hoc, it thus becomes difficult for many plaintiffs to survive a motion for summary judgment. Employment lawyers report that there has been an increase in the number of discrimination cases decided for employers on motions for summary judgment.[58] Data collected by the Federal Judicial Center on federal civil rights employment cases decided in federal courts between 1987 and 2000 show that there was an almost 30 percent increase in the number of federal civil rights employment cases decided on pretrial motion since 1987. At the same time, there was an 80 percent decline in plaintiffs' success rates on those motions.[59] It is fair to assume that almost all federal civil rights employment cases are discrimination cases and that many of the pretrial motions were motions for summary judgment. Thus the Federal Judicial Center data provide empirical support for the view that the changing workplace is making it increasingly difficult for plaintiffs to prevail on the merits on their discrimination claims.

2. Class Action Certification

Because of the onerous burden on plaintiffs who bring individual employment discrimination claims, many are turning to class actions as a vehicle for vindicating their claims of discrimination. In class actions, plaintiffs can allege either disparate treatment or disparate impact. Class-wide disparate

---

[57] Daniels v. Home Depot, Inc. 2002 U.S. Dist. LEXIS 11990, *26–27 (E.D. La. 2002), quoting Celestine v. Petroleos de Venezuela SA, 266 F.3d 343, 357 (5th Cir. 2002). *See also* Deines v. Texas Dep't of Regulatory Services, 164 F.3d 277, 279 (5th Cir. 1999).

[58] Richard Seymour, Director of the Employment Discrimination project of the Lawyers' Committee for Civil Rights, estimates that three-quarters of discrimination lawsuits are dismissed on motions for summary judgment. *See* Kirstin Downey Grimsley, *Worker Bias Cases Are Rising Steadily; New Laws Boost Hopes for Monetary Awards*, WASHINGTON POST, May 12, 1997, p. A1.

[59] Judicial Statistical Output, containing data from the Federal Judicial Center, available at http://teddy.law.cornell.edu:8090/egi-ginjs/betaall8700. (Last consulted 1/17/03.) The data are presented in appendix B.

impact claims are directed against seemingly neutral policies that have a disparate and disadvantageous impact on a protected group. Class-wide disparate treatment claims involve allegations of intentional discrimination against women or minorities. While such claims, like individual disparate treatment claims, require the plaintiffs to show that the employer acted with a discriminatory intent, class action plaintiffs can make a circumstantial case with statistics that demonstrate a pattern or practice of discrimination. The use of statistics provides an evidentiary end-run around the problem of demonstrating pretext. However, both disparate impact and disparate treatment class action plaintiffs encounter unique difficulties when the workplace has a diffuse and decentralized decision-making structure.

In practice, the success of class action lawsuits often turns on the question of class certification. If the plaintiffs manage to obtain class certification, then the companies usually settle the claim in order to avoid a lengthy, expensive, and potentially embarrassing lawsuit. Conversely, if class certification is denied, the plaintiffs often give up. Because of the central role of class certification, meeting the requirements for class certification is the crucial issue in the ability of class action plaintiffs to succeed. Under Rule 23(a) of the Federal Rules of Civil Procedure, to be certified as a class action, the moving party must show:

(1) the class is so numerous that joinder of all members is impracticable,
(2) there are questions of law or fact common to the class,
(3) the claims or defenses of the representative parties are typical of the claims and defenses of the class, and
(4) the representative parties will fairly and adequately protect the interests of the class.

These necessary elements are known, in shorthand, as the requirement for the party seeking class action status to demonstrate numerosity, commonality, typicality, and adequacy.[60]

---

[60] Rule 23 (a), Federal Rules of Civil Procedure. In addition, the moving party must show that one of the elements of 23(b) are present. They are:

(1) the prosecution of separate actions by or against individual members would create a risk of (A) inconsistent or varying adjudications with respect to individual members of the class ... (B) adjudications with respect to individual members of the class which would ... impair or impede [the other class members'] ability to protect their interests; or

(2) the party opposing the class has acted or refused to act on grounds generally applicable to the class, thereby making appropriate final injunctive relief or corresponding declaratory relief with respect to the class as a whole; or

(3) the court finds that the common questions of law or fact common to the members of the class predominate over any questions affecting only individual members, and that a class action is superior to other available methods for the fair and efficient adjudication of the controversy.

In the boundaryless workplace, the requirements of typicality and commonality are difficult to satisfy. When the claims involve individualized assessment of each class member's claim, then there is no typicality or commonality. Thus allegations of discriminatory treatment that resulted from decentralized decision making are particularly hard to aggregate into a class action.

For example, in *Allen v. Chicago Transit Authority*,[61] the court refused to certify a class action that sought to challenge the employer's promotion decisions as racially biased because it found that the company's promotion decision-making policy was not sufficiently uniform to satisfy the requirement that class actions must involve "questions of law or fact common to the class."[62] In that case, decisions concerning promotion to exempt positions were made at the department level, where departmental managers had wide discretion to decide how and whether to fill positions. The only uniform policy was a requirement that anyone selected for promotion ultimately had to be approved by the vice president of human services. A number of black employees brought suit, alleging that the decision making was biased in that qualified blacks were repeatedly passed over for promotion to jobs that were given to less qualified whites. The court considered whether the claims could be brought as a class action, and concluded that the very decentralized nature of the decision making meant that it could not be maintained on a class-wide basis. The court found:

The record shows promotion and pay decisions are made at the level of individual departments by many different people using different methods with varying human resources involvement. . . . While Czech [the vice president of human resources] was involved in some departments' decisions, he had little to do with the personnel decisions in others. . . . Furthermore, there are dozens of departments and over 1200 exempt CTA employees. It is unclear how Czech could have exercised control over all personnel decisions on such a large scale. Similarly, the record does not reveal unfettered discretion in the CTA's decisionmakers. The CTA has a written anti-discrimination and affirmative action policy. Managers are required to put the reasons for their decisions in writing. At most, the record shows that Czech and human resources shared responsibility for promotion and pay decisions with the individual department managers. This is not sufficient to establish a centralized or entirely subjective practice.

Because the company had neither a highly centralized nor an entirely subjective practice regarding promotions, the court held that the complaint failed to allege a uniform discriminatory practice that satisfied the requirement of common questions of law and fact.

---

[61] Allen v. Chicago Transit Authority, 2000 WL 1207408 (N.D.Ill.).
[62] Federal Rules of Civil Procedure, Rule 23(a).

The *Allen* case is typical of many courts' approach to the issue of class certification in the face of decentralized decision-making authority. Yet without
class action certification it is often impossible for plaintiffs to prevail in a
race or sex discrimination claim. For reasons explained above, the burden
of establishing liability for individual plaintiffs is so onerous in the boundaryless workplace that they can only prevail when they bring a class-wide
claim in which statistical data can be used to demonstrate a discriminatory
pattern and practice.

In a recent class action lawsuit against the Sodexho Marriott Corporation,
one district court judge took a different approach. The company, formerly
Marriott Management Services, provides food and facilities management
services for institutions such as hospitals, hotels, corporations, college dor-
mitories, and schools. It has over one hundred thousand employees, most of
whom work on the premises of the clients at over five thousand locations.
Each unit has one or more in-unit managers and an overall manager known
as the general manager. The general managers report to above-the-unit managers known as district managers, who have greater salaries, prestige, and
perquisites. There are also higher-level managers in the corporate headquarters in areas such as sales, human resources, and finance.

Until 1998, all managers were salaried by grades, from forty to sixty-
four, with most in-unit managers in the forties, most general managers in the
low fifties, district managers in the mid-fifties, and corporate headquarters'
managers in the top range. In 1998 the company adopted a broad band
system in which the multiple grades were collapsed into single bands, placing
in-unit managers in a relatively low band and above-the-unit managers in a
higher band.

Sodexho has decentralized promotion policies that give managers unfettered discretion in filling vacancies. Employees in any division can apply for
job openings that arise in any division throughout the company with the
consent of their supervisor. The hiring manager has total discretion about
whom to interview and there are no company rules, guidelines, or criteria
regarding the promotion process. Indeed, supervisors are not required to
take notes during interviews or to explain their choices., Thus each manager
makes promotion decisions based on whatever criteria she or he chooses,
without guidance or accountability.[63]

In 1992, the company established a Diversity Roundtable to which five
or six selected minority general managers were invited to meet regularly
with senior white executives for mentoring and advancement opportunities.
The roundtable was founded by the then president, Charles O'Dell, with the
avowed purpose of helping mid-level black managers advance to high-level
jobs. However, it failed to accomplish its goal. One member, Ellen Early,
tried to apply for a higher-level job, but her supervisor refused to let her.

[63] McReynolds v. Sodexho Marriott Services, Inc., 208 F.R.D. 428, 432–33 (D.D.C. 2002).

When she complained to a white executive on the roundtable, he refused to intervene. Other members of the roundtable reported similar experiences. After a few years, the minority members of the roundtable pronounced it a sham.[64]

In 2001, a number of black managers, including some minority members of the roundtable, filed a class action lawsuit, alleging that Sodexho's promotion policies and practices discriminated on the basis of race. They alleged that the lack of consistent policies and written records enabled white senior managers to act on subtle biases and unconscious racism in their promotion decisions. In their motion for class certification, the plaintiffs presented statistical evidence that African Americans were significantly underrepresented in above-the-unit managerial positions, holding constant seniority and other qualifications. They also showed that the African American managers were clustered in accounts that served primarily black clients and that black managers were more likely to report to another African American manager. In the company overall, blacks were clustered in the lowest pay categories, comprising 26 percent of the workforce in the four bottom rungs. In the highest paid positions – those at regional and corporate headquarters – blacks comprised merely 1.9 percent.[65]

In its opposition to class certification, the company argued that its decentralized decision-making structure and its lack of uniform promotion policies meant that there could not have been a conspiracy or policy of intentional discrimination, and hence there was no typicality in the claims. Indeed, in numerous cases with similar facts over the past few years, courts have denied class certification on the grounds that without a uniform policy, there was no evidence of discrimination. In a surprising departure, the D.C. Circuit in *McReynolds v. Sodexho Marriott Services, Inc.*, stated that the defendant's position "would permit companies to escape Title VII class actions by minimizing the amount of control that they exercise over individual managers. Such a holding," the court continued, "would run afoul of the purpose of Title VII, which is 'not to provide redress but to avoid harm' by encouraging employers to adopt antidiscrimination policies and to educate their personnel on Title VII's prohibitions."[66]

The *Sodexho* court's approach demonstrates a sensitivity to the need to tailor the class action vehicle to the modern workplace. It remains to be seen whether the *Sodexho* approach will influence other courts faced with discrimination claims in the face of diffuse and decentralized human resource practices.

---

[64] Neely Tucker, *Bias Suits Scale Corporate Ladder*, WASHINGTON POST, Nov. 30, 2002, pp. A1, A10.

[65] *Id.*, at A10.

[66] McReynolds v. Sodexho Marriott Services, Inc, *supra* n. 63.

3. Naming and Blaming the Appropriate Defendant

The new decentralized workplace, with its diffused authority structure, not only makes it difficult for victims of discrimination to prove their case, it also makes it difficult for them to bring suit against the people who are harassing them. The flattening of workplace hierarchies and the delegation of authority to peers in the workplace elevates and legitimates the power of the working group. Under contemporary human resource practices, peer groups are used to allocate work tasks, evaluate individual performances, distribute rewards and perks, and impose punishments. In some cases, peers are called upon to make decisions regarding hiring, promotions, layoffs, and discharge. And in an increasing number of firms, supervisor decisions can be appealed to a peer review appeal panel.

All of these techniques enhance the power of the working group. While the empowerment of the peer group can be an egalitarian development, it also can have deleterious consequences for women and minorities. As explained above, workers in traditionally all-male or all-white workplaces are often hostile to the introduction of minorities and women. If integration occurs as a result of an affirmative action program by which the women or minorities jump over incumbent white males in rank or salary, the hostility can be intense. Also, in workplaces that are historically predominantly male or white, the incumbents often generate a culture that communicates to women or minorities that they do not belong. Through techniques of ostracism, bullying, shunning, or other means of exclusion, the predominant whites and/or males can make the newcomers feel unwelcome, insecure, and inadequate. Furthermore, the predominant group often refuses to share knowledge of the tricks of the trade or to engage in customary forms of cooperation, thereby undermining the competence as well as the confidence of women or minorities. Thus, for example, there are numerous instances in which women fail to succeed in formerly male jobs for such simple reasons as not knowing where the toolroom is or not knowing how to fix a particularly temperamental machine.[67]

The more an employer delegates power to peers, the more the old boy networks can marginalize, penalize, and terrorize women and minorities. Many women who are victimized by these means give up in despair. Some bring discrimination claims, but the claims are difficult to win.

When a woman or minority encounters bullying, ostracism, informal sabatoge, or failure to train by coworkers, their legal recourse is to sue for harassment. However, they cannot sue the coworkers directly – they must sue the employer. To establish a claim for coworker hostile environment harassment under Title VII, the plaintiff must show (1) membership in a protected group; (2) that she was subject to unwelcome harassment; (3) the

[67] *See generally* Abrams, *New Jurisprudence of Sexual Harassment*, 83 CORNELL L. REV. at 1196–99; Schults, *Reconceptualizing Sexual Harassment*, 107 YALE L.J. at 1762–69.

harassment occurred because of membership in the protected group; (4) the harassment was so severe and pervasive as to affect a term, condition, or privilege of employment; and (5) the employer knew or should have known of the harassment and failed to take adequate remedial action.[68] Several of these requirements are difficult to establish in the boundaryless workplace.

The first problem is that when a party alleges harassment that was not overtly sexual in nature, most courts find that it does not come within Title VII. Rather, they hold that informal bullying, ridiculing, shunning, or ignoring are not sufficiently tangible harms to come within the statute. Thus, for example, in *Scusa v. Nestle U.S.A. Company, Inc*, the plaintiff was ostracized, shunned, and isolated by her coworkers and supervisors after she filed a sexual harassment complaint. The Court of Appeals for the Eighth Circuit dismissed her suit, both for the initial harassment and for the subsequent retaliation, because, according to the court, rudeness, ostracism, snubbing, and shunning by coworkers do not amount to an "adverse employment action" for purposes of Title VII liability.[69] Similarly, in *Matvia v. Bald Head Island Management, Inc.*, the Fourth Circuit characterized the uncivility of coworkers, including ignoring and spying on an employee, as "ordinary workplace strife" and held that it could not constitute an adverse employment action.[70]

In addition, harassing conduct must be "because of sex" to be actionable. When there is no overtly sexual element in the conduct, courts are reluctant to find coworker mistreatment, however egregious, to be because of sex. Often workers experience mistreatment by coworkers – slights, snubs, rude remarks, hostile glances, and so forth. Someone can be excluded from a group for any number of reasons – because they wear the wrong clothes, listen to the wrong music, have the wrong hobbies, have an off-putting personal style. None of these workplace unpleasantries are necessarily because of sex or gender. Someone can be different, or downright irritating, without being the victim of discrimination.

Courts usually find that harassment is because of sex only when there is an element of sexuality in the offensive conduct. Thus, when the unwanted conduct is motivated by desire between heterosexual parties of opposite genders – such as repeated requests for dates or sexual favors – or when conduct involves sexual aggression, such as unwanted touching or even rape – courts almost automatically will find it to be "motivated" by sex. But nonsexual mistreatment, even if pointedly directed at women, is rarely seen as "because of sex."[71]

---

[68] Jacob-Mua et al. v. Veneman, 289 F.3d 517, 522 (8th Cir. 2002); Scusa v. Nestle U.S.A. Company, Inc., 181 F.3d 958, 965 (8th Cir. 1999).

[69] 181 F. 2d at 969.

[70] Matvia v. Bald Head Island Management Inc., 229 F.3d 261, 272 (4th Cir. 2001).

[71] Schwartz, *When Is Sex Because of Sex?* 150 U. Pa. L. Rev. at 1719–28; Schultz, *Reconceptualizing Sexual Harassment*, 107 Yale L.J. at 1683.

Several feminist scholars have urged the courts to adopt an approach that focuses not on the *motive* for, but on the *impact* of, the challenged behavior. Katherine Franke, for example, contends that the essence of sexual harassment is the instantiation of "hetero-patriarchal gender norms" into the workplace, and that liability should attach to employer actions that have this effect.[72] Kathryn Abrams proposes instead that sexual harassment should be understood as actions that "preserve male control and entrench masculine norms in the workplace."[73] Vicki Schultz argues that sexual harassment should be defined as actions that have the purpose or effect of undermining a woman's competence to perform her job.[74] While all these suggestions are valuable, the courts to date have adhered to a more narrow focus on causality and require the plaintiff to show that sex or race, rather than simple distaste, caused the challenged conduct.

Finally, and most problematically, woman and minority plaintiffs who complain of coworker harassment must prove that the employer knew or should have known about the harassment and failed to take remedial measures. The plaintiff has the burden of proof on both issues, and the burden is formidable. If a worker fails to report coworker harassment for fear of subtle or not-so-subtle retaliation, her failure to report makes it easy for a firm to deny knowledge of the harassment, and thus escape liability. Some courts find that an employer is on notice of harassment if other employees have reported similar incidents, but not all courts do so.[75] Some courts find that an employer is not on notice of harassment if the employee complains to the wrong supervisor. For example, in one case, an employee reported harassment to her immediate supervisor, but the court concluded that because it was a low-level supervisor, it did not count as notification to the corporation.[76]

The "knew or should have known" standard makes it more difficult for a plaintiff to prove coworker harassment than to prove supervisory harassment. In 1998, in two cases decided the same day, the Supreme Court announced the framework for analyzing liability for supervisor workplace harassment. In *Farragher v. City of Boca Raton* and *Burlington Industries v. Ellreth*, the Supreme Court held that a firm is vicariously liable for its supervisor's harassment even if the firm was unaware of the

---

[72] Katherine M. Franke, *What's Wrong with Sexual Harassment?*, 49 STAN. L. REV. 691, 772 (1997).

[73] Kathryn Abrams, *New Jurisprudence of Sexual Harassment*, 83 CORNELL L. REV. at 1172.

[74] Schultz, *Reconceptualizing Sexual Harassment*, 107 YALE L.J. at 1762.

[75] *Compare* Madray v. Public Supermarkets, Inc., 208 F.3d 1290 (11th Cir. 2000) *with* Jackson v. Quanex Corp. 191 F. 3d 647 (6th Cir. 1999); Hurley v. Atlantic City Police Dept., 174 F.3d 93 (3rd Cir. 1999).

[76] Madray v. Publix Supermarkets, Inc., 208 F.3rd 1290 (11th Cir. 1999). *See also* B. Glenn George, *If You're Not Part of the Solution, You're Part of the Problem: Employer Liability for Sexual Harassment*, 13 YALE J. LAW & FEMINISM 133, 153–54 (2001).

harassment.[77] A firm can only escape liability for unknown supervisory harassment if it can prove that (1) the employer exercised reasonable care to prevent and correct promptly any sexually harassing behavior, and (2) the plaintiff employee unreasonably failed to take advantage of any preventive or corrective opportunities provided by the employer or to avoid harm otherwise.

The *Farragher* framework makes it easier for a plaintiff to prevail against a supervisor than against a coworker for sexual harassment. When a supervisor is the alleged harasser, the plaintiff does not have to prove anything about the employer's knowledge of the alleged harassment. Rather, the burden is on the employer to prove that it took reasonable steps to prevent harassment in the first place.[78]

The heightened requirement of knowledge in the case of coworker harassment makes it particularly difficult for Title VII to redress coworker claims. While Title VII is designed to prevent discrimination practiced by employers, the contemporary workplace is structured to push much of the authority down to lower levels. In the face of this reality, a new theory must be devised to hold the employer responsible for the oppressive and discriminatory conduct of coworkers that can result.

4. Crafting a Remedy

In addition to making it more difficult to establish liability, the new employment practices have made conventional civil rights remedies problematic. As discussed above, civil rights enforcement efforts were initially directed at corporate hiring and compensation practices in order to obtain equal pay and access to jobs for women and minorities. But it quickly became apparent that women and minorities needed not simply jobs, but good jobs. They needed access to jobs in the primary sector that offered promotion opportunities, training, job security, and benefits – that is, jobs that were part of internal labor markets. Hence Title VII plaintiffs sought not only hiring mandates, but also affirmative action to help women and minorities enter the primary labor market and move up the advancement ladders.

In an era of promotional ladders within firms, it was logical and appropriate for Title VII plaintiffs to seek remedies that gave women and minorities access to the upper rungs of the promotion ladders. Hence many lawsuits challenged employers' use of discriminatory tests and other selection devices as well as subjective supervisory assessment measures in promotion decisions.[79] They sought remedies that restructured the promotion criteria

---

[77] Farragher v. City of Boca Raton, 524 U.S. 775 (1998); Burlington Industries v. Ellreth, 524 U.S. 742 (1998).

[78] George, *If You're Not Part of the Solution*, 13 YALE J. LAW & FEMINISM at 162–63.

[79] *See, e.g.*, Price Waterhouse v. Hopkins, 490 U.S. 228 (1989) (upholding a challenge to the denial of partnership to a woman on the basis of sex stereotyping); Griggs v. Duke Power Co.,

and seniority procedures to enable minorities and women to advance quickly. They also sought, and achieved, affirmative action and quotas for hiring and promotion to the higher rungs in the job ladders.[80]

Title VII remedies for employment discrimination were tailored to redress discrimination within firms that utilized internal labor markets. Affirmative action and requirements that firms promulgate goals and timetables for measuring their compliance with equal employment objectives helped numerous women and minorities gain access to previously segregated workplaces and helped them move up within the firm. However, the remedies assumed that there were identifiable job ladders that defined advancement opportunities within firms, and operated to move women and minorities up within them. These same remedies are problematic in firms with flattened job structures that provide lateral rather than hierarchical mobility. Affirmative action in promotion is meaningless when there is no promotional ladder by which advancement can be measured. New remedies are necessary if women and minorities are to gain access to power within large corporations.

Today most Title VII suits are brought by private parties rather than by the Equal Employment Opportunity Commission (EEOC), and they seek monetary awards rather than injunctive decrees. While damage remedies such as back pay, front pay, and even punitive damages are available for victims of discrimination, these remedies provide compensation for harm done, not a correction of discriminatory conditions. Individuals can benefit from generous monetary awards, but such awards do not directly alter the working conditions for either the victim or others stuck in the same discriminatory situation. It is possible that the prospect of extremely large damage awards can shatter glass ceilings, warm up chilly climates, and help women and minorities break into the "old boy" clubs by scaring corporations into changing their practices. But runaway jury awards in Title VII cases are rare and random events. Furthermore, corporations can limit their liability for large damage awards through liability insurance or the use of mandatory arbitration.[81] Given the availability of insurance, Title VII's monetary remedies become a cost of doing business and thus a weak inducement for change.

---

401 U.S. 424 (1971) (upholding a challenge to racially discriminatory testing and selection devices).

[80] *See, e.g.,* Franks v. Bowman, 424 U.S. 747 (1976) (affirming retroactive seniority relief to remedy effects of past discrimination). *See also* U.S. v. Lee Way Motor Freight Co., 625 F.2d 918 (10th Cir. 1979), in which the court held that in light of the history of race discrimination in this firm, the court required it to adopt an affirmative action plan, modify the seniority system, and fill existing vacancies with minorities. It also remanded for the lower court to consider whether minimal height requirements had discriminatory impact on Latino-American employees.

[81] *See* Susan Sturm, *Second Generation Employment Discrimination: A Structural Approach,* 101 COLUM. L. REV. 458, 475–78 (2001) (on use of insurance against Title VII liability).

D. Proposals for Redressing Discrimination in the New Workplace

Employment discrimination in the new workplace is more subtle and intractable than in the old. As discussed, sharply drawn legal tests for liability are difficult to apply in part because the legal wrongs themselves are difficult to identify. Women and minorities experience exclusion and encounter glass ceilings, yet it is not always clear whether or how the employer has engaged in wrongdoing. The harms from such actions are far from trivial – cooperation of coworkers and access to grapevine information is often the key to success in today's workplace. Yet it is difficult to police such conduct under conventional antidiscrimination law.

Some legal scholars have addressed the problem of these "second generation employment discrimination claims" by proposing new definitions of liability.[82] While this is important, we must also devise new procedural mechanisms to determine liability and devise remedies that actually transform workplaces. Some European countries are experimenting with new theories of liability and new types of remedies in order to address the unique problems of discrimination in the changing workplace. These approaches are described below.

1. New Conceptions of Liability

Several legal scholars have recently considered the types of difficulties women and minorities encounter in the new workplace. Vicki Schultz, for example, has addressed the problem of workplace cliques that sabotage the work efforts of women who enter traditionally male occupations.[83] Schultz provides an account of the role of gender in the workplace, emphasizing the ways in which "the gender stratification of work – who does what type of work, under what conditions, and for what reward" is a more potent source of women's disadvantage than is sexual conduct per se.[84] She argues that sexual conduct is often intertwined with forms of hostility designed to demean and disable women who attempt to work in a "man's world." Shultz presents numerous examples to show how male workers use mechanisms of exclusion to retain the material and psychological privileges that accompany access to secure and well-paying jobs. To remedy these forms of sexual discrimination, Schultz urges that all types of gender-based conduct that undermine a women's competence be defined as a legal wrong under Title VII. To that end, she advocates that sexual harassment be reconceived not as a sexual affront per se, but as "conduct designed to undermine a woman's competence."[85] She proposes a legal standard by which actions by an employer or its agent that deliberately undermine the competency of

---

[82] *Id.* at 460.
[83] *See* Schultz, *Reconceptualizing Sexual Harassment*, 107 YALE L.J. at 1756–69.
[84] *Id.* at 1748.
[85] *Id.* at 1769.

a person because of his or her gender would be actionable under Title VII. Schultz acknowledges that it is often difficult to prove whether the challenged conduct is motivated by gender, so she further proposes that in contexts in which women work in traditionally male jobs, courts adopt a presumption that any competence-sabotaging conduct is motivated by gender.[86] Schultz finds support for her view in Justice Ruth Bader Ginsburg's concurring opinion in *Harris v. Forklift Systems, Inc.*,[87] in which Justice Ginsburg stated that to establish a hostile work environment, a plaintiff must "prove that a reasonable person subjected to the discriminatory conduct would find . . . that the harassment so altered working conditions as to '[make] it more difficult to do the job.'"[88]

David Yamada has written about the problem of supervisors who undermine a worker's morale and confidence.[89] His discussion is not limited to gender- or race-based harassment claims, but rather applies to all types of bullying by supervisors. He proposes a new cause of action, called the "Intentional Infliction of a Hostile Work Environment," which would make an employer liable for "intentionally subject[ing] the plaintiff to a hostile work environment."[90] If a work environment were found to be "hostile by both the plaintiff and by a reasonable person in the plaintiff's situation," the employer would be liable unless he could show (1) that he exercised reasonable care to prevent and correct the challenged conduct, and (2) that the plaintiff failed to utilize any preventive or corrective opportunities provided by the employer.[91] While Yamada's proposal is not limited to gender or racial discrimination claims, it is an attempt to address the kinds of pernicious conduct that are particularly problematic for women and minorities in the new workplace.

The proposals by Schultz and Yamada are bold and creative efforts to reach beyond existing discrimination law and address heretofore unacknowledged forms of workplace injustice. Both scholars have called attention to the problem of subtle, yet powerful, forms of disempowerment that in today's workplace can make the difference between an individual's success or failure. The virtue of the proposals is that they attempt to identify, name, define, and constrain some of the forms of harmful conduct that appear to be increasing. However, neither proposal fully contends with the problems women and minorities face in the boundaryless workplace. They both propose theories of liability to constrain actions by *supervisors* that intimidate, harass, sabotage, or otherwise bully a subordinate. But as this chapter has

---

[86] *Id.* at 1801.
[87] 510 U.S. 17 (1993).
[88] Harris, 510 U.S. at 25 (Ginsburg, J., concurring).
[89] *See* Yamada, *"Workplace Bullying,"* 88 GEO. L. J. at 480–83.
[90] *Id.* at 524.
[91] *See id.* at 524–27.

argued, the most serious forms of discrimination in the new workplace are often not the result of *supervisor* conduct but of *coworker* conduct.

In addition, both of the proposals, while thought provoking, are difficult to apply. The standards they propose for liability – Schultz's competence-undermining test and Yamada's hostile work environment test – are vague. To base liability on such standards could pose difficult issues of proof, create uncertainty, foment litigation over trivial insults, and run the danger of judicial micromanagement of employee relations. For these reasons, their proposals are best understood as providing broad new conceptions of workplace justice rather than as detailed blueprints for legal reform.

2. A New Procedure for Adjudicating Discrimination Claims

We have seen how difficult it is to address or remedy many new types of employment discrimination under the existing Title VII framework. Currently, Title VII is directed to harm caused by employers or their agents; it assumes a hierarchical authority structure. Title VII reaches coworker harassment only when the employer knew or should have known of the harassing conduct, and failed to take adequate remedial measures.[92] This is because the law prohibits those who have authority in the employment relationship from exercising their power in a discriminatory fashion.[93] While there is authority and power in the new workplace, it is often exercised through cliques and peer groups, defying traditional tools for assigning accountability. Yet, as courts frequently remind us, Title VII is not a generalized code of workplace civility. Therefore, to redress the new forms of employment discrimination, it is necessary to combine new concepts of substantive liability, such as Schultz's redefinition of sexual harassment or Yamada's proposed tort of intentional creation of a hostile work environment, with new procedures and remedies that operate on horizontal as well as vertical power relations.

At present, employment discrimination claims are brought to a court or an administrative agency such as the Equal Employment Opportunity Commission or a state human rights agency. These tribunals have the virtue of placing decision-making authority in the hands of someone who is not part of the workplace that gave rise to the alleged discrimination, and who can apply neutral, nondiscrimination norms. However, both courts and agencies are also remote from the workplace, circumscribed in the evidence they can hear and limited in the remedies they can issue. Furthermore, as Yale law professor Judith Resnik has pointed out, courts and agencies have constricted approaches to standing that prevent them from treating discrimination as the collective harm that it is. Rather, by requiring the individual targets of

---

[92] *See* Gunnell v. Utah Valley State Coll., 152 F.3d 1253, 1265 (10th Cir. 1998); Blankenship v. Parke Care Ctrs., 123 F.3d 868, 873 (6th Cir. 1997); Yamaguchi v. United States Dep't of Air Force, 109 F.3d 1475, 1483 (9th Cir. 1997).

[93] *See* Burlington Indus. v. Ellreth, *supra* n. 77 at 742, 761–62.

discrimination to bring an action, courts cannot address the ways in which a culture of harassment can arise that shapes power relationships among all individuals in a workplace.[94]

Furthermore, as discussed, much of today's discrimination takes the form of coworker conduct that marginalizes a member of an outsider group. It is difficult to imagine a court imposing civil liability on a group of workers for ganging up on a coworker or for spreading nefarious gossip unless the conduct constitutes a crime or tort, such as assault or rape. For a court to judge the subtle aspects of exclusion and marginalization that debilitate women and minorities in the workplace would involve it in micromanaging workplace etiquette, something courts are reluctant to do.

In addition, it is not always feasible for individuals to obtain redress from a court or administrative agency. Courts and agencies are inundated with complaints and have large backlogs so that they are not always able to hear cases in a timely fashion. Litigation is expensive and many victims of employment discrimination lack the resources to enforce their rights.

Even if the courts were not backlogged and litigation was not expensive, there is an additional reason why these new forms of discrimination are not best handled in an adversary procedure. The adversary process gives each side a stake in proving the truthfulness of its claims and the falsity of the opposing party's claims, even when doing so inflicts damage on a continuing relationship. Where complaints involve allegations of exclusion, marginalization, or subtle forms of harassment, the complaining party must either demonize her coworkers or risk demonization herself. For example, if a plaintiff complains she has been shunned and denied access to informal know-how, her coworkers might defend by claiming that they refused to socialize with her because they disliked her and found her to be obnoxious or even paranoid. The complaining party then must counter by impugning the motives and good faith of the dominant group, accusing them of racism or sexism or worse. That is, the courtroom setting tends to make each side exaggerate its accusations and harden its position rather than seek concilia-tory solutions. In a harassment case, this kind of name-calling occurs not as lunchroom gossip, but in the open in a public trial. Even if the accusations are true, the public nature of the setting makes it unlikely that such a dynamic will help a workplace to function better.

For all these reasons, conventional litigation is not an attractive option for remedying new types of employment discrimination. Rather, it is necessary

---

[94] Judith Resnik, *The Rights of Remedies: Collective Accountings for and Insuring Against the Harms of Sexual Harassment,* in DIRECTIONS IN SEXUAL HARASSMENT LAW (Catherine A. McKinnon and Riva B. Siegal, eds., 2003). Susan Sturm has also pointed out that the activities that produce exclusion of women and blacks are highly contextualized, and not amenable to crisp, clear rules of right and wrong. *See* Sturm, *Second Generation Employment Discrimination,* 101 Colum. L. Rev. at 475–78.

to devise a workplace-based dispute resolution procedure to supplement, not substitute for, existing procedural mechanisms.

A workplace-based dispute resolution mechanism could provide an accessible and flexible approach to remedying workplace discrimination. In recent years there has been an increased interest in utilizing alternative dispute resolution mechanisms to resolve employment discrimination disputes. Increasingly, employers are instituting mediation, arbitration, peer review, and other dispute resolution systems into the workplace. If properly structured, these workplace-based mechanisms could prove to be a useful means of resolving discrimination claims in the boundaryless workplace. However, as with any procedural mechanism, the devil is in the details.

First and foremost, alternative dispute resolution procedures to redress employment discrimination must be designed to identify rather than obscure the existence of discrimination. Such a system cannot delegate responsibility for recognizing and remedying discriminatory conduct to the work group, because the work group is often the source of the problem. Similarly, it cannot delegate those tasks to top management, because they have an interest in smooth operations, which often means condoning the discriminatory conduct. Instead, it is necessary to devise a system of workplace-specific alternative dispute resolution that utilizes neutral outsiders to scrutinize workplace conduct, identify subtle as well as overt discriminatory practices, and fashion effective remedies.

Two types of alternative dispute resolution involve the use of outside neutrals – mediation and arbitration. Mediation is a method by which an outside neutral helps parties achieve a consensual resolution of a dispute. In arbitration, an outside neutral hears evidence and imposes a resolution on the parties. While mediation is often preferable because it results in a consensual resolution, it is not always possible to resolve discrimination claims in such a forum. Mediators aspire to a stance of neutrality, yet neutrality compels them to refrain from intervening to correct preexisting power disparities that might exist between the parties – disparities in resources, sophistication, knowledge, or experience – that might compromise one side's ability to negotiate a fair settlement of the dispute. In discrimination cases, the complainant is by definition a member of a subordinate group, so that disparities in power are almost always present.

Where mediation does not work, arbitration should be used to hear claims and make an independent decision to resolve a dispute. To provide redress for subtle forms of employment discrimination, the outside arbitrator should not merely apply norms internal to the workplace, but must also serve as a check on the possibility of tyranny and capture by insider cliques. Thus the arbitrator would have to apply external antidiscrimination law.

The use of arbitration and mediation for addressing employment discrimination complaints has been growing at a rapid rate. Prior to 1991, the use of arbitration by nonunion firms to decide employment disputes was extremely rare. In 1991, the Supreme Court decided in *Gilmer v. Interstate/Johnson Lane* that an individual could be compelled to submit his age discrimination complaint to arbitration.[95] By 1995, in the wake of *Gilmer*, the Government Account Office found that almost 10 percent of nonunion firms utilized arbitration for discrimination claims, and another 8.4 percent were considering doing so. By the late 1990s, the evidence suggests that even more firms had introduced arbitration systems for their nonunion workforces. In 2001, in *Circuit City Stores, Inc. v. Adams*, the Supreme Court removed whatever doubts persisted about the application of the Federal Arbitration Act (FAA) to such employment arbitrations systems.[96] As a result, employers now have wide latitude to design alternative mechanisms to avoid costly and risky employment litigation. At present, nearly as many workers are covered by nonunion arbitration systems as are covered by union contracts.[97]

The use of arbitration to resolve employment discrimination disputes has been highly controversial. Many existing nonunion arbitration systems are biased toward employers and serve to evade, rather than enforce, external norms. They often work to employees' disadvantage through such procedural provisions as shortening the statute of limitations for bringing complaints, raising the employee's burden of proof, limiting discovery, and restricting the remedies that a victorious employee can recover.[98] Also, under current interpretations of the FAA, arbitral awards receive virtually no judicial review.[99] Under the FAA, an arbitral award may not be vacated for an error of law or erroneous fact finding, but only for arbitrator misconduct or if the arbitral award displayed a "manifest disregard of the law."[100] As a result, employees can be compelled to bring their employment discrimination complaints to decision makers who are biased in favor of the employer or who simply lack knowledge of antidiscrimination law, and yet whose decisions cannot be appealed.[101]

---

[95] 500 U.S. 1 (1991).

[96] 532 U.S. 105 (2001).

[97] See Katherine Van Wezel Stone, *Employment Arbitration Under the Federal Arbitration Act,* in EMPLOYMENT DISPUTE RESOLUTION AND WORKER RIGHTS IN THE CHANGING WORKPLACE 27, 27–28 (Adrienne E. Eaton & Jeffrey H. Keefe, eds., 1999).

[98] See Katherine Van Wezel Stone, *Mandatory Arbitration of Individual Employment Rights: The Yellow Dog Contract of the 1990s,* 73 DENVER L. REV. 1017, 1051 (1996).

[99] See Katherine Van Wezel Stone, *Rustic Justice: Community and Coercion Under the Federal Arbitration Act,* 77 N.C. L. REV. 931, 954–55 (1999) (citing cases that establish the narrow standard of review under the Federal Arbitration Act (FAA)).

[100] Wilko v. Swan, 92 U.S. 427, 436 (1953), *overruled on other grounds by* Rodriguez de Quijas v. Shearson/Am. Express Inc., 490 U.S. 477 (1989).

[101] For criticisms of employer-designed arbitration systems in the nonunion setting, *see* Stone, *Mandatory Arbitration,* 73 DENVER L. REV. at 393; Joseph R. Grodin, *Arbitration of Employment Discrimination Claims: Doctrine and Policy in the Wake of* Gilmer, 14 HOFSTRA LAB. & EMP. L.J. 1 (1996); David S. Schwartz, *Enforcing Small Print to Protect Big Business: Employee and Consumer Rights Claims in an Age of Compelled Arbitration,* 1997 WIS. L. REV. 33.

Despite the potential abuses of arbitration, it is possible to imagine an internal dispute resolution system that could address the subtle but powerful forms of discrimination in today's boundaryless workplaces. Such a system could seek to vindicate equality norms without the limitations imposed by current Title VII doctrine. For example, arbitrators could take into account many kinds of evidence, including shop history and lore, to identify departures from past practices and consider whether or not an employer's stated reasons for an action was a pretext. Furthermore, claimants could impugn the plausibility of an employer's asserted reason by showing that the action was irrational or inconsistent with sound business judgment – arguments that, while comporting with common sense, are not persuasive to a court. In addition, workplace arbitration could embrace disputes between coworkers as well as disputes between employees and employers. While a court may not find a particular type of mistreatment sufficiently serious to be actionable under Title VII, an arbitrator may be better attuned to the contextualized nature of the harm.

The Supreme Court has recently created an incentive for employers to develop workplace dispute resolution systems for handling discrimination complaints in cases involving allegations of supervisor sexual harassment. As noted earlier in this chapter, in *Farragher v. City of Boca Raton*[102] and *Burlington Industries v. Ellreth*,[103] the Court held that firms whose supervisors have engaged in sexually harassing conduct can avoid liability if they have internal procedures in place to prevent and redress harassment claims, and if the complaining employee unreasonably fails to utilize them. These decisions encourage employers to develop procedures to address harassment complaints against supervisors. While some courts have found that firms need not have very sophisticated internal procedures to prevail on a *Farragher* defense, others require more than an open-door policy or a complaint hotline; they require an in-house mechanism for filing harassment complaints and having them heard.[104]

---

[102] 524 U.S. 775 (1998).
[103] 524 U.S. 742 (1998).
[104] *Compare* Hill v. American General Finance, Inc., 218 F.3d 639, 643–44 (7th Cir. 2000) (stating that no sexual harassment procedure was necessary to satisfy the Farragher affirmative defense, and finding a policy that consisted of a leaflet stating the company intended to comply with the equal opportunity laws and to maintain a workplace free from harassment, combined with a telephone number of an official to whom complaints could be lodged, "may leave room for improvement, [but] the policies get the job done"), with Gentry v. Export Packaging Company, 238 F.2d 842, 847–48 (7th Cir. 2001) (stating that to satisfy the affirmative defense, a sexual harassment policy must provide a "meaningful process whereby an employee can express his or her concerns regarding an individual within a working environment," and finding the policy at issue inadequate because it did not tell employees to whom to report allegations of harassment). *See generally* Martha S. West, *Preventing Sexual Harassment: The Federal Courts' Wake-up Call for Women*, 68 Brooklyn L. Rev. 457 (2002).

Over time, it is hoped that more courts, when ruling on the *Farragher* defense, will scrutinize employer workplace harassment procedures for their adequacy.

If the courts were to adopt a broad interpretation of *Farragher* and *Ellreth* and apply the same framework to coworker claims, then employers would have a powerful incentive to establish dispute resolution mechanisms for these claims. To succeed, however, the dispute resolution systems would have to utilize external decision makers. By bringing in outside neutrals to adjudicate workplace disputes, such a system would offer the possibility of injecting an external standard that could transcend the rule of the clique. Some corporations are already designing systems to resolve both grievances between the employee and the firm and disputes among employees. If properly structured, internal dispute resolution systems could help counteract the development of workplace fiefdoms and cliques, redress abuses of hidden authority, and bring external norms to the workplace.[105]

In order to identify and redress subtle forms of employment discrimination that arise in the new workplace, courts would have to impose minimal standards of due process on the arbitration process.[106] Thus, for example, a court would have to ensure that the complainant had a right to counsel, to take discovery, subpoena witnesses, obtain documents, and cross-examine adverse witnesses. The arbitration procedure could not unduly shorten limitations periods, shift burdens of proof, or impose high costs on the party seeking to vindicate her discrimination claim. There would also have to be de novo judicial review for issues of law to ensure that arbitrators did not merely defer to the rule of the clique, but rather applied Title VII and other employment laws to the workplace.

The proposed workplace arbitration should be a supplement to, not a substitute for, the enforcement of statutory employment rights. Under this proposal, a worker with a claim of discrimination should be free to choose, after a dispute arose, whether to submit it to her workplace-specific arbitration procedure or whether to bring it to a court or human rights agency. If she selected arbitration, the arbitrator's decision would be binding on issues of fact, but it would be appealable on issues of law. In order to preserve the right of appeal, a record would have to be made and a written opinion rendered. Also, under the proposal, the worker would be entitled to engage in limited discovery and to have an attorney represent her in the arbitral hearing.

---

[105] Susan Sturm gives examples of internal dispute resolution systems established by Deloitte & Touche, Intel, and Home Depot to deal with complaints of subtle forms of gender bias and exclusion that decreased women's advancement prospects. *See* Sturm, *Second Generation Employment Discrimination*, 101 Colum. L. Rev. at 458.

[106] *See* Stone, *Rustic Justice*, 77 N.C. L. Rev. at 1024–28 (suggesting a mechanism to provide increased scrutiny and to inject external norms into private arbitration tribunals).

The foregoing proposal provides a mechanism for resolving discrimination disputes in the new workplace. It is a mechanism that would enable women and minorities to obtain redress for competency sabotage, bullying, shunning, harassing, and other forms of gender-based or race-based conduct that undermine their employment prospects. Workplace arbitration, as proposed herein, would cost more than most current forms of nonunion arbitration because it calls for a transcript, a reasonably full hearing, and a written opinion. However, the proposal also provides a relatively expeditious fact-finding procedure that could stave off many lawsuits. Employment discrimination suits are often factually dense matters. To the extent that documentary evidence and credibility assessments can be determined in an arbitral setting, employers and employees can often be spared lengthy and expensive litigation.

The proposal does not provide a new test for liability, but rather a new mechanism for resolving discrimination disputes. It is a mechanism that would enable each workplace to identify and impose sanctions for competency sabotage, bullying, shunning, harassing, and other forms of gender-based or race-based conduct that threaten once again to undermine the employment prospects of women and minorities. And by doing so, it is hoped that it would provide an approach to employment discrimination that would enable women and minorities to achieve true equality of opportunity to pursue an unbounded career.

3. New European Approaches to Employment Discrimination

In other countries, some scholars and policy-makers have recognized the problematic nature of existing discrimination law in the face of the types of gender-based and race-based bullying and harassment that occur in the contemporary workplace and have developed an approach that could hold great promise for the United States. The approach involves the imposition of positive duties on employers to eliminate discrimination of all types and to foster equality in the workplace. The positive duties approach is neither adversarial nor fault-based – it does not assign blame or impose penalties for past discrimination. Instead, positive duties require employers to formulate equality goals, to monitor their workplaces for inequality, and to alter practices and patterns of conduct that stand in the way of achieving their equality goals.

The positive duties approach to employment discrimination was described in a 2000 report entitled EQUALITY: A NEW FRAMEWORK, REPORT OF THE INDEPENDENT REVIEW OF THE ENFORCEMENT OF UK ANTI-DISCRIMINATION LEGISLATION, prepared by a commission chaired by Bob Hepple, Master of Clare College, Cambridge, and former head of the UK Industrial Tribunal. The report states the problem as follows:

[T]he current framework was designed largely to deal with a model of organisations with hierarchical, vertically integrated and centralised bureaucracies. This is a top-down rule-making approach which focuses on individual fault-finding and depends on retrospective investigation of an act alleged to be motivated by an unlawful ground of discrimination. . . . [Today's] [o]rganisations are flattening their hierarchies, giving more authority to lower-level managers, and demanding a high quality workforce. . . . Equality of opportunity increasingly depends, not simply on avoiding negative discrimination, but on training, improving skills, developing wider social networks, and encouraging adaptability. The present framework places too much emphasis on state regulation and too little on the responsibility of organizations and individuals. . . . [P]rocedures and remedies for individuals need to be made more effective to deal with the increasingly subtle and complex nature of discrimination."[107]

After surveying employers in the United States, Northern Ireland, and the United Kingdom and reviewing legislation in those countries, the commission concluded that equality cannot be achieved simply on the basis of voluntary compliance or the promulgation of best practices. Rather, it stated that "The first lesson which we draw from the North American and Northern Ireland experiences is that there will not be significant improvements in the representation of women and ethnic minorities in the workforce without positive action."[108]

The commissioners identified those laws in the countries studied that impose positive duties on employers to monitor and eradicate discrimination. For example, they describe legislation in Northern Ireland pursuant to which public authorities are required to make equality issues central to public debates, and private employers are required to take positive steps to achieve fair representation of both Protestant and Roman Catholic employees in their workforces. In Ontario, Canada, the Ontario Pay Equity Act of 1987 requires employers to identify pay discrimination and institute corrective measures. In the United Kingdom, the Race Relations Act of 2000 requires public authorities to promote racial equality in carrying out all public functions. The report highlights these as examples of positive duties that could help eliminate workplace discrimination by restructuring institutions.

The UK equality report made many recommendations to extend positive duties in the United Kingdom. For example, it recommended that all UK employers be required to conduct a periodic review of employment practices, including recruitment, training, promotion, and redundancy, "for the purpose of determining whether members of ethnic minorities, women and disabled persons are enjoying, and are likely to continue to enjoy, fair

---

[107] Bob Hepple, Mary Coussey, & Tufyal Choudhury, EQUALITY: A NEW FRAMEWORK, REPORT OF THE INDEPENDENT REVIEW OF THE ENFORCEMENT OF UK ANTI-DISCRIMINATION LEGISLATION 19–20 (2000).
[108] *Id.* at 70.

participation in employment in the undertaking."[109] Where an employer finds significant under-representation, it would have a duty to "draw up and implement an employment equity plan to identify and remove barriers to the recruitment, training and promotion" of members of the under-represented groups.[110] Failure to do so could make the employer liable for unlawful discrimination in an industrial tribunal, which would have the power to require positive action, set goals and timetables, order appropriate antidiscrimination actions, and award monetary penalties. The authors recommended a pyramid of enforcement devices, beginning with persuasion and encouragement of voluntary compliance, and moving up to more coercive measures including investigations by public agencies, judicial enforcement, and sanctions.[111] The authors hope that the imposition of positive duties, combined with a flexible yet firm enforcement strategy, will be able to address the new forms of employment discrimination that are resistant to current antidiscrimination laws.

Sandra Fredman of Oxford University applauds the positive duties approach as responsive to changing workplace conditions:

[T]he aim [of this legislation] is to introduce equality measures rather than responding to complaints by individual victims. . . . At the root of the positive duty is a recognition that societal discrimination extends well beyond individual acts of racist prejudice. Thus equality can only be meaningfully advanced if practices and structures are altered pro-actively by those in a position to bring about real change.

As Fredman further explains, positive duties move attention from the perpetrator of the discriminatory act to "the body in the best position to promote equality."[112] This is a great advantage in the new workplace, in which the perpetrator is often either difficult to identify or an individual who holds no power to change workplace conditions.

The concept of positive duties is gaining widespread acceptance in Europe. Thus, for example, in September 2002, the European Parliament adopted a directive amending the Treaty of Rome to require mainstreaming of gender equity issues for all public policies and decisions. The Mainstreaming Directive states that "Member States shall actively take into account the objective of equality between men and women when formulating and implementing laws, regulations, administrative provisions, policies and activities . . ."[113] The directive also requires member states to adopt measures to ensure full equality in practice between men and women in the public and private sector,

---

[109] *Id.* at 71–72.

[110] *Id.*

[111] Hepple et al., EQUALITY 59.

[112] Sandra Fredman, DISCRIMINATION LAW 176–77 (2003).

[113] Directive 202/73/EC of the European Parliament and of the Council of 23 September 2002.

including monitoring and other measures to encourage employers to promote equal treatment in a "planned and systematic way."[114]

It is too soon to know whether state-imposed positive duties requiring employers to monitor and eradicate discrimination will change employer behavior. As Fredman recognizes, the positive duties are not self-evident or self-enforcing. They require a body to identify what practices are in need of correction and what constitutes the content of the duty to correct. Yet several European countries and Canada have begun to use the law in innovative ways in order to restructure and monitor the workplace on an ongoing basis. We can learn a lot from their efforts.

E. Conclusion

The changing nature of the workplace forces us to reconsider the definitions of liability, remedies, and procedures contained in existing discrimination law. Women and minorities who have suffered workplace discrimination should receive compensation for their losses. But equally important, workplaces that exclude or disadvantage people on the basis of their gender, race, or ethnicity must be forced to restructure to remove the impediments to equality. A well-designed workplace-specific alternative dispute system might provide better redress and promote more restructuring than the existing adversarial procedures available under Title VII. In addition, the European approach of imposing positive duties on employers to monitor and redress discrimination might also be an effective approach to attaining a prospective change. Neither approach will work in a vacuum, however. First, it is necessary that the new forms of discrimination be identified and understood so that new theories, procedures, and remedies can be devised.

[114] *Id.*

9

Unionism in the Boundaryless Workplace

The new employment relationship and its corresponding job structures were initially constructed in nonunion environments, and they continue to operate almost exclusively in nonunion environments to this day. Hewlett Packard, TRW, and the General Electric Company (GE) are three leading exemplars of the new work practices described in Chapter 5. Hewlett Packard and TRW have always been nonunion, and GE engaged in aggressive deunionization efforts in some of its plants, and then instituted boundaryless workplace practices after the unions had been eliminated. The sequence of deunionization first, workplace restructuring later, was commonplace in many large corporations in the 1980s.[1] As discussed in Part I, the same sequence characterized industrial relations practices in major corporations in the late nineteenth and early twentieth centuries when internal labor markets were first established. At that time, employers first broke the unions and then instituted Taylorism and other work rationalization measures. Like the implementation of scientific management in the early twentieth century, today's boundaryless workplaces are being created in the vacuum left by the deunionization drives of the previous decade.

In the past twenty years, union density in the private sector declined from almost 16.5 percent in 1983 to 9.0 percent in 2001.[2] This decline is particularly striking in light of the fact that during most of that period, workers' real wages were declining, so that one might have expected aggressive organizing activity and union growth.[3] The union decline was most pronounced in large manufacturing firms in which internal labor markets had been the most deeply entrenched. While there has been some union growth since 1990, it

---

[1] *See* Thomas A. Kochan, Harry C. Katz & Robert B. McKersie, THE TRANSFORMATION OF AMERICAN INDUSTRIAL RELATIONS 47–80 (1986).
[2] *See* U.S. Dept. of the Census, STATISTICAL ABSTRACT OF THE UNITED STATES 411 tbl. 628 (122d ed. 2002).
[3] *See id.* at 443 tbl. 698.

has been primarily in public sector and service sector workplaces, such as health care and janitorial providers – fields that have been the least affected by the new work practices described in Part II.[4] The precipitous decline of unions in manufacturing during the 1980s gave management a free hand to restructure work practices. As a result, conventional unions have not been able to gain a foothold in the new high-technology-intensive workplaces that are expanding rapidly today.[5]

The nonunion nature of the boundaryless workplace is cause for concern. Historically, unions have been an important mechanism for identifying and redressing work-related injustice. Union-negotiated wage and benefit levels brought an unprecedented standard of living and security to millions of Americans – both union and nonunion alike. Union seniority arrangements and just cause clauses freed many workers from the whims of abusive or arbitrary foremen. In addition, union-sponsored arbitration systems have forced employers to honor their explicit and implicit contracts and prevented them from engaging in opportunistic behavior.[6] Unions have also been valuable for giving employees a voice in their workplaces.

In addition to providing representation in the workplace, unions are an essential element of a democratic polity. As Alexis de Tocqueville pointed out long ago, voluntary organizations in the United States are the vehicles by which the private concerns of citizens are shared and translated into public issues.[7] It continues to be the case that without robust voluntary organizations, it is virtually impossible for individuals to articulate shared concerns and bring their interests into the public arena. Unions play an important role both in the workplace and in the political process to ensure that the concerns of working people and other disadvantaged groups are expressed and heard. They represent millions of people who do not have any other access to the political process, providing democratic participation and voice to a sector of the population that would otherwise remain silent and unrepresented. Therefore, they are an essential element of a pluralistic democracy.[8]

The labor movement is the only significant organized group that has an interest in pressing for social legislation to regulate working conditions,

---

[4] *See* Katherine Van Wezel Stone, *The Legacy of Industrial Pluralism: The Tension Between Individual Employment Rights and the New Deal Collective Bargaining System*, 59 U. CHI. L. REV. 575, 581–82.

[5] *See* William B. Gould IV, *Some Reflections on Fifty Years of the National Labor Relations Act: The Need for Labor Board and Labor Law Reform*, 38 STAN. L. REV. 937, 942–43 (1986) (discussing the unions' inability to organize in high-tech industries).

[6] *See* Katherine Van Wezel Stone, *Policing Employment Contracts Within the Nexus-of-Contracts Firm*, 43 U. TORONTO L.J. 353, 376–77 (1994) (discussing the unions' role in enforcing implicit contracts for job security and deferred compensation).

[7] *See* Alexis de Tocqueville, 2 DEMOCRACY IN AMERICA 106 (Henry Reeve trans., 1961); *see also* Robert A. Dahl, POLYARCHY: PARTICIPATION AND OPPOSITION 20 (1971).

[8] *See* Dahl, Polyarchy 20; *see also* Thomas C. Kohler, *Civic Virtue at Work: Unions as Seedbeds of the Civic Virtues*, 36 B.C.L. REV. 279, 300–332 (1995).

promote employee protections, ameliorate unemployment, and ease transitions between jobs. Unions have also been at the forefront of lobbying efforts for civil rights, welfare benefits, food stamps, environmental protection, national health insurance, and many other issues of general social welfare. Indeed, the labor movement is the only major political institution that is dedicated to promoting the interests of working people generally.

Unions could play a unique role in shaping the legal rules to govern the emerging regime of work. They could also help ensure that employers' promises under the new psychological contract are enforced. For example, Chapter 7 described many instances in which employers promised employees training, networking, and employability, yet later attempted to capture their employees' human capital by seeking to enforce post-employment restraints. Unions can help enforce promises for training and ensure that employers do not try to usurp the human capital they promised to give their employees.[9] Similarly, Chapter 8 described the dangers of new forms of discrimination that are emerging in the changing workplace practices. Unions could help design and operate the dispute resolution mechanisms that have been proposed to help address problems of coworker as well as supervisory discrimination.

This chapter explores the prospects for employee representation in the new boundaryless workplace. It examines both union practice and labor law, arguing that the shift from the old to the new employment relationship has rendered many aspects of conventional trade unionism and existing labor law obsolete. The following chapter proposes new models of unionism and changes in labor law that embody a vision of employee representation appropriate to the new workplace.

A. The Tension Between Unionism and the Boundaryless Workplace

Despite the dramatic decline of unions in the past decade, survey evidence suggests that most employees want some form of workplace representation. Richard Freeman and Joel Rogers conducted a large survey of worker attitudes in the mid-1990s and found that 87 percent of American workers want some form of representation.[10] According to Charles Heckscher, "polls show that people want unions, but not the unions we have now."[11] Why then is the new workplace shaping up to be a nonunion juggernaut?

---

[9] *See also* Peter Cappelli, THE NEW DEAL AT WORK: MANAGING THE MARKET-DRIVEN WORK FORCE 240–41 (1999) (calling for a new infrastructure to enforce training agreements and verify credentials).

[10] *See* Richard B. Freeman & Joel Rogers, WHAT WORKERS WANT 147 (1999).

[11] Century Fund Task Force on the Future of Unions, WHAT'S NEXT FOR ORGANIZED LABOR 53 (1999) (statement of Charles Heckscher).

In order to consider the prospects for employee representation in the new boundaryless workplace, it is necessary to understand why unions have not made significant inroads there. What features of the current labor laws are rooted in the old employment relationship and therefore inappropriate for large sectors of today's workforce? What kinds of policies or practices could unions adopt that would be compatible with the boundaryless workplace? What kinds of labor law reforms would promote boundaryless unionism? These questions are addressed in this chapter.

1. Can Unions Function in the Boundaryless Workplace?

In the 1980s and 1990s, employer power vis-à-vis their unions increased as a result of many factors, including increased global competition in product and labor markets,[12] the growing hegemony of neoliberal ideology,[13] and changes in public policy that were disadvantageous to unions.[14] Some labor relations scholars posit that this increase in employer power fueled both the rise of the new employment relationship and the decline of unions – two independent results of a single cause.[15] They reason that there is no necessary incompatibility between new workplace practices and traditional unionism, but that, to the contrary, unions can instill the elements of employee cooperation and trust necessary to enable the workplace to be restructured and improve its functioning.[16] Some labor relations scholars have therefore urged unions to embrace high performance objectives as a way to become relevant to the changing workplace.[17]

Eileen Appelbaum and Rosemary Batt were among the first scholars to argue that high performance work practices are compatible with traditional trade unionism. In the early 1990s, Appelbaum and Batt studied the development of a nonunion "human resource model" of industrial relations that they found was quickly replacing the previous union-centered model.[18] The human resource model was characterized by quality circles,

---

[12] Katherine Van Wezel Stone, *To the Yukon and Beyond: Local Laborers in a Global Labor Market*, 3 J. SMALL AND EMERGING BUS. L. 93 (1999); Katherine Van Wezel Stone, *Labor and the Global Economy*, 16 MICH. J. INT'L LAW 987 (1995) (on impact of global competition on union bargaining power).

[13] Harry Arthurs, *Globalization of the Mind*, 12 CAMBRIDGE J. LEG. STUD. 219 (1997).

[14] Katherine Van Wezel Stone, *Labor and the Corporate Structure: Changing Conceptions and Emerging Possibilities*, 55 U. CHI. L. REV. 73 (1988).

[15] *See* Paul Osterman, SECURING PROSPERITY 5 (1999) (arguing that employer power in the workplace increased in the 1990s).

[16] *See, e.g.,* Jeffrey Pfeffer, THE HUMAN EQUATION: BUILDING PROFITS BY PUTTING PEOPLE FIRST (1998); Eileen Appelbaum & Rosemary Batt, THE NEW AMERICAN WORKPLACE (1994).

[17] *See, e.g.,* Barry Bluestone and Irving Bluestone, NEGOTIATING THE FUTURE: A LABOR PERSPECTIVE ON AMERICAN BUSINESS 18–30 (1992). *See generally* John G. Godard and John T. Delaney, *Reflections on the "High Performance" Paradigm's Implications for Industrial Relations as a Field*, 53 INDUS. & LAB. RELS. REV. 482, 493 (2000).

[18] Appelbaum & Batt, THE NEW AMERICAN WORKPLACE.

self-managed teams, skill-based pay, and other high performance innovations in human resource policies. Appelbaum and Batt identified two variations of high performance work practices. One, "lean production," utilized
total quality management (TQM), reengineering of work flows, and performance measurement in an attempt to centralize decision making and to
align goals between the company and its employees. The other, "team production," utilized autonomous work teams and emphasized decentralized
decision making, employee involvement, and employee participation. Lean
production, they noted, was more likely to be found in nonunion settings and
team production was more likely to be in a unionized setting. Appelbaum
and Batt compared the performance results of the two approaches. Through
case studies of the use of teams, just-in-time production techniques and total
quality programs at the unionized firms of Corning, Saturn, and Xerox –
where unions participated in making the programs work – they found that
the programs in all three companies yielded efficiency and quality gains.
On this basis, they concluded that the two approaches produced equivalent
results in terms of reducing defects and increasing efficiency.[19]

Some scholars have made an even stronger claim about the relationship
between new work practices and unions. Mary Ellen Kelly and Bennett
Harrison found that the use of team production and other high performance
work practices were most effective when they operated in a union environment. That is, they found that far from impairing efficiency, unions actually
helped to generate efficiencies.[20] Similarly, Saul Rubenstein found that at
the General Motors' Saturn plant, union involvement helped to make lean
production more effective.[21]

More recently, Appelbaum, Thomas Bailey, and others published case
studies of union-friendly firms that have been successful at combining new
work practices with a continuing commitment to providing job security.[22] In
one case study, they describe a sheet steel plant where the local union helped
establish team production, worker retraining, job enlargement, and other
forms of high performance work systems in the early 1990s in exchange for
a job security agreement in the union contract. While the examples illustrate
the potential for efficiencies that result when union-abetted restructuring is
combined with a firm-level commitment to job security, the authors also
recognize that many local unions and managements lack sufficient trust to
realize the benefits.[23]

[19] *Id.* at 127–143.
[20] Maryellen Kelley & Bennett Harrison, *Unions, Technology and Labor Management Cooperation*, in Unions and Economic Competitiveness (Lawrence Mishel & Paula B. Voos, eds.,
1992). *See also* Bluestone & Bluestone, Negotiating the Future 15–16.
[21] Saul A. Rubinstein, *The Impact of Quality Performance: The Case of the Saturn Corporation*,
52 Indus. & Lab. Rel. Rev. 197 (2000).
[22] Eileen Appelbaum, Thomas Bailey, Peter Berg, & Arne L. Kallenberg, Manufacturing
Advantage: Why High-Performance Work Systems Pay Off (2000).
[23] *Id.* at 54–56.

Jeffrey Pfeffer has also argued that new work practices can be implemented successfully with unions because unions can provide the necessary trust and cooperation to enable them to function.[24] In one example, Pfeffer describes a galvanized steel plant of the LTV Corporation in which the local union played a major role not merely in organizing production but also in human resource functions. With union support, the plant adopted many features of the boundaryless workplace, such as flattened hierarchies, elimination of executive perks, and pay-for-skills compensation systems.[25] Pfeffer reports that the company elicited the union's cooperation by committing to job security and promising not to avoid the union.[26]

While Batt, Appelbaum, Pfeffer, and others convincingly demonstrate that some forms of workplace restructuring can occur with a union present, their examples all come from cases in which a company makes a commitment to job security. Indeed, Kelley and Harrison are explicit in their conclusion that production teams work best where there is an enterprise-level commitment to job security.[27] Hence the findings do not necessarily apply to work practices that do not involve such a commitment.

Most of the cases in which unions helped to implement restructuring involved companies that have adopted a team production approach. Autonomous team production involves the use of groups of nonsupervisory workers to handle tasks of work allocation, job assignment, intragroup compensation, and internal conflicts.[28] In the 1980s, autonomous team production was introduced in many manufacturing firms, particularly those in the auto, steel, and apparel industries. Often the introduction of teams was accomplished with union cooperation.[29] But while team production is a significant departure from the hierarchical command-and-control workplaces of the Taylorist era, it is a system that also retains a commitment to job security. Teams require employment stability so that team members can learn the techniques and develop the trust essential to teamwork. Also, team production involves significant engineering changes in physical equipment and human attitudes, so that it is a long-term investment in both equipment and in employees.

While unions may be compatible with team production, many other features of the new employment relationship do not involve teams or implicit

---

[24] Pfeffer, THE HUMAN EQUATION.
[25] *Id.* at 234–35.
[26] *Id.* at 236.
[27] Kelley & Harrison, *Unions, Technology and Labor Management Cooperation* 250–51; Appelbaum et al., MANUFACTURING ADVANTAGE.
[28] Kochan et al., TRANSFORMATION OF AMERICAN INDUSTRIAL RELATIONS 99–100.
[29] *See* Appelbaum et. al., MANUFACTURING ADVANTAGE 54–58. As the new wave automobile plants of Saturn and Nummi demonstrate, when teams and unions blend their roles, the productivity results can be impressive. Rubinstein, *Impact of Quality Performance,* 52 INDUS. & LAB. REL. REV. at 214.

promises of job security. As reported in Chapter 5, Paul Osterman's survey of over 500 firms found that between 1992 and 1997 the use of all forms of high performance work organizations (HPWO) increased *except* the use of teams. This led Osterman to conclude that "teams are probably the most difficult work innovation to implement and the one that is most likely to be disrupted by turnover and restructuring."[30] Osterman also found that firms that used the high performance practices of job rotation, quality circles, and TQM provided less employment stability than other firms of their type. He found that by the late 1990s the workplaces that used high performance work practices in 1992 experienced more layoffs than those that did not. Yet he also found that the layoffs were not accompanied by overall downsizing. The constant turnover – churning of the workforce – in the HPWO firms suggests that those firms are not engaged in downsizing, but in building a boundaryless workplace.[31] In such a setting, autonomous teams – with or without a union – cannot flourish.

The failure of autonomous teams to expand in boundaryless workplaces is not altogether surprising. Autonomous teams require workforce continuity. Employees who are trained to work in teams are often given training in cooperation and teamwork skills that an employer is loathe to lose. Also, teams only work when team members trust each other – a process that requires multiple repeat interactions between team members. Teams thus rely upon the very feature that the new workplace repudiates – long-term attachment of the employee to the firm. Osterman found that those high performance practices that survived and grew throughout the decade of the 1990s were quality circles, job rotation, and TQM.[32] Unlike teams, these practices involve up-skilling but they do not require long-term employment.

Today unions face a question of major strategic and tactical significance. Should they oppose new work practices or find ways to adapt? Should they oppose broad-banding, flexible staffing, outsourcing, and other practices that erode the boundaries of the traditional work unit, or should they find methods of operation that protect workers in the face of the new employment practices? Many unions have adopted the former stance. However, like the railroad unions' demands for featherbedding in the 1960s, opposition to innovation earns unions a bad name but does not stop the train of progress. Another approach, and the one advocated here, is to identify the ways in which traditional union practices are inconsistent with the boundaryless workplace, and then try to imagine a form of unionism that is both compatible with the new workplace and capable of protecting the employees who work there.

---

[30] Paul Osterman, *Work Reorganization in an Era of Restructuring: Trends in Diffusion and Effects on Employee Welfare*, 53 INDUS. & LAB. REL. REV. 179, 186 (2000).
[31] *Id.* at 190–92.
[32] *Id.* at 186.

2. Union Practices and the Old Employment Relationship

There are several respects in which core practices of American labor unions are fundamentally at odds with the boundaryless workplace. For example, two of the most fundamental pillars of industrial unionism are seniority and narrow, precisely defined job definitions. Yet both are inconsistent with the new employment relationship. Seniority systems allocate priority and privilege on the basis of length of service. Because today's workplace practices do not embody a commitment to long-term employment, the seniority concept has lost much of its practical function. Similarly, narrow job classifications are designed to specify as precisely as possible the work that any individual is expected to perform. This protects workers against excessive demands by a supervisor, and at the same time protects them against displacement by outsiders who might otherwise be hired to perform their work. But narrow job classifications are the opposite of the flexible work practices of the new employment relationship.

Seniority and narrow job classifications were union-negotiated accommodations to management's creation of job ladders and the establishment of internal labor markets.[33] Seniority was originally a practice that large companies such as the Westinghouse Corporation, General Motors, and the Ford Motor Company instituted in order to build loyalty and encourage attachment in the early 1900s.[34] It was part of the program of personnel management to establish internal labor markets and create long-term attachment between the worker and the firm. The practice of seniority was subsequently embraced by industrial unions, so that by the 1930s seniority became a central demand of unions in their efforts to counteract job insecurity. Today seniority has become so entrenched in union practice and principle that, in the words of labor historians David Montgomery and Ronald Schatz, "many workers today find it difficult to imagine any other principle as just."[35]

The use of narrow job classifications had a similar origin. It originated in scientific management programs established by Taylor, who urged management to study, time, and then subdivide all jobs. Once jobs were broken down to their narrowest elements, they were fully specified on routing cards so that workers could be instructed in proper performance. Each job was then retimed and assigned a "scientifically correct" rate. Taylor was

---

33 For a detailed description of labor-management efforts to construct a scheme of job classifications and wage differentials consistent with scientific management, *see* Katherine Van Wezel Stone, *The Origins of Job Structures in the Steel Industry*, in LABOR MARKET SEGMENTATION 65–70 (D. Gordon, M. Reich, & R. Edwards, eds., 1975).

34 Ron Schatz, THE ELECTRICAL WORKERS: A HISTORY OF LABOR AT GENERAL ELECTRIC AND WESTINGHOUSE, 1923–1960, 19–20 (1983).

35 *See* David Montgomery, THE FALL OF THE HOUSE OF LABOR: THE WORKPLACE, THE STATE, AND AMERICAN LABOR ACTIVISM, 1865–1925, 139, 140–43 (1987). *See also* Peter Doeringer & Michael Piore, INTERNAL LABOR MARKETS AND MANPOWER ANALYSIS (1971) (describing how seniority became the standard of fairness under industrial unionism).

adamantly opposed to the notion of a standard rate – his mission was to individualize wages to the narrowly defined jobs. In the early twentieth century, the craft unions resisted Taylor's efforts to subdivide tasks, and called for a return to the standard rate. Sometimes strikes resulted, such as the one at the Watertown Arsenal described in Chapter 2. After World War I, when Westinghouse, GE, and other industrial establishments sought to introduce scientific payment schemes with disparate rates, their workers went on strike. However, unlike their craft predecessors a decade earlier, these strikers did not seek a return to a standard single rate. Rather, they sought a series of standard rates, graduated according to well-defined job definitions. By that time, unions had come to see graduated rates pegged to specific job classifications as a means to provide orderly advancement and constrain foreman favoritism.[36]

Other practices of unions that are antithetical to the boundaryless workplace are job-bidding systems that require employers to rely on internal promotion to fill openings, and bumping rights that establish specific demotion paths for employees during downsizing. Like seniority, these practices discourage cross-utilization and lateral mobility.

In addition to insisting on the use of seniority for job assignment, retention, and progression, unions bargain for compensation structures that base pay on three factors: job definition, hierarchical role, and length of service. These three factors seem fair to many because they appear to provide uniformity between similarly situated workers. In the past, corporations often utilized these same three factors to determine pay rates in internal labor markets, with or without unions present.[37] However, none of these factors are compatible with the new workplace: formal hierarchy is waning, strict job definitions are disfavored, and longevity is no longer valued.

Modern compensation theory seeks to tie compensation to the person, not to the job. Today's managers want to base pay on performance or productivity, not on job title or length of service.[38] They do not seek uniformity in compensation. Rather, workers who perform the same job may earn different amounts because of their differential performances or differential value to the firm. By insisting on uniform job-based pay rates and rejecting individual-based rates, unions today encounter fierce employer resistance.

Other union bargaining goals that are antithetical to the boundaryless workplace are scope clauses, which keep work inside the bargaining unit, and no-subcontracting clauses, which keep work inside the plant. Unions

---

[36] See Montgomery, FALL OF THE HOUSE OF LABOR 113, 122–24; Stone, *The Origins of Job Structures* 43–44.

[37] See, e.g., Stone, *The Origin of Job Structures.* 65–70. (describing the development of the pay structure at U.S. Steel in the postwar era).

[38] See Cappelli, NEW DEAL AT WORK 232–33 (describing contemporary compensation practices that are not based on seniority or hierarchy premiums).

also bargain for provisions that require supervisors to refrain from performing bargaining unit work and in this way attempt to draw tight jurisdictional lines around their certified units. These practices seek to prohibit the very blurring of departmental and firm boundaries that characterize the boundaryless workplace.

In addition, two key features of most union collective bargaining agreements are just cause limitations on dismissal and the establishment of arbitration systems. Both provisions are important sources of protection for employees against managerial discretion and favoritism. But in the new workplace they are even more of a hindrance to management than before. In today's boundaryless workplace, decision makers need to move, and to remove, people quickly on the basis of a decision maker's assessment of the individual's current and future contribution to the task at hand. Lacking job definitions and orderly progression charts, these judgments are highly subjective, ad hoc, and difficult to justify to third parties. Thus, union job security protections, as well as seniority, make flexible staffing and just-in-time production difficult.

Furthermore, unions traditionally bargain for longevity-linked pay and benefits, such as step raises, back-loaded pensions, and length-of-service-based vacation benefits. These types of union pay and benefit practices encourage longevity and are the antithesis of a just-in-time workforce.

Thus it is evident that many traditional union bargaining goals are incompatible with the essential features of the boundaryless workplace. Union-promoted measures such as seniority for promotions and downsizing, just cause for dismissal provisions, and longevity-based pay and benefits were tailored to the old internal labor markets. They helped to ensure that the former job structures operated in a fair and even-handed fashion. But those same measures now operate to impede the flexibility that employers currently seek. As a result, employers find these features of unionism burdensome and have escalated their efforts to deunionize. Where unions exist, employers are increasingly bargaining for, and unions are increasingly conceding, flexibility in work rules. According to a survey conducted by the Federal Mediation and Conciliation Service, by 1999 the subject of work-rule flexibility had become the most important topic in labor-management negotiations after wages and benefits.[39] Nevertheless, unions remain committed to seniority, just cause, and other features of the old psychological contract.[40]

The current tension between established union practice and emerging job structures finds a parallel in the 1920s. In that decade, employers waged a fierce campaign against the American Federation of Labor (AFL) craft unions. Employers wanted to eliminate AFL unions where they currently

---

[39] Joel Cutcher-Gershenfeld, *Is Collective Bargaining Ready for the Knowledge-Driven Economy?* 3 PERSP. ON WORK 20, 22 (1999).

[40] *See* BNA 1999 UNION CONTRACT PROVISIONS 140:320 (on contract clauses).

existed and keep them out of the mass production industries where they were trying to gain a foothold. As a result of the employer open-shop offensive, union membership declined from 5 million in 1920 to under 3.5 million by 1930, a drop in union density from 19.4 percent of the nonagricultural work force to 10.2 percent.[41] The AFL's weakness was in part the result of employers' aggressive open-shop campaigns, but it was also in part due to the fact that nineteenth-century craft unions had policies and programs that were not compatible with the job structures of mass production firms. The AFL craft unions emphasized control of entry to crafts and apprenticeship, practicing what has been termed "job control unionism."[42] The craft workers' job security came from their knowledge of particular crafts. The craft unions' power was linked to specific production methods; they were not agile at adapting to technological change. Thus, when employers shifted from craft production to mass production, many craftsmen found their skills obsolete and their power gone. Craft workers therefore resisted technological change mightily, rather than seeking an alternative form of job security and power.[43]

Job control through exclusive possession of skill was not particularly important to semiskilled workers in the mass production industries. For mass production workers, hierarchical job ladders ensured them training and defined their promotional opportunities. It took the vision of industrial unionism of the Congress of Industrial Organizations (CIO) in the 1930s for unions to organize successfully in mass production industries that utilized Taylorist and Fordist job structures.[44] Today unions again need to develop a new vision in order to play a meaningful role in the new workplace.

B. The Boundaryless Workplace and the National Labor Relations Act

The tendency of unions to focus their efforts on job-specific goals and bargain for employer-specific protections is fostered and reinforced by the existing labor law framework. There are many respects in which the National Labor Relations Act (NLRA)[45] is out of step with today's workplace.

1. The Concept of the Bargaining Unit

Collective bargaining under the NLRA is organized around the concept of a bargaining unit. Under the NLRA, unions exist as representatives of a

---

[41] *See* Irving Bernstein, THE LEAN YEARS 84 (1966).
[42] *See* Selig Perlman, A THEORY OF THE LABOR MOVEMENT 7 (1928).
[43] *See, e.g.*, Montgomery, FALL OF THE HOUSE OF LABOR 105–07 (giving examples of craft workers' resistance to technological change that threatened not merely their jobs, but their way of life).
[44] *See* Steven Fraser, LABOR WILL RULE: SIDNEY HILLMAN AND THE RISE OF AMERICAN LABOR 63–75 (1991); Nelson Lichtenstein, THE MOST DANGEROUS MAN IN DETROIT 65–83 (1995).
[45] 29 U.S.C. §151 (1994).

bargaining unit. If there is a sufficient showing of interest by workers in a particular workplace, the National Labor Relations Board (NLRB) determines the appropriate unit and conducts an election among employees working in the unit to determine whether a majority favor the union.[46] If the union wins the election, the union is certified and becomes the exclusive representative of the unit for purposes of collective bargaining.[47] Once certified, the employer and the union have a duty to bargain for a collective agreement to govern the terms and conditions of employment for all workers in the unit, regardless of whether the employees are union members or not.[48] Thus any contract concluded between the union and the employer applies to all jobs in the unit. The employees in the unit lose their right to take collective action apart from their certified representative,[49] and the union has a duty to represent fairly all employees in the unit – those that support the union and those that do not.[50]

The bargaining unit is thus an integral part of the statutory scheme of the NLRA. However, the statute does not provide a definition of what constitutes an appropriate unit. Rather, it leaves that question for the NLRB to determine on a case-by-case basis. The definition of the bargaining unit is often one of the most contested aspects of an organizing campaign because a union will advocate a unit in which it has majority support and an employer will advocate a unit in which union sentiment is weak. Under the statute, the NLRB is prohibited from basing the unit solely on the extent to which the union has organized.[51] Instead, the board attempts to define units of employees who share a "community of interest." Some of the factors the board uses to determine whether there is a community of interest are: similarity in kinds of work performed; similarity in compensation, types of training, and skills required; integration of job functions; and commonality of supervision.[52]

Under the community of interest test, bargaining units tend to have static job definitions and clear departmental boundaries. The community of interest test assumes a functionally delineated workplace in which work tasks are continuous and well defined. In addition, the NLRB has a preference for worksite-specific bargaining units and has adopted a presumption

---

[46] 29 U.S.C. §159(b).
[47] Under the National Labor Relations Act (NLRA), a union can also be designated as an exclusive representative by means of an employer grant of recognition after a showing of a card majority or other convincing evidence of majority support. *See* NLRB v. Gissel Packing Co., 395 U.S. 575, 592 (1969). But certification as a result of a board-sponsored election is the preferred method of obtaining representative status under the NLRA. *See id.* at 596.
[48] *See* Steele v. Louisville & Nashville R.R. Co., 323 U.S. 192, 200–04 (1944).
[49] *See* Emporium Capwell Co. v. W. Addition Cmty. Org., 420 U.S. 50, 64, 69–70 (1975).
[50] *See* Vaca v. Sipes, 386 U.S. 171, 177, 182 (1967); Steele, 323 U.S. at 200–02.
[51] *See* 29 U.S.C. §159(c)(5).
[52] *See* NLRB v. Action Auto., 469 U.S. 490, 494 (1985); NLRB v. Purnell's Pride, Inc., 609 F.2d 1153, 1156 (5th Cir. 1980). *See generally* Julius G. Getman, Bertrand B. Pogrebin, & David L. Gregory, LABOR MANAGEMENT RELATIONS AND THE LAW 30–31 (2d ed. 1999).

in favor of single facility units.[53] Yet much of today's work involves networks across multiple establishments or multiemployer tasks, defying traditional bargaining unit definitions.[54] Thus the NLRB's approach to bargaining unit determination does not fit comfortably with the cross-utilization and the blurring of boundaries that are typical of work practices today.[55]

The bargaining unit focus of the NLRA also means that terms and conditions negotiated by labor and management apply to the jobs in the unit rather than to the individuals who hold the jobs. As individual workers move between departments, units, or firms, their labor contracts do not follow them. Yet the new workplace is not job centered, nor is it made up of separable, bounded departments. It involves cross-utilization, broad banding, and other boundaryless features. As a result, in today's world of frequent movement, union gains are increasingly ephemeral from the individual's point of view.

One area in which the bargaining unit focus of the NLRA has been particularly out of step with labor market reality concerns the act's treatment of temporary employees. Indeed, the evolving law of temporary workers illustrates the difficulty of applying static notions of bargaining units to the complex employment relationships that arise with today's peripatetic work force.

Since the 1980s, temporary employment has been the fastest growing portion of the labor market. According to the U.S. Department of Labor, between 1982 and 1998, the number of jobs in the temporary help industry grew 577 percent, compared to a 41 percent increase in jobs in the labor force generally.[56] In 1999, the Bureau of Labor Statistics reported that nearly two million employees worked for temporary help agencies or contract labor provider firms.[57] Temporary employees who work for staffing agencies are

[53] *See* Charrette Drafting Supplies Co., 275 NLRB 1294, 1296–97 (1985); Haag Drug Co., 169 NLRB 877, 877–78 (1968); Metro. Life Ins. Co., 156 NLRB 1408, 1414–15 (1966); Dixie Belle Mills, Inc., 139 NLRB 629, 631–32 (1962). *See generally* Howard Wial, *The Emerging Organizational Structure of Unionism in Low-Wage Services*, 45 RUTGERS L. REV. 671, 681 n.34, 710–11 (1993).

[54] *See* Alexander J.S. Colvin, *Rethinking Bargaining Unit Determination: Labor Law and the Structure of Collective Representation in a Changing Workplace*, 15 HOFSTRA LAB. & EMP. L.J. 419, 454–58 (1998) (criticizing the single-plant presumption).

[55] *Id.* at 430–31 (noting that changes in the nature of employment create problems for bargaining unit determination).

[56] GAO, CONTINGENT WORKERS: INCOME AND BENEFITS LAG BEHIND THOSE OF THE REST OF THE WORKFORCE 16 (2000); *see also* David H. Autor, *Outsourcing at Will: Unjust Dismissal Doctrine and the Growth of Temporary Help Employment* 1 (Nat'l Bureau of Econ. Research, Working Paper No. 7557, 1999) (reporting that the temporary-help supply industry grew more than five times faster than U.S. nonfarm employment between 1979 and 1995).

[57] *See* Bureau of Labor Statistics News Release 99–362, *Contingent and Alternative Employment Arrangements*, available at http://stats.bls.gov/news.release/conemp.news.htm (Dec. 21, 1999).

often given long-term placement at particular user firms. There, the user firm supervises the work of the temp on a day-to-day basis, and the temp works alongside the firm's regular employees, with the same skills, duties, and job classifications. In this triangulated employment relationship, the NLRB has considered both the temporary agency and the user firm to be joint employers of the temporary employee.

In 1990, the NLRB ruled that long-term temporary employees could not be included in a bargaining unit with a user employer's regular employees unless both the provider-agency employer and the user employer consented.[58] Thereafter, the board refused to consider any unit that combined temporary and regular employees, absent consent of both employers.[59] Thus it was almost impossible for temporary workers to unionize.

In fall 2000, in *M. B. Sturgis, Inc.*,[60] the NLRB reversed its former position and held that regular employees and temporary employees could be in the same bargaining unit so long as they shared a community of interest.[61] The *Sturgis* ruling eliminated the dual consent requirement. The board in *Sturgis* also reiterated that temporary employees could organize into a bargaining unit of all the employees of a single temporary work agency.[62] As a result, the NLRB now permits temporary employees to be included in bargaining units that are comprised of temporary and regular employees of a single employer, or that are comprised of all employees of a single temporary agency. This ruling greatly expands the possibilities for temporary workers to claim the protection of the labor law.

2. Secondary Boycott Prohibitions

Another feature of the NLRA that assumes the existence of bounded workplaces and internal labor markets is the prohibition of secondary boycotts. In the past, unions often called for boycotts or strikes against firms that did business with the firm with which they had a dispute. For over a hundred years, courts have been hostile to efforts by unions to exercise economic pressure against entities that are not parties to an immediate dispute.[63] Courts repeatedly enjoined, heavily fined, and otherwise penalized workers who engaged

---

[58] *See* Lee Hosp., 300 N.L.R.B. 947 (1990).

[59] *See, e.g.*, Int'l Transfer of Fla., 305 N.L.R.B. 150 (1991).

[60] 2000 NLRB LEXIS 565 (2000).

[61] *See id.* at * 12.

[62] *See id.* at * 19.

[63] *See, e.g.*, Plant v. Woods, 57 N.E. 1011, 1015 (Mass. 1900) (holding pressure on an employer by a rival union unlawful); Bowen v. Matheson, 96 Mass. (14 Allen) 499, 503 (1867) (holding a boycott of a shipping agency to compel shipowners to pay union's standard rate for seamen unlawful); *see also* Loewe v. Lawlor, 208 U.S. 274, 294 (1908) (holding a combination "aimed at compelling third parties and strangers involuntarily not to engage in the course of trade except on conditions that the combination imposes" actionable under the Sherman Antitrust Act).

in these secondary strikes and boycotts.[64] The labor movement and its supporters bitterly resented and resisted the hostile judicial treatment of peaceful secondary pressure. Thus, for over a century the issue of secondary boycotts has generated passionate controversy and intense lobbying.[65]

Congress has visited the issue of secondary boycotts on many occasions. In 1914, Congress enacted the Clayton Antitrust Act,[66] which purported to legalize peaceful secondary pressure. However, in 1921, in *Duplex Printing Co. v. Deering*, the Supreme Court gave the Clayton Act an extremely restrictive interpretation that effectively nullified its labor-protective provisions.[67] Subsequent pressure by organized labor and progressives induced Congress to enact the Norris-La Guardia Act in 1932, in which Congress again attempted to legalize peaceful secondary conduct by unions.[68] The Norris-La Guardia Act was upheld and interpreted broadly by the Supreme Court in *United States v. Hutchenson* in 1941, but the legality of secondary conduct remained controversial.[69] In 1947, Congress enacted section 8(b)(4) of the Taft-Hartley amendments to the NLRA, which rendered secondary boycotts unlawful under the NLRA.[70] The scope of section 8(b)(4) and the larger issue of the lawfulness of peaceful secondary conduct remain controversial issues to this day.[71]

The labor law's ban on secondary activity assumes that union economic pressure and collective bargaining should take place within a discrete economic unit – the bargaining unit – and should not spill over beyond its boundaries. The law attempts to confine economic warfare to the immediate parties in a bounded arena of conflict. A union is permitted to exert economic pressure against a neutral firm when the neutral firm is closely related to the primary target of the union's dispute. For example, if a union is on strike, it can lawfully bring economic pressure to bear against a firm that performs the work of a struck company if it is doing so at the struck company's behest.

---

[64] *See e.g.*, Bedford Cut Stone Co. v. Journeymen Stone Cutters' Ass'n of N. Am., 274 U.S. 37 (1927); Duplex Printing Press Co. v. Deering, 254 U.S. 443, 466–68 (1921); Loewe, 208 U.S. at 292–94.

[65] *See, e.g.*, Felix Frankfurter & William Greene, THE LABOR INJUNCTION 161–62 (1931).

[66] Pub. L. No. 106–274, ch. 323, 38 Stat. 730 (1914) (codified as amended in scattered sections of 15 U.S.C.).

[67] 254 U.S. 443 (1921).

[68] Pub. L. No. 106–274, 47 Stat. 70 (1932) (codified at 29 U.S.C. §§101–115 (1994)).

[69] 312 U.S. 219 (1941). In *Hutchenson*, the court interpreted the Norris-La Guardia Act as preventing federal courts from imposing any penalties on peaceful secondary conduct "[s]o long as a union acts in its self-interest and does not combine with non-labor groups." *Id.* at 232.

[70] *See* 29 U.S.C. §158(b)(4).

[71] Courts continue to enjoin secondary activity in disregard of specific statutory directives and precedent to the contrary. *See, e.g.*, Burlington N.R.R. Co. v. Bhd. of Maint. of Way Employees, 481 U.S. 429, 437–40 (1987) (criticizing lower courts for enjoining secondary conduct by railroad workers who were not subject to the NLRA's secondary boycott prohibitions).

In addition, a union can pressure a business firm that is so closely tied to the primary employer that the two firms have integrated operations under common day-to-day control. However, these exceptions are narrow and do not extend to firms that are allied simply by common ownership or common economic interest.[72]

The NLRA's insistence that economic warfare be limited to primary participants and their close allies assumes that the unionized workplace has static borders and that disputes between the firm and its workers affect only those immediate and identifiable parties. However, it is not always easy to specify who is an insider and who is an outsider in a labor dispute.[73] Production relationships are complex, so that subcontractors, joint venturers, and suppliers are often closely intertwined with primary producers in a way that eludes precise delineation between employer and neutral.[74] In today's world of production networks and boundaryless workplaces, the assumption that there can be discrete, bounded conflict with clearly differentiated insiders and outsiders is becoming ever less plausible.

One effort to distinguish parties to labor disputes from neutrals is the work preservation doctrine. It has long been held that union efforts to preserve work that the bargaining unit has traditionally performed are lawful, while union efforts designed to further union goals elsewhere constitute an unlawful secondary boycott.[75] The work preservation doctrine incorporates the central role of bounded bargaining units with well-defined job definitions that characterized the old employment relationship. Yet when the nature of work is in flux, the work preservation doctrine becomes difficult to apply. What a union may deem work preservation may appear to an employer – and to a court – to be unlawful secondary activity.[76]

Furthermore, when an employer has subsidiaries, subcontractors, and other partners in a production network, a union may need to apply pressure on more than one part of the network to be effective. But doing so risks liability for engaging in a secondary boycott.[77] For example, in order to organize janitorial workers in Washington, D.C., and as part of its nation-wide Justice

---

[72] *See* Getman et al., LABOR MANAGEMENT RELATIONS 286–88.

[73] *See generally* Local 761, Int'l Union of Elec. Workers v. NLRB, 366 U.S. 667 (1961) (discussing the difficulty of distinguishing primary from secondary activity). *See also* Howard Lesnick, *Job Security and Secondary Boycotts: The Reach of NLRA §§8(b)(4) and 8(e)*, 113 U. PA. L. REV. 1000, 1004 (1965) (discussing the difficulty of distinguishing between primary and secondary activities).

[74] *See, e.g.*, NLRB v. Enterprise Ass'n. of Steam, Hot Water, Hydraulic Sprinkler, Pneumatic Tube, Ice Machine and Gen. Pipefitters of N.Y., 429 U.S. 507, 537–5 39 (1977) (J. Brennan dissenting).

[75] National Woodwork Manufacturers' Ass'n. v. National Labor Relations Bd., 386 U.S. 612, 644–45 (1967).

[76] NLRB v. Int'l Longshoremen's Ass'n, 447 U.S. 490, 504–6 (1980).

[77] *See, e.g.*, United Food and Commercial Workers' Union Local No. 367, and Cinnabon, Inc., 166 L.R.R.M. (BNA) 1377 (2001); Newspaper and Mail Deliverers' Union of New York

for Janitors campaign, the Service Employees International Union (SEIU) called for peaceful picketing against several Washington building owners and their building management companies. The primary employers for the janitors were two independent janitorial contracting firms hired by the building management companies, United States Service Industries, Inc. (USSI) and Red Coats. The NLRB found the union guilty of a secondary boycott, reasoning:

> Respondents were well aware of the distinctions which the law draws between primary and secondary employers. They understood full well that their primary labor dispute was with USSI and Red Coats, among others. At the same time, the record suggests that the SEIU was convinced that the law was out of sync with reality; that power over the janitors' terms and conditions of employment was concentrated in the hands of a relatively small band of property owners, including the Charging Parties. Pursuant to their perspective, the Respondents decided early on to bring pressure to bear on building owners through a variety of tactics.[78]

Unions are increasingly finding that they need to transverse traditional bargaining units and corporate boundaries to bring economic pressure to bear effectively. Yet as they apply pressure on suppliers, joint venturers, coemployers, network partners, and subsidiaries, they are finding that the secondary boycott laws are a serious hindrance.[79]

3. The Role of Arbitration

The labor law's treatment of arbitration also reflects the premise that workplaces have well-defined boundaries. Since the mid 1950s, the Supreme Court has made the grievance and arbitration procedure a central feature of the evolving system of collective bargaining.[80] In a series of cases interpreting section 301 of the Labor Management Relations Act (LMRA),[81] the Court transformed collective bargaining into a system of labor-management

---

and NYP Holdings, Inc., d/b/a New York Post, 170 L.R.R.M. (BNA) 1081 (2002). *See also* Service Employees Intern. Union Local 525, AFL-CIO, 169 L.R.R.M. (BNA) 1362 (1999).

[78] Service Employees International Union, AFL-CIO, and General Maintenance Service Co., Inc., 1992 WL 1465677 (1992),

[79] *See, e.g.*, Dowd v. Int'l Longshoremen's Ass'n, 975 F.2d 779, 783–87 (11th Cir. 1992) (finding efforts by an American union to obtain assistance of a Japanese union in pressuring a Japanese-affiliated employer to be an unlawful secondary boycott); Carpenters' Local Union No. 1478 v. Stevens, 743 F.2d 1271, 1277 (9th Cir. 1984) (finding that a collective agreement that imposed terms of collective agreement on employer's nonunion subsidiary was improper); D'Amico v. Painters & Allied Trades Dist. Council No. 51, 120 L.R.R.M. (BNA) 3473, 3480 (D. Md. 1985) (finding the effort by a union to achieve anti-double-breasting contract language to be unlawful secondary activity).

[80] Textile Workers Union of Am. v. Lincoln Mills, 353 U.S. 448, 449–51 (1957); *see also* Boys Market v. Retail Clerks, 398 U.S. 235, 242 (1970). *See generally* Katherine Van Wezel Stone, *The Post-War Paradigm in American Labor Law*, 90 YALE L.J. 1509, 1526–29.

[81] Ch. 120, §301, 61 Stat. 156 (1947) (codified at 29 U.S.C. §185(a) (1994)).

self-regulation.[82] It stated that labor and management should engage in "industrial self-government" in a self-regulatory system.[83] In this self-governing world, the parties were encouraged to determine their own norms through collective bargaining, and external norms and externally imposed sanctions were largely kept out.[84]

The self-regulatory conception of collective bargaining grew out of an ideology I call "industrial pluralism."[85] Industrial pluralism is based on the metaphor of collective bargaining as industrial self-government. Management and labor are analogized to political parties in a representative democracy in which each represents its own constituency and, as in a legislature, engages in debate and compromise in the formation of the collective bargaining agreement. In addition to the workplace legislative process – collective bargaining negotiations – and the workplace executive – management – there is a workplace judiciary – private arbitration. The metaphor of the workplace as a democracy, with a separation of powers, appears throughout postwar American labor law scholarship and judicial opinions. It portrays the workplace as a democratic institution, a microcosmic constitutional democracy in the private sphere.[86]

The industrial pluralist metaphor conveys a powerful normative message – that the unionized workplace should be permitted to self-regulate without intervention from legislatures or courts. Courts have implemented this vision through the adoption of a series of legal rules that effectively insulate the unionized workplace from external law.[87] For example, once labor and management establish internal arbitration systems for resolving disputes concerning contract interpretation and enforcement, the courts accord these tribunals almost total deference.[88] One consequence is that courts decline to enforce an individual worker's statutory rights if the claim affects an issue that is covered, or potentially covered, by a collective bargaining agreement

---

[82] *See* Katherine Van Wezel Stone, *Rustic Justice: Community and Coercion Under the Federal Arbitration Act*, 77 N.C. L. REV. 931, 1008–12, 1013–14 (describing the law of arbitration under collective bargaining as one of several examples of legally empowered self-regulating systems).

[83] *See, e.g.*, United Steelworkers of Am. v. Warrior & Gulf Navigation Co., 363 U.S. 574, 580 (1960).

[84] *See* Stone, *The Legacy of Industrial Pluralism* 622–24. *See generally* Stone, *The Post-War Paradigm* 1511–41.

[85] Stone, *The Legacy of Industrial Pluralism*, 59 U. CHI. L. REV. at 622–24; Stone, *The Post-War Paradigm*, 90 YALE L.J. at 1514–15.

[86] *See* Stone, *The Post-War Paradigm* at 1515.

[87] *See generally id.* at 1529–41.

[88] *See* Stone, *The Legacy of Industrial Pluralism*, 59 U. CHI. L. REV. at 622–25; *see, e.g.*, United Steelworkers of Am. v. Enterprise Wheel & Car Corp., 363 U.S. 593, 597 (1960) (upholding an arbitral award "so long as it draws its essence from the collective bargaining agreement"); Steelworkers of Am. v. Warrior & Gulf Navigation Co., 363 U.S. 574, 582–83 (1960) (announcing a presumption of arbitrability).

that contains an arbitration clause.[89] Thus, when unionized workers assert employment rights grounded in either state or federal law, they often find that their claims are preempted by the arbitration clause. In arbitration, the arbitrator is bound to apply the contract rather than the external law, so that unionized workers are often left with no forum in which to assert their statutory employment rights.[90]

The self-government model of collective bargaining, like the bargaining unit concept, requires a strict boundary around the unionized workplace. It presupposes that labor and management in a given bargaining unit devise the rules by which they will be governed and the procedures through which allegations of breach can be investigated, adjudicated, and remedied without outside intervention. The rules so devised only apply to the particular jobs included in the bargaining unit, and the grievance and arbitration procedure keeps the rules within those bounds. Disputes that cut across departments or workplaces, and claims based on external law are usually excluded. Thus the arbitration system, like the bargaining unit concept, is designed to keep outsiders out and insiders in, and reflects the single employer/long-term employee model of industrial relations.

4. The Definition of Employee and Employer

The NLRA only provides protections for those individuals who fall within the statute's definition of an employee. People who work for multiple employers or the wrong kind of employer fall outside the protection of the statute. For example, agricultural laborers, domestic workers, supervisors, and independent contractors are explicitly excluded from the act,[91] as well as government employees and employees covered by the Railway Labor Act.[92] In addition, the NLRB has made nonstatutory exclusions for managerial and confidential employees.[93] Furthermore, the Supreme Court has held that employees who have supervisory authority over others, or who have managerial decisions delegated to them, are excluded from coverage.[94] In today's

---

[89] *See* Allis-Chalmers Corp. v. Leuck, 471 U.S. 202, 220 (preempting an employee's state law tort claim because resolution of the claim was substantially dependent upon an analysis of the collective bargaining agreement). *See generally* Stone, *The Legacy of Industrial Pluralism* at 620–21 (contrasting the trend toward broad scope of preemption in labor law with the trend narrowing the scope of preemption in other areas of law).

[90] *See* Stone, *The Legacy of Industrial Pluralism* at 594–96, 616–28.

[91] *See* 29 U.S.C. §152(3).

[92] *See* 29 U.S.C. §152(2).

[93] *See* NLRB v. Hendricks County Rural Elec. Membership Corp., 454 U.S. 170, 177–85 (1981) (sustaining the Board's creation of confidential exclusion); NLRB v. Bell Aerospace Co., 416 U.S. 267 (1974) (sustaining managerial exclusion); In re Ford Motor Co., 66 NLRB 1317, 1322 (1946) (confidential exclusion).

[94] *See* NLRB v. Health Care & Ret. Corp., 511 U.S. 571, 578 (1994) (finding that charge nurses are "supervisors" under the statute because they assign work to nurse's aides); NLRB v. Yeshiva Univ., 444 U.S. 672, 679–82 (1980) (holding that university professors

workplace, in which hierarchies have been flattened and decision-making authority has been delegated downward, the supervisory and managerial exclusions have the potential of depriving many low-level employees of the protections of the act.

The exclusion for independent contractors has become particularly problematic for part-time and short-term temporary workers.[95] Such workers often work for more than one employer at a time, but are dependent upon and subject to the supervision of each employer for the time they are at work. Yet, when a worker has multiple employers, each employer will often claim that the worker is an independent contractor rather than an employee. Courts readily accept the employer's own definition of a temporary worker's status, thereby excluding a fast-growing portion of the workforce from unionization altogether.[96]

In general, the act's exclusion of independent contractors is increasingly difficult to justify. All at-will employees have employment contracts of uncertain duration. As the new employment relationship displaces the old assumption of steady long-term employment, the distinction between temporary and permanent employees becomes more and more arbitrary. And the line between temporary employees and independent contractors is a thin one. As regular employees' pay is increasingly pegged to individual performance and market rates, and as lower level employees are increasingly given discretion over the performance of their own work tasks, the distinction between employee and independent contractor is quickly vanishing.

5. Successorship

Another respect in which the NLRA is out of step with the contemporary workplace involves the act's treatment of corporate transformation. Unionism under the act is job centered and employer centered, not employee centered. As discussed above, bargaining units and collective agreements apply to the job and the worksite, not to the employee. So long as jobs are relatively stable – that is, the same jobs are performed over time in the same location with the same employees – bargaining units are stable as to membership, size, and composition, and collective agreements are stable as to the scope

---

are "managers" for purposes of exclusion because they exert collective decision-making authority in hiring, curriculum, and other matters).

[95] In the 1947 amendment to section 2(2) of the NLRA, 29 U.S.C. §152(2), Congress rejected an "economic reality" test in favor of a common law test for determining independent contractor status. However, the board and courts of appeal have often differed as to what that test requires.

[96] *See, e.g.*, Clark v. E.I. DuPont de Nemours & Co., 105 F.3d 646 (4th Cir. 1997) (per curiam); Abraham v. Exxon Corp., 85 F.3d 1126, 1132 (5th Cir. 1996). *But see* Vizcaino v. United States Dist. Court, 173 F.3d 713, 724–25 (9th Cir. 1999) (rejecting an employer's assertion that employees are independent contractors for purposes of eligibility for a stock purchase plan).

of their coverage. However, when businesses change hands or undergo major corporate transformations, the bargaining unit focus of the Act becomes problematic.

When there is a change of ownership such as through a sale of assets, the Supreme Court has held that the successor owner is not bound by the predecessor's collective bargaining agreement.[97] Nor does the new owner have an obligation to retain all of the former firm's employees. The new owner may have an obligation to recognize the union and bargain for the terms and conditions of the new entity, but only if a majority of the successor's employees had been employed by the predecessor, and only if there is "substantial continuity" in the nature of the work.[98] Substantial continuity involves continuity in tasks, processes, customers, and supervision. The substantial continuity test makes the union's continued existence depend upon employment continuity and stability within the employing entity.[99] Thus the successorship doctrine, like the bargaining unit concept, conditions representation on an employment relationship that is stable, bounded, and ongoing.

C. Conclusion

In sum, despite the importance of unions as an institution of employee protection and representation, there are many features of current union practice that are inconsistent with the new workplace, such as narrowly defined bargaining units, seniority, and longevity-based pay and benefit structures. The labor law, with its emphasis on discrete bargaining units and a closed labor-management boundary, reinforces conventional union practices. While such practices were effective mechanisms for employee protection under the old employment relationship, they are no longer responsive to conditions in many workplaces. If we want to promote institutions for employee representation in the new workplace, we need to imagine a new model of unionism, and a new legal regime that is suited to the evolving world of work. The next chapter suggests means by which union practice and labor law could accomplish that goal.

---

[97] Howard Johnson Co. v. Detroit Local Joint Exec. Board, 417 U.S. 249 (1974). In the narrow case in which one corporation disappears as a result of a merger, the successor corporation may have a duty to arbitrate under the collective agreement of the predecessor. See John Wiley & Sons v. Livingston, 376 U.S. 543 (1964).

[98] See Fall River Dyeing & Finishing Corp. v. NLRB, 482 U.S. 27, 43 (1987); see also NLRB v. Burns Int'l Sec. Serv., Inc., 406 U.S. 272, 277–81 (1972).

[99] See Stone, *Labor and the Corporate Structure*, 55 U. Chi. L. Rev. at 105–09 (describing the substantial continuity requirement).

10

Reimagining Employee Representation

One hundred years ago, the eminent British labor historians Beatrice and Sydney Webb identified three goals of working-class collective action and three corresponding roles for labor organizations. They were: (1) to form mutual benefit associations, (2) to create organizations to engage in collective bargaining for job-related protection, and (3) to create organizations that could lobby for legislation favorable to employees. According to the Webbs, English unions, at different times in English history, performed each of these roles.[1]

In the twentieth century, American unions have also played all three roles, but with a heavy emphasis on the second. Both the American Federation of Labor (AFL) and the Congress of Industrial Organizations (CIO) saw their primary function as bargaining for job-related protections. After merging in 1955, the AFL-CIO continued to emphasize collective bargaining and contract administration as the core function of unionism. Over the past fifty years, the individual national and international unions and the AFL-CIO federation have built highly sophisticated research and legal departments to provide support for their bargaining programs, while relegating their legislative, education, and organizing departments to secondary roles. As a result of these efforts, unions have been extremely effective in the collective bargaining arena. The strength of the AFL-CIO at its postwar zenith lay in its achievements at the bargaining table, one employer at a time.

In light of the transformation in the workplace, unions now need to develop new methods of operation. While there are many workers still working in the old employment relationship, evidence suggests that new workplace practices are spreading both across the corporate spectrum and throughout

---

[1] *See* Sidney & Beatrice Webb, THE HISTORY OF TRADE UNIONISM vii, xxii–xxiii, 1 (1894, reprinted 1950).

the employment hierarchy.[2] As careers become boundaryless and work becomes detached from a single employer, unions need to become boundaryless as well. They need to develop strategies, skills, and strengths that go beyond single contracts with single employers. They need to move beyond worksite-based collective bargaining and expand into the Webbs' other domains – that is, upward into the political domain and outward into the community.

In the political domain, unions need to expand their reach so that they represent the interests and concerns of a wider sector of the workforce. Unions have long been involved in lobbying on issues of broad concern, such as civil rights and the minimum wage. In recent years, union efforts have been especially effective in the political and legislative arenas. But an expanded role for unions in politics and the legislative process will require a major redefinition of both their mission and their membership structure. For example, unions could revise their notion of membership, or add a separate membership category, in order to give political voice to individual working people who do not have workplace representation.

In the 1990s, the AFL-CIO initiated an associate membership program in which it offered unorganized workers and unemployed members a reduced form of membership. Associate members pay lower dues and are eligible for certain union-sponsored credit card plans and other union-arranged consumer discounts. The primary goal of the associate membership program is to enlist the support of former members and workers who might go on to unionize and engage in collective bargaining.[3] The associate membership concept could be enlarged to give political voice to unrepresented workers more generally. Such an expanded concept of associate membership would help transform the labor movement into a mass-based, work-oriented political force, a work-focused analog of the American Association of Retired Persons.[4]

The current labor law discourages union participation in politics through restrictions on the use of dues money for political campaigns and other limitations on the scope of protected activity.[5] Rather than discourage unions

---

[2] *See* Paul Osterman, *Work Reorganization in an Era of Restructuring: Trends in Diffusion and Effects on Employee Welfare*, 53 INDUS. & LAB. REL. REV. 179, 180 (2000).

[3] *See* John J. Sweeney, AMERICA NEEDS A RAISE 140 (1996).

[4] The AARP, founded in 1958, gives a legislative voice to persons over the age of 50. By 2003 it had grown to 35 million members and it has been a remarkably effective lobbyist for issues such as Medicare, social security, and age discrimination. Citation http://www.aarp.org/leadership/articles/a2002-12-18-aarp factsheet.html.

[5] *See* Communications Workers of Am. v. Beck, 487 U.S. 735, 762–63 (1988) (holding that unions must give employees who so request rebates for any portion of their union dues spent on political causes to which they are opposed); Cal. Saw & Knife Works, 320 N.L.R.B. 224, 231–35, 237 (1995) (mandating that all employees in a bargaining unit be given notice of their

from participating in politics, the law should be amended to enable unions to expand their role in that domain.

Unions also need to expand their role in the community. In the boundaryless workplace, employees continue to need collective representatives to act as bargaining agents, but not merely on a single-employer basis. Employees need organizations that can bargain with groups of employers for decent wage rates, adequate and portable benefit packages, training, employability, child care, and other features of social welfare that are not adequately provided by the public sector. Thus unions need to find ways to exert influence on a multiemployer basis, across worksites, localities, and regions, and across occupational and industrial boundaries. In that way, they can help workers acquire skills, provide opportunities for retooling, ensure portability in benefits, create institutions for child care, and in other respects empower individuals to participate in the boundaryless workplace.

Unions must also reclaim their mutual assistance role. As Cornell Labor Relations Professor Samuel Bachrach has shown, unions in the nineteenth century were not merely service providers. They functioned as a community, providing mutual assistance to ease the strains of immigrant life. Union members aided each other with personal problems, family emergencies, alcohol dependency, and personal crises.[6] Unions today need to rediscover their roles as community support organizations that can encourage mutual self-help amongst members.

In recent years, some unions and labor groups have begun to perform new roles that are responsive to the changing workplace. Two different models of unionism have emerged as an alternative to traditional employer-centered unionism. The first, new craft unionism, is an occupation-based form of unionism that bargains with industry-wide employer groups to establish minimum standards and provide training, while enabling employees to move freely between employers in the industry. The second, which I call citizen unionism, is a locality-based form of unionism that uses collective pressure to induce corporations to become good corporate citizens of the geographic area in which they are located. While firm-centered unionism will continue to be effective for employees within internal labor market employment settings, these two emerging types of unionism can provide representation for employees in the boundaryless workplace.

"Beck rights," and setting guidelines for calculating Beck rebates); *see also* NLRB v. Motorola, Inc., 991 F.2d 278, 285 (5th Cir. 1993); *cf.* Eastex, Inc. v. NLRB, 437 U.S. 556, 567–70 (1978) (holding that union-sponsored political literature is protected under the NLRA only so long as there is some nexus between the issue and employees' interests as employees).

[6] Samuel B. Bachrach, Peter A. Bamberger, & William J. Sonnenstuhl, MUTUAL AID AND UNION RENEWAL (2001).

A. New Craft Unionism

Some unions have taken steps to respond to the changing workplace by se-
lectively borrowing from traditional craft union practices. One of the most
interesting examples can be found in the trades associated with the film and
television industries. The employees in the below-the-line theatrical crafts –
the workers who perform lighting, sound, camera work, props, costuming,
makeup, stagehand work, equipment loading, driving, and so forth – have
long been organized into two competing unions.[7] The National Association
of Broadcast Employees and Technicians (NABET) organizes employees on
an industrial basis, and seeks to negotiate collective bargaining agreements
between the various below-the-line crews and the major motion picture and
television studios. The International Alliance of Theatrical and Stage Employees (IATSE) is organized on a craft basis. The two unions function very
differently and accordingly have had very different rates of success in the
new workplace.

NABET began as an independent union in the 1930s and joined the CIO
in the early 1950s. It is a typical industrial union that negotiates for long-
term continuous employment with the major producers. Its collective agreements contain standard seniority, job-bidding, just-cause-for-dismissal, and
grievance-arbitration provisions. In the 1960s and 1970s, NABET developed
a reputation for militancy after conducting numerous strikes, strike threats,
and highly visible arbitrations. Since then, film and television companies
whose employees are represented by NABET have bristled under the job
security terms of the NABET agreements.[8]

Production work is often intermittent and unpredictable, so film and television companies do not want to have to support full complements of craft
workers on a year-round basis. Even in the relatively stable setting of television, the major networks do not want to pay idle crew members during
summer rerun periods. Therefore, film and television employers have tried to
cut staff and substitute temporary per diem workers for permanent workers.
Because per diem workers are paid considerably less than the NABET union
rate and are not eligible for benefits, their use has become a source of great
controversy.

In the 1970s and early 1980s, the major television network executives
tried to negotiate for the right to use per diems, but NABET consistently
refused. In 1987, the National Broadcasting Corporation (NBC) renewed

---

[7] The International Brotherhood of Electrical Workers also represents broadcast engineers and
technicians in the industry, but they are omitted from discussion because they do not have a
major presence in the other below-the-line crafts. *See* Lois Gray & Ronald Seeber, *The Industry
and the Unions: An Overview*, in UNDER THE STARS 15, 34–42 (Lois Gray & Ronald Seeber,
eds., 1996).

[8] *See* John Amman, *The Transformation of Industrial Relations in the Motion Picture and Television
Industries: Craft and Production*, in Gray & Seeber, UNDER THE STARS 113, 118–21.

its efforts to utilize per diem and freelance workers, but NABET refused to even discuss it. Eventually NBC implemented its demands unilaterally and the union responded with a strike. After eighteen weeks, during which the network operated with supervisors, clerical staff, and nonunion strikebreakers, the union capitulated and granted the network every major concession it sought, including the right to use temporary workers.[9]

The NBC strike emboldened the other networks to obtain the right to use unlimited numbers of per diem employees. In 1987, the Columbia Broadcasting System (CBS) bargained hard on the issue and won its objective. The American Broadcasting Company (ABC) also began to increase its use of per diem workers. Escalating tension at ABC about the extent to which the network could utilize per diem workers led to a lockout in the fall of 1999, after which the company's position prevailed.

As the use of temporary workers has increased, regular employment at NABET-organized companies has declined. Accordingly, since the early 1990s, NABET membership has also been declining. In 1990, NABET's largest film local, Local 15, merged with IATSE, and, in 1992, the remainder of the union merged with the Communications Workers of America.[10]

IATSE operates in a manner that is very different from its industrial union counterpart. IATSE engages in a modern variation of the nineteenth-century insider-contractor system, in which lead workers hire their own crews on an individual job basis. For example, a film producer who wants to produce a film in New York City contacts a lighting technician, sound engineer, or other craft worker in New York and asks that individual to put together a crew. The one who was called becomes the head lighting technician or head sound engineer for the job, and that person contacts others to assemble a crew. Each individual in the crew makes his or her own contract with the employer-producer within the framework of the IATSE local's basic agreement.[11]

IATSE engages in a form of collective bargaining that combines collectively negotiated terms with individually negotiated ones. In this "embedded contract bargaining" model, the union negotiates a basic agreement that provides for individually negotiated agreements consistent with its terms. A basic agreement sets forth some terms of the labor-management relationship and requires employees covered by it to establish other terms through individual contracts with the employer. For example, the typical IATSE basic agreement provides for union recognition and contains some general terms such as workplace health and safety protections, a requirement that the employer provide housing during out-of-town production assignments, and mandated

[9] *See id.* at 134–35.
[10] *Id.* at 135–53.
[11] Much of the information that follows comes from a series of interviews. Interview with Franklin Moss, Esq., International Alliance of Theatrical and Stage Employees counsel, Lipton, Watanabe, Spevak & Moss, in New York, NY (May–June 2000).

employer contributions to the joint pension and health funds. It also sets the minimum pay for each day worked. However, the agreement contains no seniority, just cause, or arbitration provisions – in fact, there is no provision for job security at all. To the contrary, the basic agreement contemplates that workers will be hired on an as-needed basis and will work from job to job, sometimes on more than one job at a time.[12]

The most significant aspect of the basic agreement is that it specifies that the employer must give each worker it hires a specific individual employment contract, called a cover sheet, which is contained in an appendix to the basic agreement. The cover sheet is a one-page agreement, negotiated between the producer-employer and the individual employee, that fixes the level of pay and other terms relating to compensation for the specific job. The cover sheet also authorizes a dues check-off on behalf of the relevant IATSE local.

IATSE's collective bargaining agreement is an umbrella that contains and defines the parameters of individual bargains that are embedded within it. Most of the significant terms of compensation and hours of work are thus derived from individual bargaining between a union member and the specific employing company. I call this form of collective bargaining "embedded contract bargaining" because it permits individually negotiated terms to be embedded in a collective agreement. It has proven to be a means for unions to provide minimum terms and protections and yet be compatible with the new boundaryless workplace. Because it is an arrangement that permits employers to reward superstars with mega-salaries, embedded contract bargaining is also used for the talent groups in the entertainment industry, such as screen writers and actors, as well as for professional athletes.

Whereas the use of per diem workers in the film industry posed a serious threat to the industrial union model of NABET, it did not pose a similar threat to IATSE. Instead, the IATSE contract permits employers to use temporary workers without having to go outside the union. Indeed, under an IATSE contract, all employees are hired temporarily and an employer pays for exactly the amount of labor it needs, on a job-to-job, or even on a day-to-day, basis. As a result, IATSE has been growing rapidly in the industry even though the overall level of full-time employment has shrunk. At the same time, many NABET workers have shifted to IATSE. The employer's desire to use temporary workers has proved to be an opportunity rather than a threat to IATSE.

While IATSE was not threatened by temporary workers, it was threatened by changes in technology and industry structure. As a craft union, IATSE can only protect its members if most of the workers in a craft are unionized. If there are significant numbers of nonunion workers available, employers will seek to utilize them rather than comply with union standards.

---

[12] *See, e.g.*, United Scenic Artists, Local 829 Agreement with the League of Resident Theaters (Sept. 1, 1992–Aug. 31, 1996) (copy on file with author).

In the mid-1980s, IATSE experienced growing competition from nonunion workers employed by low-budget independent film producers who could not afford the minimal rates and terms of the IATSE basic agreement. Some IATSE members argued that the low-budget film workers should not be permitted in the union, but IATSE then-president Tom Short disagreed. Short took the position that having any workers in their craft outside the union was a great threat. If they were outside, he reasoned, the low-budget, low-cost workers would constitute a source of trained strikebreakers, presenting the companies with a constant temptation to eliminate the union. Thus the leadership of IATSE negotiated contracts with special concessionary rates for low-budget film producers and, at the same time, brought the new workers into the union. Although it generated dissatisfaction among some incumbent members, the IATSE strategy succeeded in keeping the union strong and in keeping its strongholds, like New York City, almost 100 percent union.[13]

The IATSE approach to the low-budget films illustrates the difference between new craft unionism and the old craft unionism still found in many of the building trades today. The old craft unions were notorious for restricting membership and using patronage networks and nepotism to ration the privilege of membership. These membership practices resulted in unions that were almost exclusively white and male, and subjects of well-founded charges of racial, gender, and ethnic discrimination. Further, the exclusive practices of the craft unions ultimately weakened them because as crafts became easier to learn and as training opportunities proliferated, there were many nonunion workers who were ready, willing, and able to underbid the unionized workers.[14] In contrast, IATSE's inclusion of newcomers enabled the union to retain the flexibility of craft unionism without generating a pool of underprivileged outsiders.

Also, in the past, many craft unions declined when technological change made their craft skills obsolete. IATSE has attempted to prevent skill obsolescence by pressuring employers and equipment manufacturers to provide training for its members. In addition, many IATSE locals provide training themselves. For example, the New York stagehand local sends members to courses all over the country in computerized lighting and other technical innovations and pays for the courses out of union dues.[15]

IATSE is not the only union that has developed mechanisms for dealing with the boundaryless workplace based upon traditional craft union models. Rutgers labor historian Dorothy Sue Cobble finds examples of similar

[13] *See* Amman, *Transformation* 142–48; Moss Interview, *supra* note 11.

[14] *See, e.g.*, David Montgomery, THE FALL OF THE HOUSE OF LABOR: THE WORKPLACE, THE STATE, AND AMERICAN LABOR ACTIVISM, 1865–1925, 199–201 (1987) (describing how craft unionism in metal trades became all-white and all-male).

[15] *See* Gray & Seeber, *The Industry and the Unions* 42–48. Moss Interview, *supra* note 11.

practices in early-twentieth-century waitress unionism.[16] Cobble studied the Hotel Employee and Restaurant Employees Union's all-female waitress locals that existed from 1900 until the 1950s. These unions combined conventional practices of highly skilled craft unions with practices developed by nonfactory, unskilled workers such as longshoremen and teamsters. Like the longshoremen, the waitress unions established hiring halls and used closed shop agreements in order to obtain employment security, benefits, and minimal standards in restaurants in their locality. Like the craft unions, the waitress unions attempted to define occupational standards for waitressing. The waitress locals developed work rules, set craft standards, and established training and apprenticeship programs. By maintaining standards of competence, the waitress union hiring halls gave employers a source for obtaining well-trained and reliable workers, while at the same time giving the union control over the labor supply.[17]

Waitress unionism had many similarities to IATSE. It was occupationally based rather than employer- or worksite-based. Also, like IATSE, the waitress union contracts did not provide protection against layoffs or unjust dismissal. The collective agreements of the waitress union occasionally contained embedded contract provisions that permitted individual employees to negotiate their own wage bargains. And like IATSE and other craft unions, the waitress union had portable union-run benefit funds. However, unlike IATSE, the waitress workers had no identifiable skill, so that the success of their union depended upon their ability to maintain a closed shop.[18]

Cobble traces the decline of occupational waitress unionism in the 1950s and 1960s. In part, the rise of large hotels with unions organized on an industrial union model undermined the waitress union's power. In addition, the union's fate was sealed by a 1955 Supreme Court decision that held that hotels and restaurants fell under the National Labor Relations Act (NLRA).[19] Thereafter, the act's prohibition on closed shops and its ban on supervisors in bargaining units spelled the demise of the union's essential practices. By 1970, the Hotel and Restaurant Employees International Union had merged the craft- and gender-specific locals, ending the tradition of occupational unionism in the industry.[20] Cobble uses history to argue that occupationally based craft unionism could be a successful form of representation today.[21]

Several contemporary unions have adopted some of the practices of the new craft unionism described above. For example, the Service Employees

---

[16] *See* Dorothy Sue Cobble, *Organizing the Post Industrial Work Force: Lessons from the History of Waitress Unionism*, 44 INDUS. & LAB. REL. REV. 419, 421–23 (1991).

[17] *Id.* at 420–27.

[18] *See id.* at 425–32.

[19] *See* Hotel Employees Local No. 255 v. Leedom, 358 U.S. 99, 99 (1958); *see also* Floridan Hotel of Tampa, Inc., 124 N.L.R.B. 261, 263–64 (1959).

[20] *See* Cobble, *Organizing the Post Industrial Work Force* at 430.

[21] *See id.* at 431–35.

International Union (SEIU) initiated a Justice for Janitors program in 1985 to organize janitors on a geographic basis and to attempt to induce employers to commit to a standard agreement.[22] The union has since developed a referral service for janitors and has successfully organized janitors in twenty cities.[23]

Howard Wial of the Working for America Institute uses the examples of SEIU's Justice for Janitors campaign, the Hotel and Restaurant Employees' citywide organizing drives, and other similar experiences to advocate a form of geographic and occupational unionism that would enable low-wage service workers to organize loosely defined occupational groupings within a geographic area.[24] Wial describes how many low-wage service workers share a common "job mobility path," that is, a series of jobs between which workers move regularly. He argues that employees who regularly move between jobs along the same mobility path should be organized into a single union.[25] Under Wial's proposal, unions would attempt to get employers to agree to both a set of area-wide standard wages and benefits and a benefit package that permits portability for those in the mobility path. Wial writes, "In occupations like janitorial work, where workers move frequently between a large number of small worksites in a relatively small geographical area, the area-wide uniformity of wages and benefits that results from multi-employer bargaining raises workers' standard of living and removes it from labor market competition."[26]

At the other end of the skill spectrum, there are a growing number of membership organizations in Silicon Valley comprised of semi-professionals such as system administrators, web designers, technical communication specialists, technical writers, and graphic artists. Some of these organizations are unions but most are not. These organizations operate on a regional scale to provide their members with networking opportunities, skill development, job listing services, and general career development.[27] While they do little to change employment conditions in the workplace, they help their members succeed in the boundaryless regional labor market of Silicon Valley.

Several unions have also adopted training programs characteristic of new craft unionism. Economist Stephen Herzenberg et al. describe union-negotiated training programs in the construction industry, in which employers contribute to funds for apprenticeship programs that are administered by

---

[22] *See* Elise Blackwell, *A Commitment to Organization: Justice for Janitors*, BEYOND BORDERS, Spring 1993, p. 16.

[23] *See* Howard Wial, *The Emerging Organizational Structure of Unionism in Low-Wage Services*, 45 RUTGERS L. REV. 671, 702 (1993).

[24] *See id.* at 693–98.

[25] *See id.* at 694–701.

[26] *Id.* at 694 (citation omitted).

[27] Chris Benner, WORK IN THE NEW ECONOMY: FLEXIBLE LABOR MARKETS IN SILICON VALLEY 130–175 (2002).

joint union-employer boards.[28] These training programs are designed to enable workers to keep their skills up to date. Similarly, in 1993, the unions at twelve hotels in the San Francisco area set up a joint training fund administered by unions and employers to upgrade their workers' skills.[29] The hospital workers' union, District 1199, has a training program in Philadelphia and New York that is designed to give entry level hospital employees the skills necessary to move up to higher occupational levels.[30] In 1992, the Wisconsin Regional Training Partnership was formed by approximately forty unionized manufacturing firms and their unions in the Milwaukee area to provide job development for the firms' current workers and workers who were laid off.[31] Also, the Communications Workers of America and the Washington Alliance for Technology Workers (WashTech) induced Cisco Systems to establish a national training program for technical workers in Seattle.[32] These union-sponsored training programs have differing goals, from job performance improvement to individual career development, but together they demonstrate that some unions understand the necessity of training as a matter of employee survival in a world in which neither work nor skills are steady.

The emerging examples of new craft unionism address many of the problems facing workers in the boundaryless workplace. Members of such occupationally based unions are not guaranteed jobs, but they are able to develop networks with which to find them. Similarly, new craft union members are not guaranteed income, but they work under contracts that guarantee minimal terms to ensure a living wage. Further, members are not guaranteed protection of their skills from technological change, but the unions provide a mechanism for continual learning.

Overall, then, nonexclusive craft unionism, with embedded contract bargaining and a job-to-job insider contracting employment system, is better suited to the modern workplace than is the industrial union model. However, this form of unionism does not solve all the problems of the boundaryless workplace. While it is inclusive rather than exclusive, the insider contract form of job placement still favors insiders and reinforces established cliques. Thus it poses a serious danger that long-time members will use their own contacts and prerogatives to monopolize employment opportunities and exclude newcomers, particularly on racial and gendered lines. Chapter 8 described the dangers of informal discrimination in

---

[28] See Stephen Herzenberg, John Alic, and Howard Wial, New Rules for a New Economy 131–33 (1998).

[29] See id. at 134–35.

[30] See Joan Fitzgerald & Virginia Carlson, *Ladder to a Better Life*, Am. Prospect, June 19, 2000, pp. 54, 56–57.

[31] See Herzenberg et al., New Rules for a New Economy 135–36.

[32] Danielle Dorice Van Jaarsveld, *Collective Representation Among High-Tech Workers at Microsoft and Beyond: Lessons from WashTech/CWA*, forthcoming in 42 Indus. Rel. (2004).

employer-controlled workplaces; the same danger is posed by worker-controlled job structures. To avoid replicating past exclusionary practices, a union hiring hall or a union-maintained referral list would be preferable to the inside contracting method of allocating job assignments. Such mechanisms would permit external monitoring for fair employment practices.[33]

Another limitation of the new craft unionism is that it may only be suitable for skilled work. If a job requires no skill or training, an employer has no incentive to turn to the union to fill it. In such cases, if a union cannot maintain a closed shop, it cannot protect low-skilled workers or workers who do not have clearly delineated occupational mobility paths. But if the laws policing discrimination were strengthened, and if the laws prohibiting the closed shop were eliminated, new craft unionism could prove to be an effective vehicle for boundaryless unionism.

B. Citizen Unionism

Another form of unionism that is emerging to address the problems created by the changing workplace is geographically based organization rather than workplace-based, firm-based, or skill-based organization. Locality-based unions, or citizen unions, operate by enlisting all employees in a locality or region to pressure area employers to provide the labor market protections workers need to survive and thrive in the boundaryless workplace. Notwithstanding the globalization of production, consumption, and knowledge, most people today still look to their local city, town, or county for schools, hospitals, libraries, parks, museums, and other accoutrements of daily life. Also, while Americans change their residences frequently, most of these moves are within the same county or metropolitan area.[34] Thus, most people would benefit from improvements in their locality's social infrastructure and have a strong incentive to work toward that end. Citizen unionism draws on those impulses.

A geographically based citizen union is a cross between a central city labor council, a worker-based civic association, and an old-fashioned benevolent association. It includes as members working people of all types, from all types of workplaces and industries in a given locality. Its goal is to pressure area-wide employers to provide area-wide workers with the income, benefits, and training they need to operate in the boundaryless workplace. Citizen unionism is evocative of the One Big Union movement that flourished briefly in Canada in the early years of the twentieth century, in which all workers in a given town or locality organized around the goal of conducting a general

---

[33] *See* Cobble, *Organizing the Post Industrial Work Force*, 44 INDUS. & LAB. REL. REV. at 432–34.
[34] *See* U.S. Bureau of the Census, http://www.census.gov/press-release/www/2000/cb00-107.html at 63.

strike.[35] In recent years, some worker groups have formed locality-based organizations with the goal not of calling a general strike but of creating an effective political and economic pressure group. Citizen unionism is just in its incipiency, however, so this conception of boundaryless unionism can only be described in a sketchy form.

1. The Role of a Citizen Union at the Local Level

Citizen unionism is neither industrial nor craft based, but rather geographically based. It is a form of unionism that addresses the needs and concerns of employees in their roles as citizens as well as in their roles as workers.[36] By reconceptualizing employees as citizens who collectively have an interest in the health, education, well-being, and employabilty of the entire population of their locale, citizen unionism makes it possible for workers to bring their collective strength to bear on issues that concern them both inside and outside the workplace. Some of the issues on which a citizen union might bring pressure are:

(a) Benefits. Citizen unions could pressure employers in a given locality to provide portability and uniformity in their pension and health benefit offerings. Alternatively, a citizen union could operate its own plan that provides uniform benefits and portability and does not impose waiting periods or sanctions for job hopping. Citizen unions could also monitor employer efforts to redesign benefit plans and negotiate with benefit providers to ensure portability and satisfactory benefit levels.

(b) Training. Citizen unions could pressure employers to pay for training and retraining throughout an employee's lifetime. They could also sponsor their own training programs to help employees learn job-related skills. Citizen unions could also negotiate with area employers to establish local and regional training, retraining, and up-skilling centers (TRUCs), paid for by employers, with a board of directors comprised of area unions, employers, and members of community groups representing contingent workers and the unemployed. The TRUCs could offer free training to all residents of the locality in skills required by area employers, regardless of whether they are union members, currently employed, or formerly employed by a contributing employer. The purpose of the TRUCs would be to enable local employees to acquire the necessary skills to participate in the boundaryless workplace.

---

[35] *See* Wial, *Unionism in Low-Wage Services*, 45 RUTGERS L. REV. at 690–91 (discussing the organizational structure of the "One Big Union" movement in Canada).

[36] Raymond Miles has a similar conception of geographically based unionism. *See* Raymond E. Miles, *Adapting to Technology and Competition: A New Industrial Relations System for the 21st Century*, CAL. MGMT. REV., Winter 1989, pp. 23–25.

(c) **Child Care.** Citizen unions could advocate employer-financed, cross-workplace child care centers akin to the TRUCs described above. Indeed, they could be part of the same program, a TRUC-4-Kids. These too should be available free of charge to all residents of the locality in order to enable them to participate in the boundaryless workplace. Such an institution would make it possible for employees to move between jobs without having to worry about displacing a child from his or her current child care situation. Such centers could also provide care for older children, such as after-school programs, school vacation and snow-day coverage, educational programs, and homework assistance.

(d) **Wages.** Citizen unions could pressure local employers to adhere to a local wage schedule, or local minimum wages, for broadly defined categories of work. They could pressure for wage subsidies for low-paid work. The living wage campaigns in many cities are current examples of attempts by citizen-union coalitions to mobilize local political pressure to achieve a local minimum wage above the national rate. In addition, a citizen union could monitor employers that pay substandard wages and report violations of wage and hour laws to the appropriate governmental authorities.

(e) **Legal Assistance to Individual Employees.** Citizen unions could provide legal assistance to individuals who are bringing lawsuits to enforce laws regarding minimum wages, occupational safety and health, pension security, antidiscrimination, and other worker protection measures. In addition, they could represent employees in the nonunion dispute resolution procedures that have proliferated in recent years in the wake of the Supreme Court's decision in 1991, in *Gilmer v. Interstate/Johnson Lane Corp.*, which upheld the use of predispute arbitration systems to resolve employees' discrimination complaints.[37] Unions have considerable expertise in the area of arbitration, and they could use it to assist nonunion workers in these employer-crafted tribunals. Union business agents could press for fair procedures, help workers select arbitrators, and supply representation in the proceedings. By doing so, unions could ensure that legislative gains in employment standards are enforced in these employer-crafted tribunals.

(f) **Corporate Citizenship.** Citizen unions could act at the local and regional level to pressure corporations to become good corporate citizens. Citizen

---

[37] *See, e.g.,* Stone, *Employment Arbitration Under the Federal Arbitration Act,* in EMPLOYMENT DISPUTE RESOLUTION AND WORKER RIGHTS IN THE CHANGING WORKPLACE 27 (Adrienne E. Eaton & Jeffrey H. Keefe, eds., 2000) (discussing the rapid growth of nonunion arbitration systems); *see also* Joseph R. Grodin, *Arbitration of Employment Discrimination Claims: Doctrine and Policy in the Wake of Gilmer,* 14 HOFSTRA LAB. & EMP. L.J. I (1996) 4–5 & n.6 (reporting on studies that found rapid growth of nonunion arbitration since the *Gilmer* decision).

unionism is animated by the proposition that because employers in a boundaryless workplace draw on the collective skills, knowledge, experience, and expertise of the local workforce, they should contribute to the welfare of that workforce generally. Employers should contribute to the local school systems, libraries, museums, cultural programs, sporting events, and hospitals. They should also fund enrichment programs for children. Corporate contributions of this sort would benefit all working people in the communities in which they operate. Citizen unions could use their clout to induce employers to become corporate citizens at the local and regional level.

2. Citizen Unionism and Bargaining Power

To be effective, citizen unionism has to have more than good intentions: it must have power. What kinds of power could a citizen union have to compel local corporations to comply with its demands? What economic weapons could it use to exert pressure on employers? Why would corporations submit to these kinds of social citizenship demands when they can always move away?

The bargaining power of a citizen union arises from several sources. First, it can exert public pressure on local corporations through publicity campaigns, informational picketing, and shaming in the local press. It can publicize bad working conditions and breaches of implicit promises to provide training, child care, or other basic benefits. A citizen union could publish annual lists of good corporate citizens and of bad corporate citizens, urging people to patronize the former and shun the latter. It could publish each company's on-going donations to important civic causes like the local school system or the local library. Local plant managers who live in a community are surprisingly vulnerable to pressures of these types from their neighbors, colleagues, and fellow country club members.

Second, citizen unions can organize boycotts of products or services produced by bad corporate citizens. The union-sponsored product boycott was a powerful economic weapon for labor during the nineteenth century, and it could be revived.[38] Corporations that produce products directly for consumers are sensitive to changes in demand. Those that do not produce consumer products often operate in networks with corporations that do produce for direct consumption, or have buyers and suppliers that do so. Exerting economic pressure on a buyer or supplier in order to affect the labor conditions or corporate behavior of a target corporation would run afoul of the current secondary boycott laws, but part of the legislative program of citizen unionism would be to change the secondary boycott laws to permit such tactics.

---

[38] On the role of the boycott for nineteenth-century unionism, see Montgomery FALL OF THE HOUSE OF LABOR, 147–48.

Citizen unions could also use public pressure and boycotts to induce corporations to sign codes of conduct in which they pledge to provide certain specified terms to its employees, such as training, child care, and portable benefits. These codes could be drafted in a way that made them enforceable by the citizen union in a federal or state court.

In addition to applying direct pressure on area employers, a citizen union could be a potent force in the political process. On the local level, it could run candidates and push for legislation to provide some of the measures mentioned above, including portability of benefits, a local minimum wage, publicly funded wage supplements, publicly funded child care, and training programs. A federation of citizen unions could play a similar role in state and national politics.

On the national level, a federation of citizen unions could serve as a potent force to lobby for measures that promote equality and justice in the workplace and in society more generally. It could press for antidiscrimination legislation, occupational safety and health protection, minimum-wage increases, universal health insurance, and other worker protection measures. In addition, because a citizen union defines its members both as workers and as citizens of a locality, a state, and a nation, it can go beyond traditional labor issues and address issues of concern to working people more generally.

None of the activities of citizen unionism described above depend upon National Labor Relations Board (NLRB) certification of a majority representative. Rather, they envision a union that functions as a hybrid of a local-improvement civic association and a citizens' lobbying group, emphasizing issues emanating from the workplace. Citizen unionism as thus described could supplement and support plant-level collective bargaining by individual unions in settings in which they exist.

3. Citizen Unions, Runaway Shops, and Local Agglomeration Economies

One possible objection to these proposals is that the more unions exert pressure on corporations at the local and regional level, the more temptation there will be for corporations to relocate to avoid union demands. This is the well-known danger of the runaway shop, or race to the bottom, and it results from the fact that capital is generally more mobile than labor. It is often posited that absent some reason for remaining in a particular locale, corporations will tend to move to locations that have the lowest labor costs.[39]

While there is considerable evidence that corporations do race to the bottom, or at least away from the top, there are circumstances in which corporations do not move to the lowest labor cost location. Sometimes

---

[39] *See* Katherine Van Wezel Stone, *Labor and the Global Economy*, 16 MICH. J. INT'L L. 987, 992–94 (1995) (citing race-to-the-bottom studies); Katherine Van Wezel Stone, *To the Yukon and Beyond: Local Laborers in a Global Labor Market*, 3 J. SMALL & EMERGING BUS. L. 93, 96–98 (1999).

corporations want to take advantage of a specifically trained labor force or be near particular markets or raw materials.[40] Furthermore, in today's world, corporations often want to be near others that produce in their field in order to take advantage of agglomeration economies.

Economists began to study the effect of agglomeration on economic growth in the 1980s. They found that firms producing certain types of goods and services were likely to locate near others of their type, such as the diamond district on 47th Street in New York City or the clusters of used car lots found on the periphery of most small cities.[41] This led economists to hypothesize that when certain types of firms were located in proximity to one another, they all received value from agglomeration that was independent of any single firm's contribution. Since then, a great deal of empirical work has confirmed the existence of localized agglomeration economies that play a powerful role in the locational choices of firms.[42] One well-known study is by Anna Lee Saxenian, a professor of Regional Development at the University of California, Berkeley. Saxenian describes the dramatic effects of agglomeration in the Silicon Valley computer industry.[43] Other examples of successful localized agglomeration economies are the clusters of biotechnology firms around Princeton, New Jersey, of banking and financial firms in New York City, and of computer hardware manufacturing firms around Austin, Texas. Regional economists attribute much of the positive effects of agglomeration economies to the skills and knowledge that is concentrated in, and shared among, the locality's workforce. A trained yet transient local workforce is seen as the key to successful local economic development because the workers who move constantly acquire and spread up-to-date knowledge among the firms in the locale.[44]

When locational choices of firms are influenced by the prospects of valuable agglomeration effects, those firms will be less likely to move overseas, or across the country, to escape rising labor costs. Indeed, many of the measures for which citizen unions might mobilize are measures that would enhance the value of a region's human capital, and thus increase the value of agglomeration. For example, corporate contributions to adult education and training programs can help make a locality's workforce more flexible and skilled, thereby providing a benefit to all area employers. Yet no individual

---

[40] *See* Stone, *To the Yukon*, 97–98.

[41] *See generally* John M. Quigley, *Urban Diversity and Economic Growth*, J. ECON. PERSP., Spring 1998, p. 132 (describing studies).

[42] *See, e.g.*, Matthew P. Drennan, *National Structural Change and Metropolitan Specialization in the United States*, 78 REGIONAL SCI. 297, 314–15 (1999) (describing an empirical study finding agglomeration economy in information-intensive industries in urban areas). *See generally* Edward L. Glaeser, *Are Cities Dying?* J. ECON. PERSP., Spring 1998, pp. 148–50 (citing studies).

[43] *See* Anna Lee Saxenian, REGIONAL ADVANTAGE: CULTURE AND COMPETITION IN SILICON VALLEY AND ROUTE 150 (1994).

[44] *See generally* John McDonald, FUNDAMENTALS OF URBAN ECONOMICS (1998).

employer has an incentive to establish such programs unilaterally because it would have no means of capturing all the benefits for itself, or preventing their capture by a competitor. However, if a citizen union pressures firms in an area to contribute jointly, then they all would share in the benefit. Similarly, if enough corporations contribute to a local school system to raise the level of educational attainment, that would help attract a highly skilled workforce and thus benefit all local firms. In this way, the prospects of agglomeration economies combined with increased reliance by corporations on human capital could provide the glue to keep corporations in place and prevent them from bolting each time a citizen union demands that local firms adopt good corporate citizenship behavior.

4. Emergent Examples of Citizen Unionism

Elements of citizen unionism can be found in organizations that are forming regional alliances and in unions that are broadening their role. For example, centers for contingent workers are appearing in many metropolitan centers to assist temporary workers with work-related problems. These centers address problems of contingent workers of all occupational types on an area-wide basis. The Boston Center for Contingent Work (CCW) uses media and other mechanisms to pressure companies that hire contingent workers to adopt codes of conduct that specify minimum rights and benefits. CCW is also active in lobbying the Massachusetts state legislature to enact a Workplace Equity Bill that would end discrimination in wages and benefits for contingent workers. To date, the bill has garnered significant support. CCW also works with Boston area labor unions to encourage them to provide for wage and benefit parity for contingent workers in their collective bargaining agreements.[45]

Recently CCW has joined with contingent worker organizations from more than twenty-five cities to form the National Alliance for Fair Employment (NAFFE). NAFFE is lobbying to get temporary workers the same rights under the labor and employment laws as permanent employees. NAFFE has also proposed a Temporary Industry Code of Conduct, which would require temporary employment agencies to provide temporary workers with written job descriptions, adequate safety equipment, on-site orientation, training, sick pay, holiday pay, health insurance, and transportation to work sites that are not publicly accessible.[46] The code further specifies that temporary workers may join unions at client employers if the existing

---

[45] Interviews with Tim Costello and Gail Nicholson, Director & Associate Director of Center for Contingent Work (CCW) in Boston, Mass. (May 2000).

[46] *See* National Alliance for Fair Employment, Contingent Workers Fight for Fairness 29–33 (May 2000) (unpublished manuscript on file with author), available at http://www.fairjobs.org.index.php (last visited Jan. 24, 2001).

collective agreement so permits.[47] It also provides that "[t]he agency will pay welfare-to-work participants a living wage consistent with local standards and benefits."[48]

Another example of citizen unionism is the Workplace Project on Long Island. Begun in 1992, the Workplace Project attempts to organize Latino immigrant workers on Long Island into membership organizations.[49] It seeks to bring together people who work in multiple occupations to address their common economic, social, and political problems. The Workplace Project, like CCW, organizes across industry and occupational lines and exerts pressure within a single locality or region. Its long-term plan is to develop workplace committees in each of the industries in which its members work, such as restaurants, landscaping services, and housecleaning, that can press for improvements in minimum wages and health standards.[50] The Workplace Project has also been active in lobbying for changes in state laws that affect immigrant workers. In 1997, it joined with other workers' rights groups in New York to secure the passage of the Unpaid Workers Prohibition Act, the strongest wage enforcement law in the country.[51]

There are also examples of cross-workplace organizations that involve workers with different types of skills within the same general industry. For example, WashTech involves technology workers of all types in the Seattle area. It is a community-based membership organization that uses publicity and lobbying to address the labor-related issues of high-tech firms. WashTech was founded in 1998 by a group of temporary workers at Microsoft, but has since expanded to include workers from Amazon.com and other high-tech industries.[52] Its goals are benefit portability, training, assistance with networking, restrictions in the use of noncompete covenants, and parity and fair treatment for temporary workers – many of the issues raised by the new employment relationship.[53] WashTech currently includes lower- to middle-skilled technical workers in high-tech industries in the Seattle area. It has a web page, a Listserv, and a staff to address the labor-related issues of high-tech firms.

---

[47] *See id.* at 32.

[48] *Id.* at 33.

[49] Jennifer Gordon, *We Make the Road by Walking: Immigrant Workers, the Workplace Project, and the Struggle for Social Change,* 30 HARV. C.R.-C.L. L. REV. 407, 428–29 (1995).

[50] *See id.* at 449.

[51] *See* Jennifer Gordon, THE CAMPAIGN FOR THE UNPAID WAGES PROHIBITION ACT: LATINO IMMIGRANTS CHANGE NEW YORK WAGE LAW (Carnegie Endowment, Working Paper No. 4, 1999).

[52] *See WashTech: A Voice of the Digital Workforce,* at http://www.washtech.org. (Last visited June 10, 2003.) *See also* Van Jaarsveld, *Collective Representation Among High-Tech Workers at Microsoft,* forthcoming in 42 INDUS. REL. (2004).

[53] The WashTech Mission Statement states: "WashTech is an organization of high-tech workers and allies joining together to provide an effective voice in the legislative and corporate arenas, and to advocate for improved benefits and workplace rights." *WashTech* at www.washtech.org.

In 2001, WashTech affiliated with an established labor union, the Communications Workers of America (CWA). Since then, WashTech attempted to engage in collective bargaining on two occasions, but each time, the units it was seeking to organize were sold and/or moved overseas. As a result, the organization primarily focuses on two other features of unionism – providing mutual aid and political action. For example, WashTech has set up a regional training center in Seattle for high-tech workers that offers low-cost training to IT workers in programming techniques and web design skills. It also participates in a national training program that the Communications Workers of America has established with Cicso Systems. WashTech helps high-tech workers resist noncompete clauses, and offers its members job-listing services and training classes.[54] WashTech also engages in extensive publicity and lobbying on behalf of temporary workers' interests. For example, WashTech helped defeat a proposed state law that would have eliminated overtime for computer professionals. It also lobbied successfully for a law to protect public sector temporary workers from misclassification or other attempts to deny them benefits they are entitled to under state law or collective bargaining agreements. Currently it is attempting to enact legislation that would force temporary employment agencies to inform their employees of their pay, work schedules, and other conditions of employment.[55]

Perhaps the most comprehensive example of a community-wide organization involved in work-related issues is the Industrial Areas Foundation (IAF). The IAF is a multi-issue organization that works at the grass-roots level on local issues such as social services, education, and employment. It has established organizations in a number of cities, including Chicago, Baltimore, Los Angeles, New York, and Boston, and has particularly been active in the Southwest. For example, in Texas, it has chapters in Dallas, Houston, Fort Worth, El Paso, San Antonio, and the Rio Grande Valley. The IAF's goal is to build broad-based coalitions that can exert pressure at the local and state level on issues of job training, living wages, education, local economic development, health care, social services, and housing. It works through existing organizations such as churches, schools, unions, community groups, health centers, and other local organizations, attempting to integrate concerns at the neighborhood, family, and workplace level. The IAF organizing style is to identify leaders within existing organizations and teach them to mobilize others and exert political power. It has had a number of successes and has become a potent political force in many cities.[56]

---

[54] Van Jaarsveld, *Collective Representation Among High-Tech Workers at Microsoft*, 42 INDUS. REL. at 15–16.

[55] *Id.* at 17.

[56] For a thorough and insightful description of the history and current operation of the Industrial Areas Foundation, *see* Paul Osterman, GATHERING POWER: THE FUTURE OF PROGRESSIVE POLITICS IN AMERICA (2002).

The IAF is involved in so many types of activities that it is impossible to catalog them fully. Of particular interest for present purpose are the IAF's activities in the labor market. In the early 1990s in San Antonio, the IAF developed an innovative job training program called Project QUEST. The program enrolled trainees for an eighteen-month intensive skill-training course. It utilized local community colleges to provide the classroom instruction. It also secured commitments from 650 local businesses to provide jobs to the QUEST graduates. According to Paul Osterman, who evaluated Project QUEST for the Ford Foundation, the program "led to substantial gains for its participants, gains that far exceed that of typical training efforts." Osterman found that the program's graduates saw substantial enhancement in their earnings power, and that the program provided other tangible benefits to the community. It led firms to raise their wage levels generally because QUEST insisted that participating employers pay trainees a living wage. The program also improved the community colleges because by working with QUEST, they were persuaded to revise their curricula in ways that better served the labor market needs of all their students.[57]

The IAF has also been involved in workplace safety campaigns and living wage campaigns in numerous cities. In the Rio Grande Valley, it is currently attempting to build an employees' association. According to Osterman, the association will be a broad-based employee organization that includes all types of workers – low-wage workers, contingent workers, unemployed workers, public employees, semi-self-employed, and full-time workers. It plans a living wage campaign for health care workers, and hopes that the campaign will affect wage levels throughout the community. The association is planning to offer training programs, job placement assistance, or other services to its members. However, it will not engage in conventional collective bargaining.[58]

Citizen unionism is an umbrella concept that could bring together all these different types of grass-roots organizing efforts into an effective community-based worker organization. It is compatible with traditional workplace-based local unions and other organizations, such as professional associations, that have similar interests. A citizen union could have local unions as affiliates and work with them on job-related issues that cut across workplaces. The AFL-CIO's Union-Community program currently engages in locality-based projects of this type.

Citizen unionism is also compatible with company-specific employee caucuses. Such caucuses are emerging with increased frequency in nonunion workplaces, usually around a single issue or comprised of a specific racial or ethnic group.[59] For example, IBM technicians recently organized

---

[57] *Id.* at 163–64.
[58] *Id.* at 167–68.
[59] *See* Alan Hyde, *Employee Caucus: A Key Institution in the Emerging System of Employment Law*, 69 Chi.-Kent L. Rev. 149, 159, 601 (1993).

themselves into a powerful protest group when the company converted its pension plan to a cash balance plan in such a way that threatened to defeat many long-term workers' expectations of continually increasing pension benefits. They held meetings and utilized e-mail, media, and stockholder resolutions to exert pressure on the company, the Securities and Exchange Commission, and Congress. Eventually they succeeded in getting the company to change its policy.[60] The IBM workers' network was comprised of computer specialists, engineers, and technicians – workers who have until now eschewed conventional unionism. The network they formed around the pension issue has affiliated with the CWA. Other single-issue employee caucuses have become a common form of employee protest. These efforts focus on a single occupation, job category, or employer. Such local organizations and employee caucuses would benefit from having a citizen union in their locality to give publicity and support to their campaigns, boycotts, and strikes.

C. Labor Law Reform to Facilitate Boundaryless Unionism

Changing work practices will activate new forms of unionism which will in turn create pressure for change in the labor laws. We have already seen some of the ways in which the National Labor Relations Act embodies the old employment relationship's assumption of long-term stable employment. The centrality of the bargaining unit in the labor law creates and reinforces hard boundaries between individual establishments and between departments within establishments. Other aspects of labor law such as the secondary boycott prohibition and the industrial pluralist treatment of arbitration similarly reinforce separatism and discourage boundaryless organizational forms. As the workplace changes and new union practices emerge, there will have to be reforms in the labor law to accommodate new forms of employee representation. Some of the reforms necessary to promote new forms of employee representation are discussed here. Some of the proposed changes would require amendments to the statute, and some would require modifications in existing doctrine by the National Labor Relations Board. None will magically transform the workplace and reverse the dynamics of union decline, but they would expand the possibilities of restoring democracy, accountability, and equity to the workplace.

1. Legal Change to Facilitate Inclusive Craft Unionism

In many respects, the labor law hinders the development of the types of new craft unions described above. To facilitate the formation of new forms of craft unions, the labor laws must cease treating the unionized workplace as an isolated and separate sphere. To this end, the NLRB should encourage

---

[60] *See* http://www.allianceibm.org/resolutions/resolutions2.htm (last visited Feb. 1, 2001), for information and documents pertaining to the IBM pension conversion battle.

multiemployer bargaining. One step in this direction would be to abandon the presumption in favor of single establishment bargaining units. Instead it should adopt a presumption in favor of multiemployer bargaining whenever a union requests it. In addition, the Labor Board should reverse the current requirement, under the joint employer doctrine, that each employer-member of a proposed multiemployer unit consent before certifying a multiemployer unit. Rather than make multiemployer bargaining the exception, the NLRB should make it the default rule.[61]

In order to encourage cross employer unions, the NLRB should modify the "community of interest" test for determining a bargaining unit. Rather, bargaining units should include occupational clusters and mobility paths that extend beyond the firm. In addition, Congress should amend the statute to permit bargaining units to be determined according to the wishes of the employees involved. [62]

There are other changes that Congress could make in the NLRA that would bolster the effectiveness of new craft unions. First, it could change the secondary boycott laws to permit unions to bargain for terms and conditions of workers at establishments within a production network, including an employer's subsidiaries or its joint venture partners. And rather than ban closed shops, the law should permit unions that maintain nondiscriminatory hiring halls or other nondiscriminatory job referral systems to bargain for closed shops. In addition, if Congress amended the definition of supervisor in section 2(11) of the NLRA so that lead workers could be union members, unions would be able to develop variants of the insider contracting system used by nineteenth-century steelworkers or by IATSE locals today. Finally, Congress should modify the independent contractor exclusion in section 2(3) of the NLRA by the adopting of an "economic realities" test for determining who is an employee.[63] This change would enable unions to organize workers who have employment relationships with multiple employers.

2. Legal Change to Facilitate Citizen Unionism

There are many respects in which Congress could amend the labor law to facilitate the formation of citizen unions and enable them to bargain with employers in a locality for area standards in compensation, benefits, health and safety, training, and child care. One of the legal reforms that would facilitate

---

[61] *See, e.g.*, Herzenberg et al., NEW RULES FOR A NEW ECONOMY 155, 161–66 (proposing legal changes that would favor multiemployer bargaining).

[62] To determine bargaining units by the wishes of employees would require a change in the statute, *see* 29 U.S.C. §159(c)(5) (1994).

[63] *See* 29 U.S.C. §152(3); NLRB v. Hearst Publ'ns, Inc., 322 U.S. 111 (1944) (adopting an "economic facts" test to determine whether an individual is an employee or independent contractor for purposes of NLRA). *Hearst* was repudiated by Congress in the 1947 Taft-Hartley Amendment to section 23 of the NLRA.

area-wide bargaining for regional employment standards and portable benefits is to change the presumption against multiemployer bargaining so as to enable more cross-employer bargaining. In addition, Congress could adopt European-style extension laws that extend negotiated standards to all firms of the same type in the same locale. To give a citizen union significant bargaining power, Congress should repeal section 8(b)(4) of the NLRA and permit unions to engage in peaceful secondary activity.

One of the main arenas for citizen union action is the political arena. Hence Congress and the NLRB could remove current impediments to union political action. For example, Congress could overturn the Supreme Court's decision in *Communications Workers* v. *Beck* that prohibits unions from using agency fees to influence elections and thereby permit unions to engage in more effective lobbying campaigns.[64] In addition, the NLRB could alter its definition of concerted protected activity so that workers are protected in their efforts to act collectively to affect legislation and politics.

D. Conclusion

There are emerging forms of employee organization that are more appropriate to the emerging workplace than existing bargaining-unit-based organization. The new forms are not limited to particular workplaces or bounded by relationships with particular employers. Two such forms, new craft unionism and citizen unions, have been described in this chapter. Yet, in many respects, the current labor law stands in the way of these initiatives. Several types of labor law reforms have been proposed that would facilitate their growth. Some of the proposals are minor revisions in existing rules, some challenge fundamental aspects of the statutory scheme. None of the proposals will magically produce boundaryless unionism; rather, they are aimed at removing some of the legal obstacles to this goal.

While attempts at labor law reform have not succeeded in the recent past, it is useful to articulate directions for reform because doing so makes it possible to envision legal change and to begin to build a coalition able to bring change about. Actually to produce a form of representation appropriate to the new workplace will require both a bold vision with broad reach and, at the same time, many small-scale experiments by many local unions, national unions, and other types of workers' groups. Many such experiments are arising in disparate locations and with different goals and differing foci. It is primarily out of these efforts that it may be possible to close the representation gap and bring democratic voice to workers in the new, boundaryless workplace. Legal reforms of the sort proposed could support these efforts and help realize their goals.

---

[64] 487 U.S. 735 (1988).

PART IV

SOCIAL JUSTICE IN THE DIGITAL ERA

The Crisis in Benefits and the Collapse of the Private Welfare State

Mobility is both the bane and the opportunity of the boundaryless workplace. On the one hand, the emerging digital era employment relationship creates a more interesting work environment and offers workers more autonomy and freedom than did the industrial era job structures. Yet on the other hand, for many it creates uncertainty, shifts risk, and fosters vulnerability.

Some of the groups that are disadvantaged in the new work regime can be easily identified. For example, older workers caught in the transition are heavy losers. Having been led to expect a good job and a secure future, they instead discovered that their expectations were chimeral.[1] Another group that has not fared well is the low-skilled – those who have neither the necessary training nor the ability to reinvent themselves, retool, and adapt to new labor market demands. A third disadvantaged group is the risk-averse – those who were comfortable with the stability and certainty that internal labor markets offered, and lack the desire or initiative to seek out opportunities, to network, and to build their own careers.

In addition to the older, the unskilled, and the risk-averse, all workers now face heightened risks at certain points in their working lives. Given the churning and constant change that characterize the new workplace, all face a high likelihood that their working lives will be peppered by occasional periods of unemployment. Therefore every worker requires a reliable safety net to ease the transitions and cushion the fall when they are left behind by the boundaryless workplace.

---

[1] A case study of white-collar workers laid off at IBM and Link Aerospace in Binghamton, New York – two companies known for their paternalistic long-term employment relationships – concluded that "downsizing and displacement change the expectations about the relationships among workers and between employers and workers." C. Koeber, *Corporate Restructuring, Downsizing and the Middle Class: The Process and Meaning of Worker Displacement in the "New" Economy*, 25 QUALITATIVE SOC. 217, 219 (2002).

Part III proposed changes to the law of intellectual property, employment discrimination, and collective bargaining in order to address issues of unfairness for incumbent workers in the boundaryless workplace. Part IV considers the problems of those left outside the boundaryless workplace and proposes mechanisms by which the law could offer them social protection. The present chapter addresses the crisis of social insurance that is created by the new employment relationship. Chapter 12 addresses the problem of widening income dispersion. Taken together, Part III and Part IV address the twin ideals of fairness and social protection – two necessary elements to ensure social justice in the digital era.

A. The Benefit Coverage Crisis

The boundaryless workplace is not a frictionless one. Each time employees moves across a corporate boundary, their social insurance, and hence their security, is at risk. For some, a move means losing health insurance coverage for preexisting conditions such as diabetes or heart problems. For others, it means waiting periods that spell risky gaps in their medical insurance coverage. Yet others can lose large sums in unvested pension rights or back-loaded pension plans.

As seen in Part I, the social insurance system in the United States was initially designed to complement job structures of the industrial era. In the early twentieth century employers deliberately structured health insurance and pension plans to tie the worker to the firm. These arrangements fit well with the long-term commitment that employers were seeking. But now, when employers neither desire nor offer long-term commitment to their employees, the design of most benefit plans is dysfunctional from the workers' point of view. Workers who change jobs frequently risk losing their benefits, yet those who do not change jobs out of fear of losing benefits – a condition termed "job lock" – cannot succeed in the current labor market.[2]

In the United States, workers' primary source of health insurance, pensions, disability, long-term care, and most other forms of social insurance is their employer, not the state. The federal government mandates some insurance through the social security program, particularly old-age assistance and insurance against disability and accidental death. In addition, state governments provide insurance against workplace injury through their workers' compensation systems and insurance against unemployment through their unemployment insurance programs. However, these programs provide bare bones protection at best. Thus since the mid-twentieth century, most American workers looked to their employer for health insurance, long-term

---

[2] On the problem of "job lock," see Katherine Elizabeth Ulrich, *You Can't Take It with You: An Examination of Employee Benefit Portability and Its Relationship to Job Lock and the New Psychological Contract* 19 HOFSTRA LAB. & EMPL. L.J. 173 (2001).

disability insurance, and meaningful pension coverage. Employers are not legally obligated to provide social insurance, and when they do, it is often because they have been forced to do so by unions.

The employer-centered nature of the American social insurance system contrasts sharply with the state-centered social welfare systems of Western Europe. The European welfare states provide residents with a wide range of benefits – family assistance, medical care, parental leave, unemployment insurance, retraining allowances, pensions, and so forth – financed by employer contributions as well as general tax revenues. The European social welfare system is available to all residents, whether working or not.[3]

Changes in the nature of work have had a two-fold impact on employee benefits in the United States. First, because social insurance in the United States is tied to employment, the increased job mobility that characterizes the new employment relationship contributes to the erosion of the social safety net because as employees move from job to job, they typically lose whatever employer-sponsored benefits they once had. Even if one's new employer offers benefit plans comparable to those of the former employer – an increasingly unlikely event given current cutbacks in benefit offerings – the new plans often impose waiting periods for health coverage and contain exclusions for pre-existing conditions that leave many effectively uninsured. Second, employers are restructuring their benefit plans just as they are restructuring their employment practices. In keeping with the ethos of the new workplace, the new benefit plans represent a retreat from the principle of risk sharing and a shift to a principle of individual choice. The new plans are designed to shift more risk of uncertainty onto employees, and by doing so, they weaken the social safety net. Changes in health insurance and pension practices will be described below.

B. Revamping Health Insurance

1. Declining Coverage

While the overwhelming majority of employees in the United States obtain their health insurance from their employer, the percentage of employees who have coverage has declined sharply in recent decades. Between 1983 and 1997, the number of full-time workers in medium and large establishments in the private sector who had medical care benefits from their employer decreased from 97 percent to 76 percent.[4] Furthermore, the percentage of

[3] Maurizio Ferrara & Anton Hemerijck, *Recalibrating Europe's Welfare Regimes*, in GOVERNING WORK AND WELFARE IN THE NEW ECONOMY 88–128 (Jonathan Zeitlin & David M. Trubek, eds., 2003).

[4] *See* U.S. Dept. of Labor, Bureau of Labor Statistics, EMPLOYEE BENEFITS SURVEY, Compensation Series Id EBUALLRET00000ML (available at data.bls.gov/servlet/SurveyOutput Servlet).

all workers with no insurance increased from 13.9 percent to 16.3 percent of the private sector workforce between 1990 and 1998.[5] According to the Congressional Budget Office (CBO), the number of individuals who are uninsured at any point in time is much larger than these numbers suggest. The CBO found that between 57 and 59 million people lacked health insurance at some point in 1998, a number that amounted to about a quarter of the nonelderly population.[6]

In addition to the declining incidence of coverage, medical insurance coverage has become less comprehensive, imposing more exclusions and limitations on coverage. Cutbacks in the types of coverage mean that many employees have insurance plans that do not cover basic health care needs.

At the same time, there has been a rapid rise in the cost of insurance, and a large share of the increase in insurance premiums has been passed on to employees. Between 1980 and 1998, the total cost of health insurance increased more than 300 percent – a rate that was three times faster than wages increased.[7] Employers have responded to the escalating costs of insurance by shifting some of the expense to employees, so that today more than 80 percent of full-time employees who have health plans are required to pay part of the cost.[8] Plans differ markedly as to the amount an employee is required to pay. The average employee contribution for medical coverage increased from $10.13 per month to $39.14 per month between 1983 and 1997, an increase of nearly 400 percent.[9] For the past four years, the amount employees are required to pay has increased at double-digit rates each year.[10] In addition, plans have imposed co-payments and raised deductibles, further raising the cost of medical care to employees. According to a report by the Kaiser Foundation, workers with employer-sponsored health plans are paying 48 percent more than they were just three years ago in employee contributions, copayments and other out-of-pocket expenses combined. As

---

[5] U.S. Dept. of the Census, STATISTICAL ABSTRACT OF THE UNITED STATES 102 tbl. 144 (121st ed. 2001).

[6] Robert Pear, *New Study Finds 60 Million Uninsured During a Year*, NEW YORK TIMES, May 13, 2003, p. A22.

[7] Albert E. Schwenk, *Trends in Health Insurance Costs*, COMPENSATION & WORKING CONDITIONS, Spring 1999, pp. 24, 26. While the rate of increase slowed in the mid-1990s – from almost 7 percent a year between 1988 and 1993, to 1 percent a year between 1993 and 1997 – evidence suggests that the rate of increase is rising again. David M. Cutler, *Employee Costs and the Decline in Health Insurance Coverage* (Nat'l Bureau of Econ. Research, Working Paper 9036, July 2002).

[8] Schwenk, *Trends in Health Insurance Costs* at 24.

[9] Cutler, *Employee Costs* 16–17.

[10] Milt Freudenheim, *Employees Paying Ever-Bigger Share for Health Care*, NEW YORK TIMES, Sept. 10, 2003. The Kaiser Foundation found that two-thirds of employers had increased the amounts employees are required to contribute in 2003, and 97 percent said they will do so again in 2004. Kaiser Commission on Medicaid and the Uninsured, UNDER-INSURED IN AMERICA: IS HEALTH COVERAGE ADEQUATE? (2002).

a result, the report found that many workers decline coverage because it has become too expensive.[11]

The decline in coverage is also a result of a decline in eligibility. As the amount of part-time, contingent, temporary, and other atypical types of work has increased, more and more workers are not eligible for employer-sponsored insurance.[12] Also, workers who move jobs frequently may decline coverage because of waiting periods and exclusions for preexisting conditions that render the insurance less valuable to them.

2. Redefining the Insurance Concept

The changes in scope and cost of coverage are related to changes in the very concept of health insurance. In the past, health insurance plans consisted of large risk pools that combined the healthy with the unhealthy, thereby spreading the risks and costs amongst numerous heterogeneous individuals. The large-pool approach reflected the view that insurance was about risk spreading and cross-subsidies in which the healthy helped subsidize the infirm. Today's trend is to the contrary: the trend is to decrease the size of pools and subdivide covered workers into discrete risk subgroups – skimming off the healthy, increasing the price for the less healthy, and denying coverage altogether for those deemed to be high risk.

In addition, many employers now offer flexible benefit plans, called "cafeteria plans," in which employees can choose to allocate a certain sum to whichever programs they select. They can often choose between a wide array of benefits, such as different levels of health coverage, dental benefits, short-term disability, long-term disability, child care, additional vacations, and even cash. According to the American Compensation Association, "As the employer role in employee benefits changes from 'provider' to 'facilitator,' many employers are finding flexible benefit plans to be a valuable tool."[13]

The cafeteria plans are touted because they increase employee choice while limiting employers' costs. However, such plans also foster adverse selection because younger and healthier individuals opt for health clubs, fertility treatment, and child care rather than long-term health coverage. This leaves the older and less healthy workers in the risk pool, raising the cost of health insurance for them. While cafeteria plans appear to optimize choice, they

---

[11] Kaiser Commission on Medicaid and the Uninsured, UNDER-INSURED. This finding was confirmed by labor economist David Cutler, who conducted a regression analysis of data from the Current Population Surveys since 1987. *See* Cutler, *Employee Costs* 25–27.

[12] Susan N. Houseman, *The Benefits Implications of Recent Trends in Flexible Staffing Arrangements*, in BENEFITS FOR THE WORKPLACE OF THE FUTURE 89, 104–05 (Olivia S. Mitchell et al., eds., 2001).

[13] Richard Sanes & Joseph L. Lineberry, IMPLEMENTING FLEXIBLE BENEFITS: AN APPROACH TO FACILITATING EMPLOYEE CHOICE 1 (American Compensation Association, 1995).

also undermine the risk-spreading ideal that lies at the heart of the concept of insurance.

Recently the Internal Revenue Service (IRS) has approved the use of defined contribution plans for health insurance. Under this approach, employers can give employees a determined amount toward their insurance which employees can spend as they choose in the private insurance market. Employees can tailor their plans themselves and even supplement the employer contributions to buy the insurance that best suits their individual and family needs. Many benefit consultants are advising their employer-clients to adopt these plans in order to reduce insurance costs and maximize individual employee choice.

Cafeteria plans and defined contribution health plans express a paradigm shift in the conception of benefits that has been dormant in benefit discussions for the past several years. Instead of seeing health insurance as a benefit conferred on employees by employers – whether for paternalistic reasons, the result of union bargaining, or as part of a larger human resource strategy – the new paradigm views health insurance as the individual's responsibility. In this new paradigm, the rationale for employer contributions to employees' health insurance is not its employee welfare or morale-building effects, but simply the fact that an employer can provide more coverage at less expense than can an individual. The employer has access to group rates and also is eligible for tax deductions for health insurance that are not available to employees. These features mean that employers can provide coverage more cheaply than an employee can obtain it.[14] In the new paradigm, the employer provides insurance because it is the least-cost provider, and the insurance is a form of in-kind salary to its employees.

There are legal developments that further move health policy discussions away from a group-based cross-subsidy approach toward an individual responsibility approach. Since the early 1980s, the IRS has permitted employers to offer their employees flexible spending accounts (FSAs). These are accounts in which the employees can set aside a portion of pretax income – up to a ceiling of $5000 – to pay for uninsured medical expenses. In effect, FSAs permit employees to enjoy some of the tax benefits for health-care costs that had previously been reserved to employers.[15] Recently there have

---

[14] *See* Greg Scandlen, *MSA's Can Be a Windfall for the Rest of Us Too*, 49 CATH. U. L. REV. 679 (2000). In 1996, Congress enacted a program of medical savings accounts that permit the self-employed and employees of small employers to set aside a certain amount of pre-tax dollars to pay for health needs. This program, a part of the Health Insurance Portability and Accountability Act of 1996 (HIPAA), permits those groups of individuals to enjoy some of the tax benefits for health insurance that previously were reserved to employers.

[15] For a detailed and enlightening description of the origin of flexible spending accounts, *see* Daniel C. Schaffer & Daniel M. Fox, *Tax Law as Health Policy: A History of Cafeteria Plans, 1978–1985*, 8 AM. J. OF TAX POL'Y 1 (1989). *See* 42 U.S.C. §§ 300gg-300gg-92 (1996 and Supp. 2001).

been changes to the program to increase the amount an individual can set aside and to make the program more user-friendly for employees. These changes would give individuals more of the tax benefits for medical reimbursement accounts that were previously reserved to employers, and would thereby undercut the least-cost-provider rationale for employer-provided benefits.

The trends in health insurance do not bode well for the future of employer-centered health insurance. If employers are not the least-cost providers, they may have no incentive to provide health insurance at all. They could easily decide to let individuals make their own choices about how much insurance to buy. However, there are two fundamental fallacies in the new individual responsibility and employee choice paradigm for health insurance. First, low-paid employees are unlikely to purchase sufficient insurance to cover their unanticipated health care needs. Thus the declining extent of employer-provided coverage will foster resentment, vulnerability, and discontent. Second, employers also lose when employees do not have adequate medical insurance. Employees who have insurance are more likely to get health care when they are sick and therefore have fewer and shorter absences from work. Some insurance plans also provide preventative programs for heart ailments, back injuries, and other potentially chronic conditions. Even though today's employers do not value long-term attachment from their employees, they also do not want sporadic and unpredictable absences of indeterminate duration. Employee health insurance helps employers maintain steady production schedules with reliable employees.

3. Legislating Health Insurance Reforms

The reform agenda for health insurance has to address two goals that are not entirely compatible. First, health insurance has to be *portable* if it is to be meaningful for employees in the boundaryless workplace. Second, it must be *affordable*. If there were a national single-payer scheme as is found in most of Western Europe and Canada, both goals would be met. Health insurance would not be linked to employment so workers would have coverage even as they moved from job to job, and it would be affordable for individuals because it would be financed from general tax revenues. But in the absence of such universal coverage, other reforms are necessary in the United States if individuals are to retain health coverage as they move around in the new flexible labor market.

In the past two decades, there has been some movement toward greater portability in the area of health insurance. In 1986, Congress put a provision into the Consolidated Omnibus Budget Reconciliation Act that requires employers who have health insurance plans to offer departing beneficiaries the opportunity to continue their coverage for 18 months.[16] This provision for

---

[16] P.L. 99–292.

continuation of benefits, known as COBRA, has been amended, modified, and expanded several times. In 1996, Congress further expanded portability in the Health Insurance Portability and Accountability Act (HIPAA), which requires group plans to reduce waiting periods for preexisting conditions when employees move from one health plan to another. HIPAA also raised the tax deductibility of health insurance premiums for individuals who are self-employed. These provisions make it easier for individuals to retain health coverage as they move between workplaces, but at their own expense. While employees are generally required to pay for their COBRA coverage themselves, it nonetheless means that if they had insurance with a former employer, they do not automatically lose their health insurance when their employment terminates.[17]

There are other proposals to expand health insurance portability currently under consideration. One proposal is to expand medical reimbursement accounts by permitting individuals to get tax deductions for health insurance coverage, thereby delinking health insurance from employment. Another measure that would enhance portability would be to permit individuals to deduct the full cost of health insurance premiums from their income for tax purposes. This change would permit individuals to select their own health insurance plan and thus side-step employer-sponsored plans altogether.[18]

Although COBRA, medical reimbursement accounts, and the proposed tax deductions for health insurance would enhance portability for individuals who can pay the cost of health insurance, they would not address the problem of affordability. As the costs of health insurance go up and up, and as incomes at the middle and bottom of the income distribution stagnate, health insurance becomes a luxury many cannot afford. So while there are viable proposals for portability, they must be combined with a program to make health insurance affordable if it is to have an effect on the incidence of health insurance coverage.

Health insurance is one issue that could be treated at the local and/or regional level by the kind of citizen union proposed in Chapter 10. A locality-based citizen union could exert pressure on local employers to establish an area-wide health insurance plan that provides both portability and affordability to employees working at participating establishments. Such a plan could form a partnership with public providers of insurance such as Medicaid to include coverage for the unemployed and under-employed. There have been experiments with public-private locality-based health insurance plans in Wisconsin and other places that could serve as a model for

---

[17] Sharona Hoffman, *Unmanaged Care: Towards Moral Fairness in Health Care Coverage*, 78 IND. L. J. 659, 677–78 (2003).

[18] This proposal is put forward by Marina v.N. Whitman, NEW WORLD, NEW RULES: THE CHANGING ROLE OF THE AMERICAN CORPORATION 174–75 (1999).

multi-workplace-based or non-workplace-based forms of affordable and portable health insurance.[19]

4. Shifts in Private Sector Pension Policy

In addition to the declining scope and adequacy of health insurance over the past two decades, there has been a decline in the incidence and adequacy of old-age assistance. Between 1985 and 2000, the number of full-time workers in large establishments in the private sector who have retirement plans of any type has declined from 91 percent to 70 percent.[20] Furthermore, employees who change jobs, whether voluntarily or involuntarily, lose valuable pension rights. In addition, the same movement from a paternalistic, collectivist approach to an individual responsibility approach to benefits that we saw with health benefits has affected pensions. Thus, in the past two decades, there has been a dramatic shift in the nature of pensions, a shift that has moved risk and responsibility away from the firm and placed it on the employee.[21]

(a) Defined Benefit Plans. In the past, most private pensions were "defined benefit" plans. In a defined benefit plan, each employee is guaranteed a specified benefit level at the time of retirement. The actual benefit usually varies with length of service and final out-going salary level, but it is part of a fixed schedule on which the worker can rely. The benefits are paid from a fund to which employers contribute on behalf of their covered employees, sometimes with employee contributions as well. The IRS and the Department of Labor monitor employer contributions to defined benefit plans in order to ensure that employer contributions are sufficient to cover future plan liabilities. A federal agency, the Pension Benefit Guaranty Corporation (PBGC), insures the plans and pays benefits to beneficiaries if a fund becomes insolvent.

Most defined benefit plans are structured so that an an individual's pay-out is a function of their final year's earnings and their length of service. That is, the pay-out amounts are back-loaded to provide greater benefits to long-term employees. This structure means that employees who depart before reaching their highest earning rate forfeit significant pension benefits.

Mobile employees not only lose the back-loaded benefits of their plans, they lose all their benefits if they change jobs before their benefits vest. The

---

[19] For a detailed description of the Wisconsin initiatives, *see* Louise G. Trubek, *Working on the Puzzle: Health Care Coverage for Low-Wage Workers*, 12 HEALTH MATRIX: J. L.-MED. 157 (2002).

[20] U.S. Dept. of Labor, BLS, EMPLOYEE PARTICIPATION IN DEFINED BENEFIT AND DEFINED CONTRIBUTION PLANS, 1985–2000 (Mar. 26, 2003) (available at www.bls.gov/opub/cwc/em20030325tbo1.htm, last checked Sept. 19, 2003).

[21] For a detailed discussion of the recent shifts in pension practices and its impact on risk, *see* Edward Zelinsky, *Defined Contribution Plans After Enron* (unpublished manuscript on file with author 2003).

Employee Retirement and Security Act (ERISA) requires that defined benefit plans must either vest gradually over a three-to-seven-year period, or vest all at once (known as "cliff vesting") within five years of employment under the plan.[22] Workers in defined benefit pension plans who leave their employment before becoming fully vested lose some of the contributions they accrued while on a job. Those who depart after their benefits have vested also stand to lose a lot. Vested benefits in a defined benefit plan remain frozen in amount until the individual reaches retirement age. They do not grow and are not protected from inflation. Also, as mentioned, departing workers lose the benefit of the back-loading. Because many employees view pension contributions as recompense for a lower salary, a mobile employee loses on both scores.[23]

At present, defined benefit plans are under siege. Because most pension assets have been invested in stocks, the long bear stock market of the early 2000s has been devastating to defined benefit plans. As a result, many plans do not have sufficient assets to cover their estimated pension liabilities. As of September 2003, 353 of the Standard & Poor's 500 companies offered defined benefit plans, and it is estimated that 322 of them are in debt. The total debt of those companies was estimated at $226 billion.[24] The PBGC estimates that as of May 2003, total U.S. corporate pension deficits amounted to $300 billion.[25]

(b) Defined Contribution Plans. In the 1980s, many employers began to shift from defined benefit plans to defined contribution plans. In defined contribution plans, the employer contributes into an account for each worker based on the number of person-hours worked. Typically, the worker makes a contribution as well. Usually workers are given some choice about how the funds in their accounts shall be invested. Upon retirement, the amount of each worker's pension is determined by the value of the account at that time. If the funds were invested well or if the market did well overall, the worker's pension might be ample. But if the funds were invested poorly or if retirement occurred amidst a market downturn, the pension could be small.

---

[22] Internal Revenue Code, 26 U.S.C. § 411 (a)(2)(A) & (B). Employer contributions to defined contribution plans have similar vesting requirements.

[23] A study by the Pensions Institute of the University of London found that a typical individual in Great Britain loses almost 30 percent of their benefits from a defined contribution plan due to job mobility. David Blake & J. Michael Orszag, *Portability and Preservation of Pension Rights in the United Kingdom* 9–10, in REPORT OF THE DIRECTOR GENERAL'S INQUIRY INTO PENSIONS vol. 3, Office of Fair Trading, July 1997.

[24] David R. Francis, *Pension Funds Pinched, Stirring Calls for Reform*, CHRISTIAN SCIENCE MONITOR, Sept. 3, 2003.

[25] Special Report on Corporate Pensions, *Nest Eggs Without the Yolk*, ECONOMIST, May 10, 2003, p. 59.

In a defined contribution plan, the risk both of market decline and of bad investment decisions fall on the individual employee.[26]

In the past twenty years, defined contribution plans have overtaken defined benefit plans as the dominant form of employer-provided pensions in the United States. Defined benefit plans covered approximately 80 percent of full-time workers in medium and large establishments in the private sector in 1985, but by 2000 that number had declined to 36 percent.[27] Today more than 50 percent of workers who have pension plans are in defined contribution plans, and 90 percent of employer plans are now defined contribution plans. One commentator writes:

Defined contribution pensions are said to reflect an employer's desire to limit long-term financial exposure, and a shift in employers' priorities away from retaining workers with eroding industrial skills to attracting new workers with up-to-the-minute skills. Defined contribution arrangements tend to attract mobile workers because they are more adaptable to the needs of workers who change jobs or follow varied career paths.[28]

Defined contribution plans are attractive to employers for the obvious reason that they shift risk of stock market fluctuations onto the employee. Defined contribution plans are also attractive to mobile workers because the benefits generally vest sooner than in defined benefit plans, and because such plans usually pay a lump sum distribution to departing employees. Furthermore, even if employees do not take lump sums at the time of departure, the benefits in their accounts continue to grow during their working careers. Thus while defined contribution plans impose a new level of risk on employees, they are in many respects more adaptive than defined benefit plans for today's mobile workforce. Yet despite their attractiveness, defined contribution plans leave many vulnerable to stock market downturns and Enron-style pension malfeasance.[29]

---

[26] *See* Edward A. Zelinsky, *The Cash Balance Controversy*, 19 VA. TAX REV. 683, 692–93 (2000).

[27] U.S. Dept. of Labor, BLS, EMPLOYEE PARTICIPATION IN DEFINED BENEFIT AND DEFINED CONTRIBUTION PLANS. *See also* Richard A. Ippolito, *Tenuous Property Rights: The Unraveling of Defined Benefit Pension Contracts in the United States*, in PENSION POLICY IN AN INTEGRATING EUROPE (O. Castellino and E. Fornero, eds., 2003); U.S. Dept. of Labor, BLS, EMPLOYEE BENEFITS SURVEY.

[28] Ulrich, *You Can't Take It with You*, 19 HOFSTRA LAB. & EMPL. L.J. at 186.

[29] In December 2001, Enron Corporation, a multibillion-dollar company ranked seventh in the Fortune 500, declared bankruptcy. The collapse of Enron was the biggest corporate collapse in history. Enron's demise was a product of a cat's cradle of secret partnership deals, shady accounting practices, stock manipulation, and regulatory malfeasance. For an unusually lucid account of Enron's demise, *see* Kurt Eichenwald with Diana B. Henriques, *Web of Details Did Enron In As Warnings Went Unheeded*, NEW YORK TIMES, Feb. 10, 2002. *See also* Gretchen Morgenson, *How 287 Turned into 7: Lessons in Fuzzy Math*, NEW YORK TIMES, Jan. 20, 2002. For Enron workers, the behemoth's collapse spelled the end not only of their jobs, but also of their retirement savings. Enron had a 401(k) retirement plan into which it contributed company stock, encouraging employees to do so as well. Approximately

Even more risky for employees is a type of defined contribution plan that has enjoyed increasing popularity in recent years – 401(k) plans. These plans are employer-sponsored arrangements by which employees can purchase stock using pre-tax dollars. Some plans provide for matching employer contributions up to a fixed maximum amount. Many 401(k) plans require the funds to be invested heavily in the employer's own stock. The popularity of 401(k) plans has increased steadily, so that today 55 percent of all full-time employees in medium and large companies participate in such plans.[30]

One benefit of a 401(k) plan is that the employee's money grows in the stock market and all taxes are deferred until the time of retirement. Because both the contributions and the fund's earnings are tax-deferred, many employees use these devices as a substitute for individual retirement savings. However, many 401(k) plans place restrictions on the types of stock investments individuals can make and impose limits on when funds can be withdrawn. A plan that requires investment of a substantial part of each employee's 401(k) funds in the company's own stock puts that employee at great risk from business downturns. If the firm becomes insolvent, the employees will lose both their jobs and their retirement savings. Indeed, this form of investment runs afoul of modern portfolio theory, which counsels investors to diversify their investments. Section 401(k) plans channel employees' investments into the very same company where their human capital is already invested, thereby accentuating their exposure to risk.[31]

Currently, defined contribution plans are undergoing a subtle but significant transformation. Employers are reducing their contributions and permitting employees more options about how the funds are invested. These changes shift the plans from an employer-provided benefit to a personal savings plan. In addition, increasingly defined contribution plans are permitting employees to take out loans from their accounts, a trend that undercuts the potential of a defined contribution plan to ensure retirement security. Additionally, most defined contribution plans do not offer employees a lifetime annuity at retirement age, but offer a lump sum payment instead. These changes undercut the concept of pensions as a vehicle for lifelong retirement security.[32]

---

51 percent of Enron employees participated in the plan, with the lion's share invested in Enron stock. On October 17, 2001, the company froze the plan's assets and did not permit employees to withdraw Enron stock. The freeze occurred just when the executives knew that there would be imminent disclosures of the company's shaking financial condition and questionable accounting practices. As a result, 15,000 workers lost $1.3 billion in their retirement savings. See Richard A. Appel, Jr., *Employees' Retirement Plan Is a Victim As Enron Tumbles*, NEW YORK TIMES, Nov. 22, 2001; Louis Uchitelle, *The Rich Are Different: They Know When to Leave*, NEW YORK TIMES, Jan. 20, 2002.

[30] U.S., Dept. of Labor, BLS, EMPLOYEE BENEFITS IN MEDIUM AND LARGE PRIVATE ESTABLISHMENTS (1997, available at http://stats.bls.gov/beshome.htm).

[31] *See* Susan Stabile, *Defined Contribution Plans*, 77 N.Y.U. L. Rev. 71, 90–91 (2001).

[32] Olivia S. Mitchell with Erica L. Dykes, *New Trends in Pension Benefit and Retirement Provisions*, in Mitchell et al., BENEFITS FOR THE WORKPLACE OF THE FUTURE 110, 128–30.

(c) Cash Balance Plans and Other Hybrid Plans. In the 1990s, many corporations adopted a new type of pension plan that was a hybrid between a defined benefit and defined contribution plan. These plans, called cash balance plans have multiplied quickly in recent years.[33] A cash balance plan works as follows: each employee has a hypothetical account to which the employer contributes a percentage of the worker's compensation and an interest payment, at a predetermined rate, that compounds to the worker's retirement date or when the worker leaves the plan. When employees leave employment, they can either take their accumulated accounts as lump sums or leave them to continue to compound at the interest rate set, until withdrawal at a later date.

The distinctive feature of a cash balance plan is that it is a defined benefit plan but it is not back-loaded. Instead, a cash balance plan enables employees to accrue benefits at an even rate. When employees depart, they can either take the full value of the contribution made on their behalf as a lump sum or freeze it in an account that will continue to grow. Thus cash balance plans offer portability for younger and mobile workers because they do not penalize job changes. However, such plans have been challenged on the ground that they discriminate against older employees in the rate of benefit accrual. Under a cash balance plan, as an individual approaches retirement, the even rate of accrual of benefits means that the annuity value amount of the benefit accrual declines. At least one court has found cash balance plans to be discriminatory for that reason, and others may follow suit.[34]

Many cash balance plans were introduced as conversions of traditional defined benefit plans, and the process of conversion had catastrophic effects on older, long-term workers.[35] This was because companies often underestimated the value of existing accrued pension rights and utilized formulas for future pensions that prevented older employees from accumulating new pension benefits for a substantial period of time. However, some pension analysts have proposed methods of converting to cash balance plans that do not impose significant losses on older employees by grandfathering accrued and vested benefits.[36]

C. Achieving Benefit Portability and Continuity

If the pension system is to provide genuine old-age assistance, it must provide both portability and security. Presently, the system does not offer either to

---

[33] For a detailed analysis of the role of tax policy in fostering the growth of cash balance plans, see Ippolito, *Tenuous Property Rights.*

[34] Cooper v. IBM Personal Pension Plan 2003 WL 21767853 (S. D. Illinois, 2003).

[35] For an excellent discussion of the barriers to portability in pension and health insurance plans, and recent changes to make plans more portable, *see* Ulrich, *You Can't Take It with You,* 19 HOFSTRA J. LAB. & EMPL. L.J. at 222–51.

[36] Deana Saxinger, *Cash Balance Plans: They Work for Employers but Do They Work for Employees?* 34 J. Marshall L. Rev. 345 (2000).

workers who move frequently between firms and in and out of the labor market. Hence pensions need to be restructured to provide a cushion against the risks of the digital era workplace. There have been some modifications in the laws and practices governing pensions and health insurance in the past two decades that move in this direction, but for reasons that will be explained, they are not sufficient.

On several occasions in the past decades, Congress has amended the laws governing pensions to enhance their portability. In 1984 and again in 2001, Congress amended the Employee Retirement Security Act of 1974 to decrease the vesting periods for defined benefit and defined contribution plans, thereby enhancing their portability. In 1984, Congress lowered the maximum vesting period from ten years to five. And in 2001, an amendment lowered the maximum vesting periods for employer contributions to defined contribution plans to three years for cliff vesting and two to six years for gradual vesting. In addition, in 1992 Congress expanded the situations in which employees who change jobs could roll over assets accumulated in their pension accounts to a new plan without incurring tax or penalty liability.[37]

Other legislative reforms that enhance pension portability have taken the form of expanding the possibilities for individuals to participate in individual tax-preferred retirement savings programs, through expanding the use of individual retirement accounts (IRAs), providing for 401(k) plans, and providing for medical expenses accounts and educational savings accounts. These measures permit individuals to enjoy some of the tax benefits that employers' previously enjoyed, thereby giving individuals freedom to structure their own retirement arrangements. Because IRAs are established by individuals, they are entirely portable. All these measures embody the individual responsibility approach to pensions, and they all share many of the problems of defined contribution plans. They shift the risks of bad investment and market decline to individuals. Individuals are notoriously bad at making investments, so that while an individualized approach to pension investment may sound good in principle, it is usually ill-advised in operation.[38]

The further danger of the move to individualized retirement savings is that it will further encourage employers to cease offering retirement plans altogether. As we saw in Chapter 2, pension plans were initially set up as a means for employers to bind employees to their firms, thereby promoting long-term attachment between the employee and the firm. Because employers no longer value that kind of attachment, they have scant incentive to offer retirement plans in the first place. Already, as defined benefit plans become increasingly expensive and debt-laden, employers are converting them to defined contribution and cash balance plans. The next logical step

---

[37] Economic Growth and Tax Reconciliation Act of 2001, P.L. 107–16.
[38] For studies about individual investment choices, *see* Stabile, *Defined Contribution Plans*, 77 N.Y.U. L. Rev. at 86–90.

advocated by some management consultants is to terminate the employer's role in pensions altogether and permit each individual to choose for him- or herself whether to invest salary dollars into present consumption or a tax-preferred savings vehicle.[39] Where unions are present, they will undoubtedly continue to bargain for pension plans as part of their wage packages, but with unions declining and job structures transforming, it is altogether possible that private pensions will become a vestige of an earlier era.

If private employers get out of the pension business, it will become necessary to use public funds to provide old-age assistance because not all individuals will do so on their own. Yet at present, it is not conceivable that Congress would restructure the endangered Social Security system to provide *increased* protection for the aging workforce. So unless we can foresee major social security reform, it is necessary to devise reforms to the private pension system that will increase portability and income security. While shortening vesting periods and increasing rollover opportunities contribute to pension portability, these reforms do not go far enough. Defined contribution plans are inherently risky for employees, so that the shift away from defined benefit plans may promise illusory benefits at best. A better solution would be to foster portability within defined benefit plans by requiring immediate vesting and 100 percent rollover.

D. Conclusion

The sustainability of the boundaryless workplace depends on the existence of a social safety net that can effectively ease worker transitions when they change jobs or move in and out of the workplace. At present, the private safety net that has been in place in the United States since the 1930s is not only unsuitable to the emerging era, it is also unravelling. Thus it is necessary to reinvent the social benefit system, both for health insurance and for old-age assistance. In the area of health insurance, that means providing portability and, at the same time, affordability. In the area of pensions, it means providing portability while ensuring that pay-outs are adequate. In both areas, portability could be achieved by the formation of regionally based, multi-employer pension and health plans. Such plans could operate on a regional basis and enable all employees in a locality to participate. A community-based benefit plan of this type could be sponsored by a community-based citizen union of the type discussed in Chapter 10. Indeed, a citizen union might be the only type of organization that can initiate a plan of this type. Thus reforms in the labor laws that facilitate the formation of community-based unions would also facilitate the development of institutions to shore up the social safety net.

---

[39] Special Report on Corporate Pensions, *Nest Eggs Without the Yolk*, 59, 61 ECONOMIST, May 10, 2003, p. 61.

The Working Rich and the Working Poor: Income Inequality in the Digital Era

The changes in the employment relationship described in Part II have been accompanied by a marked deterioration in the income distribution. The U.S. income distribution has become considerably more unequal since 1970, a trend that accelerated in the 1980s and 1990s. Despite the economic boom of the 1990s, the working poor now comprise the fastest growing portion of the workforce. The burgeoning inequality threatens the integrity and moral authority of the social order. Those locked out of the world of economic opportunity are locked into a perpetual underclass, and often exhibit antisocial behaviors such as drug use, alcoholism, and crime. The extent of income inequality offends our sense of decency and undermines the possibility of social cohesion. It stands as a quiet but persistent reminder that current economic arrangements are not moving in the direction of economic justice.

The widening of the income distribution has occurred in the same period in which firms have dismantled their internal labor markets and begun to implement boundaryless human resource practices. The correspondence suggests that there may be a relationship between the two developments. This chapter explores the deterioration of the income distribution and its possible relationship to the changing job structures. It argues that one important factor that is driving the trend toward increased income inequality is the changing nature of the employment relationship. It further argues that in evaluating programs designed to promote income equality, we should choose those that help cushion the shocks and ease the transitions of workers as they experience the vicissitudes of the boundaryless workplace.

A. The Facts of Rising Income Inequality

While there are many ways to measure income inequality, all measures tell the same story: There has been a steady increase in income inequality in the United States since 1970 and a particularly sharp increase in the late 1980s and mid 1990s. For example, the share of total income going to those in the highest 10 percent of the income distribution – called the top decile – increased from under 32 percent in 1970 to nearly 42 per cent in 1998. Of this, the lion's share of the increase went to those at the very top. The share of total income going to the highest 1 percent of the population has more than doubled between 1970 and 1998, from 5 percent to 11 percent in 1998. And the share going to the top 0.1 percent more than tripled in that period, rising from under 2 percent to 6 percent.[1]

Since the late 1970s, only those with incomes in the highest 7 or 8 percent have seen increases in their hourly pay.[2] The income of wage earners in all other groups experienced declines. The share of income going to the bottom 20 percent – the bottom quintile – has declined most severely. Between 1977 and 1999, the incomes of families in the bottom quintile declined in absolute terms by 9 percent, shrinking from 5.7 percent of total income to 4.2 percent. In the same period, the share of total income going to the middle quintile declined from 16.4 percent to 14.7 percent, while the share of those in the highest quintile grew from 44.2 percent to 50.4 percent. According to the Center for Budget Priorities, "In 1999, for the first time in the years CBO [the Congressional Budget Office] has examined, the top fifth of the population is expected to receive slightly more after-tax income than the rest of the population combined."[3]

One method economists use to measure income inequality is to compare the income of those in the top 10 percent of the income distribution with those in the lowest 10 percent. This produces a number known as the 90/10 ratio. Between 1970 and 1998, the 90/10 ratio for men increased from 3.85 to 5.31, and for women, it increased from 3.41 to 4.33. This indicates a substantial increase in inequality between those at the top and those at the bottom of the income distribution.[4] To put the contrast even more starkly, as of 1999, the share of income of the top 1 percent, some 2.7 million Americans, is approximately the same as that of the 100 million Americans with the lowest incomes.[5] This dramatic rise at the very top of the income distribution has created a small group earning mega-salaries, a group known as the "Working Rich."[6]

[1] Thomas Piketty & Emmanuel Saez, *Income Inequality in the United States, 1913–1998*, 118 Q. J. ECON. 1, 11 fig. 1 (2003).

[2] Gary Burtless, Robert Z. Lawrence, Robert E. Litan, & Robert J. Shapiro, GLOBALPHOBIA: CONFRONTING FEARS ABOUT OPEN TRADE 77–78 (1998).

[3] Isaac Shapiro & Robert Greenstein, *The Widening Income Gulf*, Center on Budget Priorities (Sept. 9, 1999). *See also* Frank Levy, THE NEW DOLLARS AND DREAMS: AMERICAN INCOME AND ECONOMIC CHANGE 199 tbl. A.1 (1998).

[4] U.S. Bureau of the Census, Current Population Reports, THE CHANGING SHAPE OF THE NATION'S INCOME DISTRIBUTION, 3 tbl. 1 (June 2000).

[5] Shapiro & Greenstein, *Widening Income Gulf* 2. *See also* Piketty & Saez, *Income Inequality*, 14 & fig. III (showing percentage income share of top 0.01 percent of earners increased fivefold from 1973 to 1998).

[6] Piketty & Saez, *Income Inequality* 17 & fig. 4.

In addition to comparing the top to the bottom, economists also measure inequality by looking at whether there has been a dispersion or a convergence between the bottom and the middle of the income distribution. To measure growing inequality in the lower part of the income distribution, economists compare the share of total income going to the group in the middle, those in the 50 percent decile, with the share going to the bottom, the 10 percent decile. This comparison, the 50/10 ratio, has also increased in the past thirty years. The 50/10 ratio for men increased from 2.14 to 2.43 between 1970 and 1998, and for women it increased 1.98 to 2.08 in the same period. These numbers reveal that while the income spread between the top and the bottom has been increasing dramatically, inequality between the middle and the bottom has also been increasing, although not as markedly.[7]

Yet another measure of income inequality compares average executive pay to the average wages of a salaried full-time worker. This inquiry reveals that the ratio of CEO pay to average worker pay has widened substantially, particularly since 1980. As recently as 1980, an average CEO of a large American company earned 42 times the earnings of the average worker; twenty years later, in 2000, the same CEOs earned 419 times an average worker's pay.[8] Between 1970 and 1999, the pay of the top-paid 100 CEOs increased by more than 400 percent while that of the average salaried worker remained flat.[9]

When the income distribution figures are broken down in more detail, two features stand out. First, there has been a dramatic increase in the incomes of the highest earners. Indeed, the higher the income group, the greater the increases. For example, the percent increase for the top 5 percent of the income distribution was considerably greater than the increase for those between the 90th and the 95th percentile.

Second, the returns to education have increased dramatically. Wages of lower-skilled workers – those workers with only a high school diploma or less – have declined precipitously in the past three decades, while those with college degrees or higher educational attainment have increased disproportionately. For example, male high school dropouts experienced a decline of 20.8 percent in their real median income between 1967 and 1999. Males with a high school diploma but no additional schooling experienced declines of 6.5 percent. Yet in the same period, males with a college degree or more have seen a rise in their median incomes of 13.4 percent. Or, to put it

---

[7] *Id.*

[8] Robert H. Frank, *Higher Education: The Ultimate Winner-Take-All Market?* (paper on file with author). There is a similar statistic in Robert Frank, LUXURY FEVER 33 (1999), reporting that in 1973 CEOs of large companies earned 35 times that of the average worker, and in 1999 they earned about 200 times as much.)

[9] Piketty & Saez, INCOME INEQUALITY fig. 18.

differently, a college-educated man earned 149.7 percent of what a high school graduate earned in 1967, and 181.4 percent in 1999.

The change in the education wage premium for women has also been pronounced. In 1967, women who completed college earned 151.1 percent more than women who had only completed high school; by 1999, college-educated women earned 181 percent more than their high-school-educated peers.[10] Concomitantly, occupational wage differentials have moved in a direction that indicates rising returns to education. Between 1970 and 1987, incomes of professionals and managers rose considerably while those of clerical workers, craftsmen, operatives, and laborers fell.[11]

The increasing returns to education for both men and women support the dominant theory of growing income inequality – that recent rising income inequality is the result of skill-biased technological change. However, as explained in the next section, the dominant theory leaves much unexplained and must be supplemented with other explanations for the growing gaps in the income distribution.

B. The Theories of Rising Income Inequality

Economists agree about the facts of growing inequality, but they disagree about its cause. Some of the factors cited to explain the phenomenon are the decline of unions, the decline in the minimum wage in real dollars, increased international trade, rising trade deficits, the shift from manufacturing to service sector production, and technological change. Of these, the most frequently cited explanation is that technological advances, particularly the advent of computerized technologies, have created greater demand for higher-skilled and more-educated workers and diminished demand for less-skilled and less-educated workers. By means of a simple application of the laws of supply and demand, this theory posits that skill-biased technological change has driven up the wages of the higher skilled and driven down those of the lower skilled.[12]

1. Skill-Biased Technological Change
The skill-biased technological change explanation has become the overwhelmingly dominant explanation for rising income inequality. If skill-biased technological change is the whole story, then we might understand the present level of income inequality as a transitory phenomenon – the result of

[10] Francine D. Blau, Marianne A. Ferber, & Anne E. Winkler, THE ECONOMICS OF WOMEN, MEN AND WORK 267–68 (4th ed. 2002).

[11] Chinhui Juhn, Kevin M. Murphy, & Brooks Pierce, *Accounting for the Slowdown in Black-White Wage Convergence*, in Marvin H. Kosters, WORKERS AND THEIR WAGES: CHANGING PATTERNS IN THE UNITED STATES, 107, 135–39 & tbl. 4–7 (Marvin H. Kosters, ed., 1991).

[12] *See, e.g.*, Levy, NEW DOLLARS AND DREAMS 86–87; Burtless et al., GLOBALPHOBIA 83–84.

a time lag. With the dizzying pace of technical change, the theory suggests, some people failed to get skills, or the right skills, to succeed. Whether due to individual ineptitude or institutional failure, their poverty is the result of inadequate education, training, or talent. The solution, according to this view, is to improve training and education for the ill-equipped and hope that those coming after them obtain better, or at least more current and flexible, skills.

However, there is a growing chorus of economists who argue that skill-biased technological change cannot be the sole explanation for dramatically growing income dispersion. Thomas Piketty, of the Centre for Economic Policy Research in London, and Emmanuel Saez, of the Department of Economics at the University of California at Berkeley, challenge the thesis on the ground that the timing of the shifts in income disparities does not support it. Using Internal Revenue Service (IRS) data to examine changes in the U.S. income distribution since 1913, Piketty and Saez found that income distribution narrowed during World War II due to wage controls, remained compressed until 1970, and then began to widen steadily. Piketty and Saez contend that widening income disparity cannot be simply a response to technical change or changes in the supply of educated workers, because if this were the case, inequality would have increased immediately after the wartime wage controls were removed rather than remain compressed until 1970. Similarly, they contend that the huge increase in income inequality since the 1970s is not compatible with the explanation because the lion's share of the increases in income is highly concentrated among the very highest earners. That is, the theory cannot account for the rise of the working rich.

Piketty and Saez instead posit that changing social norms is an important factor in explaining the recent increase in income inequality, particularly in the rise of mega-incomes for the very top earners. They argue that the redistributive policies of the New Deal period and pressures from labor unions constrained wage inequality in the United States from World War II until the mid-1970s. In recent years, those social norms and union pressures have been replaced by free market ideology, allowing the incomes at the very top to rise disproportionately.[13]

Like Piketty and Saez, New School economist David Howell argues that institutional factors explain the collapse of wages for those in the lower 70 percent of the income distribution in the 1980s and 90s.[14] Howell argues that the ideological shift toward laissez-faire markets and the globalization of production ushered in a host of public policies that undermined workers' bargaining power. Some of these policies were a decline in the real minimum

---

[13] Piketty & Saez, *Income Inequality* 26–28.
[14] David R. Howell, *Theory-Driven Facts and the Growth in Earnings Inequality*, 31 REV. RAD. POL. ECON. 54, 64–70 (1999).

wage, an increase in legal and illegal immigration, welfare reform, and public and private policies that undermined unions.[15]

Some economists have pointed out that if skill-biased technological change were the sole explanation, we would expect to observe similar trends in the income distribution in other countries that experienced similar technological advances during the same period. To the contrary, however, countries that experienced the same technological changes have experienced vastly different effects on their national income distributions. In France, for example, the share of total income going to the highest decile declined between 1970 and 1998 from almost 33 percent to 32 percent, with a dip to 30 percent in the mid 1980s. In Canada, in the 1980s, family inequality actually fell.[16]

Cornell economists Francine Blau and Lawrence Kahn conducted a comparative study of income distribution in Western Europe and concluded that technological change alone did not explain differing experiences with inequality. They found that it was also necessary to factor in the differential role of labor laws, unions, and other wage setting institutions.[17] Blau and Kahn's findings are consistent with those of Piketty and Saez and Howell to the effect that public policies and private practices can exacerbate or mitigate the dis-equalizing impact of skill-biased technological change.

Labor economists Barry Bluestone and Bennett Harrison also dispute the skill-biased technological change thesis. They argue that if it were correct, we would expect to find the most wage growth in science and technical fields. But this is not the case. Rather, they show that between 1979 and 1995, "the real winners in the earnings derby were not those on the forefront of the new computerized technologies, but medical doctors (up 43 percent), lawyers (24 percent) sales representatives and brokers (24 percent), and managers (15 percent)."[18] Bluestone and Harrison conclude that inequality must be

---

[15] David Howell, *Skills and the Wage Collapse*, 11 AM. PROSPECT 74 (June 19, 2000).

[16] On income inequality in France, *see* Howell, *Theory-Driven Facts* at 62–63; Piketty & Saez, *Income Inequality* 35–37 & fig. 12. On inequality in Canada, *see* David Card & Richard B. Freeman, *Small Differences That Matter: Canada vs. The United States,* in WORKING UNDER DIFFERENT RULES, 189, 193 (Richard B. Freeman, ed., 1994). For other cross-country comparisons, *see* Francine D. Blau & Lawrence M. Kahn, US LABOR MARKET PERFORMANCE IN INTERNATIONAL PERSPECTIVE: THE ROLE OF LABOR MARKET INSTITUTIONS (2003); David Rueda and Jonas Pontusson, *Wage Inequality and Varieties of Capitalism*, SZ WORLD POL. 354 (2000).

[17] Blau & Kahn, US LABOR MARKET PERFORMANCE; Bjorn Gustafsson & Mats Johansson, *In Search of Smoking Guns: What Makes Income Inequality Vary over Time in Different Countries,* 64 AM. SOCI. REV. 585 (1999) (explaining different experience with inequality in Sweden, the United States, and Finland in the 1980s on the basis of differences in trade union density). *See also* Richard B. Freeman & Lawrence F. Katz, *Rising Wage Inequality: The United States vs. Other Advanced Countries,* in Freeman, WORKING UNDER DIFFERENT RULES 29, 51–56.

[18] Barry Bluestone & Bennett Harrison, GROWING PROSPERITY: THE BATTLE FOR GROWTH WITH EQUITY IN THE TWENTY-FIRST CENTURY 193 (2000).

seen as a combination of factors such as deindustrialization, deunionization, global trade, immigration, and the trade deficit.[19]

The arguments of Piketty, Saez, and the others cast serious doubt on the view that skill-biased technological change is the sole explanation for rising income inequality. This conclusion is not to deny that technological change plays a significant role, but only to insist that there are other factors at work, factors that still need to be identified.

2. *The Shift from Manufacturing to Service Industries*

One factor that has contributed to rising inequality is the shift of workers from relatively high-wage manufacturing jobs to low-wage service sector jobs that has transpired in the United States over the past twenty years. Several economists have argued convincingly that this shift, termed "de-industrialization" by Bluestone and Harrison, has caused the incomes of those at the bottom to deteriorate. The growing service sector jobs, such as waitressing, lawn cutting, or working in dry-cleaning establishments, tend to be labor intensive and subject to intense wage competition. Further, productivity in service sector jobs grows slowly and service jobs are less likely to be unionized. As economists Frank Levy and Richard Murname write, former craftsmen and basic industry factory workers have "become 'hamburger flippers' in the service sector – rather than engineers and market specialists."[20] Thus the shift from manufacturing jobs to service jobs since the 1970s has led to more inequality.[21]

While the shift away from manufacturing accounts for some of the increased inequality, it too cannot tell the whole story. This is because there has been an increase in inequality within the service sector as well as within the manufacturing sector. In the 1980s and 1990s, both the service and the goods-producing sectors experienced the same pattern of widening disparities. In a report commissioned by the National Policy Association, Harvard Professor of Economics Richard Freeman found that between 1979 and 1995 the dispersion of earnings increased within the majority of occupations examined, which included both service and manufacturing positions.[22] Economist Thomas Hyclak studied wage inequality in twenty urban labor markets and also found a consistent increase in wage variance across all

---

[19] *Id.* at 196. Barry Bluestone & Bennett Harrison, THE DE-INDUSTRIALIZATION OF AMERICA: PLANT CLOSINGS, COMMUNITY ABANDONMENT, AND THE DISMANTLING OF BASIC INDUSTRY (1982).

[20] Frank Levy & Richard J. Murnane, *U.S. Earnings Levels and Earnings Inequality: A Review of Recent Trends and Proposed Explanations*, 30 J. ECON. LIT. 1333, 1347 (1992).

[21] Levy, NEW DOLLARS AND DREAMS 60–62.

[22] Richard B. Freeman, WHEN EARNINGS DIVERGE: CAUSES, CONSEQUENCES, AND CURES FOR THE NEW INEQUALITY IN THE U.S. 11 (1997).

types of occupational groups between 1975 and 1991.[23] Thus some other factors must also be at work.

3. Income Dispersion Within Firms

In addition to increased income inequality within industries, firms, and specific jobs, there has also been an increase in earnings inequality within groups that are similar as to age, education, occupation, and other observable characteristics.[24] These trends are inconsistent with the skill-biased, technological-change hypothesis. In order to understand the income dispersion within firms and industries it is necessary to look at the impact of changing human resource practices on intrafirm and intra-industry income patterns.

A recent series of case studies financed by the Sloan Foundation test the skill-biased technological change thesis by exploring the impact of technological change on industry-level and firm-level income distribution. These researchers found that for industries that experienced technological change in the past twenty years, technological factors were not the sole, or even the dominant, cause of either widening income disparities or lowering incomes at the bottom tiers. Rather, they found that changing work practices are a significant factor in explaining widening income disparities.[25]

For example, labor economists Thomas Bailey, Peter Berg, and Carola Sandy studied the steel and apparel industries, where they found that workers in firms that used high performance work practices received higher pay. They defined high performance practices as participation on self-directed teams, assignment to high autonomy work tasks, and opportunities to communicate across departmental boundaries. Bailey, Berg, and Sandy found that those workers who were on self-directed teams or engaged in other high performance practices received not only higher pay, but also more variability in pay.[26]

Some of the researchers in the Sloan project found that skill-biased technological change had had an indirect effect on income inequality when it operated in conjunction with changes in human resource practices. Cornell Professor Rosemary Batt, for example, studied telecommunications services and sales workers. She found that there had been significant wage dispersal

[23] T. Hyclak, RISING WAGE INEQUALITY: THE EXPERIENCE IN URBAN LABOR MARKETS 39 (2000). *See also* Lawrence Mishel, Jared Bernstein, and Heather Boushey, THE STATE OF WORKING AMERICA 2002/2003 169 (2003).

[24] For a summary of studies that find increasing intra-firm and intra-industry wage dispersion, *see* Levy & Murname, *Earnings Levels and Earnings Inequality*, 30 J. ECON. LIT. at 1367.

[25] Harry C, Katz, *Industry Studies of Wage Inequality: Symposium Introduction*, 54 IND. & LAB. REL. REV. 399 (2001).

[26] Thomas Bailey, Peter Berg, & Carola Sandy, *The Effects of High-Performance Work Practices on Employee Earnings in the Steel, Apparel, and Medical Electronics and Imaging Industries*, 54 IND. & LAB. REL. REV. 525 (2001).

since the break-up of the Bell system in 1983. In the same period, the introduction of new technologies made many new marketing and service offerings possible. Analyzing data from 354 service and sales centers, Batt concluded that business strategy and human resource policies were more significant than skill-biased technology per se in explaining patterns of wage inequality.[27] Batt also found significant wage differentiation between call center establishments. Establishments that utilized variable pay and other high performance work practices had higher overall wage levels than those that did not.

The impact of changing work practices on intrafirm wage structures is illustrated vividly by a case study on human resource practices in the banking industry in the 1980s and 1990s by Larry Hunter, professor of management and human resources at the University of Wisconsin, John Paul Mac Diffie, professor of management at the Wharton School of Business, and Lorna Doucet, professor of business at the University of Illinois. In that period, banks were adopting a host of new technologies, such as new hardware and software systems for handling accounts and automated teller machines (ATMs) for customer service. Also in that period, deregulation led to greater consolidation in the industry and intensified price competition among banks. With the repeal of the Glass-Steagall Act in 1999, banks and other financial institutions were able to diversify their services, so that banks began to compete with brokerage houses and mutual funds to sell investment products as well as checking accounts and loans.[28]

Hunter and his coauthors report on the human resource restructuring undertaken by two banks in the face of this increased competition and technological change. In both banks, there was a growing gap in the functions and the earnings between the bank tellers and the "platform workers," the people who open accounts and receive loan applications. Tellers remained responsible for providing routine services such as check cashing, while the job of the platform worker was redefined. Those in the latter jobs, renamed "Personal Banker" or "Financial Specialist," became responsible for promoting sales of a variety of banking products and providing financial counseling to high-yield customers who required personalized services. To appeal to the high end of the customer population, the banks required a college degree for the Personal Banker positions. They selected workers with a professional demeanor for these new positions. These newly professionalized jobs paid considerably more than the teller jobs. The banks' impetus to hire college graduates was not skill-biased technological change but rather a desire to

[27] Rosemary Batt, *Explaining Wage Inequality in Telecommunications Services: Customer Segmentation, Human Resource Practices, and Union Decline*, 54 IND. & LAB. REL. REV. 425 (2001).

[28] Larry W. Hunter, Annette Bernhardt, Katherine L. Hughs, & Eva Skuratowicz, *It's Not Just the ATMs: Technology, Firm Strategies, Jobs and Earnings in Retail Banking*, 54 IND. & LAB. REL. REV. 402 (2001).

engage in strategic customer segmentation, by which the more profitable customers were routed to the more professional types of workers.[29]

These studies and others suggest that the adoption of the high performance work practices of the boundaryless workplace operate in conjunction with, but independently of, technological change to provide at least a partial explanation for the rising inequality of the past twenty years. When jobs are redesigned to provide greater flexibility, their skill requirements also increase. When this occurs, change in firm-level income distribution that mirrors changing differential skill levels is as much a result of new employment practices as it is a response to changing technology.[30]

4. The Impact of Digital-Era Employment Practices on Wage Inequality

The dismantling of internal labor market job structures leads to more dispersion in pay rates for several reasons. First, in internal labor markets, wages were set by institutional factors such as seniority and longevity rather than by the external market. Internal labor markets, like labor unions, thus have promoted wage compression and provided a cushion for workers from external labor market forces. The dismantlement of internal labor markets and the decline in unions remove pressure for wage compression and permit wages to be pegged to other factors.

There are other respects in which the new workplace produces widening disparities in income between and within firms.[31] New compensation practices such as incentive pay schemes, skill-based pay, and market-based pay almost by definition generate wide pay differentials within firms. In jobs where performance is highly variable, the trend is to base wages on individual performance wherever possible. In jobs where performance is routine and predictable, benchmarking is used to set wages according to the going rate for the particular job, and thus break the lock-step wage patterns of internal labor market or union compensation schedules.

Another way that new employment practices generate intrafirm inequality is through the talent wars to obtain superstars. As Robert Frank, professor of economics at the Cornell University Johnson School of Business, and Philip Cook, professor of economics at Duke, have documented, a large number of occupations have become "winner-take-all markets" in which the very best commands a price far beyond that of its nearest competitors.[32] The top

---

[29] *Id.* at 419–21.

[30] Annette Bernhardt & Thomas Bailey, *Improving Worker Welfare in the Age of Flexibility*, 41 CHALLENGE 16 (1998). *See also* Peter Cappelli, *Are Skill Requirements Rising? Evidence from Production and Clerical Jobs*, 46 IND. & LAB. REL. REV. 515 (1993).

[31] Levy, NEW DOLLARS AND DREAMS (summarizing data on rising income inequality in the 1980s and 1990s); *see also* Robert Frank & Philip J. Cook, THE WINNER-TAKE-ALL-SOCIETY 211–31 (1995) (discussing the increasing gap in income between the top and the bottom in the U.S. labor market).

[32] Frank & Cook, THE WINNER-TAKE-ALL SOCIETY.

firms want top performers and are willing to pay a disproportionate price to get them. As part of the talent wars, firms use the carrot of off-scale salaries and generous compensation packages to lure and retain those it deems to be top performers. Over time, such practices lead to vast disparities between employees at the same level, as similarly situated employees are differentially rewarded.[33] The talent wars also foster gaping earnings disparities between individuals at different levels, because the more highly skilled occupations are those in which competition for talent is most aggressive. Both compensation practices that generate wage dispersion within firms, and income tournaments at the top are features of the new workplace that accelerate the other processes generating income inequality.

Another feature of the new employment relationship that is creating an increase in income inequality is the precarious nature of jobs. Many workers no longer can expect to work twelve months a year every year until retirement. Rather, employment is periodic, punctuated by episodes of unemployment or partial unemployment. Thus even if wages were constant or rising, a worker who had a period of unemployment in any given year would have a lower annual income for that year. Annualized income data for all workers does not separate those who worked year round and those whose work was interrupted. If employment precariousness were a condition that was distributed equally throughout the income distribution, then this factor would not explain income dispersion. However, those at the very top of the income pyramid have controlled their risks with golden parachutes and stock options, so that their incomes do not necessarily fall even if they lose their jobs. Thus the precarious nature of work accentuates the gap between the working rich and everyone else.

5. The Impact of Globalized Production on Income Inequality

While changing human resource practices and skill-biased technological change are factors in the widening income distribution, so too is the increase in global production and the policies of trade liberalization. With increased global trade and the relaxation of import barriers, goods produced with low-cost labor are able to out-compete domestically manufactured items. As a result, domestic low-wage workers are forced to compete with low-wage workers in developing countries for jobs. The same results follow when domestic manufacturers shift production to low-wage countries for those parts of their operations that can utilize foreign, low-wage labor. Workers for any company whose goods are traded in the global market, or whose company

---

[33] *See, e.g.,* David Lebow, Louise Sheiner, Larry Slifman, & Martha Starr-McCluer, RECENT TRENDS IN COMPENSATION PRACTICES 8 (1999) (reporting on a Federal Reserve study that found firms are increasingly using compensation systems that permit greater differentiation among employees).

makes goods that compete with goods traded in the global market, is vulnerable to downward pressure on wages.[34]

The impacts of technological change, new employment practices, and global production on income distribution are intertwined. Flexible wage practices are most frequently adopted by firms that are most exposed to foreign trade.[35] For example, Princeton economist Marianne Bertrand finds that companies that face competitive pressures from the global marketplace are more likely to adopt flexible wage policies.[36] Increasing global competition subjects many firms to increased market pressure, which in turn induces them to adopt the kinds of boundaryless work practices that involve a dispersal of firm-level incomes.[37] And as firms dismantle internal labor markets and rely on an external labor market for their hiring needs, they have less incentive to protect their workers from the dynamic of decline.

C. Promoting Equality, Opportunity, and Stability in the Digital Workplace

For the reasons discussed above, it appears that the factors of technological change, new human resource practices, global competition, and the rise of free market ideology all play a role in the deteriorating income distribution. A multifactored understanding of the causes of rising inequality means that no single public policy cure can reverse the dynamic. Once we move beyond the skill-biased explanation to a multifactored one, we are forced to abandon a singular emphasis on training policy and instead entertain a wide range of policy proposals at the macroeconomic and political level.

Because the new human resource practices and the consequent emerging digital-era job structures play a role in generating income disparity, we must confront a choice if we want to reduce income inequality. We can try to arrest the spread of new workplace practices, or we can develop a macroeconomic and political program to ameliorate their effects. The former approach would involve opposing high performance work practices at the plant level and advocating legislative change in the at-will doctrine to require companies to provide workers with job security protection. In light of the continuing decline in union strength, the failure of labor law reform efforts, and the competitive nature of the global marketplace, these strategies are unlikely

---

34 Adrian Wood, NORTH-SOUTH TRADE, EMPLOYMENT AND INEQUALITY: CHANGING FORTUNES IN A SKILL-DRIVEN WORLD (1994).

35 Geoff Mason, *Product Strategies, Workforce Skills and "High-Involvement" Work Practices: US-European Comparisons*, in EMPLOYMENT STRATEGIES: WHY EMPLOYERS MANAGE DIFFERENTLY 193, 211–12 (P. Cappelli, ed., 1999).

36 *See* Marianne Bertrand, *Changes in the American Workplace*, in PROC., 52D ANN. N.Y.U. CONF. ON LABOR & EMP. L. (1999).

37 Robert C. Feenstra & Gorden H. Hanson, *Globalization, Outsourcing and Wage Inequality* (Nat'l Bureau of Econ. Research, Working Paper 5424, 1996).

to succeed. Furthermore, attempting to halt the spread of digital-era work practices would be a form of twenty-first century Ludditism – a romantic but futile effort to pillage the future and recapture the past. Instead, it is more useful to devise policies to redress the rising inequality and those forms of vulnerability that are created by the new work practices.

There are a myriad of proposals currently circulating to address the widening income distribution and the growing underclass. They include proposals for increasing the minimum wage, expanding the earned income tax credit, and providing wage subsidies. These proposals are employment-centered policies that are explicitly designed to redistribute earnings income. In addition, there are a number of proposals to assist the long-term poor, including a negative income tax, providing cash grants to the poor, and establishing a system of universal citizen stakeholding. These measures operate independently of labor market participation and aim at poverty reduction.

In order to choose between these social policies, it is first necessary to decide whether the ultimate goal should be income redistribution or poverty reduction. The elimination of poverty is not the same as raising the earnings of those at the bottom of the income distribution. More than half of adults living in poverty do not work, so that programs to raise earnings do not help them directly. Rather, redistributive measures directed at enhancing earnings of those at the bottom of the income distribution assist the working poor, not all of the underclass. Because public funds for social welfare are a scarce resource, a choice must thus be made between the competing goals of poverty reduction and augmenting the earnings of those at the bottom.

In this section, I describe the major programs for earnings enhancement and for poverty reduction that are currently on the public agenda. I also present the debate between advocates of earnings redistribution and advocates of antipoverty measures. While both types of measures are valuable, I believe it is important to further another goal as well, the goal of helping people prepare for and survive within the digital-era labor market. That is, programs should be adopted that respond to the particular vulnerabilities and problems created by the digital job structures. At the end of this chapter I describe several measures that have this potential. Some are explicitly redistributive and some are not, but all are designed to give individuals the flexibility they need to participate in today's labor market.

1. Earnings-Enhancement Policies

The principal policy measures available to enhance the earnings of low-wage workers are the minimum wage, the earned income tax credit, and wage subsidies. These programs are designed to assist those who participate in the labor market. They are described below.

(a) *The Minimum Wage.* The minimum wage is probably the best-known social program for redistributing income. Enacted in 1935 as part of the Fair

Labor Standards Act, the federal minimum wage sets a floor for wage rates for employees whose jobs are involved in interstate commerce.[38] While the minimum wage level has been raised from time to time, it is not indexed for inflation. It peaked in 1969 at over $7.50 per hour in 1999 dollars, but has never come close to that level since. The minimum wage declined sharply in the 1980s because Congress failed to adjust it for nine years, reaching a low in 1989. Several increases in the 1990s partially corrected the trend. However, even with the increases of the 1990s, inflation has so eroded its purchasing power that today the minimum wage is 21 percent lower than it was in 1979.[39]

The federal minimum wage has long been popular with the public but anathema to economists. Mainstream economists contend that it raises wages above the competitive level, thereby causing employers to reduce employment. This results in a loss in employment opportunities for workers whose value to employers is less than the minimum, and in a sub-optimal level of output for society as a whole. Thus the criticisms of the minimum wage are primarily directed at its efficiency-defeating impact.

However, some research has demonstrated that the minimum wage does not always have deleterious employment effects. Economists David Card and Alan Kreuger conducted an empirical study of fast food industry workers and found that increases in the minimum wage do not necessarily lead to declines in employment opportunities. Prior to 1992, New Jersey and Pennsylvania had the same minimum wage. In 1992, the minimum was raised in New Jersey but not in Pennsylvania. Card and Kreuger found that after 1992, the predicted drop in employment in the New Jersey fast food restaurants did not materialize, but rather, employment in the New Jersey establishments increased relative to those in Pennsylvania. This led them to hypothesize that small increases in the minimum wage could lead to expanded employment opportunities and thus to increased efficiency.[40]

The Card and Kreuger finding initially generated considerable controversy within the economics profession because it appeared to challenge one of the basic tenets of the neoclassical model. However, many economists have since conceded that modest increases in the minimum wage might not be detrimental to employment levels, particularly in a period in which the minimum wage has failed to rise with inflation. If the minimum wage is set at a level below the competitive wage rate, then arguably increases would not lead to employment losses.[41]

---

[38] 29 U.S.C. §§201–219.

[39] *See* National Economic Council, The Minimum Wage: Increasing the Reward for Work, A Report, chart 2 (Mar. 2000).

[40] David Card & Alan B. Kreuger, Myth and Measurement: The New Economics of the Minimum Wage 20–69 (1995).

[41] Francine D. Blau & Lawrence M. Kahn, *Institutions and Laws in the Labor Market*, in 3 Handbook of Labor Economics 1400, 1442 (O. Ashenfelter & D. Card, eds., 1999).

For present purposes, the efficiency effects of the minimum wage are not as important as its distributional effects. The widespread popularity amongst the public of the minimum wage stems not from its impact on overall production but from its impact on wages. That is, there is a widespread belief that the minimum wage puts upward pressure on all wages.

Card and Kreuger looked at the distributional impact of the increase in the federal minimum wage in 1990 and 1991. They found that the raise in the minimum wage, while small, provided a significant boost to the economic well-being of many low-income earners.[42] They also found that the 1990 and 1991 increases in the minimum wage affected overall income distribution. They report that the increases "rolled back a significant fraction of the cumulative rise in wage dispersion from 1979 to 1989 ... [and] led to significant increases in the 10th percentile of family earnings, and to a narrowing of the gap between the 90th and 10th percentiles of family earnings."[43] Rebecca Blank, dean of the University of Michigan School of Public Policy and former member of the President's Council of Economic Advisors, similarly found that the increases in the federal minimum wage in 1996 and 1997 helped low income families.[44]

These findings support the popular belief that the minimum wage is an effective mechanism for redistributing income toward the lower end of the income distribution. However, because less than half of the poor work, and because those that do often work part-time or intermittently, increases in the minimum wage do not translate into significantly higher incomes for the poor. Rather, the minimum wage is best understood as a means of protecting the wages and labor standards of the working poor who otherwise could face a downward spiral as employers bid down the price of labor of those working near the bottom of the income distribution.[45]

(b) The Earned Income Tax Credit. The largest federal redistribution program presently is the earned income tax credit (EITC). The EITC is a refundable tax credit for low-income working families with children. Eligible individuals who earn less than the specified target amount get a tax credit for each dollar earned up to a set maximum benefit. The credit can be either a reduction in tax liability or, if tax liability is less than the credit, a check from the IRS for the difference. Currently, a family with two or more children with parents working at the minimum wage would receive a rebate through the EITC that would be the equivalent of a $2 per hour increase in pay. Or, a single

---

[42] Card & Kreuger, MYTH AND MEASUREMENT 276–77.
[43] Id. at 279.
[44] Rebecca M. Blank, Fighting Poverty: Lessons from Recent U.S. History, 14 J. ECON. PERSP. 3, 14 (2000).
[45] See Timothy J. Bartik, JOBS FOR THE POOR: CAN LABOR DEMAND POLICIES HELP? 278–84 (2001).

wage-earner with two children earning $8500 a year can receive approximately $3370, bringing them above the poverty line.[46]

Between 1975, when the EITC was established, and 1999, the size of the program grew from $3.9 billion to $31.9 billion. It is currently the largest federal welfare program in the United States, dwarfing other federal programs for the poor, such as food stamps, which came to $19 billion in 1999, and Temporary Assistance for Needy Families (TANF), which came to $16.7 billion in 1999. Unlike these other welfare programs, the EITC enjoys considerable popular and political support. In 1998, the EITC raised an estimated 4.4 million Americans above the poverty line.[47]

The EITC is widely viewed as a valuable policy tool for redressing inequality. Rebecca Blank says the expansion of the EITC in the 1990s "may be the most important anti-poverty policy implemented during this decade."[48] Economists Barry Bluestone and Teresa Ghilarducci point out that the EITC not only raises wages but also provides "wage insurance for the temporary poor in an era of job instability and earnings insecurity."[49]

Some have expressed concern that the EITC could lower wages by inducing employers to hire the same workforce for less and simply letting the government pay the difference. In that event, the EITC would prove to be a subsidy for low-wage employers rather than a raise for the working poor. To counter that potential negative consequence, Bluestone and Ghilarducci argue that the EITC should be combined with raising the minimum wage and indexing it for inflation.[50] Rebecca Blank also argues that the EITC should be expanded and combined with an increased minimum wage. If raising the wage floor were combined with an expansion of the EITC, Blank reasons that more nonworkers would join the labor force. The combination could combat the negative employment effects of the minimum wage and would make "full-time, full-year work much more attractive."[51]

Francine Blau and Lawrence Kahn also argue that the EITC is a valuable approach to ameliorating income inequality, but they see it as an alternative rather than as a complement to the minimum wage. They prefer the EITC

---

[46] V. Joseph Hotz & John Karl Scholz, *The Earned Income Tax Credit*, 1–8 (Nat'l Bureau of Econ. Research, Working Paper No. 8078, Jan. 2001); Joel F. Handler, *Low Wage Work "As We Know It,"* in HARD LABOR: WOMEN AND WORK IN THE POST-WELFARE ERA 3, 13–14 (Joel F. Handler & Lucie White, eds., 1999)

[47] Council of Economic Advisors, 1998. *See also* Bartik, JOBS FOR THE POOR 77–80; Katherine S. Newman, NO SHAME IN MY GAME: THE WORKING POOR IN THE INNER CITY 271 (1999); Council of Economic Advisors, 2000.

[48] Rebecca M. Blank, IT TAKES A NATION: A NEW AGENDA FOR FIGHTING POVERTY 113 (1997). In addition, Timothy Bartik says there is "little doubt that the EITC's effect is to truly raise net wages after taxes for many of the working poor." Bartik, JOBS FOR THE POOR 80.

[49] Barry Bluestone & Teresa Ghilarducci, MAKING WORK PAY: WAGE INSURANCE FOR THE WORKING POOR, 28/ 1996 Public Policy Brief (1996).

[50] *Id.*

[51] Blank, IT TAKES A NATION, 114–16.

to increases in the minimum wage because, they say, the EITC raises after-tax wages of low-income workers without interfering in the labor market. It enables employers to hire more workers without increasing their labor costs, and thus, unlike the minimum wage, it does not induce employers to reduce employment levels.[52]

(c) Wage Subsidies. Rather than give subsidies to employees to bring their earnings above the poverty level as the EITC does, some analysts have pro-posed a government subsidy paid to employers to raise the wages of low-income workers. In the past, wage subsidies have been used to assist certain targeted groups for a limited period of time. In 1979, Congress enacted the Target Jobs Tax Credit, and in 1996 it enacted the Work Opportunity Tax Credit, both of which gave private-sector employers a subsidy to employ cer-tain targeted groups, such as welfare recipients, disadvantaged youths, and ex-criminals. The results of these programs were mixed. Several researchers found that they had a negative effect on the employment of the targeted work-ers. They surmised that the subsidy stigmatized the targeted job seekers and thus made employers reluctant to hire them despite the financial inducement to do so. According to economist Lawrence Katz, sending in a welfare recip-ient to a job interview with a wage subsidy voucher is like saying, "Hi. I'm a lemon – give me a job!" Others, however, claim that the stigma factor was exaggerated, and some have found that the programs yielded positive effects on the job opportunities of some categories of disadvantaged workers.[53]

One of the most ambitious wage subsidy proposals has been put forward by Edmund Phelps in his 1997 book, REWARDING WORK.[54] Phelps attributes the low wages of the working poor to their low productivity. In addition, he contends, the advent of information-intensive production increases the low-wage workers' disadvantage. The less well educated are not likely to be selected for jobs that involve handling and/or processing information, so that "the flow of new technical information widens the gap between low-wage and median-wage workers." Similarly, employers are unwilling to invest in training for low-educated workers, so their relative disadvantage in the labor market increases. For these reasons, Phelps argues, neither traditional welfare programs nor employment-based social insurance can reverse the low-wage cycle of low-educated workers. Rather, Phelps proposes that the

---

[52] Blau & Kahn, US LABOR MARKET PERFORMANCE.

[53] On the negative consequences of targeted wage subsidies, *see* Lawrence F. Katz, *Wage Subsidies for the Disadvantaged* (Nat'l Bureau of Econ. Research, Working Paper 5679, 1996); Gary Burtless, *Are Targeted Wage Subsidies Harmful?* 39 IND. & LAB. REL. REV. 105 (1985). On the positive effects of targeted wage subsidies amongst certain discrete populations, *see* Newman, NO SHAME IN MY GAME 270–71; John H. Bishop & Mark Montgomery, *Does the Targeted Jobs Tax Credit Create Jobs at Subsidied Firms*, 32 INDUS. REL. 289 (1993). *See also* David Whitman, *Take This Job and Love It*, U.S. NEWS & WORLD REP., OCT. 14, 1996.

[54] Edmund S. Phelps, REWARDING WORK (1997).

federal government pay employers to raise the wages of their low-income employees.[55]

The Phelps proposal is ambitious and expensive, costing taxpayers an estimated $132 billion in 1998. This enormous sum, he claims, would be offset by increased taxes and by the savings from reduced crime, unemployment benefits, Medicaid, welfare payments, and the elimination of the EITC. For example, an employer whose employees cost $4 an hour in wages, benefits, and payroll taxes would receive a subsidy from the state to bring up its workers' wages to some set minimum amount, posited at $7. To avoid perverse incentives, he proposes that the subsidy be structured to decline as hourly wages increase. As Phelps explains, "The subsidy is thus like a matching grant rewarding the firm for as many workers as it employs, particularly workers whose private productivity is low (as evidenced by the low hourly labor cost that firms are willing to incur for their services)."[56] Unlike the targeted wage-subsidy programs attempted in the past, Phelps' proposal would give subsidies to employers of all types of low-wage workers. He claims that the subsidy would not only pull up wage rates, but also reduce unemployment by giving employers an incentive to hire some whom they would not have employed otherwise.

Phelps justifies wage subsidies on the ground that existing wages reflect only a worker's private productivity to an individual employer. The subsidy, on the other hand, would bring up the wage to the worker's "social productivity" – the contribution of the employee to society.[57] According to Phelps, the social benefit of employment is the benefit workers confer on the rest of society "from their position as participants in the business life of their community and the country, earning their own keep and supporting their children and setting an example for others growing up in their neighborhood."[58] Ideally, he says, the size of the income subsidy should make the wage equal to the worker's external productivity – the private benefit and the social benefit that the worker provides. In this way, he argues, wage subsidies would have benefits for the taxpayers who would be called upon to pay for them.

Phelps's proposal conditions the subsidy on having a job. He argues that a redistributive program should encourage labor market participation because employment is more than a means of self-support – it is "the vehicle for personal growth and the sense of belonging and being needed."[59]

A number of analysts have criticized wage subsidies for their extremely high cost. The price tag for the Phelps plan is over $132 billion, making it an

[55] *Id.* at 65–68.
[56] *Id.* at 106.
[57] *Id* at 106–9.
[58] *Id.* at 124.
[59] *Id.* at 112.

expensive gamble.[60] Yale Law School professor Anne Alstott has attacked wages subsidies in particular, and employment-linked redistribution policies in general, on a number of grounds.[61] Alstott contends that the Phelps plan, by requiring work, could discourage individuals from obtaining additional education and training and hence could impede their labor market opportunities in the future. In addition, she argues that the program is not well targeted. Because it gives subsidies to all low-wage earners, it assists middle-class teens and secondary earners as well as the poor.[62]

Some economists have criticized wage subsidies on the grounds that they could give employers a windfall by inducing them to lower wages and then hire subsidized workers to replace unsubsidized ones. This danger is serious with regards to the Phelps plan because the employer knows which workers are eligible for the subsidy, and can downwardly adjust their wages to offset the subsidy while keeping the unsubsidized workers pay at a level sufficient to keep them employed. With the EITC, on the other hand, the employer does not know which workers are subsidized, because the employer does not know the workers' total family income. In that case, if the employer lowers wages, it risks losing its unsubsidized workers who will refuse to work at the lower pay rate. The fact that employers cannot know which worker is eligible for the subsidy under the EITC leads many economists to prefer the EITC because it has more likelihood of actually raising the wages of the program's beneficiaries.[63]

There is an additional problem with wage subsidies. The Phelps proposal would only assist full-time workers, and thus would impose a full-time work requirement on its beneficiaries. The EITC, on the other hand, assists those whose work is part-time. Thus the EITC permits workers to retain the benefit while adjusting their work schedules to their own life exigencies. In addition, as Bluestone and Ghilarducci point out, the EITC benefit is triggered by low income rather than low pay, so that it assists workers who suffer temporary layoffs or other employment transitions. Thus it is responsive not only to the low pay, but also to the other vicissitudes and vulnerabilities of the boundaryless workplace.

2. Poverty-Reduction Measures
Some policy analysts propose that the problem of growing inequality be addressed through measures that provide cash grants to those outside the

---

[60] Bartik, JOBS FOR THE POOR 242–44.
[61] Anne L. Alstott, *Work vs. Freedom: A Liberal Challenge to Employment Subsidies*, 108 YALE L.J. 967, 1056–58 (1999).
[62] *Id.* at 1042–45.
[63] *See* Rebecca Blank, *Enhancing the Opportunities, Skills, and Security of American Workers*, in A WORKING NATION: WORKERS, WORK AND GOVERNMENT IN THE NEW ECONOMY 105, 117–18 (David T. Ellwood, Rebecca M. Blank, Joseph Blasi, Douglas Kruse, William A. Niskanen, Karen Lynn-Dyson eds., 2000).

labor market, without conditioning benefits on labor market participation.[64] In this vein, some advocate a return to the federal welfare program Aid to Families with Dependent Children (AFDC) that Congress abolished in 1996, a system that focused assistance on the nonworking poor with dependent children. Others propose a negative income tax – using the tax system to provide cash grants to the working and nonworking poor, with a phase-out of the benefit as income rises. Yet others have proposed a stakeholder program that would give a cash grant to every young adult in the country upon the attainment of majority, financed by the federal income tax. Some of these proposals are discussed here.

(a) Cash Grants. The policy of giving public assistance to the disadvantaged goes back many centuries and has taken many forms. In the United States, since the 1930s there has been a federal welfare program that provides cash grants to the disadvantaged. The Social Security Act of 1935 contained a program called Aid to Dependent Children, later renamed Aid to Families with Dependent Children (AFDC), which provided cash grants to poor women to enable them to stay out of the labor market to raise children. The program was expanded considerably during the Great Society's war on poverty in the 1960s and 1970s, and in the 1970s it was supplemented by a federal program to provide food stamps to the needy. However, as welfare was expanding, it also began to lose political support. By the 1980s and 1990s, American values had shifted considerably, so that the goal of keeping women out of the labor force in order to raise children was no longer palatable to large numbers of the population. Rather, women who were on welfare were stigmatized as lazy, opportunistic, or simply caught in a cycle of dependency. By the mid 1990s, political support for the welfare system had evaporated.[65]

In 1996, Congress repealed AFDC and replaced it with the Personal Responsibility and Work Opportunity Act, which established a program called Temporary Aid for Needy Families, or TANF. The proponents of TANF renounced the premise that public assistance should be a source of long-term support for the needy, and instead sought to re-create public assistance as a transition into the labor force. Accordingly, TANF places a five-year lifetime limit for an individual receiving federal welfare and requires states to pressure recipients to find work.[66] Under TANF, states have broad discretion to decide who is eligible for benefits and in what amount, so long as they do not give benefits to any individual beyond 60 months. Also under TANF, states

[64] Alstott, *Work vs. Freedom*, 108 YALE L.J. at 977–87.
[65] *See* Michael B. Katz, THE UNDESERVING POOR: FROM THE WAR ON POVERTY TO THE WAR ON WELFARE 66–69 (1989). For an excellent overview of AFDC and discussion of criticisms of such programs, *see* Blank, IT TAKES A NATION 133–77. For an account for the waning political support for cash assistance in the 1980s and 1990, *see id.* at 123–26.
[66] Pub. L. No. 104–93 (1996).

face fiscal penalties if they fail to meet specified targets for the percentage of recipients working or participating in a work-related activity. Thus, under TANF, public assistance is no longer a universal program of aid to the poor. Rather, it is a time-limited safety net for those who fall outside the labor market, to tide them over and help them get back in.[67]

(b) Stakeholder Proposals. A variation on the cash assistance proposal that avoids its political pitfalls is the proposal for the establishment of a system of universal stakeholding. Yale law professors Bruce Ackerman and Anne Alstott, in their recent book, THE STAKEHOLDER SOCIETY, propose a program to give every child in America a "stake" of $80,000 upon reaching maturity. The stake could be used to finance a college or technical education, open a business, buy a home, or any other use that the individual chooses. If an individual uses it to finance a college education, he or she would receive it at age eighteen; otherwise he or she would receive it at age twenty-one. The only requirement for obtaining the stake would be the completion of high school and U.S. citizenship. Initially the stake would be paid with a 2 percent tax on wealth. And those who receive a stake would be required to pay it back, with interest, in their estate when they die. Thus while the initial federal outlays would be substantial, over time the repayments would accumulate in a fund to finance future stakes.[68]

Ackerman and Alstott argue that their stakeholder proposal would give young adults significant resources at a time when they most need them to shape their economic prospects. Thus, they claim, it is a step toward providing equality of opportunity, comparable to the public education system that at one time represented a commitment to providing all children with the tools for building their futures. Ackerman and Alstott also argue that the proposal would help to solidify a meaningful sense of citizenship by giving each citizen a concrete stake in his or her country. In this regard, they compare their proposal to the GI Bill that gave citizen-soldiers funds early in their adult lives. In keeping with the goal of redressing inequality and at the same time creating a robust form of citizenship, Ackerman and Alstott also advocate that social security be transformed into a citizen pension rather than a pension linked to employment status. This way, they argue, the issue of old-age financial security would express our society's "commitment to the ideal of a dignified old age," not to a particular role in the labor market.[69]

Ackerman and Alstott claim that their citizenship stakeholder proposal would partially overcome those aspects of inequality that stem from

---

[67] *See* Mark Greenberg, *Welfare Restructuring and Working-Poor Family Policy: The New Context,* in Handler & White, HARD LABOR 24–32.
[68] Bruce Ackerman & Anne Alstott, THE STAKEHOLDER SOCIETY (1999).
[69] *Id.* at 140–54.

intergenerational privilege.[70] While it would not affect relative incomes in the short run, it is a measure for equalizing opportunity over the long run.

3. Assessing Non-Employment-Linked Proposals for Redistribution

While the foregoing proposals for cash assistance and universal stakeholding are social welfare measures that do not depend upon employment, they differ greatly in their ability to position people in the labor market. The cash assistance program is a safety net that shores up the very bottom of the economic ladder without affecting the labor market directly. If the cash grant were sufficiently generous, it might make it more difficult for employers to obtain low-wage labor and thereby indirectly exert an upward pressure on wages. However, none of the proponents are proposing a cash grant large enough to do that. Thus the cash assistance proposals would create an alternative to the labor market rather than revise the distribution of earnings generated by the labor market.

The stakeholder proposal, on the other hand, does more than simply provide assistance to the poor. It endows individuals with tools they can use to play a meaningful role in society, whether through education, training, or entrepreneurial activity. And because the stake is a one-time grant to young adults, it does not create long-term disincentives to joining the labor force. Rather, it creates opportunities for those who otherwise would not have them. It does not discourage labor market participation but rather operates as an enabler of more widespread and robust participation.

In addition, because the stakeholder benefits are available to all without a means test, it would encounter less political resistance than a cash grant program. For all these reasons, the stakeholder proposal is an approach to long-run inequality that has great promise. Standing alone, an $80,000 cash grant to young adults will not create equality of educational opportunity, reverse the talent wars, or revitalize the labor movement. However, it can help level the playing field.

D. Poverty Reduction Versus Earnings Enhancement

The choice between poverty reduction and earnings enhancement is ultimately a philosophic and normative question. Anne Alstott characterizes the choice between employment-linked redistribution such as wage subsidies and the EITC, and poverty-alleviation programs such as unconditional cash grants, as a choice between work and freedom. She argues that public assistance that is conditioned on employment interferes with the freedom to determine one's own trade-off between remunerative and nonremunerative activities. Alstott claims there is no reason to privilege labor market participation – some individuals may want or need to spend their time taking care

[70] *Id.* at 24–34.

of children or pursuing other objectives. Accordingly, she terms TANF "unconscionable" for imposing a work requirement and a time limit on welfare recipients. [71]

Alstott argues that both the nonworking and the working poor would fare better under a system of unconditional cash grants or a negative income tax than they would under a redistributive program that requires participation in the labor market. Her argument is that cash grants give the working poor a choice as to how to allocate their time between work and leisure. With cash grants, low-wage earners can choose to enhance their standard of living by working full-time, or choose to live frugally and not work at all, or strike some balance in between. For example, a cash grant would give a mother the freedom to choose to forgo earnings in order to spend time at home while her children were young, a choice that employment subsidy denies. According to Alstott, this kind of choice is an important aspect of freedom.[72]

There are, however, several problems with the outright cash assistance approach to income redistribution. First, since the English Poor Laws if not before, public charity has been permeated with judgments about the moral character of the poor. Public charity has long distinguished between the worthy poor and the unworthy poor in determining how to distribute public largesse. This point was made comically in the long-running Broadway musical *My Fair Lady* in which Eliza Doolittle's ne'er-do-well pauper father, Alfred Doolittle, lectures Professor Henry Higgins on the plight of the *undeserving* poor. As Doolittle laments, speaking from personal knowledge, the lazy, the drunks, and the ne'er-do-wells should be pitied above all others because, unlike the deserving poor, they receive neither charity nor sympathy from the public. In a more serious vein, social historian Michael Katz writes:

The undeserving poor have a very old history. They represent the enduring attempt to classify poor people by merit. This impulse to classify has persisted for centuries partly for reasons of policy. Resources are finite. Neither the state nor private charity can distribute them in unlimited quantities to all who might claim need. On what principles, then, should assistance be based? Who should – and the more difficult question, who should not – receive help?[73]

We see the distinction at work when victims of natural disasters and terrorist attacks are treated more generously than derelicts and drug addicts.

The impulse to distinguish the worthy from the unworthy poor frames modern welfare policies. For example, it is out of skepticism about the spending habits of the poor that public and private charity efforts often involve the distribution of goods, such as food, shelter, or clothing, rather than

[71] Alstott, *Work vs. Freedom*, 108 YALE L.J. 967.
[72] *Id.* at 987–88.
[73] Michael Katz, THE UNDESERVING POOR 9. For a history of attempts to classify the deserving from the underserving poor prior to the twentieth century, *see id.* at 11–16.

distributions of cash. Because of an implicit moral judgment that the able-bodied poor are unworthy rather than merely unfortunate, public charity has usually been structured not only to provide subsistence to the poor, but also to change their behavior, beliefs, and character. Hence public and private charities often couple assistance with intrusive inquiries into the private conduct of recipients. The requirement that the recipients of public relief perform work for their dole is justified not merely in instrumental terms, but also in moral ones. The working population has a deep resentment of those on welfare and it is a moral resentment, a belief that "I work, they should work too."[74]

Because of the history of moralizing and coercion that pervades outright cash assistance, it is a program that breeds mutual distrust and ill will between the givers of assistance – that is, the taxpayers – and the recipients – the needy. It fosters not social cohesion but its opposite. As a result, political support for non-work-based income redistribution has almost entirely evaporated. In this context, it is difficult to see how proposals for ameliorating income inequality by increasing cash grants to the needy are likely to succeed.

In addition, it is not clear that a cash grant approach is ultimately beneficial to the poor. Unconditional cash grants create incentives for individuals to stay out of the labor force. While they may be useful, indeed necessary, for certain limited periods to enable care giving for children or aging parents, they are not a means to foster independence and dignity over the long term. In today's world, work plays a central role in one's sense of identity and connection to the larger world that cash assistance programs cannot deliver.

Harvard anthropologist Katherine Newman, in NO SHAME IN MY GAME, paints a vivid portrayal of the way work creates personhood and paves the way to fulfillment in our society. Newman interviewed a group of inner city youths in Harlem, New York, who held jobs at a fast food hamburger establishment. She found that in numerous respects those in Harlem who have jobs inhabit a different world than those who do not. Job holders not only had more money than their nonworking peers, they had more stability, self-respect, direction, sense of connection to the larger world, and the means for a richer life. For example, one black teenage girl told her:

"When I got in there, I realize it's not what people think. It's a lot more to it than flipping burgers. It's a real system of business. That's when I really got to see a big corporation at play. I mean, one part of it, the foundation of it. Cashiers. The store, how it's run. Production of food, crew workers, service. Things of that nature. That's when I really got into it and understood a lot more."[75]

---

[74] *See* Robert H. Haveman, *The Clinton Alternative to "Welfare as We Know It": Is It Feasible?* in THE WORK ALTERNATIVE: WELFARE REFORM AND THE REALITIES OF THE JOB MARKET 185, 194 (D. Nightingale & R. Haveman, eds., 1995),

[75] Newman, NO SHAME IN MY GAME 103 (1999).

According to Newman, "What they have that their nonworking counterparts lack is both the dignity of being employed and the opportunity to
participate in social activities that increasingly define their adult lives. This
community gives their lives structure and purpose, humor and pleasure, support and understanding in hard times, and a backstop that extends beyond
the instrumental purposes of a fast food restaurant."[76] Newman concludes
by observing that:

Our culture confers honor on those who hold down jobs of any kind over those
who are outside the labor force. Independence and self-sufficiency – these are virtues
that have no equal in this society. But there are other reasons why we value workers
besides the fact that their earnings keep them above water and therefore less in need
of help from government, communities, or charities. We also value workers because
they share certain common views, experiences, and expectations. The work ethic is
more than an attitude toward earning money – it is a disciplined existence, a social
life woven around the workplace.[77]

If we understand work as producing not merely income but, as Newman's
study vividly demonstrates, a means to personhood, then it makes sense to
design public policies to further rather than hinder that goal. Public largesse
is not infinite, so if our social welfare dollars are spent on unconditional
cash grants, there will be little available to encourage labor market participation and assist the working poor. While Alstott characterizes the choice
between employment-linked redistribution such as wage subsidies and the
EITC, on the one hand, and unconditional cash grants on the other, as a
choice between work and freedom, it is equally possible to pose the choice
as one between dignity and dependency. Dependency is not real freedom,
but rather "the liberty of the outcast."[78] Viewed from that perspective, the
employment-linked programs do not "lure people into the labor market,"
as Alstott contends, but are instead programs that offer individuals the opportunity to experience a richer and more meaningful way of life.

E. Addressing Vulnerability in the Boundaryless Workplace

In order to help people to achieve the type of self-actualization that comes
from participation in the labor market while at the same time addressing the
vulnerability and inequality that are generated by the digital-era workplace,
it is necessary to draw on some elements of both the poverty reduction and
the earnings enhancement approaches. Any program that only assists current
workers will omit those who move in and out of the workforce due to the
precarious nature of today's jobs. Also, any program that fails to assist people in obtaining training will not meet the needs of today's employees. Thus

---

[76] *Id.* at 120–212.
[77] *Id.* at 119.
[78] Guy Standing, GLOBAL LABOUR FLEXIBILITY: SEEKING DISTRIBUTIVE JUSTICE 341 (1999).

increasing the earned income tax credit, together with raising the minimum wage, would offer a promising approach to short-term income redistribution. At the same time, the Ackerman-Alstott proposal for universal stakeholding would enable low-wage workers to enhance their human capital at an early stage in their work lives, and hence would be redistributive over time.

Despite their promise, each of the programs discussed so far can only have limited effectiveness in the new workplace. They all involve after-the-fact adjustments to the dynamics of the digital era firm. None of the measures will induce firms to generate more equalizing compensation practices in their day-to-day operations, none will reverse the trend toward more and more winner-take-all markets for talent, and none will directly assist workers as they navigate the tumultuous new world of work.

This section considers some recent U.S. programs that address the vulnerabilities that the new workplace creates. These are programs designed to assist in periods of transition and help workers attain and upgrade their skills. It then presents a European proposal that attempts to address the problem of increased worker vulnerability directly: the proposal for social drawing rights.

1. Current U.S. Approaches to Economic Transitions

(a) Training. In 1998, Congress enacted the Workforce Investment Act[79] (WIA), as a complement to the Personal Responsibility and Work Opportunity Reconciliation Act of 1996, which ushered in welfare reform. The WIA provides federal funds for states to establish "career centers" that are to be one-stop delivery systems for the unemployed and job seekers. These One-Stop career centers administer unemployment insurance but they also do a lot more. They provide a clearing house for job-placement services, offer job-training information, provide computer training, run workshops on résumé writing, and offer free faxing and Internet access. They also provide information on labor market trends, the availability of training providers, and evaluations of local training options. According to Linda Angello, New York State's labor commissioner. "We've been working hard to change our image from the unemployment people to the employment office. There's been a change in philosophy and a change in the way we do business."[80]

Under the WIA, localities are required to establish a Workforce Investment Board comprised of local employers to match the One-Stop career services to the local job market. WIA also provides funds for Individual Training

---

[79] 29 U.S.C. §2801 (West 2000).
[80] Susan Saulny, *New Jobless Centers Offer More Than a Benefit Check,* NEW YORK TIMES, Sept. 5, 2001, p. A1.

Accounts (ITAs) for workers who require job training.[81] Training can include occupational skills training, on-the-job training, cooperative education, private sector training, skill upgrading and retraining, entrepreneurial training, job readiness training, and adult education and literacy activities.[82]

At present, most cities are in the process of establishing One-Stop centers. New York City opened a One-Stop center in Queens a year ago, and plans five more in the next two years. Los Angeles has opened 18 centers, Chicago has 17, and San Francisco has only three. In Austin, Texas, three One-Stop centers and four satellite offices have been established. These centers have utterly transformed the old unemployment offices, which used to be primarily surveillance mechanisms to ensure that recipients were able, available, and actively searching for work – more like parole offices than places to get assistance. The new centers offer job search facilities and counseling that are not only attuned to the local labor market, but also to the local populations. Large city centers are offering services in many languages to cater to their diverse populations. Their services are designed to provide assistance in finding employment at all levels, including offering workshops on self-employment. One worker, a former Cable News Network employee laid off in May 2003, said of her experience with the Queens One-Stop, "My experience was remarkable. I was very impressed. They treated us like professionals rather than problems."[83]

While the WIA is relatively new, and One-Stop centers are just being established in most locations, it is a program that could help workers weather career transitions. One commentator has criticized the program for its overreliance on the principle of consumer choice.[84] Under the statute, individuals are given vouchers to pay for training on the theory that it will help create a market-based system for training services. Law professor Nan Ellis is critical of the use of vouchers for job training on the grounds that job seekers too often cannot make informed choices about either their labor market prospects or about the quality of the training options available to them.[85] But if the One-Stop centers ensure informed and reasoned choice among job seekers by providing them with reliable information about training opportunities in readable and comprehensible form, the centers could become effective mechanisms for dealing with the vicissitudes of the boundaryless labor market. If they were funded at a level that enabled them to offer significant and on-going training programs for all who wanted them, and if they included local unions and community groups on their Workforce Investment

[81] For a description of the Workplace Investment Act, *see* Nan Ellis, *Individual Training Accounts Under the Workforce Investment Act of 1998: Is Choice a Good Thing?* 8 GEO. J. ON POVERTY L. & POL'Y 235 (2001).

[82] 29 U.S.C. 2864 (West, 2000)

[83] Saulny, *New Jobless Centers*, NEW YORK TIMES, Sept. 5, 2001 at B6.

[84] Ellis, *Individual Training Accounts* at 241.

[85] *Id.* at 251–52.

Boards, they would begin to resemble the Worker Retraining and Upskilling Centers described in Chapter 10.

(b) Child Care. In addition to the WIA, there has been some expanded support for child care as part of the welfare-to-work programs established under the Personal Responsibility and Work Opportunity Act. A 1996 enactment established the Child Care Development Block Grant to consolidate four federal programs that made funds available for child care for AFDC recipients moving into the workforce and for certain other low-income working families. The new program gives block grants to the states to establish and design their own child care programs. The program is poorly funded, but the law permits states to use some of their TANF funds for child care as well.[86]

These programs do not go nearly far enough. Lack of affordable quality child care is a major impediment to full labor force participation for women. The new welfare philosophy that mandates workforce participation cannot succeed without providing the necessary infrastructure of child care. Adequate child care is necessary for women throughout the income distribution, but especially for those at the bottom. When women are forced to miss work to stay home with a sick child, or leave work early to attend doctors' appointments, and when women are forced to fill gaps for school holidays and snow days, they are penalized in the labor market. The new workplace requires flexibility on the part of employees but it does not promise them flexibility in return. Without reliable child care women are not only penalized for missing days or coming in late, they experience new types of disabilities as well. Women with children are often unable to take advantage of after-hours training opportunities, unable to engage in informal networking in bars and cafés after work, and are less available for travel. Even though some enlightened employers are willing to give employees flex-time or make other accommodations, without funded and reliable child care women workers will always be living on the edge and sometimes falling off.

Child care needs to be understood as part of the social infrastructure required for our economic system to operate. Once we abandoned a cash grant approach to welfare and chose instead to encourage work, then we became obligated to ensure that the preconditions for women's participation in the workforce were in place. We finance a public education system in order, in part at least, to enable individuals to be productive members of society, and we provide a system of junior colleges and adult education programs to provide lifetime learning possibilities. For the same reasons, we need to finance adequate child care.

---

[86] *See* Greenberg, *Welfare Restructuring and Working-Poor Family Policy* 33–34.

2. The European Approach to the Changing Workplace

A very different approach to the problems of inequality and vulnerability has emerged in Europe. In 1996, the European Commission convened a group of labor relations experts to consider the impact of changes in the workplace on labor regulation in Europe. The group, of which Alain Supiot was the chair, studied the changing industrial relations practices in Europe, and in 2000 issued what has become known as the Supiot Report. The report describes a changing employment landscape in Europe that mirrors the changes that have occurred in the United States – a movement away from industrial-era job structures toward more flexible industrial relations practices. It finds that the new work practices have entailed a loss of job and income security for European workers. The report calls for new mechanisms to provide workers with "active security"– a means to equip individuals to move from one job to another. They contrast this need for active security with the welfare type of security of the past:

Rather than making welfare a type of compensation made available after supposedly unavoidable economic damage has been done, it should be turned into something which gives individuals and intermediary groups their own resources, which, in turn, will enable them to equip themselves with active security to cope with risks.... It therefore follows that security in the form of guarantees of a minimum standard of life, as traditionally provided by social security systems, has to be supplemented, because of the need for economic flexibility, by the objective of shaping, maintaining, and developing people's competencies during their lifetimes.[87]

The Supiot Report contains a number of suggestions for changes in the institutions regulating work to provide active security. Their most visionary proposal is for the creation of "social drawing rights" to facilitate worker mobility and to enable workers to weather labor market transitions. The concept of social drawing rights is derived from existing arrangements in which workers have rights to time off from work for specified purposes such as union representation, maternity leave, sabbaticals, and so forth. The report refers to these existing types of leave to observe that "we are surely witnessing here the emergence of a new type of social right, related to work in general."[88]

Under the Supiot Report proposal, an individual would accumulate social drawing rights on the basis of time spent at work. The drawing rights could be used for paid leave for purposes of obtaining training, working in the family sphere, or performing charitable or public service work. It would be a right that the individual could invoke on an optional basis to navigate career transitions, thereby giving flexibility and security in an era of uncertainty. As Supiot writes, "They are *drawing* rights as they can be brought into effect

[87] Alain Supiot, ed., BEYOND EMPLOYMENT: CHANGES IN WORK AND THE FUTURE OF LABOUR LAW IN EUROPE 197 (2001).

[88] *Id.* at 56.

on two conditions: establishment of sufficient reserve and the decision of the holder to make use of that reserve. They are *social* drawing rights as they are social both in the way they are established . . . and in their aims (social usefulness)."[89]

The purpose of the social drawing rights is to give individuals the flexibility to take time away from the workplace in order to manage transitions and build human capital. This approach responds to the new conditions of work lives, in which careers unfold in unpatterned ways and require an individual to operate both inside and outside the formal labor market at different and unpredictable times. Social drawing rights would smooth these transitions and give individuals the resources to retool and to weather the unpredictable cycles of today's workplace. Like the Ackerman-Alstott proposal for stakeholder grants, it would be an equalizing measure, not because it is overtly redistributive but because it would help to equalize opportunity. Also like the Ackerman-Alstott stakeholder proposal, social drawing rights would be a social investment in the ability of all to participate as equals in the emerging economic order.

The Supiot Report does not specify how the social drawing rights would be funded other than to suggest that they be funded by a combination of contributions from the enterprise, the state, social insurance funds, and perhaps individual savings. The question of funding may not be a major concern in Europe because most European countries already make substantial expenditures on social welfare that could, at least theoretically, be redeployed in this fashion. But to transpose the idea of social drawing rights to the United States would require a major reorientation in our social policy.

In the United States, we have precedents for the concept of paid time off with reemployment rights to facilitate career transitions or life emergencies. There are well-established precedents for paid leaves for military service, jury duty, union business, and other socially valuable activities. Some occupations also offer periodic sabbatical leaves. The concept is also built into the idea of temporary disability in state workers' compensation and other insurance programs that provide compensation and guarantee reemployment rights for temporary absences. The recent Parental Leave Act extends the concept of leave time to parenting obligations, although it does not mandate that such leave time be compensated. These programs all reflect and acknowledge the importance of subsidized time away from the workplace to facilitate a greater

---

[89] See *Id.*; Alain Supiot, Maria-Emilia Easas, Peter Hanau, Anders Johansson, Pamela Meadows, Enzo Mingione, Robert Salais, Paul Vander Heijden, *A European Perspective on the Transformation of Work and the Future of Labor Law*, 20 COMP. LAB. L. & POL'Y J. 621, 628 (1999). *See also* David Marsden & Hugh Stephenson, *Discussion Paper, Labor Law and Social Insurance in the New Economy: A Debate on the Supiot Report*, Centre for Economic Performance (July 2001).

contribution to the workplace. They could serve as the basis for developing a more generalized concept of career transition leave.[90]

Like the stakeholder proposal, the proposal for social drawing rights is an innovative policy proposal that is directly responsive to the needs of individuals in the face of the changing workplace. It preserves worker autonomy and freedom while at the same time equalizing opportunity, creating conditions of success in the changing workplace, and reinforcing the central role of work in our lives. For these reasons, it deserves to be taken seriously on both sides of the Atlantic.

F. Conclusions

Many of the programs and policies described in this chapter have the potential to enable individuals to participate in the new labor market in a meaningful way. Expanded child care and training programs and benefit portability would work in conjunction with programs like the EITC and the minimum wage to alleviate some of the problems that stand in the way of success in the boundaryless workplace. Even then, however, such programs cannot ensure success for everyone. The new workplace presents new challenges and will generate a new mix of winners and losers. Those who are not flexible – who have personal situations or personality traits that lead them to require stability, certainty, and routine – will not fare well. The proposal for universal stakeholding would provide some measure of assistance to permit individuals, at a crucial time in their life-cycle, to start with a solid foundation. And the European proposal of social drawing rights is directly responsive to the need to provide flexibility and bolster people's ability to weather career transitions. All these measures are a far cry from the old safety net provided by AFDC and general relief. Yet these measures have the potential for providing a new kind of safety net – a safety net of empowerment and opportunity, rather than a safety net of minimal subsistence and stasis.

---

[90] For a comprehensive approach arguing for the necessity of reforming family, work, and the state in order to accommodate dependency, care-taking, and paid work, see Martha Albertson Fineman, THE AUTONOMY MYTH: A THEORY OF DEPENDENCY (2004).

Summary and Conclusion

This book has argued that in the past decade there have been changes in the workplace as momentous as those that occurred at the turn of the last century. Guided by the postulates of scientific management and personnel management, early-twentieth-century industrialists repudiated the labor relations systems of the artisan era and constructed a new labor relations system in its place. They erected a system of industrial practices comprised of job ladders, internal promotion schemes, seniority, welfare benefits, and inducements for long-term employment – a system known as an internal labor market – that has dominated major U.S. firms throughout the twentieth century.

At the beginning of the twenty-first century, the internal labor market job structures themselves have begun to dissipate. Employers, faced with increased competition in the product market and technological change in production methods, are seeking more efficient and effective ways to organize the workplace. Out of these efforts, a new constellation of job structures is emerging, structures that are increasingly defining the new digital-era workplace. They include an explicit rejection of job security and a replacement with promises of training and opportunities for human capital development, a flattening of hierarchy, opportunities for lateral movement within and between firms, market-based pay with steep performance incentives, opportunities to network, an emphasis on quality and customer satisfaction at all levels, and plant-specific dispute resolution mechanisms to foster and preserve a perception of procedural fairness.

The new labor system offers both freedom and vulnerability to the working population. For some, it signifies an escape from the rigid hierarchies of the past, hierarchies that were often racially or gender biased in their operation. It also promises to free many from the mind-numbing narrowness of work tasks that were required by the precisely defined job classifications of the past. Yet the new system also creates great vulnerability. It shifts many of the risks of the employment relationship from the firm to the individual. Gone is the individual job security and reliable income and benefits of the past. Individuals must manage their careers, market their talents, and take their compensation as the market measures their value.

The new workplace also generates a number of new concerns about workplace fairness and social justice – new forms of discrimination that are difficult to eradicate, new dangers for employees to forfeit their own human capital and intellectual property, new difficulties for union organizing, new impediments to collective representation and voice, and new ruptures in the social safety net. Our existing legal framework of labor and employment regulation is based upon the template of the old employment relationship. Thus the existing labor laws assume the existence of long-term stability of employment, hierarchical promotion opportunities, and long-term attachment between the employee and the employer. Because those assumptions no longer pertain, many of the problems in the new workplace elude legal remedy.

In Part III, I analyzed the inability of present legal rules to protect employees' human capital, enforce employer promises of human capital development, remedy new forms of employment discrimination and provide employee representation and voice. These problems arise in a legal vacuum because the labor and employment laws do not fit the workplace practices of the digital era. I presented proposals to remedy these types of workplace specific problems.

In Part IV, I analyzed some of the larger social problems that stem from the changing nature of work, including the crisis in social insurance and the deteriorating income distribution. I argued that existing legal rules and social welfare programs do not address the social needs that the new workplace creates. I then explored various proposals to provide benefit portability, child care, training, and to redress inequality in the new era. These proposals are designed to reframe the legal issues and reinvigorate public debates about how to ensure justice and equity in the new workplace. Specifically, I argued that the proposals that have the most promise of effectively reversing the growing inequality of the current era are (1) expanding the earned income tax credit, (2) adopting a generous stakeholder program, (3) expanding programs for job training, child care, and benefit portability, and (4) implementing a program for career transition leave, akin to the European proposal for special drawing rights, that would provide income support for the inevitable and necessary periods of transition. These proposals, each in a different way, has the potential to effectuate meaningful redistribution and redress the vulnerabilities imposed on workers by the digital-era workplace.

While the programs and proposals discussed in the preceding chapters have considerable merit, political realism compels me to acknowledge that the prospects for their adoption is dim. There is presently no organized group that can effectively press for reforms that can address the problems faced by workers in this new world of work. With the precipitous decline of unions in the past two decades, the ability of organized labor to achieve redistributive public policies either in the workplace or at the political level has been severely compromised. Thus at present, the prospects for any redistributive policies depends not upon the collective strength of organized labor but upon the altruism and largesse of the liberal branch of the general citizenry. At best, then, the proposals in Part IV are policies and programs that an organized constituency could promote. Possibly they could form the platform of a political party dedicated to redistribution. Possibly they could frame the issues around which a renewed union movement could lobby. Hopefully in this way they can become not merely utopian proposals but aspirational goals.

Beyond the specific proposals, the analysis presented demonstrates the need for a mechanism to realize the social goals. One lesson to draw from labor history is that to address the ongoing conditions that perpetuate unfairness in the workplace and generate widening income disparities, there must be a union movement that can act as a political constituency for progressive social change. Unions must reinvent themselves as forces that can press for legal and policy change at the national level and address macroeconomic policies in the arenas of public debate. The proposed model of unionism based on local citizenship – a citizen union that includes working people at all points in their work lives, regardless of whether they are attached to a particular workplace or in an employment relationship – could provide the nucleus of such an organization. Such citizen unions, if united with existing workplace, craft, and occupationally based unions, might prove to be the only interest group available to promote such redistributive programs.

In conclusion, the changes in the nature of work do not make labor unions obsolete. Rather, in the digital era, unions are more necessary than ever. They alone have the potential to enable workers to participate meaningfully in the boundaryless workplace and to ensure that the new workplace offers fairness, equity, and dignity. But unionism has to change. Because of the boundaryless quality of the workplace, unionism cannot be grounded solely in a specific employing relationship or even a specific industry or craft. Rather, as the boundary between workplaces softens, the boundary between work lives and nonwork lives will also become blurred. Workers' identities will meld into their identities as citizens. Today's boundaryless workplaces can give rise to boundaryless labor organizations – organizations that welcome the unorganized as well as the organized, the permanent as well as the contingent, the full-time as well as the part-time, regular employees as well as atypical ones. In such an organization, the boundaries between industrial, corporate, and civic citizenship will also become blurred, making it possible for labor organizations to address not only issues of worker rights but also social rights more broadly.

It is my hope that the history, analysis, and proposals I have set forth will make it possible to imagine a legal and policy framework that can promote justice, equality, dignity, and fairness in the emerging workplace. Once such a framework exists in the imagination, it becomes possible to construct it in the real world.

Index

Accident and Disability Insurance, 6
Ackerman, Bruce, 278, 287
Affirmative Action, 164, 177, 179, 183
AFL-CIO, See American Federation of
  Labor-Congress of Industrial
  Organizations
Age Discrimination, 189. See also
  Employment discrimination
Age Discrimination Act of 1967, 124
Agglomeration economies, 232, 233
Aid to Families with Dependent Children
  (AFDC), 277, 285, 288
Alstott, Anne, 276, 278, 287
Alternative dispute resolution, i, 98, 188
Amalgamated Association of Iron, Steel and
  Tin Workers, 25
American Association of Retired Persons
  (AARP), 218
American Federation of Labor (AFL), 21, 28,
  61–62, 205–6
American Federation of Labor-Congress of
  Industrial Organizations (AFL-CIO),
  217, 218, 236
  Associate Membership Program, 218
  Union-Community Program, 236
American Law Institute, 149, 150
American Socialist Party, 28
American Society of Mechanical Engineers
  (ASME), 28–29, 31, 33
  Discussing labor problems, 29
Americans with Disabilities Act of 1990, 124
Appelbaum, Eileen, 108–201
Apprentices, 13, 14, 19, 20
Apprenticeship, 19–20, 22, 28, 41, 42, 52,
  153, 163, 206, 225
Arbitration, 98, 188, 189, 190, 191, 212,
  213, 222, 229, 237
  Arbitral review, 192
  Arbitration process and procedure, 191,
  214

Arbitration systems, 62, 63, 86, 121, 189,
  197, 205, 213, 214, 229
Artisanal production, 4
Assembly line, 5, 38, 44, 45, 46, 57
At-will employment, 23, 49, 59, 123, 130,
  136, 152, 154
  Implied contract exception, 84
  Just cause, 59, 62, 84, 121, 135, 154, 197,
  205, 220
  Just cause liability, 84
  Tort of unjust dismissal, 123
AT&T Co., 71
Automobile industry, 62, 77
  Big Three, 77, 79
  Delphi Automotive Systems, 79
  Ford Motor Company, 39, 44, 45,
  203
  General Motors Company, 83, 200
  Visteon Corporation, 79
Autonomous work teams, 200
Autor, David, 84, 85

Back pay, 183
Bailey, Thomas, 140, 200, 265
Bakers and Confectioners Workers
  International Union, 18
Baldridge Award, 107
Bargaining unit, 121, 125, 204, 206–8, 224,
  237, 238, 239
  Community of interest test, 207, 238
  Single establishment bargaining units,
  238
Barth, Carl, 36
Batt, Rosemary, 199–201, 265–66
Becker, Gary, 57, 140, 145–46, 159
Benchmarking, 113
Bertrand, Marianne, 269
Bethlehem Steel Company, 35, 36, 38
Blau, Francine, 162, 263, 273
Bloomfield, Meyer, 39–40

Bluestone, Barry, 263, 264, 273, 276
Bonus plans, 31. *See also* Compensation
  systems
Boot and Shoe Workers' Union, 20
Boundaryless career, 92–94, 125, 152
Boundaryless labor market, 284
Boundaryless workplace, i, 9, 93, 114–16,
  125–26, 144, 157, 165, 167, 168, 172,
  176, 177, 180, 185, 190, 196–206, 219
Boycotts, 209–10, 230, 237
Brandeis, Louis Dembitz, 35
Broadbanding, 93
Brotherhood of Painters and Decorators of
  America, 18

Card, David, 271–72
Career management, 88
Career wage model, 56
Carnegie, Andrew, 40, 58
Carnegie Corporation, 25
Cash balance pension plans, 237, 255
Center for Contingent Work (CCW), 233–34
  Workplace Equity Bill, 233
Child care, 161, 219, 229, 230, 285, 290
Cigar-Makers International Union, 18
Cigar workers, 17
Citizen unionism, 219, 227–28
  Bargaining power, 132, 230, 262
  Informational picketing, 230
  Legal assistance, 229
  Training, Retraining, and Upskilling
    Centers (TRUCs), 228–29
Civil Rights Act of 1964, 124, 157, 158
Civil Rights Laws, 157–58
Civil Service Reform Act of 1978, 123
Class actions, 166, 175–78
  Class certification, 174
Clayton Antitrust Act, 210
Closed shop agreements, 224
Coal miners, 16, 23
Cobble, Dorothy Sue, 223–24
Collective action, 4, 7, 21, 25. *See also*
  Concerted action; Unionism
Collective bargaining, 52, 119–20
  Appropriate bargaining unit, 207
  See also National Labor Relations Act of
    1935
Collective bargaining agreements, 69, 233,
  235
Commerce Clause, 120
Commitment, 1, 3, 38, 49, 68, 70, 90, 91,
  94–95, 110–16, 129, 147, 154, 200–3,
  236, 278
  Affective commitment, 94, 95
  Continuance commitment, 95
Common law conspiracy doctrine, 4, 21
Communication Workers of America (CWA),
  235

Compensation systems, 201
Competency-based organizations, 92, 100–2,
  107
Concerted action, 119. *See also* Collective
  action; Unionism
Congress of Industrial Organizations (CIO),
  62
Consolidated Omnibus Budget
  Reconciliation Act (COBRA), 249–50
Contingent employment, 68, 72, 73
  Atypical employment, 69
  Contract employment, 69
  Flexible staffing, 68, 80
  Leased employees, 69
Cook, Philip, 267
Corporate citizenship behavior, 233
Corporate welfare programs, 28, 38, 43–44
  Stock subscription plans, 43
Covenants not to compete, 128–33, 144, 153,
  155, 156
  Confidential employees, 214
  Confidential information, 130, 132, 136,
    137, 143, 146
  Confidentiality agreement, 142
  Common law origins, 153
  Customer lists/customer contacts, 138,
    139, 141, 142, 143, 146, 149
  Employee hardship, 141
  General business information, 149
  Legitimate interest test, 139, 141,
    143
  Rule of reason approach, 132
Craft unions, 4, 18–23, 24, 28, 31, 52, 58,
  61, 204, 205, 206, 223–24, 237
  Craft governance rules, 19
  Old craft unionism, 223
  Skill acquisition and transmission, 41
  See also New craft unionism
Craft workers, 4, 8, 15, 16, 18, 22, 27, 36,
  63, 206, 220
Cross-functional work teams, 101, 105

Davenport, Thomas, 91, 96
De Tocqueville, Alexis, 197
Defined benefit pension plans, 251–52, 253,
  255, 256, 257
Defined contribution pension plans, 252–54,
  255, 256, 257
Deming, W. Edwards, 104–7
Deming Prize, 104
Deskilling, 35, 46, 63, 92
  Differential piece rate, 31, 33, 36, 45. *See
    also* Compensation systems; Scientific
    management
Digital era, 5–6, 7, 9, 244, 267, 269, 270,
  282, 283, 289, 290
Digital production, 4, 5, 6, 8
Digital workplace, 7, 87, 256, 269

Discrimination, *see* Employment discrimination
Dispute resolution, 63, 98, 99, 113, 190, 191, 198, 289
Doeringer, Peter, 53–54, 55, 56, 60, 61
Downsizing, 59, 70, 90, 116, 202
Drucker, Peter, 91, 94, 111
Duty of loyalty, 130, 131

Earned Income Tax Credit (EITC), 270, 272, 283, 290
Economic weapons, 230
Employability, 8, 111, 112, 125, 144, 198, 219
Employability security, 111, 124, 147
Employee benefits, 108, 125, 245, 247
    Sick leave, 121
    Vacation benefits, 205
    See also Pensions
Employee involvement, 114, 200
Employee leasing, 69. *See also* Contingent employment
Employee mobility, 129, 155
Employee participation, 108
Employee representation, 7, 9, 125, 198, 199, 216
Employee retention, 47
Employee Retirement and Income Security Act (ERISA), 256
Employer recruitment, 2
Employment conditions, 225
Employment discrimination, 9, 123, 244, 290
    Adverse employment action, 170
    Anti-discrimination laws, 7, 9, 124, 125, 159, 231
    Anti-discrimination policies, 176, 178
    Bullying, 179, 180, 185, 192
    Competence-undermining test, 186
    Coworker harassment, 158, 181–82
    Discrimination claims, 174, 179, 185, 186–89
    Discriminatory motive, 169–71
    Discriminatory treatment, 169, 176
    Disparate impact, 174
    Disparate treatment, 174
    Gender pay gap, 124
    Gender stratification, 184
    Hostile environment, 179
    Intentional discrimination, 171, 175, 178
    Intentional infliction of a hostile work environment, 185
    Job segregation, 158, 163
    Pay discrimination, 193
    Race-based harassment claims, 185
    Second generation employment discrimination claims, 184
    Sex segregation, 164

Sexual harassment, 166, 180, 181, 182, 184, 190
Statistical discrimination, 159–64
Supervisor liability, 181
Taste for discrimination, 159
Unconscious racism, 178
    See also Equal Pay Act of 1962; Title VII of the Civil Rights Act of 1964
Employment laws, 62, 68, 84, 119–28, 191, 233
Employment manuals, 58, 83
Employment security, *see* Job security
Entire contract doctrine, 23–24
Entry-level jobs, 161
Equal Employment Opportunity Commission (EEOC), 164, 186. *See also* Employment discrimination
Equal employment opportunity laws, 164
Equal Pay Act of 1962 (EPA), 124, 158. *See also* Employment discrimination
European welfare states, 245
External labor market, 52, 54, 55, 91, 267

Factory system, 17, 22
Fair Labor Standards Act of 1937, 119
Farber, Henry, 80–82
Featherbedding, 202
Federal Arbitration Act (FAA), 189. *See also* Arbitration
Federal Mediation and Conciliation Services, 205
Federal Rules of Civil Procedure, 175
Federation of Organized Trade and Labor Unions (FOTLU), 21
Film and television industries, 220
Firm-specific human capital, 54, 55, 163
Firm-specific skill, 42, 52
Firm-specific training, 41, 42, 53, 55, 57. *See also* Training
Fixed-term employment contract, 134
Flexible benefit plans, 247–48
Ford, Henry, 44, 58
Fordism, 46
Foremanship, 38
Frank, Robert, 267
Free labor, 14
Freedom of contract, 120
Freeman, Richard, 198, 264
Frick, Henry Clay, 25
Front pay, 183

General Electric Company, 6, 39, 71, 196
General knowledge, 147
General training, 145–47. *See also* Training
Glass blowers' union, 16
Global production networks, 5
Globalization, 100, 227, 262
Gonos, George, 68

Great Depression, 119
Grievance arbitration, 63, 220. *See also* Arbitration
Grievance procedures, 38, 63. *See also* Unionism
Guild, 4, 153

Halsey, Frederick, 31
Harassment, 157, 166, 167, 179–92. *See also* Employment discrimination
Harrison, Bennett, 200, 263, 264
Hawthorne experiments, 47, 88
Health insurance, 6, 121, 122, 125, 198, 231, 244, 245–51, 256, 257
See also Employee benefits
Health Insurance Portability and Accountability Act (HIPPA), 248–49, 250
Heckscher, Charles, 93, 198
Hewlett Packard Company, 6, 196
Hierarchical promotional systems, 42. *See also* Personnel management
High performance work practices, 114, 115, 116, 144, 200, 265, 266, 269
High performance work systems, 92, 107
Highland Park Factory, 44
Hiring halls, 52, 163, 224, 238
Homestead Steel Works, 25
Horizontal flexibility, 130, 144
Hospital Workers' Union, District 1199, 226
Hotel Employee and Restaurant Employees Union, 224
Waitress unionism, 224
Howell, David, 262, 263
Human capital, i, 5, 8, 19, 54–55, 96, 111, 125, 128–56, 162, 163, 198, 232, 233, 283, 287, 290
Human relations school, 47
Human resource model, 45, 199
Human resource practices, 68, 79, 86, 87, 106, 108, 129, 158, 179, 258, 265, 268, 269
Bureaucratic organizations, 47

Implicit contracts, 70, 152–63, 197
Implied promises, 58
Income distribution, 9, 126, 258, 285, 290
Education wage premium, 261
Occupational wage differentials, 261
Working rich, 259, 262, 268
Income inequality, 9, 258–81. *See also* Income distribution
Income security, 24, 48, 163, 239, 286
Indenture, 153
Independent contractor, 15, 70, 73, 214, 215, 238. *See also* Contingent employment

Individual Retirement Account (IRA), 256
Industrial Areas Foundation (IAF), 235
Industrial common law, 63, 168
Industrial engineering, 28, 29
Industrial era, 6, 8
Industrial espionage, 130
Industrial pluralism, 213
Industrial relations system, 47
Industrial union model, 222, 226
Industrial Workers of the World, 28
Inevitable disclosure doctrine, 151. *See also* Trade secrets
Informal work groups, 47
Information-based workplace, 128
Injunctions, 119, 134
Inside contracting system, 27
Inside contractors, 15, 16
Intellectual capital, 5
Intellectual property, 5, 125, 290
Internal dispute resolution systems, 190, 191. *See also* Dispute resolution
Internal labor market, 5–8, 28, 48, 49–57, 60–63, 68, 70, 73, 76–83, 86, 93, 94, 95, 113, 121–23, 145, 154, 158–65, 182, 196–205, 209, 243, 258, 267–69, 289
Internal promotion, 38, 40, 52, 53, 61, 160, 204, 289. *See also* Personnel management
International Alliance of Theatrical and Stage Employees (IATSE), 220, 221–24, 238
Basic agreement, 221–22, 223
Dues check-off, 222
Joint pension and health fund, 222
International Association of Machinists, 18, 20
International Harvester Company, 22, 44
International Union of Bicycle Workers, 18
Interstate Commerce Commission, 35
Involuntary job loss, 6, 81, 83
Iron and steel foundry industry, 80
Iron Molders' International Union, 20

Jacoby, Sanford, 46, 61
Job analysis, 32. *See also* Scientific management
Job classifications, 52, 92, 108, 203–9
Job definitions, 5, 63, 93, 101, 109, 203, 204–11
Job insecurity, 74, 110, 203, 289. *See also* Job security
Job ladders, 5, 38, 44, 45, 47, 99, 206
Changes in, 92, 93, 94, 110
Discrimination and, 125, 128, 160–62, 165, 167
Internal labor markets and, 52, 53, 57
Personnel management and, 40–43
Unions and, 63, 203

Job lock, 244
Job mobility, 9, 129, 225, 245
Job rotation, 114–16, 202
Job security, 3, 5, 122, 123, 269
    At-will rule and, 48–49, 59–60, 84, 85,
        123, 154
    Changes in, 6, 70, 72–83, 94, 97, 110, 111,
        113, 129, 154, 289
    Craft workers and, 206, 220, 221
    Discrimination and, 163, 182
    Human resource practices and, 42–43, 46,
        109–10, 200, 201
    Internal labor markets and, 56–59, 60,
        163
    New Deal and, 122, 123
    Psychological contract for, 88, 92
Job stability, 81
Job structures, 4–8, 227, 270
    Artisanal era, 15, 16
    Assembly line, 44–45
    Changes in, 94, 196, 258, 267, 286, 289
    Critique of internal labor market, 99,
        110
    Discrimination and, 159–65, 183
    Income distribution and, 269
    Internal labor market, 28, 53, 57–63, 80,
        82, 87, 119, 163
    Scientific management, 29, 47, 51
    Temporary work, 68
    Unions and, 205–6
Job tenure, 74–83
Joint union-employer boards, 226
Journeymen, 14–19, 153
Just-in-time production, 86, 200, 205. *See
    also* Lean production
Justice for Janitors, 225. *See also* Service
    Employees International Union

Kahn, Larry, 263
Kaizen, 106
Kanigel, Robert, 32
Kanter, Rosabeth Moss, 3, 103, 110,
    112
Katz, Lawrence, 274
Kerr, Clark, 51–52, 60
Klein, Janice, 111
Knights of Labor (KOL), 21–22
Knowledge sharing, 42, 48, 58
Knowledge transfer, 41, 42
Krueger, Alan, 271

Labor law, 68–69, 213, 216, 263, 269
    Arbitration and, 212
    Existing, 6, 7, 9, 198–99, 206, 218
    Need for change in, 7, 125
    New Deal, 119–23, 199
    Reform proposals, 237–39
    Secondary boycott prohibition, 210

Temporary workers, 209
    See also National Labor Relations Act of
        1935
Labor-Management Relations Act, 212
Labor unions, *see* Unionism; *individual unions
    by name*
Labor unrest, 39, 44
Lasters, 17, 20
Lateral mobility, 94, 154, 204
Lawler, Edward E. III, 100–3, 166
Layoffs, 6, 14, 46, 68, 90, 93, 116, 123, 179,
    202, 224, 276
Lean production, 200
Learning organizations, 100, 104
Living wage campaigns, 229, 236
Long-term commitment, 244
Long-term employment, 7, 57, 58, 70, 73,
    74, 77, 97, 121, 154, 215, 289
Long-term loyalty, 45

Mandatory arbitration, 183
Master-servant law, 23
Mediation, 98, 188
Merchant manufacturers, 14, 15
Metalworkers, 16
Microsoft Corporation, 5, 69, 234
Middle management, 89
Midvale Steel Company, 32, 48
Migrant workers, 122
Minimum wage, 120, 123, 218, 229–34, 261,
    262, 270–74, 283
MIT Sloan School of Management, 111
Molders, 16, 36
Montgomery, David, 18, 203
Morale, 27, 38, 45, 48, 58, 90, 163, 185, 192

Multiemployer bargaining, 238–39
Multiemployer unit, 238

National Alliance for Fair Employment
    (NAFFE), 233–34
National Association of Broadcast
    Employees and Technicians (NABET),
    220–22
National Conference of Commissioners on
    Uniform State Laws, 149
National craft unions, 18, 21–22
National Establishment Survey, 114, 115
National Industrial Conference Board, 33, 46
National Institute of Standards and
    Technology, 107
National Labor Relations Act of 1935, 62
National Labor Relations Board (NLRB),
    119
National Labor Union (NLU), 20–21
National Typographers Union, 18, 20
Networks, 5, 8, 92, 104, 111, 125, 151, 167,
    179, 208, 220, 226

New compensation practices, 267
  Incentive pay schemes, 267
  Market-based pay, 289
  Performance-based pay, 106, 107, 109
  Skill-based pay, 102–3, 200, 267
  Wage dispersion, 113
New craft unionism, 9–227
  Nonexclusive craft unionism, 226
  Embedded contract bargaining, 221,
    222
  Job-to-job contracting, 226
New Deal, 119
  New Deal labor legislation, 124
New deal at work, 3, 6, 83
New employment relationship, 3, 8, 9,
    87–116
  Discrimination and, 159, 165
  Income inequality and, 268
  Post-employment restraints, 129, 138, 147,
    151, 152, 154, 155
  Terms of, 110–13
  Unions and, 125, 196, 199, 203
New York Workingman's Assembly, 21
Newman, Katherine, 281–82
Noncompete covenants, *see* Covenants not to
  compete
Nondisclosure agreements, 130, 132. *See also*
  Covenants not to compete
Nonunion arbitration, 189, 192, 229. *See
  also* Arbitration
Nonunion dispute resolution, 98, 229. *See
  also* Dispute resolution
Nordstrom, 96
Norris LaGuardia Act of 1932, 119, 210

Occupational mobility paths, 227
Occupational safety, 123, 229
Ombudsmen, 98
Open shop, 206. *See also* Unionism
Organ, Dennis, 97
Organizational citizenship behavior (OCB),
    92, 94–99, 107, 110, 147
Osterman, Paul, 60, 114–16, 202, 236
Outsourcing, 93, 94

Part-time employment, 73
Peer-based decision making, 166
Peer review, 98–103, 166, 179, 188. *See also*
  Dispute resolution
Pensions, 7, 43, 95, 121, 141, 205, 237, 245,
    251–57
  Pension portability, 255–57
  See also Cash balance pension plans;
    Defined benefit pension plans; Defined
    contribution pension plans; Employee
    benefits
Pepsico. Inc., 150–51
Per diem workers, 220–22
Personnel department, 39, 40, 46, 172

Personnel management, 28, 38–44, 46–47,
    51, 56, 72, 162, 203
  Personnel management theorists, 39, 42
Phelps, Edmund, 274–76
Piece-rate system, 30, 33. *See also*
  Compensation systems
Piketty, Thomas, 262–64
Piore, Michael, 53–54, 55, 56, 60–61
Pipe fitters, 16
Polygraph Act, 123
Post-employment restraints, 128–35, 155. *See
  also* Covenants not to compete; Trade
  secrets
Precarious employment, 70. *See also*
  Contingent employment
Pressmen, 23
Primary labor market, 162, 163, 182
Primary metals industry, 80
Primary sector, 122, 182
Procedural fairness, 97–99
Procedural justice, 96–99
Producer cooperatives, 20
Producers' alliance, 21
Production networks, 211
Profit-sharing plans, 16, 43, 109
Promotion criteria, 182
Promotion ladder, 46, 121, 161
Promotion policies, 28, 40, 46, 166, 177
Protected activity, 218
Psychological contract, 58, 88–92
  Bilateral exchange, 89
  Changes in, 71, 83, 91–94
  Discrimination and, 163, 165
  Employer breach of, 154–56
  Labor law and, 199, 216
  New, 3, 88, 99, 112, 115, 121, 125, 126,
    215
  Promise of training in, 147–48
  Unions and, 198, 205

Quality circles, 58, 114, 115, 199, 202

Railway Labor Act, 214
Redundancy, 193
Résumés, 2
Retirement security, 122. *See also* Employee
  benefits; Pensions
Roosevelt, Franklin D., 119
Rousseau, Denise, 88, 89, 91

Sabotage, 27, 33, 58, 184, 185, 192
Saez, Emmanuel, 262–64
Saxenian, Anna Lee, 232
Schwab, Charles, 38
Scientific management, 5, 7, 8, 28, 33–41,
    44, 46–49, 56, 72, 100, 110, 203
  Functional foremanship, 35
  Planning department, 34–45
  Routing cards, 36, 41

Routing systems, 34
Soldiering, 29, 33, 48
  See also Taylorism
Secondary boycott, 209–12, 230, 237, 238
Secondary labor market, 163
Secondary strikes, 210
Self-managed teams, 109, 110, 115, 116, 200

Self-regulation, 5, 121, 213
Semiskilled workers, 28, 41
Seniority, 46, 47, 52, 59, 60, 61, 63, 68, 77,
  95, 121, 125, 178, 183, 197, 203–5,
  216, 220, 222, 267, 289
Sennett, Richard, 71, 83
Service Employees International Union
  (SEIU), 212, 224
Sexual harassmen, *see* Employment
  discrimination,
Sherman Antitrust Act, 21
Shoe workers, 17, 18, 20
Skill development, 4, 39, 99, 107, 147, 154
Slichter, Sumner, 39, 40
Social insurance, 6, 9, 121, 222, 244, 245,
  274, 287
Social Security Act of 1935, 62, 277
Social welfare benefits, 6
Specialized knowledge, 147, 149
Statute of Apprentices of 1563, 153
Steel industry, 16, 29
Step raises, 205
Stevens Institute of Technology, 28
Stewart, Thomas, 92, 127
Stonecutters, 23
Strikes, 18, 19, 30, 33, 63, 155, 204, 209, 220
  Strikebreakers, 25, 26
  See also Economic weapons
Subcontractors, 15, 68, 211, 268
Successorship, 215–16
Supiot, Alain, 286
Supiot Report, 286, 287
  Active security, 286
  Social drawing rights, 283, 286–88
Suppliers, 105, 107, 112, 144, 211, 230
Sylvis, William E., 20

Tabor Manufacturing Company, 37
Tacit knowledge, 5, 104
Talent wars, 2, 3, 267, 268, 279
Taylor, Frederick Winslow, 30–38, 41
Taylorism, 37, 45, 46, 51, 88, 92, 95, 99, 110,
  196. *See also* Scientific management
Teamwork, 106, 167, 201, 202
Temporary employment, 67, 68, 73, 85
  Long-term temporary employees, 208, 209
  Manpower, Inc., 67
  Permatemps, 69
  Staffing agencies, 208
  Statutory employer, 69
  Temporary agency employees, 70

Temporary employees, 69, 80, 85, 90
Temporary employment agencies, 67, 68,
  69
Temporary help industry, 68
Temporary industry code of conduct, 233
Temporary work, 70
Triangulated legal arrangement, 68
  User firm, 68–69
Third Restatement of Unfair Competition,
  150
Time and motion study, 32, 33, 36. *See also*
  Scientific Management
Tin Plate Workers, 18
Title VII of the Civil Rights Act of 1964, 124,
  158, 167
  Class actions under, 178
  Coworker harassment claims, 179–82
  New workplace and, 168–74
  Proposed new approaches to, 184–91
  Remedies under, 182–83
Total Quality Management (TQM), 104–7,
  114, 115, 116, 144, 200, 202
Trade schools, 42
Trade secrets, 8, 128, 129, 131, 137–42, 145,
  146, 149–52, 156. *See also* Inevitable
  disclosure doctrine
Traditional pay systems, 101
Training, i, 2, 5, 262, 269, 285, 288,
  289–90
  Assembly line and, 45
  Bureau of Labor Statistics Survey of
    Employer Provided Training, 114
  Citizen unions and, 228–36, 238
  Commitment and, 95
  Competency-based organizations and,
    100–4
  Craft unions and, 14, 19, 20, 27
  Discrimination and, 158–62, 167, 182,
    193–94
  Employer promises of, 128, 130
  High performance work systems and,
    107–10, 114, 202
  Income distribution and, 274, 276, 279,
    282
  Industrial era and, 27, 28, 29, 38, 40,
    41–43, 48, 206
  Internal labor markets and, 52–60
  New craft unionism and, 223–27
  Noncompete covenants and, 138, 144–49,
    153, 156
  Psychological contract for, 88–89, 111,
    112, 154–55, 198
  Social drawing rights and, 286
  Total Quality Management and, 102–7
  Training costs, 53, 60, 147, 148
  Training repayment agreement, 148
  Unions and, 198, 219
  Vocational education, 41–42
  Workforce Investment Act and, 283–85

TRW Company, 98
Turnover, 8, 38, 48, 72
   Assembly line and, 45
   Internal labor markets and, 53, 56–58, 60, 161
   Promotion systems and, 38–41
   Psychological contracts and, 90
   Teamwork and, 202
   Welfare programs and, 44

U.S. Department of Labor, 67, 70, 71, 126
U.S. Industrial Relations Commission, 37
U.S. Steel Corporation, 40–43
Unemployment programs, 121
Uniform policies, 172
Union density, 123
Union hiring hall, 61
Unionism, 61, 62, 125, 167, 198, 202
   Firm-based organization, 227
   Geographically based organization, 227
   Locality-based unions, 227
   Skill-based organization, 227
United Hatters of America, 18
United Kingdom (UK) Equality Report, 193–94
United Mine Workers of America, 18
United Shoe Workers of America, 20
Universal Health Insurance, 231. *See also* Social insurance
Unjust dismissal, 133, 155, 224. *See also* At-will employment
Unpaid Workers Prohibition Act, 234
Unskilled workers, 14, 21, 23–28, 48–49
Upskilling, 156. *See also* Training

Wage gap, 124. *See also* Employment discrimination
Wage inequality, 262, 264, 266. *See also* Income distribution
Wage payment systems, 31
Wage plans, 46. *See also* Compensation systems
Wage standardization, 40

Wage structure, 40, 52, 62, 113
Wage subsidies, 229, 270, 274–79, 282
   Targeted Jobs Tax Credit, 274
   Work Opportunity Tax Credit, 274
Wagner Act, *see* National Labor Relations Act
Wal-Mart, 96
War Labor Board (WLB), 63
Washington Alliance of Technology Workers (WashTech), 226, 234
   Regional Training Center, 235
Watertown Arsenal, 36, 37
Webb, Beatrice and Sydney, 217, 218
Welch, Jack, 71, 91
Welfare, 270, 276, 277, 279, 281, 282
Western Electric experiments, *see* Hawthorne experiments
Whistleblowers, 123
Wildcat strikes, 47
Williamson, Oliver, 56–60
Wisconsin Regional Training Partnership, 226. *See also* Training
Work rules, 21, 25, 26
Worker Adjustment and Retraining Notification Act (WARN), 123
Worker compensation systems, 244
Worker loyalty, 28
Worker motivation, 4, 28
Workforce empowerment, 104
Workforce Investment Act, 283
   Child Care Development Block Grant, 285
   Individual Training Accounts, 283
   One-Stop Centers, 283–85
   Workforce Investment Board, 284
Workplace-based dispute resolution procedure, 188. *See also* Dispute resolution
Workplace justice, 4, 186
Workplace Project, 234
Workplace representation, 218
Workplace restructuring, 109
Workplace rules, 18